Edmondo de Amicis, Wilhelmina W Cady

**Military life in Italy**

Edmondo de Amicis, Wilhelmina W Cady

**Military life in Italy**

ISBN/EAN: 9783337229641

Printed in Europe, USA, Canada, Australia, Japan

Cover: Foto ©Andreas Hilbeck / pixelio.de

More available books at **www.hansebooks.com**

# MILITARY LIFE

## IN ITALY

### SKETCHES

BY

EDMONDO DE AMICIS

ARMY OFFICER

TRANSLATED BY

WILHELMINA W. CADY

*WITH ILLUSTRATIONS*

NEW YORK
G. P. PUTNAM'S SONS
27 & 29 WEST 23D STREET
1882

"Two files marched on the right and two on the left of the road."

(*Page* 1.)

# AUTHOR'S PREFACE.

SOME time ago, in speaking of one of these sketches, two readers, who were exceedingly emotional, unwittingly revealed the double purpose I had in view when writing this book.

A working man said: "When I had finished reading it, I would have gladly pressed the hand of the first soldier whom I happened to meet."

A soldier said: "It is a story full of consolation, which inspires a man with good-will for his duties."

Let the one wish well to the soldier and the other be a soldier from the heart. Should I succeed in obtaining these two results in any of my readers, I should feel well repaid for my pains, and my liveliest and most earnest desire would be fulfilled.

TO MY MOTHER,

## THERESA BUSSETTI DE AMICIS,

I DEDICATE THIS BOOK,

REGRETTING THAT I CANNOT UNITE HER DEAR NAME WITH A WORK LOVELY AS HER HEART, CHOICE AS HER VIRTUES, AND HOLY AS HER LIFE.

# LIST OF ILLUSTRATIONS.

PAGE

"Two files marched on the right and two on the left of the road."
*Frontispiece*

"He rushed breathless to the door, opened it, looked around, and saw —the officer of the day, erect, immovable, and rigid." . . 28

"Saying which, he sprang at him, seized him by the collar of his jacket and shirt, pinned him with one dash against the wall, raised his clenched and trembling fist," etc. . . . . 38

"That was a large café, lighted and gleaming with mirrors, full of staff-officers, aides-de-camp," etc. . . . . . . 146

"At the same moment she dashed with one spring upon the lieutenant, seized him with superhuman force about the waist, and began to kiss him furiously on his face, neck, chest," etc. . . 186

"Apart from the others, and turned in the opposite direction from the ship's course, were a young man and girl leaning on the railing, arm in arm," etc. . . . . . . . . 188

"Oh! here is a door; enter quickly with lowered bayonets; a courtyard, the enemy, a flag; courage, on to them! Around the flag is a bulwark of breasts, bristling with motionless bayonets." . 200

"Little by little the people, armed with scythes, picks, guns, assembled," etc. . . . . . . . . . . 378

# MILITARY LIFE.

## A MIDSUMMER MARCH.

It was a beautiful day in August; not a cloud was to be seen, nor was there a breath of wind stirring; the air was still and burning. The road along which the regiment was marching was broad, straight, long, and seemingly endless, and covered with a very fine dust, which rose in clouds, forcing itself into the eyes, mouth, and under one's clothes, and whitening the beard and hair. On the right and left of the road were neither trees, bushes, not a palm's breadth of shade, nor a drop of water. The country was dry, bare, and deserted; in the few houses scattered here and there, reigned such absolute silence that they seemed abandoned. We could not rest our eyes on the road, the walls, or on the fields, the sun beat so strongly on them all. We walked on with drooping head and half-closed eyes. In short, a beautiful August day, but a very terrible one for a march.

The regiment had been moving for more than an hour. Despite the dust and suffocating heat, the soldiers were still as fresh and gay as at the moment of their departure. Two files marched on the right and two on the left of the road, and from one side to the other there was a continuous fire of jokes and bon-mots, with an unceasing interchange of coarse but witty remarks. From time to time there was a burst of laughter or a noisy clapping of hands, that was always followed by a "To your place, forward, order!" which instantly restored quiet and silence. Sometimes three, four, or five voices would break out at once into some gay Tuscan *stornello;* further on was heard a pathetic southern romance, or still beyond, the war song of the Alps; then some would leave off and others begin, and a thousand different accents and dialects would succeed and mingle with each other. The march continued according to regulations—the lines compact, the step free, the officers in their places; every thing in perfect order. On and on we went. . . .

But—oh, look there; the second man of the first line begins to flag! Now I will set him right. "Ho, there! Will you fall in or not?"—He falls in.

Another ten or twelve paces,—another. "Ho, there! Will you march in your place or not? Just look how that flank is moving! *Corpo di*—. Courage, let's fall in; quick step." A rapid run, a great bumping of canteens against the hips, a noisy dancing of cartridges in their boxes, a confusion, a cloud of dust which envelops and covers every thing. . . . The rear falls in now. We must take breath; there is no help for it. One would really need a pair of iron-bound lungs for this sort of thing. It is terrible marching to-day,—the sun burns the brain,—the dust stifles us,—this road will never end,—and these caps,—if there were only a tree, a palm's breadth of shade, a drop of water! But there is nothing. This is really a desert.

The songs we heard a little while ago have fallen off a

note; the dialogues are less vivacious; the lines a trifle less compact.  The commander of the first battalion is already at the head of the second; the commander of the second is at the rear of the third.  You can see now that the regiment has been marching for three hours.

The straight road comes to an end and begins to curve. The eye can no longer follow the road and comfort itself with the view of the roofs in a distant village, the bell-tower of a little church, or any thing, in fact, that gives indication of habitation and promises a halt, a short rest, a breathing-space—a moment of life.  Heavens, what a road!  We cannot see a hundred steps ahead.  Courage—forward; five minutes more and we shall reach a turn.  Who knows but, in turning, far away in the distance a little hamlet or clump of trees may appear, where we shall make a halt!  Hope gives vigor; we steady our steps, have reached the turn, rush on to reach the new direction, stretch our necks, glance quickly ahead—houses? trees? villages? halts?  Nothing! the road, and nothing but the road, to be seen!  A feeling of desperation takes possession of all.  The heads sink on the chest, the eyes seek the ground, the backs bend beneath the knapsacks; the lines, closed up from the momentary pressure, fall apart; the rear gives the step; the commander of the first battalion is already at the head of the second, the commander of the second at that of the company which follows; the captain—where can the captain be?

The songs we heard two hours since have fallen off two notes.  The men sing because they began to do so: perhaps they would not begin again.  The conversation is forced; the jokes have lost their sharpness.  Ah! you can see that the regiment has been four hours on its march.

On—on—on we go. The foreheads, scorched by the sun, dripping with perspiration, are black, contracted, and disfigured; the breathing is labored; the lips hang down; the tongue has thickened; the hands are swollen and heavy; the soles very painful; there is a drowsiness and utter abandon throughout the entire body; the knapsacks have slipped over the loins, the cartridge-boxes on to the thigh, the cloaks up around the begrimed and soaking throats; the cravats become loosened; the caps are shoved over the nape of the neck or, if the head be bowed, on to the nose. The eyes, blinded by the strong light, are either fixed motionless upon the road-side, or wander here and there in search of a brook, a fountain, a—puddle even; so that the frightful heat which is burning up the body may be mitigated. Oh, what thirst! At this point varied and confused recollections of cafés formerly frequented (when we were happy) spring up before the excited imagination; we see the usual habitués of the place slowly sipping great mugs of frothy, iced beer; or springs of living water burst foaming from a rock. We hear its murmur and see it winding and losing itself in crystalline splendor amid the grass. Oh, to reach it!

"If I ever do reach a spout I will drink enough to kill me! I will fly to a café, empty a bottle in one breath, two, or if that be not enough—three." . . .

On and on we go. The songs have ceased; conversation is dead. A forced joke falls occasionally from the lips of the most vigorous, but in vain; it is received with arid silence. Silently we march. Many who were at the head, now, limping, find themselves at the rear. The strongest who were at the rear, involuntarily take the lead. The companies get mixed. "To your place, to your place! Is that the way to march?" . . . No one pays any attention; we might as well preach to stone walls. "Ho, there—why do you stop? Forward, courage." "Lieutenant, I cannot go another step." "It's nothing, nothing, rouse yourself, forward." . . . It's useless, he is already sleeping. "Close up there. Courage. There is only a short distance now."

"Ah, yes, only a little way! That's what they always say, but meantime we don't come to a halt,—and the soup this morning was water,—and they have n't given the loan yet. With such a sun they might have allowed us to start earlier. We don't halt at all,—and the broth,—and the loan" . . .

"Make way there!" "What is it? Who is coming?" There is the mad dashing by of a horse, a cloud of dust,—he has passed. It was a staff-officer.

"Yes, here is one of the people who make us run. It is quite easy for him on horseback to shout out forward to us on foot! If he had the knapsack——Oh, ho, lift up those feet of yours; is n't there enough dust already?"

Many stop; many, slackening their pace, let their own company pass on in order to stop unseen. The voices of their superior officers sound more irritable than authoritative. The orders come more and more rarely. The commander of the first battalion——Where is the commander of the first battalion? Ah, you can easily see that the regiment has been marching for five hours!

"Hullo! what's this?" The blast of a trumpet is heard. A prolonged *oh!* resounds from one end of the column to the other. All halt, and then begins a confusion, a hurly-burly, a tossing up of knapsacks, a falling of muskets, a rolling away of caps into the ditches by the way-side, a running to right and left. In two minutes the regiment has disappeared. In those ditches on either side of the road, there is a pushing, a shouting, a disputing with the elbows, and by well-aimed thrusts, for a palm's breadth of shade, or a bit of turf. Through the fields there is a coming and going of thirsty men in search of water. Some are looking, some run into each other, while others come to a standstill, like a procession of ants on the bark of a tree. There is a begging for a drink in lamentable tones of voice, refusals irritably uttered, or forced concessions, and pulling away of the canteens in jealous fury. Little by little the tumult subsides, the general movement diminishes, quiet returns; all, comfortably or uncomfortably, as the case may be, lie stretched out on the ground, close their eyes, and rest. One moment more, and the entire regiment will be sleeping.

"Make way, make way there, boys! A little room only—Heigh, there! lookout or the wheels will pass over you. Take up that knapsack from the middle of the road—A little more room, so—make way for me." "Ha, here's the bearer of life, here's the friend of brave men—here's Providence, the sutler!" The sleeping stir, rub their arms, rub their eyes, raise themselves on their elbows—up—up—here they all are on their feet. They rush and gather round the cart, and dash over it as waves do over a ship in a gale. Above that crowd there is a raising of hands, a stretching out of arms, a giving and receiving of money, angry complaints of having been there an hour without getting a thing, a persistency both threatening and supplicating. The poor man who is breathless, perspiring, and puffing, begs for a little space, a little breathing-room.

Another blast of the trumpet; it is the *Attention!* which is followed by a long murmur of surprise and discontent. "There is n't time to swallow a mouthful! It would have been better not to have stopped at all! They certainly want to kill us!" The crowd disperses slowly; those lying down sit up wearily; some rise to their feet slowly; others stand there and enjoy the last moment, the last instant; little by little all have sprung from the ditches on the way-side, the knapsacks are on their shoulders, the lines are formed. Another blast, the first company moves, the second, the third—the entire regiment is in motion. "Fall in there, eh! Don't let us have any repetition of the former confusion."

For a half hour things go a trifle less badly than before, though the entire body feels painfully the shortness of the rest, and not all the men were able to quench their thirst. "But look how that rear is marching! Will you close up there?" For a half hour, as I said, things go a trifle less badly than before; the lines are compact, the man who was behind has caught up with his company, the officers are back at their posts. "But how this sun burns! This is African heat! It 's impossible to stand it!" The feet have no longer strength enough to raise themselves from the ground, they drag along; the arms hang at the side, the belt slides over the hips, the straps of the knapsacks clasp the shoulders, the cloak weighs heavily on the stomach. "And we don't reach our destination! Where are they taking us to?"

"A fountain! a fountain!" A cry of joy greets this news. The lines break up; all run forward, by fives, sixes, and tens, dashing breakneck fashion on the water; then follow blows, pushes, squabbles, shouts, and thrusts. "To your places, to your places, for Heaven's sake!" shouts an indignant officer. The throng breaks up and spreads in all directions; many, whose stomachs are loaded down with water, try in vain to regain their places; others reach theirs after a breathless run, and are obliged to stop shortly thereafter; some stop for another moment, if only to give a last glance at the blessed water! Strength is failing, the vacant spaces grow larger, the ditches are filled with the exhausted; all are tottering and falling. Suddenly, at a turn of the road, a bell-tower and a village appear in sight. "It is the station! it is the station!" The cry spreads in an instant from head to the rear; the effect is miraculous; strength returns, the lines close up, the companies re-form, the stragglers run forward, and every thing is changed. The music starts up; we are at the village; we enter. The doors of the factories, the openings of the streets, the windows and balconies fill with inquisitive people; here and there little faces full of tender curiosity appear at the window-sills. "Poor fellows, how tired they must be!" Oh, the effect of those eyes! The man who was walking doubled up straightens himself, with a supreme effort, for the last time; he who was limping assumes a resolute gait; and he who was just ready to drop, utterly worn out, takes courage and pulls on. "Ho, there! where are you going?" "A swallow of water, lieutenant." "Not a bit of it! Back to your place!" "Oh, how cruel!" murmur the compassionate mammas who happen to be standing around; "how they do treat those poor boys! Not even a swallow of water!"

The regiment has passed, stacked arms, pitched the tents. Oh, what a gay and animated camp! And are the fatigues and trials of the marches remembered?

Ah, not even in their dreams!

## THE ORDERLY.

They had been living together for four years; nor had either of them forgotten for a single moment that one was the officer, the other the soldier. The former was austere as a soldier, the latter correspondingly submissive. They loved each other; but with that hard, rough, silent affection, which never makes any display, nor reveals itself, and which conceals a demonstration of tenderness under a rude action; is eloquent when sient, embarrassed when speaking; inimical to blandishments, and accustomed, when feeling the desire to weep, to bite the lips and withhold the tears for fear of appearing weak and unmanly. They used a laconic language to one another; understood each other by monosyllables, glances, and signs. Their common interpreter was the watch, which regulated every thing, even their steps and words, with the strictest discipline. "Lieutenant, do you wish any thing more?" "Nothing." "May I go?" "Go." This was the daily form of dismissal. Not one word more. So days, months, and years had passed—four years in all—in quarters, at home, in camp, on the march, and in war, and little by little a deep, stern sort of affection, almost unknown to them, had grown up in their two hearts. There was in that invariable taciturnity, that soldierly way of speaking, the fugitive exchange of glances which meant on one side, "Do this," and on the other, "I understand," for any one who knew the natures of these two, as much courtesy, kindness, and warm feeling as could be found in the most expansive interchange of tenderness.

They had stood side by side on the battle-field at solemn moments, within a few paces of the enemy's cannon, and at every whistle of the shot one had glanced quickly around in search of the other, and on finding him had heaved a sigh while thinking, "This, too, has passed." They had stood guard together on the outposts more than one cold and rainy night, with their feet in the mud, the wind blowing on their faces, and in the morning, when the relief arrived, had exchanged smiles, as if to say: "Now we are going back to camp; keep up your spirits, for you can rest." Many times, on a long summer's march, both had looked at the same moment to count the mile-stones on the way-side, and often found them to have numbered more than forty, exchanging, when they reached the last, a glance full of comfort and pleasure, which seemed to say: "There are two more—one more—here we are!" More than one evening in camp, when they were preparing their minds for the musket-shot that was to wake them before morning, after one was stretched out under the tent and the other had arranged his overcoat to protect him from the night air, the soldier said in moving off, "Good-night, lieutenant," and the officer, fancying that the voice trembled slightly, and that the last word had not come out in full force, returned the salute in the same tone. At other times, while one handed the other a letter, and the latter put out his hand impatiently to take it, a slight smile had passed over their two faces:—"It is a letter from home: I recognize the writing; it is from your mother." One meant to say, "Thanks"; the other had intended to reply, "You have anticipated my pleasure."

After which they both returned to their customary silent and severe modes of address. Not once, in presenting himself before, or upon leaving his superior, did the proud soldier forget to put his hand to his cap in a resolute manner, raising his head as he did so, and fixing his eyes upon his face, and when he went away, his right-about-face was always performed according to regulations.

They had only been living together for four years; but the soldier, who had been made an orderly after the first year of duty, was completing his term of service.

One day the commandant of the corps received orders to dismiss the class to which the orderly belonged.

That day, between the officer and the soldier, there passed few more words than usual, but their two hearts talked at length. "Do you require any thing more?" "Nothing." "The order to dismiss your class has arrived; you will leave in ten days."

A brief silence followed without their eyes meeting. . . "May I go?" "Yes, certainly." This time a *certainly* was added, and this was a great step on the road to tenderness.

They were both sad at heart, but not to an equal degree. One lost his friend—in fact, more than a friend, a brother, who loved him with an almost religious devotion. The other, too, lost a friend, a brother; but the former remained, the latter returned to his home, and this was a great comfort. To return home! After so many years, so many perils; after having asked himself so often of an evening—when the long, sad notes of the bugle give the signal for extinguishing lights, and under the tents they died out, and through the movable city of linen spreads a deep quiet—after having asked himself so often of an evening, while leaning his head on his hand in moments of melancholy, and, thinking of his mother: "What is the poor woman doing now?" After having heard so many times in camp, here and there in the groups of peasants, the notes of the rural *ritornelli*, the same that he had listened to at home, in summer, when watching in the fields where the bright moonlight fell, and among so many voices of friends and relations he heard distinctly, one, clear, silvery, and tremulous, which so well knew its way to his heart; to return! after having so often blessed those songs as a greeting from the absent mother. To return unexpectedly and see once more the country and houses, recognize from a distance the well-known roof, to hasten his steps, arrive breathless in that dear meadow, see the little sister now grown up, and the younger brother now quite a stripling, appear before his eyes. The others gather at their cry, and he dashes into their midst, then breaks away from all, runs to the house, calls the old mother, sees her come forward with outstretched arms and eyes filled with tears, throws himself on her neck, and feels the pressure of those beloved arms and experiences the most profound of human joy—these are things of which the thought alone suffices to sweeten any bitterness and heal any wound.

Yet the idea of being obliged to leave his officer cuts the poor fellow to the quick. Then, too, a true soldier never takes off the coat which has served so many years as a covering and a pillow, and upon which he has expended so much labor with soap and brush, without feeling a certain sinking at the heart, an anxious and scornful tenderness, like the separation from a friend who has often offended us, and with whom we should like to keep up the quarrel, but who has always been esteemed and loved. Those pockets at the back, where in prison he concealed his pipe at the appearance of the officer of the guard and for which (until he has overcome the old habit) he still searches with his hands. . . . What a nuisance not to find it any longer there!

The good officer had become pensive and had added not one word to his usual formula. So it was with the soldier too. But their glances were more frequent and longer, and they seemed to say: "You are suffering, I know." The soldier performed his duties more slowly, in order to remain longer in the house and compensate himself, during those last days, for the approaching separation. At first he proceeded with a certain slowness; then with a sluggishness, apparently studied; at last pretended to dust the tables and chairs; but more often absorbed in his sad thoughts, he moved his cloth quite blindly without touching anything. Meanwhile, the officer, erect and immovable, with arms crossed before the mirror, which reflected the figure of his soldier, followed his steps, the movements of the face, and avoided the other's glances by quickly raising his eyes to the ceiling in an abstracted manner. "Lieutenant, may I go?" "Yes, certainly." And the soldier took his departure. He had not gone down two steps when from within came a hurried: "Come here," and he returned. "Do you require any thing else?" "Nothing. I wished to tell you." . . . "Nothing—nothing; you can do it to-morrow—go now." Perhaps he had called him back to see him, and, on his moving off again, he continued to fasten his eyes upon the door through which he had passed.

Finally, the day for departure came. The officer was at home seated at the table opposite the half-closed door. Half an hour later the soldier would be obliged to come, take leave, and go away. He was smoking, blowing the clouds of smoke into the air, and with his eye lazily followed its slow and tortuous course until it melted into the atmosphere. The smoke which got into his eyes made the tears gather, and he wiped them away from time to time with the back of his hand, wondering why such big tears should fall just as if he were crying. He attributed it all to the smoke, wished to delude himself as to his emotion, dissimulate to himself, and ascribe to the cigar that which really belonged to the heart. He thought : Yes—he might have expected it. So why should he take it so to heart ? Did n't I know when I took him that I could not keep him always ? Did I not know that the term of service was five years ? And this man has a home, a family, where he was born and has grown up, which he left with sorrow, and to which he will return with joy ? Could I expect that he would continue a soldier out of affection for me ? I should be an egotist—in fact I am one. What tie of gratitude binds him to me ? What have I done for him ! What does he owe me ? Oh, a great deal certainly. I have never been other than harsh to him. I have always been to him like a father of the inquisition. It 's my temperament, to be sure, what can I do ? It is useless. I cannot find words with which to express certain thoughts. And, then, . . . they must not be uttered. But at least I can give a rather more human expression to my face. . . . Now he is going away, is going back to work in the fields, to take up his old life again, and little by little he will lose all his military habits and will forget everything, . . . his regiment, comrades, and officers. Never mind, so long as he is contented. But shall I be able to forget him? How much time will have to elapse before I become accustomed to a new face? Upon waking in the morning, shall I not seem to see him hard at his work in a corner of the room, but so quietly that he scarcely moves for fear of arousing me before the time? How many times, when half asleep, shall I not call him by name. So many years of companionship, devoted attachment, affectionate service, and then . . . To see him go away . . . from one day to another. Bah! it is our profession, and there is nothing to be said. We must be resigned. . . . What a good fellow! What a heart he has!

If sometimes when marching, overcome by fatigue, burned by the sun, choked with dust, I stopped a moment and glanced around as if in search of a little water, a canteen instantly appeared before me and a voice at my side said: "Do you wish a drink, lieutenant?" It was he. He had left the ranks, run to fetch water * * * at a distance perhaps, who knows where, had, in the twinkling of an eye, returned panting, dripping with perspiration and exhausted, and came behind me to wait until I had shown a desire to drink. In camp, if I fell asleep under the shade of a tree, and the sun gradually began to shine in my face, a careful hand raised a green bough at the side, or stretched a tent, or placed three or four knapsacks on top of one another, or spread a cloak over a stack of arms; whose hand was it? His always. Hardly had we arrived at a station, after six, seven, or eight hours' march, barely were the tents unfolded, when he disappeared; and I began to look for and call him at the top of my voice all over the camp, then getting angry : where is he? who knows where he has hidden himself? What a scamp he is. Is this the way to do? Just wait till he comes and I 'll fix him, and so on in this tone. A moment later I saw him appear in the distance bent under a great load of straw, with uncertain steps and great bounds, shouting to right and left at the people who wished to carry off a handful, tripping over tent cords, leaping hedge and ditches, hitting the knapsacks and shirts stretched out in the sun, stumbling into those sleeping, and drawing down upon his devoted head a regular shower of oaths and imprecations. He reached my side, threw down the straw, heaved a great sigh, wiped his forehead and said : " Lieutenant, I have kept you waiting, haven't I ? but you must excuse me for I had to go so far ! " Then he would stretch the straw on the grass the length of my body, pile it up on one end, put his knapsack under it as a pillow, and turning to me, would say : " Will that do, lieutenant ? " Good fellow, I thought, I was wrong to get angry with you. " Go," I said then, " go and rest, for you need it." " But is it all right ? " he insisted ; "if not, I 'll go and fetch some more." "Yes, yes; it 's all right; go and rest; go; do not lose any more time." And on a march at night, if I were seized by sleep and walked, as one is apt to do, staggering and tottering from one side of the road to the other, and in doing so came too near a ditch, a light hand was placed on my arm and pushed me gently toward the middle of the road, while a subdued and timid voice murmured : " Look out, lieutenant, there is the ditch." It was always he ! What have I done to this man that he should overwhelm me with the care and tenderness of a mother?

What am I that he should love me with so much devotion? What do I deserve that he should live only for me? and I am sure he would give his life for me. For what reason and in what way has this poor young fellow with his rough features, hands hardened by the spade, his frame toughened by discomforts and fatigue, without culture or education, born and brought up in a humble hut in the country, quite unused to all the ways of the city, become as bashful and gentle as a girl, so that he holds his breath for fear of disturbing my slumbers, and touches my clothes with his hand to ward off some danger from me, hands me a letter holding it with his finger tips, as if he feared to profane it, and feels happy at a kind smile, a polite word, a sign, or a look that says, "All right." How is this? Ah! one must confess that the human heart learns in these garments new throbs unknown to him who is not or has not been a soldier. People do not suppose that we are stirred by other sentiments than those which fill the soul in days of war. But people in truth know little of us. They do not understand that in being a soldier the heart never grows old, but is rejuvenated, and reopens to the lovely affections of early life, and lives and exults in them much more than in the stormy and terrible excitement of war. . . . Oh, no one who is not a soldier will ever comprehend what a feeling of affection binds me to this young fellow. It is impossible. You must have passed many nights in camp, have made long marches in the month of July, have been on picket duty in a pouring rain, have suffered hunger and thirst until ready to drop, and have had a friend at your side who has placed his cloak over you to protect you from the cold, has dried your clothes, has brought you a swallow of water, offered you a piece of bread, depriving himself of that which he offered you. Servant, domestic,—could any one call him this? Oh, he exclaims (giving vent to a movement of scorn and repugnance), it is libel! Yes, . . . because when this man comes to the doorway and salutes me, and gives that look full of timid and affectionate submission, I feel that the sign I give in order that he drops his hand, is as full of respect as the act which he performs in raising it. . . . This man is going away from me—leaves me alone—and I shall see him no more. No, that can't be; I will go and look him up; I will go and find him when he is dismissed; I know the name of his town, I will ask that of his parish and little farm, and then I will surprise him at work in the fields and call him by name. "Don't you remember your officer?" "Whom do I see! lieutenant, you here!" he will say, overcome by emotion. "Yes, I wanted to see you. Come here my dear good soldier and embrace me!"

At this point he hears a light, slow, unequal step on the stairs, like that of a person who is lingering as if trying to delay his ascent. He listens attentively without turning his head; the step approaches; his heart strings tighten; he turns; here he is—it is he—the orderly.

His face wore a disturbed expression and his eyes were red; he saluted; took a step forward, and stood looking at the officer. The latter kept his face turned away.

"Lieutenant, I am going away."

"Good-by," replied the latter pressing his lips at every word, and continuing to look in the other direction. "Good-by. A pleasant journey . . . return home . . . work . . continue to live like a good man, as you have lived up to this time. Good-by."

"Lieutenant!" exclaimed the soldier in a trembling voice, taking a step toward him.

"Go, go, or you will be too late; go, it's late already—hurry."

And he stretched out his hand—the soldier pressed it warmly.

"A pleasant journey to you, and remember me. Remember your officer sometimes."

The poor fellow wished to reply; tried to utter a word, and gave a groan; pressed the hand once more, turned, looked at the door, glanced again at the officer who continued to keep his head turned away, took a long step forward. "Ah, lieutenant!" he exclaimed with a sob, and fled.

The other left alone, looked around, remained for a short time gazing at the door, then placed his elbows on the little table, rested his head on his hands, and tears formed in the corners of his eyes; shone there for a moment, and then slipped quickly down his cheeks as if afraid of being seen. He passed his hand over his eyes, looked at his cigar; it had gone out; ah, this time they were real tears; he buried his face on one arm and let them flow, for he felt the need of them.

---

# THE OFFICER OF THE GUARD.

AFTER having had the tattoo beaten, the officer of the guard gave a glance at the court of the quarters; there was no one there; he went to the staircase leading to the dormitories,—no one; raised his eyes to the balconies; no one there; a look at the door; closed; a peep into the guard-room; all correct there; the lights on the landings and corridors were all right; every thing was in order; all was quiet, and the regiment asleep. What was left for the officer of the guard to do? Nothing but to sleep; and this he thought he would do. He glanced around once more, above and below, approached the cellar door, tried it with his hand; it was shut; he listened attentively; not a sound was to be heard. "Now I can go to sleep," he said to himself, as he moved off toward his room. He whispered a few words in the ear of the sergeant of the guard: "You understand, eh?" and having received in reply a respectful: "Trust me!" accompanied by the placing of the hand on his breast as an assurance of good faith, he entered, closed his door, took off his cap, sword, sash, approached the bed, arranged the sheet, carried his right hand to the first button of his jacket . . . "Bah, and the round?" he thought, making a slight motion of the head as if putting the question to some one else. Then taking the light in an impatient way, he went and planted himself as straight as a pole in front of the orders for the day, fastened to the wall under the portrait of the king. He placed his forefinger at the bottom of the sheet and began to run it along under the lines, reading rapidly and masticating the words in an angry and inarticulate way, until he suddenly stopped and pronounced in a distinct voice: "'Round in the interior of the quarters at eleven o'clock'—*Sacre* . . . !" he added, turning instantly toward the bed and setting down the candlestick with a bang on the little table, "I was sure of it!" And he stood there erect and immovable, with his eyes fastened on the pillow and his hands in the act of unbuttoning his jacket.

"The round! the round!" he began again, slipping the buttons one by one from the button-holes; "after having been on your feet all day, after having run here and there; up and down without a minute's rest, and being breathless from shouting from morning till night, finally the hour comes when you ought to rest your poor bones in bed, and enjoy a moment's peace; but, *no, sir!* there's the round, the round at eleven o'clock. You ought to take your good lantern in hand and go around again, poking and screaming about to see if they are all in bed, that no one has slipped out of the window, and so on, as long as necessary. Finally . . . "

Meanwhile he had thrown his jacket over a chair near the bed.

"Anyhow, I am made of flesh and blood like the rest, and I do not intend killing myself in the service. No, not much! Really one cannot go on in this way, it's out of the question. Joking aside, there really is n't time to eat, and that order for the day proves it too. There is nothing easier . . . "

And the trousers had gone to keep company with the jacket.

"Nothing easier than to arrange orders for the day, seated at table after an excellent dinner, with a seven centime cigar in the mouth ; nothing easier. The discomfort falls to the lot of the poor devils who have to keep to them. It is always low down in the ranks that the hard work falls. Can't a poor officer of the guard have time to digest his food? Oh, what difference does it make to certain fine gentlemen ? Dig, dig ; and if a mistake is made the punishment follows. Well, in the end . . . "

And the rest of his raiment was thrown down with his other garments.

"After all, who is likely to turn up here at ten o'clock ? Who will take it into his head to come and see whether I am going the round or not ? Outside it 's bitterly cold ; there is a wind that fairly freezes the face ; then a road in which you could break your neck. The colonel lives at the end of the town, and then he is not in the habit of giving surprises. The major . . Oh, he 's married, and there is no danger of his making his appearance. The officer of the day is at this hour taking a hand at *Tarocchi*,[1] and he certainly won't be seized by a caprice to drag himself over here. Then, if he did come,— he will have . . . "

Meantime he had dashed into bed, trembling with the cold, and nestling and rolling himself up softly under the comfortables, gave a little smile of indolent content.

"He will have to rap in order to be admitted ; and before the corporal of the guard has heard him, stirred, found the keyhole, and opened the door, five minutes will have elapsed, and I 'll have had time to dress myself in some sort of fashion,

---

[1] A sort of chequered cards.

fly to the door, open it, seize the lantern in the guard-room, and away through the dormitories to play my part . . . "

Here he blew out the candle, drew the counterpane over his head, turned on to his side, sought a comfortable position, and closed his eyes, thinking :—" And away through the dormitories to play my part."

" Oh, it *is* a luxury to dash into bed after working all day! What a profession! And to think that with all my efforts I can never satisfy that old dotard of a captain. The meat is underdone! Whose fault is it? Mine. The stairs are dirty! Who is to blame for it? I; the devil! The dormitories are in disorder! Who gets hauled over the coals for it? I, I, always I. No one but me. Whew! What a good bed! And to hear certain people say that we have nothing to do but fill the cafés with smoke and run after the girls. Let them try for themselves, now that the whole world is looking on with expectancy . . . with that magnificent pay . . . and the taxes . . . "

Little by little, wandering along in this defence of himself, his thoughts and ideas grew confused ; the captain, the major, the wife, the expectation, the taxes, grew into a curious muddle, which ended finally in profound slumber.

But he had not fallen asleep without a little anxiety and remorse. Every time the idea of the round came to his mind he felt a slight twinge of conscience. The same thing happens to the truant from school who goes off to make snow-balls with his companions ; the image of his master and his mother assail him from time to time, and the more he attempts to drive them away the more they return to torment and bite him like a fly.

He dreamed. One after the other the ten or twelve most wretched, undisciplined soldiers in the whole regiment, who are noted for the nocturnal escapades, revelling in taverns, and rascally adventures, which always end successfully, passed before his mind; some noted for getting off scot-free; others famous, on the other hand, for assignments, imprisonment, and so forth, to *number eighteen;* and it seemed as if each one in passing whispered just above his breath: "Sleep, sleep, and I'll play you a trick." Then these melted away, and all the most elegant and bedecked subalterns of the regiment, with cigar in mouth and a bunch of flowers in the hand, those who carry the cap-band under the lip, wear small high-heeled shoes, have lady-loves in town, and when they can escape in the moonlight do not wait for a second inspiration, seemed to pass before him murmuring softly: "Sleep, sleep, and we will get the better of you." The sergeant of the guard, who a short time before had given him that respectful "trust to me!" that reassuring sign, now, in recollecting it, seemed to have eyes gleaming with malice, and to have curled his lips under his moustache, as much as to say: "Go to sleep, do, and I'll play you a trick!"

Then came something else. He seemed to lie in the middle of a road, back of the barracks, and to be looking around to see if the sentinels were awake and at their posts. They were all there. In fact, he discovered one not unknown to him, a soldier belonging to his company, the roundest, laziest conscript of all, and, to make matters worse, short-sighted and deaf. "Just see," he thought, "doesn't it look as if they had put that stupid there just out of disrespect to me? He is not good for any thing!" And he watched him. The sentinel stretched his neck outside his box, looked to the right and left to see if any one were coming, placed his musket in a corner, wrapped himself in his cloak, sat down, put his head on his knees, and went to sleep. The poor dreamer grew enraged at the rascal, seized him by the shoulder, shook him, and opened his mouth to utter some imprecation.

At that point he thought he heard a slight noise above his head; he raised his eyes to the windows. From one of the sills there projects and moves with uncertainty something black, which stretches out, descends very slowly, and reaches the ground; it is a rope. After having followed it with his eyes to the ground, he raises them to the window, sees a head project, two shoulders, and an entire body turn warily around, seize the rope, descend, and disappear. He instantly dashes after him, is close to him, comes up with him, stretches out his hand to catch hold of him by his clothes . . .

At that moment he seems to be before a door,—the door of the cellar. He tries it lightly with his hand; it gives. Whew! What an uproar! Clattering of dishes, a clinking of glasses, a shouting of hoarse and discordant voices, a confused sound of oaths and songs, and an odor of pipes that drives one backward. He stopped an instant, pushed the door again, and threw it wide open. What a spectacle! The room was crowded with soldiers, some dressed, some in doublets, some with the cape over the shoulders like a Spanish mantle, and the cap thrown back, bravado fashion; others seated on the tables, some astride, others on their faces, some stretched indecently on the floor, their eyes shining glassy and stupefied, their faces heated; others tipsy, others still more intoxicated; some dozing, the rest sleeping soundly. A few tried to rise to their feet and fell back heavily on to their seats; some, who had succeeded in getting up, staggered shouting around the room and making the tables shake and the bottles and glasses tremble. On every side there were piles of cards and money, and a cutting of the air with hands in cabalistic signs, shouts, laughter, and every thing was enveloped in a dense cloud of smoke, enough to suffocate one in ten minutes. "Out of this! out of this!" the poor dreamer seemed to shout; "sergeant, sergeant, take all their names, put them all in the guard-house, in irons, all . . ."

Now he seemed to hear behind him a creaking like a large door moving slowly on its hinges; he turned, looked around, and discovered that he was in the hall, near the door of the quarters. A black shadow advanced suspiciously close to the wall, like the figure of a perambulating *bass-relief;* it moved two steps, paused, gazed about, began moving on again, stopped once more, as if it were afraid; reached the door, laughed, dragged its feet, and behold! on the sill of the guard-room door another figure like the first, cautious and quiet as possible. They exchanged a few words in an undertone, the door opened, and one of them slowly disappeared. "Ah, I recognized him!" thought the dreamer; "he is the sergeant of the eighth." And he turned and saw another, behind this one a third, then a fourth, the sergeant of the fifth, the commissary of the sixth, the commissary of the third. "Ah, traitors!" he dreams that he cries, "to the hall all of you! to the hall all of you! sergeant of the guard! sergeant . . ."

At this moment he seemed to strike his hand against something soft and woolly. He turns, it is a bed. Behind this another, then another, another still,—a long row of beds. He looks around and discovers that he is in a dormitory, a little light at the end of the room dimly illumines all the objects therein; all are silent, one could hear a fly stirring. Suddenly one of the sleepers begins to snore, lightly at first, then more heavily, finally so as to be heard in the street. Some one wakes. A man near by stretches his arms, yawns, rubs his eyes, and exclaims: "Oh, there, could n't you sleep a little more like a christian?" No change, he does not seem to have understood. "Do you understand? You are to sleep more like a christian," the man shouts louder still. It had no effect, one might as well talk to a stone wall. "Body of a bomb shell!" cries the infuriated man springing out of bed. "I'll fix you now!" He approaches, seizes him by both his arms, gives him such a vigorous shake that he makes his bed and all those around about tremble. The snorer stirs, wakes, half sees and understands, gives a kick to the counterpane, a shout, a spring, is on his feet in a moment with a pillow in his hand, and down it comes on the neck of the unfortunate aggressor with a blinding blow. The latter gives as good as he takes; the first one pursues him, a third rushes to the assistance of the weaker; a fourth to the defense of the first, a regular scuffle ensues, all dash from their beds, the uproar increases; the light goes out; the men get mixed up; a window pane is broken, another too, the knapsacks come down from the shelves, the sheets from the beds, the muskets from the racks. . . . The poor dreamer dazed, trembling, hardened by rage, is just about to give a loud shout that will be heard above that infernal racket, and bends himself in order to dash into the thick of the fight. . . .

At that point he heard some one knocking vigorously at the door, and it seemed as if a voice called his name. Trembling, terrified, bathed with perspiration, he rose wearily to a sitting posture, listened attentively, and held his breath. "Lieutenant! lieutenant! the officer of the day," said the voice again.

"Heavens! quick, my stockings, my stockings; where are those stockings? Well, no matter. My trowsers . . . where are they? Ah, here they are! . . . Quick, my jacket! one arm, the other . . . the jacket is on. My sword! where in heaven's name is my sword? The scarf, now, the scarf! . . . Ah, here it is! At last. . ."

And dressed thus carelessly, his jacket unbuttoned, without stockings, cravat, or drawers, he rushed breathless to the door, opened it, looked around, and saw . . . the officer of the day, erect, immovable, and rigid, with his hands crossed on his breast, and the visor of his cap over his eyes, and his eyes flashing under his knitted brows like two burning coals.

"Have you gone the rounds?"

For a moment the lieutenant hesitates, then says boldly, "I have done them."

"I understand," mutters the captain to himself, "you have *done* me."

. . . . . . . . .

Now I ask you: is it worse to have a dream of this kind, or to catch an attack of pleurisy, or bark your shins against some bed in the dark? I go in for the bruised shins and influenza, and I fancy the majority of my readers would do the same.

---

"He rushed breathless to the door, opened it, looked around, and saw—the officer of the day, erect, immovable, and rigid."

(*Page* 28.)

# THE WOUNDED SENTINEL.

It was growing dark. The streets of the city were full of people. Those shops which are generally open during the evening were in great part closed, and the remainder were being shut one by one. Here and there, at the corners, on the squares, in front of the cafés, on the steps of the churches, were groups of men and boys, who were talking in low and excited voices, turning from time to time to look around them in order to see that no suspicious person was listening. There was a continuous descent of people from the houses to the street; they stopped a moment on the door-way, looked to the right and left as if uncertain which way to go, and then mingled in the crowd. In the whispering of the crowd, although it was much denser and more noisy than usual, there was perceptible a suppressed and almost timid tone. Now and then a knot of people crossed the street hurriedly, and behind them a long train of gamins who made way for themselves between the legs of the people with their elbows and shoulders, whistling and shrieking as they did so. At the sound of any voice which made itself heard above the general murmur, many stopped and turned back to ask what was the matter. It was only some one who had made use of an expression a little stronger than the others—that was all. After the people had looked at him a moment and he at the people, every one went on his way. A moment later a great blow was heard on one side of the street; every one turned in the direction of the sound. Who is it? What is it? What's happened? It was a shopkeeper who had closed and barred his door. The carriages passed slowly, and the coachmen begged the crowd to make way, with an unusually polite smile, and a motion of the whip that was excessively courteous. On the corners, by the light of the lamps, were seen those poor newspaper venders assailed by ten people at a time, who, holding out the sou with one hand, seized the desired sheet with the other, drew to one side, then unfolded it in haste, and searched with avidity for some important news. Some of the passers-by stopped, formed a circle around the possessor of the journal, and the latter read in a low voice while the others listened attentively.

Suddenly all the people are seen running toward the end of a street; there is instantly a great press, a loud shout, a tremendous confusion; above the heads can be seen four or five muskets knocked here and there; a clapping of hands is heard; the crowd vacillates, falls back, opens on one side; four or five dark figures appear with muskets in their hands, give a glance about them with an air of triumph, turn into an alley, and off they dash; a troop of boys, howling and whistling, follow them. What was it? What's happened? Nothing, nothing. A patrol of the national guard has been disarmed. A moment later, the crowd opens on another side and four or five unfortunate fellows appear, with pale faces, bare heads, dishevelled hair, and clothes torn and disordered. Round about them there rises a murmur of compassion; some sympathetic person takes them by the arm, leads them out of the throng, and accompanies them home, exhorting them by word and gesture to be courageous.

Meanwhile confusion, great excitement, and deafening noises have sprung up in the multitude. "Give way there! Make way there!" is suddenly shouted on one side of the street. All turn in that direction. Who is it? What is it? What's happened? "Make way there! Make way there!" The crowd divides, falls back rapidly, forms a hedge on the sides of the street, and a company of sharpshooters traverse it on a run. A dirty, noisy troop of gamins follow them. The crowd closes up again.

Suddenly a confused sound of angry menacing voices breaks out on another side; the crowd gathers and forms at this point; above the heads two or three carabineers' hats appear and disappear, then a burst of applause, the crowd opens, a man breathless and disfigured runs out and disappears. "They wanted to put handcuffs on him," some one remarks in a tone of satisfaction, "but they did not succeed in doing so; there were some strong people who took his part. We should like to see them!"

The crowd proceeds slowly in one direction, and reaches the corner of a street. Suddenly the people in front stop and those behind press on to them; the former recede a few steps, the latter are violently forced back, then begin to push forward again, and then recede once more; all of which gives rise to indescribable disorder. "What is the matter? Who is preventing our going on? Forward, forward!" "Oh, yes, it is very fine to say forward! There is a company of soldiers with bayonets fixed who are barring the passage." Then follow shouts, hisses, oaths, and imprecations. "Down with the oppressors! We don't want oppression, down with those muskets, give us a free passage—out of the way!" All at once the crowd turn their backs on the soldiers and take flight, leaving the pavement strewn with the fallen and invade in less than a moment the side streets, cafés, vestibules, and courts of the neighboring houses. The soldiers have lowered their bayonets.

"Make way there! Make way there!" they shriek, on one side. From one of the side alleys comes the sound of horses' tramp and the clinking of swords; it is a squad of cavalry that is advancing; the gleam of the first helmets is seen; a troop of horses break through the crowd, which spring to the right and left against the walls of the houses; the squad passes in the midst of profound silence; when it is almost by, a voice or a hiss is heard here and there; it has passed—then follow shouts, whistles, reproaches, and a shower of cabbage-heads and lemon-peel on to the last horses. The squad stops, the last horses back a few paces, the crowd turns and clears the street for a hundred steps.

In the nearest group is heard from time to time a furious outburst of oaths, a beating of sticks, a sharp cry, a feeble moan, and then a long whisper followed by a timid silence. "What has happened? What was it? Nothing, nothing; they have driven a few inches of steel into the back of a public guard." The crowds draw back on the right and left, and a carabineer, with bare head and both hands buried in his hair, crosses the street tottering and staggering like a drunken man. "What is the matter? What have they done?" "They have given him a blow on the head." "To the square! To the square!" suddenly shouts a powerful voice. "To the square!" comes the unanimous response from all sides. And the multitude burst tumultuously into the nearest street and start toward the square.

All this occurred not many years since in one of the principal cities of Italy, while in a neighboring street in the midst of the tumult a band of eight soldiers passed with a corporal and sergeant, to relieve another body standing guard at a public building in a little square near by. The squad moved slowly, and the soldiers looked curiously on this side and that. Just in this street the excitement seemed greatest and the conduct of the people most resolute.

The patrol passed near a large group of those people who are only seen on certain evenings, and who with surly and heated faces hold forth loudly in the midst of roughs, around whom there is always a group of gamins. One of the group sees the patrol, turns, and pointing his finger at the soldiers, exclaims, *sotto voce:* "Look at them!" The whole circle turns in that direction, and one after the other, gradually raising his voice, begins to say: "Yes, look at the men who never fail to come out when the people wish to make their rights felt. They reason with the butt-end of their muskets; the bayonets are made to drive holes in the bodies of those who are hungry. They don't lack bread, you understand, but others starve; what does it matter to them? Powder and lead for those who are hungry!"

The soldiers went on without turning back. The group moved forward, and, preceded by an advance guard of gamins, followed them. In a moment they caught up with them and accompanied them for a few paces. The soldiers continued to march without turning their heads.

One of the group begins to cough; another sneezes; a third coughs harder; a fourth makes ready to expectorate, and, turning toward the band, spits with a rattling sound, which ends in a burst of incontrollable laughter; all the others clap their hands. The small boys whistle, scream, and, instigated by the larger ones, slowly approach the soldiers. The latter continue to march without giving any sign of having noticed any thing. The former approach nearer and walk beside the soldiers, looking them in the face with an expression intended to say: "I defy you." One of them begins to imitate quite grotesquely their regular step, crying in a nasal tone, as he does: "One, two! one, two!" Another mimics the gait of the soldiers bent and limping under the weight of the knapsacks. A third, urged on by one of those at the rear, seizes the hem of the corporal's cloak, gives a tug, and runs off. The corporal turns and raises his hand as if to give him a box on the ear.

"Eh! eh!" they shout all around. "Now we'll see. Give a blow to a boy! Shame! The time of the Croats has passed! You must try other methods now! A blow to a boy! Try again!"

One of the soldiers, on hearing these words, bites his finger, planting his teeth well in, and uttering a groan of rage. At that point he feels his canteen struck a hard blow; the blood rushes to his head; he turns and gives a hit on the shoulder of the gamins who had struck him, throwing him back several paces.

"Here! Here!" breaks out menacingly from the crowd. "Here are the ruffians! Worse than the Croats! Worse than the bailiffs. Now we'll give them a lesson; we'll make you pay, you dog! Oppressors! Worse than Croats! For shame to beat an unarmed boy!"

The boys, emboldened by the anger of the mob and the surety of impunity, went and stuck their heads between the soldiers, whispering in a hoarse and aggravating voice: "Ugly soldier! Ugly hangman! Traitorous, bread-eater! Convict officer! Burst, you face of a dog!"

And the throng all around: "Shame! To beat an unarmed boy!"

"You cowards!" said the poor soldier to himself, biting, meanwhile his lips until he drew blood. "Cowards! An unarmed boy! Don't you know that there are words which kill? Hangman! Croat! To me! To me! Oh!"—And he bit his hand again, shaking his head in a desperate way.

After a few moments, followed always by the people, the squad arrived at the square and entered the guard-house, which was a little, low, squalid room, lighted by one lantern. The sentinel at the door of the palace was instantly changed twenty or thirty feet from the guard, the squad who had been there first went off, and those newly arrived began arranging their knapsacks on the racks, and hanging their haversacks and canteens on the hooks.

On arriving within fifty paces of the guard-room, the people who had followed the squad stopped, and from there began provoking the soldiers by words and deeds, but the latter paid no attention to them. Seeing that there was no way of exciting a riot, they were on the point of moving off, when one of them observed that the soldier in the sentinel-box was the one who a short time before had given the boy a blow on the shoulder. "Is it really he?" "Yes." "Really?" "Yes, I tell you it is that rascal," "You wretch. Now we'll fix you. Just wait!"

And they all moved toward the sentinel. At the distance of about thirty paces they stopped, drew up in line, and began to look at him out of the corner of their eyes. The soldier stood there, near his box, motionless and firmly, with his head erect and his eyes fixed on those provoking faces which were ranged before him. Suddenly, out of the group steps a ragged youth, with a hat crushed over one ear, the stump of a cigar in his mouth, moves forward with his hands in his pockets, humming in a mocking way, and comes and plants himself within fifteen paces of the sentinel, looking insolently into his face, crossing his arms and assuming an attitude of defiant impertinence.

The soldier looked at him.

Then the man whirled suddenly on his heel, turned his back, bursting into a concerted laugh with the others, who stood watching him and urging him on by signs.

The soldier shook his head two or three times, bit his lips, uttered a sigh, tapping the ground impatiently with his foot as if to say: "Ah, patience! patience! it is hard to bear!"

The rough turned, facing the soldier once more, and, after a moment's hesitation, took from his mouth the cigar stump and threw it at his feet, retreating eight or ten paces to place himself beyond the reach of a sudden assault.

The soldier turned pale, raised his eyes to heaven, clinched his fists, and ground his teeth; his mind was growing confused. "Why do you do this to me?" he then said sadly to himself, turning his eyes and face toward those people as if he were really speaking to them. "What have you against me? Have I done any thing to you? I have done nothing. Why did I give that boy a blow? But why did he come and insult me? Who had provoked him? Who was annoying you? What do you wish of me? I have offended no one, I do not know you even; I am a poor soldier and am doing my duty, and stand here because I am ordered to do so. Yes, ridicule and hiss at me, you do yourselves honor to treat your soldiers in such a way . . . just as if they were brigands!"

At that point, a stump of cabbage thrown with great force grazed the ground, and bouncing and whistling fell at his feet. "God! God!" he murmured in a desperate tone of voice, covering his face with one hand and resting his forehead on the other which was leaning on the mouth of his gun. "I shall lose my head! I cannot control myself much longer. The blood is rushing to my head! . . ."

"But it is quite useless," he added a moment latter in a trembling and stifled voice; "it is useless to make us wear these" . . . and he gave a hard blow on the two medals that he wore on his breast, making them hit each other and resound; "it is useless for them to give us medals because we have fought for our country, if afterward they are to throw cigar stumps and cabbage heads in our faces! Oh, you wish to make me abandon my post, do you? You wish me to betray my trust. If you were fifty, or even a hundred, you could not force me to move from here; if you should all spring upon me at once, I would sooner be torn to pieces like a dog. Come on, you cowards! Don't insult me from a distance. Yes, yes, I understand, it is useless for you to make signs at me; I know that you have knives in your pockets; but you won't quite dare to plant them in my stomach in broad daylight. You would prefer sticking them into my back at night . . . when . . ."

Suddenly he uttered a sharp cry, let his musket fall, covered his face with his hands, tottered, and fell at the foot of his sentry box: a stone had hit him on the forehead.

All the soldiers rushed forward, the crowd dispersed and disappeared; the wounded man was carried into the guard-room with his face and chest bleeding; the wound was instantly washed, his head bound up, he was given something to drink, and a bed was prepared for him on the table with the camp blankets of the other soldiers. While they were all gathering around him, and overwhelming him with questions and words of comfort, and the sergeant was scolding him for not having asked assistance at the first insult of those people, an officer suddenly entered, and behind him the first file of a squad of soldiers. At the same moment, plunged forward by a vigorous push, there dashed into the middle of the room a man with distorted face, hair hanging over his forehead, and clothes in rags. He had been arrested on that same little square by the soldiers of a squad who were passing, and to whom he had offered a violent resistance.

At the first appearance of the prisoner the wounded soldier sprang up from the table, made a dash at him, placed himself face to face with him, looked at him a moment with flashing eyes, uttered a cry, which came broken and hoarse from between his clinched teeth, took a step backward, and resting proudly on his right foot, and raising his left hand, with the first finger pointing to the face of the man, who was watching him with fear: "Ah, you are the one! he shrieked in a tone that froze one's blood; "I recognize you! You called me hangman in the street and have broken my head with a stone on the square; now it's your turn!" Saying which, he sprang at him, seized him by the collar of his jacket and shirt, pinned him with one

"Saying which, he sprang at him, seized him by the collar of his jacket and shirt, pinned him with one dash against the wall, raised his clenched and trembling fist," etc.

(*Page* 38.)

dash against the wall, raised his clinched and trembling fist, and aimed at his head with angry, bloodshot eyes. . . . All this took place in an instant, those present interfered, separated them, held the wounded man by the arm, a corporal supported the other who was ready to drop, and both stood for a moment looking into each other's eyes, panting and gasping; the one white from fear, his arms hanging and his head bowed; the other with his face flaming and haughty, his fists clinched, and his whole body shaken by a violent tremor. Meanwhile a crowd of inquisitive people had gathered before the guard-room door.

The officer looked from one to the other, and asked the sergeant the cause of the trouble. The latter related all that he knew. The officer then turned toward the prisoner, who held his chin down on his chest, and in the midst of a profound silence, said in an extraordinarily quiet tone:

"I can understand that, from a barricade, a man may cast things at a battalion, with some end or aim in view, but this useless and stupid insult to an inoffensive soldier, who has neither the responsibility or right to defend himself, is one of the most disgusting pieces of cowardice that can stain a citizen."

A murmur of approbation was heard among the crowd at the door.

"Take that man away!" added the officer, lighting the end of a cigar in the flame of the lantern.

"And you," he said, turning toward the wounded soldier, while the patrol lead the prisoner off, "forgive . . . and forget."

The soldier gave a nod in the affirmative.

"And keep up your spirits," concluded the officer, putting the cigar in his mouth.

"As for me," . . . replied the soldier, closing his teeth on the cigar and taking it between his forefinger and thumb, "I am always in good spirits; but you must understand, lieutenant, that these are things that try one."

So the drama ended with a laugh.

# THE MOTHER.

When the winter sinks gradually into spring, on the evenings of those clear, quiet days without any wind, in which we keep the doors and windows open for the first time, stretch out of the window sill summer clothing, and carry the flower-pots on to the terraces; on those beautiful clear, starry nights, even the cities (not alone that everlasting country of the poets) offer a lovely spectacle full of gaiety and poetry. In walking through the streets we feel from time to time a soft, fragrant breath, from what? what flowers or grass? who knows? they are perfumes quite vague and unknown, filled with the freshness of youth and life. We inhale the air with delight, opening wide our mouths and dilating our nostrils, and it seems to refresh body and soul. "Oh, what a fine air!" we exclaim from time to time, as almost involuntarily, almost without being aware of it, from corner to corner, street to street, on we go until we find ourselves outside the walls, on the boulevards surrounding the city, in the gardens, and we bare and raise our heads in order to feel that soft air blowing over our faces and playing with our hair.

On these evenings it is impossible to stay at home, or if one is obliged to do so, they will be spent in leaning out of the window, looking down into the unusual crowd, and feeling annoyed that it is impossible to mingle with the people below; for to go to bed betimes, and not enjoy even from the window so beautiful an evening, would seem a shame.

In the principal streets there is a regular hive. The houses are quite empty. The large families, even the most domestic, decide to creep out of their shell; the "papa" goes to the window, looks down and then up at the sky, and exclaims: "Fine weather!" then turning to the family, who are behind him, and only waiting a sign from him, he says gaily: "Let us go out"; so after much shouting and running about hither and yon from room to room, clapping their hands and turning the house upside down, in search of wraps and hats in the dark, the boys are ready, and the troop puts itself in motion. Even the grandmamma, poor old lady, feels several years slip off from her shoulders, and, despite her habitual complaints, goes out too, leaning on the arm of her best-behaved grandson. The party stretches along the street, two by two, the boys in front, jumping and singing among themselves, and knocking with heads and hands into the legs of the passers-by. The old people behind, limping and coughing, try to keep out of the way of the carriages and not lose sight of the children. The newly married pairs and the betrothed couples wander about the quietest streets and garden paths arm in arm, their heads nearly touching, their fingers giving a furtive squeeze now and then, close together, and talking, talking, talking, and exchanging fond glances and long pressures of the hand, as they exclaim from time to time, their eyes turned heavenward: "How beautiful the moon is to-night!" The little dressmaker is returning home from the shop, swinging her small self along, close by the walls, and pretending not to see the high hat which is keeping pace with her behind, and will appear at the turning of a certain dark corner in such a pleasant way. The poorest girls, who have worked at home from sunrise to sunset, come dashing down the stairs, meet at the door-way their neighbors who were waiting for them, form a little circle, begin a vivacious conversation, and grouping their heads together, like flowers in a bouquet, and swinging around their forefingers the ribbon which fastens the scissors to their belt, reply to the words whispered by the young fellows who pass : Charming! in their hearts, and with their mouths : Impudence! then turn their backs in a scornful manner, not so fully, however, that they are unable to measure them from head to foot out of the corners of their eyes, to see who they are and what they are like. Others, drawn up in fours and fives, all arm-in-arm, bareheaded, arrive at the end of the street, hitting each other with their elbows as they pass, whispering in their ears, laughing aloud, and turning now and then to chide with a maternal air the younger ones who are rambling about. Meanwhile the young men are leaving the factories and workshops with their hats pushed down over their ears, their jackets slung carelessly over their shoulder, the stump of a cigar in their mouths and twisted and turned indifferently between their black lips. They come down the street in shoals, moving their shoulders in a rough fashion, shouting the latest *stornello*, meet the girls, approach them, hit them with their elbows and knees, puffing a mouthful of smoke into their faces ; and the latter scatter with a shriek, coughing, and passing their hands over their tear-filled eyes. The gamins loosen the theatre placards with their nails and then tear them down from the walls ; the small children play in the squares ; and the mothers, standing in groups at the door-ways, their babies in their arms, delay giving the usual cry : "To bed!" thanks to the softness of the air and the clearness of the sky. Along the streets, from the shops on either side of the way, comes the continuous sound of the closing of shutters, the loud noise of the bars, and a slipping of bolts into rings, and the interchange of good-nights among the clerks who are going home. The finest shops, gleaming and well-lighted, remain open still, their door-ways filled with curious people; as do the book-stores, with their tobacco-smelling literary habitués, who sport long, untidy locks and who gather in a corner at the back to grumble over old politics and disinterred parchments ; and the cafés crowded with customers enveloped in a cloud of smoke, from which, at every opening of the door, there sweeps into the street in waves a deep, full clamor of voices.

It was upon such an evening as this that my regiment, which had arrived that morning in one of the largest cities of Italy, was scatterred through the streets waiting for the barracks we were to occupy to be emptied and for the *retreat* to sound.

The soldiers were still in full marching equipment, the gaiters buttoned over the trousers, the cartridge-box at the belt, the flasks and knapsacks on the shoulder-straps. Weary from the march, their clothes and hair white with dust, they stood still in groups on the corners, their backs against the walls, their arms crossed on the breast, one leg resting over the other, or motionless before the jewellers' establishments, contemplating, open-mouthed, those show-windows filled with medals and crosses of every form and color, at which old employés and well-advanced majors cast longing glances and sighs as they pass. Many of them were seated in the hostelries reviving themselves with a swallow of wine ; others, less exhausted, wandered through the streets. All, or nearly all, however, had serious faces, were silent, or talked in a low tone with an effort; a little from their extreme fatigue and sleepiness, and a little from that confusion one generally feels in finding himself for the first time in an unknown and noisy city.

In the midst of the grave silence reigning in a small group of soldiers who were seated on the steps of a church near the barracks, was all the more noticeable the restless gaiety and incessant chatter of one of them, short of stature, of slender build, with beardless face, made most attractive by two great blue eyes, who continually ran up and down the steps, jumping about like a boy. Now he would stop near one, now beside another, and fill their ears with gossip. Then he would pull the hem of this one's coat, now take off the tassel from another's fatigue cap and place it on his knee, or pass his hands over the eyes of a third, crying out as he did so: "Guess who it is!" It seemed as if he were made of quicksilver. In passing before the church I noticed him; I stopped on the other side of the street and stood looking at him for some moments, wondering what could be the reason of such strange gaiety. The frank and pleasing face of that soldier was fixed upon my mind. I moved off.

The following day I learned, by the merest chance, what I had asked myself the evening before. That soldier had been four years in the service, and by a series of accidents which it is not necessary to relate, from the day of his departure until that time he had never been able to obtain leave, not even for the shortest time, in order to return home and see his family. Four years! To a soldier, as I knew him to be, full of heart, much attached to his relatives and the place where he had been born and brought up, of a mild, gentle disposition, knowing nothing of the revels which dull the liveliest affections and clearest memories ; to a soldier like this, four years passed without seeing his family and his home must have seemed long indeed ! And so they had been ; he had always appeared a little melancholy and taciturn in the barracks, and always alone when outside. In his hours of freedom, while his comrades lounged around in the public gardens to bestow hairy caresses on the children under the care of pretty girls, he used to pace the parade ground in its length and breadth, his chin resting on his chest ; or was seated on a stone bench at the end of a solitary avenue, drawing puppets in the sand with the end of his foot. He was always thinking of his relatives, friends, and the places that he had not seen for four years, and above all of his mother, who was a poor old, infirm peasant, but with a genial and true-loving nature and the heart of an angel. Of all her children, the one whom she loved with the greatest tenderness, and also with a particular feeling of solicitude and pity, was the soldier son ; which was also natural. He wrote, or had some one write frequently ; and his letters, read and re-read, kissed and re-kissed, then placed in her bosom like the relic of a saint, mitigated much of the bitterness of their separation. And such was the case with the son and his mother's letters? Yes, indeed. Paper, in the end, is paper, and loving mothers wish to see them (their children), wish to have them under their eyes, to touch them with their hands, and kiss them on the forehead, twice, ten times in one breath ; and the children are not satisfied with the knowledge that that dear head with its white hair is at home and thinks of them ; they wish to take that head in their arms, and place their lips on those white locks. Yet the good old woman, like her dear soldier boy had lived through those four years a life of continual hope and deluded expectations, melancholy, anxiety, and heart-beats. The son, who left a little district in northern Italy, had been taken, with his regiment, to Sicily, and detained there two years (in Sicily, poor woman, with all that water between them); from Sicily he had passed into Calabria, and spent a year there, and then a year in central Italy. Finally, one fine day, the rumor of departure spread through the regiment. "Where are we going?" asked our soldier of the sergeant of the squad, and he waited with bated breath for the reply. "Into northern Italy," was the answer. His heart gave a bound. "Where?" he asked again, growing pale; the sergeant named the city; it was the one nearest his home. "Ah!" he cried, and a little more and he would have kissed the sergeant and been put into prison. That same night, when he found time to do so, he wrote home.

This was the reason of his gaiety that evening; that city was within a few miles of his native village.

Now, with what I afterward learned, with what I saw, and with what I could not help imagining, but which must have taken place, I will tell you a story that may perhaps rouse in you the desire to kiss your own mother more fervently.

Two days had elapsed since the return. Our soldier was still talking about asking a few days' leave in order to fly home, when, one fair evening, the quarter-master looks him up in the dormitory of the company, and on finding him, says, while handing him a letter: "Come nearer." He had hardly taken it before its seal was broken, and it was unfolded in the light of a lantern in a corner of the room, by two trembling hands, and under two dilated eyes, which were glistening with two big tears. He read the letter very rapidly, accompanying the movements of his eyes with a motion of his head, and muttering the words quite hastily. When it was read he pressed it in his hands, and let his arms drop, raising his great eyes to heaven; and the two drops, after trembling uncertain on the lids, fell, ran down his cheeks without breaking, and dropped quite warm upon his hands. The letter was from his mother, and said: "To-morrow I shall come to town on foot. It is four years since I have seen you. Oh, my son, I can contain myself no longer, and I must throw my arms around your neck!"

That night he could not close his eyes. He dashed about restlessly under the counterpane, and found no peace; and therefore nothing but twist and turn, now upon one side, now upon the other, now on his back, now on his face; always quite in vain, for the coverlid seemed so heavy, and he felt in such a feverish state,—a great weight on his chest, a restlessness, a desire for motion, and a tormenting desire for fresh air. Every moment he seized the hem of the coverlid and pushed it down to his knees, sighing and gasping as if he had been in front of a furnace. From time to time he sat up in bed and looked around at his comrades who were all sleeping quietly and soundly as one is accustomed to sleep in spring. Then he looked at the bit of starry sky, which appeared through the small window on the other side, and thought: "Oh if I were in the country to breathe that air!" He glanced at the lantern placed in a distant corner, which gave a tremulous light that appeared and disappeared in turn, and it seemed to him that that light increased his anxiety and made time longer. Then he stretched himself out in bed again, and began thinking of the morrow, shutting his eyes and remaining immovable to try and fall asleep with that sweet thought, but always in vain. Still that sweet thought did not bring him peace; his body was motionless, his eyes closed, but his heart kept on beating as if to say: "You shall not sleep; you shall not sleep!" so that after a short time he was obliged to open his eyes and look around again. So many long hours passed. Finally weariness conquered; the heart was silent, and the busy fancy still. He slept; dreamed of the morrow; dreamed of his mother. He seemed to see her there, erect and smiling beside his pillow; he seemed to feel her pass her hand over his brow, and he dreamed that he seized and placed his lips upon it. Then, suddenly, he felt that he had become a child again, at home; and, one by one, there came to his mind a hundred little scenes from his early life, and in those scenes his mother was always comforting him when weeping, or defending him when threatened by his father, or nursing him if hurt by a fall, taking care of him when ill; and always full of pity and solicitude, always loving, always the mother! Then he dreamed he was grown up; recalled the day of his departure; his mother's tears, the long embraces, words of farewell, and comfort given and received; and he felt his heart-strings tighten just as they did that day; he felt around his waist the arms of his mother who would not let him go; tried to free himself, could not do so, uttered a groan, and awoke. He looked around, thought, came to himself, and that was a moment of joy which can be better imagined than expressed.

Down in the court-yard of the barracks a noisy sound of drums broke out. All dashed from their beds. He dressed in haste, and with the others performed all the duties of the morning cheerfully and with a calm face, but with a burning fever and agitated heart. He tapped the pavement with his feet, bit his lips, passed and repassed his hand over his heated brow, asked all around what the hour was, looked from his head to his feet every moment to see if he was neat and had every thing in order. Finally the desired mid-day arrived. Desired, because his mother, in leaving home at nine o'clock as she had said in her letter, ought to arrive in the city between noon and one o'clock, taking into account the distance that she had to come and the slowness with which, poor woman, she could accomplish it. Just at that hour the soldiers had to leave their quarters and go to the single-stick school.[1] Our good young fellow, by using his mother's letter, obtained a release from that exercise. The soldiers went out, the dormitories were deserted, he ran up the stairs, flew to his bed, placed his hand upon it, stood still for a moment, for he felt as if his legs refused to hold him, and panted.

A little while thereafter he seated himself on the bed; planted his elbows on his knees, rested his face on his hands, fixed his eyes on the floor, and thought: "She is coming; she is coming here to the barracks!" And laughing hysterically he rubbed his forehead with both hands. "It is four years since I have seen her! Four years!" Then he counted four on his fingers. "How long they have been!" And then he went over in his mind all his fits of melancholy, discouragement, and past sufferings. "Oh!" he exclaimed in a low tone full of loving pity, clasping his hands, shaking his head gently, with his eyes fixed upon a point on the wall, as if to say: "Poor

---

[1] A species of fencing with sticks instead of foils, now no longer in vogue in the Italian army.

mother!" and "Poor mother!" he did say in fact. "So you are coming from such a distance to see me, quite alone too and on foot; you have to walk so many miles in the sun; you will arrive in this great city, among all these people, without knowing where I am; and you will have to ask where my barracks are; then be on your feet for so long a time, alone, old, ill, and exhausted; and perhaps you will lose your way and wander about, worrying that you cannot find me. . . . Ah, poor old woman!" He kept his hands clasped and his eyes fixed upon the wall, biting one lip and then the other, and closing his eyelids to keep back the tears which were ready to fall. Then repeated from time to time: "Poor old woman!"

After which he passed both hands over his face, shook his head, gave a sigh, sprang to his feet, and paced the room with the hurried steps of a traveller. After a little he suddenly stopped. "It must be time for her now!" He ran to the window on the street, leaned out, looked to the right and left, once, twice, thrice, but no one was to be seen. The blood rushed to his head. "Let me think of something else!" he said to himself; and so tried to drive the image of his mother from his mind in order to pass this season of anxious expectation. Drive away that image! Poor fellow! It was out of the question, so he abandoned the idea.

"Look, mother," he said aloud, shaking his two open hands before his face, "I love you so well, so well!" . . . He looked around; there was no one; he continued: "More than any thing else in the world!" And letting his clasped hands fall upon the bed, he continued to shake his head gently as if to signify more clearly by act the meaning of his last words. "More than any thing in the world." Then suddenly he roused himself: "It must be time now!" he said, and again he went to the window, then stopped suddenly, and turned his back: "No," saying to himself as he did so, "you must not look." He tapped the floor with his foot as if to repeat, No. But smiled, and the smile meant: "Ah, I cannot help it!" and in fact, a moment later he again went to the window and looked out. Still no one in sight.

He returned to the bedside and tried to invent some method for passing time. He bent one arm with his forefinger against his chin, raised the elbow of that arm with the palm of the other, and, fastening his eyes upon the bed while resting a knee on the edge, he ran homeward in his mind, saw his mother make up a bundle of shirts and handkerchiefs to bring him, saw her take leave of the family and start, then accompanied her along the road in his mind's eye, that long, long road! under the burning sun, in the midst of clouds of dust raised by carts and carriages which were passing rapidly. He saw those carts graze the poor woman's skirts, touch her, shake her, She, so old, tired, and infirm had not the time to avoid them, when another one rushes on, is near her, is about to hit her. "Ah, move out of the way!" the son exclaims above his breath; making, without being aware of it, a motion with his hand as if to seize her by the arm and drag her to one side. He pointed out the curbings she was to avoid, and the bits of the road filled with stones, and the edges of the ditches. After much walking he seemed to see the poor old woman totter, bent under the weight of her bundle, quite exhausted, thirsty, and he was worried, groaned, and said to himself: "Oh, poor woman, give me that bundle; let me carry it for you; take my arm." He moved his right elbow and seemed to feel between his arm and body a trembling arm, and with his left hand, keeping his eyes quite motionless all the time, he felt the air to the right, as high as his side, in search of his mother's hand.

Then he came to himself; the thought that within a few moments he would embrace his mother returned clearly to his mind, and he felt, as at first, all its sweetness; his eyes brightened, his lips trembled, all his features gleamed with joy. A slight smile, then a broad one, then came a convulsive laugh; his chest and shoulders rose and fell as after a breathless race; and finally he threw himself upon the bed with his face in his hands and gave way to a mixture of tears and laughter, still shaking his head as if to say: " Poor mother ! "

"Are you going mad?" shouted the corporal while crossing the dormitory and stopping at the door-way through which he was to pass out.

The soldier started, rose to his feet, turned, and looked at him with his eyes full of tears, his lips parted with a smile; he had not understood him. The corporal disappeared murmuring: "He is mad; he is mad!"

When left alone, he stood meditatively for a moment; then, struck by a sudden thought, seized his knapsack leaning against the bread-shelf, drew it down on to the bed, opened it after having played for a time with the buckles of the straps, dove into it with both hands, and drew out hurriedly brushes, combs, boxes, and rags; placed them all on the coverlid, seized a brush, put his foot on the edge of one of the bed slats, leaned over, and began to polish his boots with all his might, stopping from time to time to see if they were shining well.

"I must be clean," he said to himself with a serious face, continuing his work with the brush; "I wish to shine like a mirror; I wish to make a fair soldier of myself, for I want to please her." When the boots were polished he seized his clothes brush, then the comb, then dove into the knapsack again, drew out a little round glass, opened it, and looked at himself. . . . When the soul is deeply moved by a strong and lovely affection, and the mind quite full of sunny thoughts and fancies, the eyes and smile assume such an impress of the sweetness of that affection and the serenity of those thoughts, that even the plainest face, at such a moment, is lighted up by a ray of beauty; so the good soldier, in looking in the glass and seeing his soul shining on his face, smiled with satisfaction.

At that instant he heard a quick step on the stairs; listened attentively; the sound was approaching; it was the corporal of the guard; he entered, looked about, saw our young man. "See here," he exclaimed, in catching sight of him, and calling him by name, "there is a woman at the door who is looking for you!"

"My mother!" shouted the son, running rapidly through the dormitories; he dashed down the stairs, across the court, into the vestibule; caught a glimpse of the woman, sprang toward her. She opened her arms, he fell on her breast, and both of them uttered a cry. The son placed his hands on his mother's temples, passed them through her gray hair, bent back her head, looked into her eyes, then pressed that dear head against his shoulder, covered it with his arms, and fastened his lips upon her hair, from which the handkerchief had fallen. The good woman stifled her sobs against the shoulder of her son, and seizing him around the waist, passed her thin hands over the rough jacket, which for her, at that moment, was worth a hundred times more than the most beautiful kingly mantle. The soldiers of the guard grouped respectfully on one side, looked motionless and silently upon that holy embrace, and I looked too, as I was on guard duty that day, and stood near in the door of my room.

"Come, compose yourself, mother ; be brave ; don't cry so. My God ! why should you weep ? " the son kept saying in a caressing tone, as he pushed back behind her ears with both hands the hair which had been scattered over the forehead in the impulse of the first embrace. The old woman continued to sob hard, without weeping or without words ; until, in raising her eyes to her son's face, she smiled, drew a long breath, as if lifting a weight from her heart, and murmuring, "My son ! " embraced him again. "Are you tired ? " asked the soldier anxiously, tearing himself from her arms. "A little," replied the woman, smiling. She glanced around in search of a place where she could lay down the great bundle which she had brought with her. "Come in here," I said, throwing open the door of my room. "Oh, the officer ! " she said, turning toward me, and making a courtesy ; "thank you, sir." The soldier was a trifle confused. "Come in," I repeated ; "come in." They both entered timidly, and approached the little table ; the old woman laid her bundle on it, and I moved to one side.

"Let me see you, my son ; turn around ; let me look at you," the woman began to say. The soldier, smiling, turned to show himself on every side. And the mother drawing back, glancing at him from head to foot, and clasping her hands, exclaimed affectionately : "How handsome you are, dressed like this ! " And the poor old woman felt herself rejuvenated, and was almost seized with the desire to dance around him. She approached him, then moved off, returned to his side, and devoured him with her eyes. She placed her hands on his shoulders, and let them fall down the arm until they reached his hands; put her face close to his breast in order to see the buttons; then noticing that she had dulled the cross on his belt with her breath, she rubbed it with the hem of her apron; finally, after having looked and looked again at him for some time, she threw her arms around him once more, calling him lovingly by name as she did so. Then she suddenly let go of him, and asked anxiously: "And the war?" The son smiled. She repeated: "And the war? Tell me, my son, when are you going to war?" "Oh, heavens! who has been talking to you about the war, good woman that you are?" "Oh, there is n't any war, then?" she asked, quite content. "You will never go to war, will you? Never again?" "I can't say never again, my dear." "Oh, then, you are going! tell me the truth, my son." "My good mother, what do you suppose we soldiers know about it?" "But if you who go don't know," the mother replied in that tone of profound persuasion, "who can, then?"

Having said which, she stood still awaiting his reply with such a curious expression of face and form, with such a charmingly pleasing smile on her lips, and a certain ineffable light in her eyes, that her son, smiling too, was almost entranced in looking at her; and she pleased him so much at that moment, he felt such a new and strong impulse drawing him to her in his heart, that he sprang toward her with one bound, pressed her head between his hands, kissed her, shook her playfully as they do children, and placing his lips on her forehead, murmured smiling: "My poor, dear old mother!"

And I, standing there with my back against the wall and my arms crossed on my breast, thought:

"Here is a man who adores his mother! He cannot help being a good, respectful, well-disciplined soldier, full of *amour propre* and courage. Yes, courage too, because the souls which feel deeply and strongly can never be cowardly. That soldier there, taken on to the battle-field, would allow himself to be killed without fear, and he would die with the name of his mother upon his lips. Teach him what his country is; make him understand that the country is a hundred thousand mothers and a hundred thousand families like his own, and he will love his country with enthusiasm. But one must begin with the mother. Oh! if we could discover the germ of all the lovely affections and all the honest and generous actions of which we are proud, we should almost always discover them in the heart of our mothers. How many medals of military valor ought to gleam on the breasts of the mothers instead of the sons! and how many wreaths of laurel ought to rest upon an old, bald head instead of upon the brown one of youth! Oh, mothers, you should never die! You should remain at the side of your sons, and accompany them to the end of the journey of life. Before you, even when we are old, we would always be children, and love you ever with the same love. Instead, you leave us alone . . . oh no! no! not alone; your sweet memory remains with us, your dear image is always before our eyes, your loving counsels are ever present to the spirit, and this is enough. Every time that a weariness of life assails us, and some hard disillusion raises in our hearts a feeling of hatred and aversion for men, we will call up your holy, benign, and peace-giving image; we shall feel that we hear your dear voice, which chided us when children, calling us by name; and we will bend our knees irresistibly and clasp our hands before your image, asking your pardon!"

At that moment the major comes grumbling into the barracks: "Where is the officer of the guard?" he asks of some one outside the door. I here started to go out, and planting myself pale before him, with my hand at my cap, and cry: "Present!"

He looks at me fixedly and makes a sort of face, as if to say: "What the devil is the matter with you?"

---

# THE SON OF THE REGIMENT.

## I.

CHILDREN of the two sexes, until a decided difference in form begins to become apparent, may have their playthings and amusements in common : but when, while the softness and gentleness of outline remain in the girl, in the boy the characistics of the man begin to show themselves, the resemblance changes little by little, and one sex turns and attaches itself definitely to dolls, the other to guns, trumpets, and drums. Together with the fancy for arms, there usually awakes in boys a passion for soldiers : in some temperaments it is only passing ; in others violent, irresistible, and lasting. And it is exactly in this that the difference in the two natures manifests itself first and most noticeably ; for while the woman seeks and loves that which signifies peace, weakness, and love, the man dashes with ardor toward that which represents strength, power, and glory.

After the members of the family and household, our first affection, our first outburst of enthusiasm is for the soldier. Soldiers are the first figures which we draw on the school-room walls and the book covers ; soldiers the first persons whom we turn back to look after in the street, stopping and obliging the person who is holding our hand to do the same. The first cent we receive is spent at a bookseller's for a sheet of colored soldiers; and all that which belongs to soldiers,—weapons, uniforms, galloons, feathers, trinkets, and sash,—becomes the object of our most ardent desires and our dearest hopes; so much so that we feel that, despite any sacrifice or any opposition, we shall enlist as soldiers when the proper time arrives; yes, soldiers, soldiers, even if the world falls; mamma will cry, papa growl out in that deep voice which he reserves for the most daring escapades: no matter; the matter is decided, we will be soldiers.

Here the mania for arms begins, and we search, prowl about, dive into every thing to see if there is not even a cane, stick, or leg of a broken table in the house, which, having been shaped by the blade of our penknife, may not serve, for a longer or shorter length of time, as a rapier, dagger, or gun. Who of us has not passed long hours astride a chair, with his breast against the back, working his legs as if spurring on a horse, waving aloft the handle of a broom, and holding forth in a certain slow, deep, solemn tone, like a general who is commanding a division? Who does not remember the first sword which he received from an uncle, godfather, or some retired officer, an old friend of the family, on his birthday, or as a reward for good conduct at school? But let it be understood, not one of those ordinary wooden swords, bound in silver paper, mere playthings for children, which do not even frighten flies; but a real sword, a genuine blade, such as they use in war. . .
Oh! the first sword is a great source of delight!

Then those beautiful spring mornings (which take away the desire for books, and put a fever into one's legs, as Giusti says) when, seated at the table, yawning and dozing over a fable of

Fedro to be turned into Italian, we suddenly hear a great outburst of trumpets and drums down in the street. To the devil with books and copy-books, and down the stairs, at a break-neck pace, behind the soldiers, until we reach the parade ground, and can contemplate with ecstasy that bright gleaming of bayonets, appearing and disappearing like a flash above the heads of the battalions, and hear that noisy and prolonged hurrah of the besieged, which stirs our blood, and makes us feel our strength doubled as we involuntarily clench our little fists;—who does not remember those beautiful mornings? It is true that on returning home, we have to confront the angry look of papa, or something worse; but that being able to say: "I have been on the parade ground,"—ah! it is a great relief to the conscience, an excuse which one can adduce, and which in fact one does adduce without humility or fear.

How well, also, do we remember the first soldier with whom, after a little persistency, we succeeded in making friends? And again, the first time that, on the parade ground, or at target-shooting, we have had the honor of going to fetch a little water from a neighboring spring in our own broken bowl? We brought it so full that it would have overflowed at the slightest movement; yet not one drop was spilled, so careful were we with eyes and arms, making every possible effort of body and soul to discharge our honorable task worthily! Then to be seen on the promenade with a corporal of the sharp-shooters, for instance! It is one of those pleasures in thinking of which I wish to be a boy again, in order to experience it once more, or to experience it as a man, even at the cost of appearing childish. Then in the evening, at the hour of retreat, when we accompanied our young corporal to the door of the barracks and said good-night, or secured the promise of a meeting for the following day in a loud voice, so that all the boys round about might hear it; and the next day we took a charming walk together outside the city, and on reaching a solitary spot, begged our friend to let us see his poniard; to which he replied that it was forbidden, and we continued teasing him; he refusing, and we saying: "Do me the favor for a moment only, only just one moment"; until the poor corporal, after glancing around, drew out the dagger from its sheath with a certain air of mystery, and the sight of that beautiful, bare, gleaming blade sent a shudder through our veins. Then we touched it lightly with our finger, asking if it were sharp, and if one blow would kill a man . . . Oh, the friendship of a corporal is a great thing for you! That, among others, of always having in your pocket some beautiful new cartridges, sometimes powder too, and, perhaps, even a beautiful cross of an old plate, or bruised metal buttons, and even—but these are fortunes which rarely fall to one's lot. You may become the possessor of a couple of bits of gold lace, a trifle worn perhaps, but always in such a condition as to cut a stupendous figure on the sleeves of your house-jacket. And all the boys in the neighborhood will respect you.

The idea which one has, as a child, of the superiority of soldiers over other citizens, is something really marvellous. There can be no soldiers who are not prodigies of courage. There are absolutely no soldiers who are weaker than the strongest civilian. No one in the world can run like a sharp-shooter; the handsomest beards in town belong to the sappers; there is nothing more terrible on earth than an officer with an unsheathed sword—especially if it has just come from the hands of a knife-grinder. And in fact, when we set the marionettes dancing, and improvised comedies, there might be a fierce struggle on the stage between ten armed characters, or there might be even princes and kings to make a great deal of racket with their swords in hand; but at the appearance of two soldiers with muskets slung across their shoulders, all the other wooden heads suddenly were quiet, and on their good behavior, and sometimes even the crowns bowed before the fatigue caps. When late at evening, suddenly hearing down in the street, before the door of a tavern, a confused sound of angry and threatening voices, oaths, blows, and cudgels, and a crying of women and children, and on going to the window we could see the daggers gleam, we understood that there was a fight between the soldiers and workmen, did n't we always pray that the former should do all the killing, and the latter be beaten? And if the contrary occurred, how provoked were we!

This intense affection of children is returned by the soldiers with an affection naturally less enthusiastic, but not less strong. Conscripts who have just come into the regiment, or even old soldiers who have barely arrived from an unknown city, pray, where do they seek and find their first friends? In that crowd of gamins who hang around the drummers when the regiment goes to the parade ground. From them come the first smiles, the first hand-shakings; with them the first meetings, the first genial and confidential conversations, the first solitary walks in the country, the first outbursts of rage against their all-powerful superiors, the first laments over the severity of the discipline, and from them the first words of comfort and consolation. They let them write and read their letters from home, and relate all the most insignificant particulars of their family life, and listen with pleasure, and sometimes with a certain tender melancholy, because, far as they are from their own relatives, these conversations revive in their hearts that affectionate feeling for home which one never experiences in the noisy rooms of the barracks. By means of these children, they form, little by little, a friendship with the porter; and through the latter succeed in a short time in enlarging the circle of their friendly relations, so that, in case of need, they know to whom they can have recourse, and, in any case, with whom they can exchange a little gossip, all the more if among their friends there be some good woman who has a soldier son. Thus, to the sympathy and affection in their hearts for these children is added a feeling of gratitude; and by means of them their little friends, too, form new friendships; little by little, in such and such a company, in such and such a battalion, there is no unknown or indifferent face, and their affection, the first burst of enthusiasm past, takes deeper and more lasting root. When the regiment goes away. . . . I have experienced it, we seek our mother, go and sit down beside her, and remain there with a serious face in order to be asked some question that will provoke an outburst of our grief.—" What is the matter, child?" And we do not reply. " Don't keep me in suspense; what has happened to you? what has occurred?" Then we throw ourselves into her arms and tell her what it is; and our mother, quite moved, passes her hand over our forehead, exclaiming as she does so: "Oh, poor boy! Be comforted, others will come." Then we return comforted to our swords and drums.

O mothers, let your boys come with us; we will love them like brothers, like sons; and on leaving us they will return to your bosom stronger and more loving, because among soldiers one learns to love, and with a depth of affection that softens both heart and soul.

In proof of which I will relate an incident that took place some years ago in a regiment of our army, and which was told me by a friend who played an important part in it. I will try to recall to mind his own words.

## II.

Upon one of the last evenings of 1866, our division, which in the afternoon had left Battaglia (a large place on the eastern slopes of the Euganen Hills), entered the city of Padua by the Porta Santa Croce, as they were to pass through it *en route* to Venice. Although many other corps had passed through the town, and the streets we crossed were farthest from the centre and the least frequented, yet the welcome accorded us by the people was very warm. I, however, only remember it as I would a dream; I retain a faint recollection of it, as one does of the first conversation with his inamorata, when he trembles all over, becomes white in the face, and every thing grows black around him. Yes, in approaching Padua, the first great city in the Venetian district that we reached, my heart beat wildly and my thoughts grew confused. When we entered later, and an immense multitude, breaking out into a loud cry, dashed into our ranks, broke them, surrounded and scattered us in a few moments on every side, so that there was no trace of order in the columns, then my sight as well as my mind became clouded. I remember feeling myself squeezed around the throat and waist several times by two convulsive arms, and tapped on the shoulder and arms by two trembling hands; of feeling myself kissed in the face by burning mouths, with the same fury with which a mother would kiss her son on first seeing him after a long absence; of having felt the contact of many gloves wet with tears; of having stopped several times to disengage my sword from the hands of some boy who was shaking it violently in order to make me turn around and take notice of his small "*evviva*"; then of having walked quite a distance with half a dozen bunches of flowers in my jacket, so that I looked like a country bridegroom; and, finally, of hearing resound about me a continuous and very loud hurrah. . . . But nonsense, they were not hurrahs, but inarticulate cries, broken by sobs, stifled by embraces; they were groans coming from chests oppressed and exhausted by the depth of joy; voices with a tone that my ear had never heard before, but which had sounded many times in my mind, when imagining the expression of a joy greater than human strength. The crowd mingled with a dizzy rapidity, and, flowing along, bore the soldiers here and there, always, however, advancing in the direction that the column had taken on its entrance; and above the heads of the multitude could be seen a great waving of arms, muskets, and banners, and this one and that one rushing violently together and instantly separating, according to the impetuosity of the embrace and the rapid separation of the civilians and soldiers. The boys seized the soldiers by the hems of their coats or by the sheath of the bayonet, and jealously disputed their hands in order to press their lips on them; and the women, too, young, old, of the people, or of rank, pressed the hands of the soldiers and put flowers in the button-holes of their coats, asking them gently if they had come from far and felt tired. They handed them fruit and cigars, offered their table and house, scorning with amiable affection their refusals, and warmly renewing invitations and prayers. There was not one face in that multitude that was not transfigured by emotion,—eyes dilated and flaming, cheeks pale and tear-stained, lips trembling; and in every attitude, every gesture, every cry, something feverish and convulsive, which stirred your blood and made you tremble in every fibre, so much so that you were tempted to reply to the salutations and benedictions of those people, and yet could not utter one word. The houses were covered with flags: at every window there was a group of persons, one above the other; the last erect on chairs with their hands on the shoulders of the foremost, the former so pressed against the sill as to be almost crushed. Some were waving handkerchiefs, others their hands in the way of a greeting, and some throwing down flowers; all with their necks outstretched and their mouths wide open like little birds in a nest at the appearance of the mother. Some children held in their mothers' arms waved their wee hands toward us, and uttered a small cry which was lost mid-air in the noise of the crowd. The openings of the streets, the door-ways of the workshops and stores were full of people. I saw many of those good operatives place a cigar in the hands of one of the boys, point out a soldier, and push him toward him. I saw some excellent women put their children out to the officers so that they might kiss them, as if that embrace were a benediction from heaven. I saw tottering old men pressing the heads of the soldiers against their breasts, and holding them fast as if they could never let them go. . . . In the midst of so many and such forcible demonstrations of gratitude and affection, the soldiers, poor fellows, were quite stupefied, and laughed and cried at once, not being able to find words with which to return thanks, or if they found them they could not utter them, but tried by signs to say: "It is too much, too much! We do not deserve all this! Our hearts cannot bear it!"

As we approached the gate by which we were to go out, the crowd began to thin and the soldiers fell slowly into line.

The gate through which we were to pass is called by the people of Padua the Portello. We were accompanied to the limit by many citizens, the majority, gentlemen, mixed with the soldiers, arm in arm with them, and all engaged in a lively, noisy, rapid, and broken conversation; for after the first outburst of enthusiasm, which had only found vent in tears and cries, there had followed a great desire for words, a thousand questions and protestations, they interrupting themselves from time to time to look well in each other's faces, with a smile that meant: "Is this really an Italian soldier whom I have on my arm!" "Are we really here in the midst of the blessed Paduans!" And here a long pressure of the hand and a reciprocal shake of the arm, which signified: "You are here; I feel you; I shall not let you escape." In that half hour which was employed in crossing the city, many friendships were made, many promises to write were exchanged, many propositions to meet on the return were made, and meetings arranged and noted down in the pocket-books with names and addresses. "You will write me first!" "I the first. As soon as we arrive in camp." "You promise me?" "Yes, I promise you." Then another warm pressure of the hand, another shake of the arm, and the regiment approaches the gate, the dialogues become warmer and noisier, the gestures more excited, and the expression of the faces more animated ; then they repeat the cries and hurrahs which had ceased for a short time, and the soldiers begin to get into disorder again, until on arriving at the gate the greater portion of the crowd stop. There, again, you can imagine a confusion and shouting that is indescribable ; an embracing and kissing ; a loosening of the arms from one in order to throw themselves into the arms of another ; and so on, hurriedly exchanging good wishes, salutations, and benedictions. Finally, the regiment was outside of the gate and ranged in marching order, two files to the right and two files to the left of the road. For a short time the soldiers turned now and then toward the gate, where the crowd, still stationary, went on waving handkerchiefs and uttering cries of farewell ; but little by little, as it grew dark, the crowd could no longer be seen, the cries ceased, the soldiers began marching in order, and the officers, who at first had been walking in groups, fell into their proper places.

We had been on the march for many hours ; before arriving at Padua we were tired and had already begun to move slowly and in disorder ; yet on coming out of the city we marched as if we had just then started from the camp after a long rest. The soldiers walked erect, separate, and quickly ; the lines were closed up, and a chit-chat was heard on every side. There were so many things to be said.

### III.

Now that night had fallen the lanterns were lighted. The appearance of the light brought me to myself, and showed me that we had not even left Padua ; then looking here and there with dilated eyes, as we do when we wake in the room of a hotel and do not understand for a moment where we are or why we are there, I saw by the light of a lantern two small boys whom the soldiers were leading by the hand. I turned in the opposite direction, and saw another; looked farther away, and saw two more: in fact, there were any number of them. They were all led by hand by the soldiers, and were talking in a low voice, hiding themselves as much as possible in the shade, so as not to be seen by the officers, who, perhaps, might send them home, as that was not the hour to leave the city and keep their families in suspense. The majority of the boys, one could see from their clothes, were poor; but there were not a few who were in comfortable circumstances, as their faces, timid manners, and clean clothing showed. At every ten or twelve paces one stopped, and after shaking hands and exchanging some affectionate salutation, turned back. It is impossible to tell what an amount of sweetness, heartiness, and delicate feeling of sadness lay in those leave-takings. Then, the peculiar accent of the Paduan dialect which lends itself so fully to the expression of warm affection, and the profound emotion, and the night, and the silence that began to spread through the ranks; in fact, every word of those boys touched me deeply. I shall always remember one of them who, in taking leave and saying good-by to all the soldiers, exclaimed in a sweet, trembling voice, in which one could hear the soul : "God protect you all!"

"Thanks, dear boy," I said to myself; "may God bless you with every good thing, may your mother never die, may you enjoy every day of your life some happiness like that which touches my soul this evening. Farewell, farewell!"

Little by little all the boys turned homeward, first the smallest and most timid, then the largest; and over the regiment fell a deep silence, broken only by the sound of weary, dragging steps and the monotonous tic-tac of the points of the bayonets against the ends of the poniards. We began to doze and staggered here and there like drunken men who are walking arm in arm, I dozing and staggering more than all the rest.

Suddenly I felt some one touch my arm; I turned; it was a boy. "Who are you?" I asked, stopping, in a very sleepy voice. He hesitated to reply, because he was dozing too. "Carluccio," he then said, in a low and trembling voice. "Where do you come from?" "From Padua." "Where do want to go?" "With the soldiers." "With the soldiers! And do you know where the soldiers are going?"

He did not reply; so I began again: "Return home, go home, you have got too far away. Who knows how anxious your father and mother may be about you at this hour. Take my advice and go home." He neither replied nor moved. "Won't you go back?" "No." "Why not?" He did not answer. "Are you sleepy?" "A little." . . . "Here, give me your hand, then."

I took him by the hand, rejoined my company, which had got quite a distance ahead, and, thinking that to send him back to his home and make him go all the way alone at night would expose him to some great fright, I decided to take him with me to the station. When we reached the station I knew I could find some means of sending him back.

"We have a recruit," I said to one of my comrades, as I passed him. He approached me, and after him several others who had heard my words, and while they all were gathering about the boy, and asking me who he was and where I had found him, we heard a blast of the trumpet and the regiment stopped. While the ranks broke up and the soldiers threw themselves down, I, dragging behind me the little fugitive, entered a field on the right of the road, and the others followed me. About ten paces from the ditch we stopped; a soldier with a lantern came up; we gathered around the boy, and throwing the light on to his face, bent down to look at him. He was beautiful, but pale and exhausted, and had in his eyes—two beautiful, great dark eyes—a very strange expression of sadness for a child of his age, as he could not be more than twelve. His old, worn, and ill-fitting garments were a strong contrast to his delicate and gentle appearance. He wore an old straw hat to which a great portion of the brim was lacking, a blue handkerchief around his neck, a fustian jacket large enough for a man, a pair of trousers that only reached his ankles, and two old shoes laced with twine. But he was neat and not ragged; he had his handkerchief knotted with a certain grace; his hair arranged; and face, hands, and shirt quite clean. He looked first in the face of one and the other with wide-stretched, motionless eyes.

"But don't you know that you are alone?" I asked.

He looked at me fixedly without replying.

"All the other boys have gone back," said one of my friends, "and why did n't you go back with them?"

Then another: "What do you wish to do here with us? Where do you wish to go?"

He looked first at one and then at the other, with his eyes always wide-stretched; then dropped them and was silent.

"Speak up, now; say something," said one of us, shaking him lightly by the shoulder; "have you lost your tongue?"

But he never opened his mouth, and kept his eyes fastened on the ground, so obstinate and immovable that it was really provoking. I made another attempt: I took his chin between my forefinger and thumb, and, raising his head gently, asked:

"What will your mother say when she sees that you do not return?"

He raised his eyes and looked at me, no longer with that astonished, almost stupid expression that he had worn before, but with brows knitted and his mouth open, as if only at this point he had begun to understand our words, and were waiting for us to interrogate him and make him tell what he had not had the courage to say.

"Why did you run away from home?"

He was silent a moment after that question, and then burst out crying, and between his sobs he murmured:

"They—beat me!"

"Oh, poor boy!" we all exclaimed, putting our hands on his head and shoulders, and patting his cheeks and chin. "And who is it that beats you?"

"My—mother."

"Your mother?" we all asked at once, with astonishment "How's that?"

"But—she is not—my own mother." Here the poor boy, after being urged, told us that his father had been dead for some time; that he had no one left but his step-mother, who only loved her own children and could not bear him; and that as he had been suffering for some time, he had run away from home with us. He had not finished speaking, when we began to pet and comfort him. "You shall come with us, good boy; don't worry about any thing. You will have as many fathers as there are officers, and as many brothers as there are soldiers. Don't be anxious." Then wishing to quiet him and make him smile, I said: "And if any one asks you whose son you are and where you have come from, you must answer that you are the son of the regiment, and that we found you in the folds of our flag; do you understand?"

He smiled slightly, and made a sign in the affirmative.

"And meanwhile," I continued, "as soon as we start, you shall come with me or with some one of us, and keep beside us, and walk as long as your legs will permit; then when you are tired, you are to say so, do you understand? and we will put you in a wagon."

Poor Carluccio, who could not comprehend so many demonstrations of kindness and feared he was dreaming, made a sign in the affirmative by bowing and raising his head and looking at us with his eyes full of surprise.

"How do you feel now? Are you tired? Are you thirsty? Do you want something to eat? Do you wish a little coffee, or a little *rosolio*?"

"No, thank you, I am not thirsty"; and he tried to push back the flask of *rosolio* which an officer held out to him.

"Drink, drink, it will do you good and make you strong; drink."

"Do you want something to eat? There is nothing but bread just now.—Oh! lantern there, give us a piece of bread!"

The soldier holding the lantern drew quickly from his pocket a bit of bread and handed it to him.

"No, thank you, I am not hungry."

"Eat, eat; you have been walking for a long time, and ought to refresh your stomach."

He hesitated a moment, then seized the bread with both hands, and bit into it with the avidity of a hungry animal.

At that moment we heard the sound of the trumpet, and put ourselves *en route*. After a little more than a half hour Carluccio was overcome with sleep. I took him by the hand and led him to the rear of the column, where, after exchanging a few words with the commissary, I had him placed in the wagon, while he kept saying: "I am not really sleepy. . . . I am not really sleepy." And off he dropped into a sound slumber, murmuring that he did not need any sleep, and that he wished to march. An hour afterward the regiment stopped again for some moments. Hardly had the trumpet sounded, when the soldiers of the last company, who had seen me take Carluccio to the commissary, ran and gathered about the wagon. One of them took the lantern from his musket and put it at the boy's face, then they all bent over to look at him. He continued to sleep peacefully, his head resting on a bag of bread, and his eyes still red, and his cheeks wet with tears. "What a beautiful little rascal!" said a soldier, *sotto voce*. "How well he is sleeping!" murmured another. A third stretched out his hand and pinched his cheek with two of his fingers. "Down with that hand!" shouted the corporal, and all the others cried out: "Leave him alone! Let him sleep!" Carluccio waked at that moment, and seeing himself surrounded by the soldiers, was a trifle frightened, but was instantly reassured and smiled.

"Whose son are you?" asked one of the soldiers.

Carluccio hesitated for a moment and then, remembering my advice, he replied seriously: "I am the son of the regiment."

All the soldiers began to laugh. "Who brought you to us? Where did they find you?"

The boy replied with the greatest gravity: "They found me in the folds of the flag!"

The soldiers burst out laughing again. "Your hand here, comrade!" shouted the corporal, extending his hand. Carluccio put out his and clasped it. "Give it to me too," said another soldier, and Carluccio pressed his also. Then every one followed suit, and the boy shook hands with them all. The last one said aloud: "We are firm friends, are we not, child?" and he replied: "Yes, firm friends." At that moment the trumpet sounded, and the soldiers moved off laughing, and I, appearing suddenly before Carluccio, asked him: "Well, what have you to tell me?" He looked at me, and replied smilingly, in a tone of perfect content: "The soldiers like me."

## IV.

We arrived in camp about midnight; I do not remember how many miles we made from Padua up, nor at what point we pitched the tents. There must have been some village near the camp; but there was not the top of a steeple to be seen in any direction. The sky, which had been dark and cloudy so that we could not see the stars, had become clear. The field where the regiment was to encamp was all lighted by the moon, and surrounded by great thick trees, which cast a dense shade all around. It was a spot full of dark, gloomy beauty, and in it reigned a profound quiet; so struck were we by it, that we all entered the camp without speaking, and drew up in line in silence, looking with amazement here and there, as if we were in an enchanted garden.

In a short time the camp was in order, the wagons were taken to their places, the sentinels given their posts; the companies were re-arranged without arms, among their own tents; and the sixteen orderly-sergeants began the roll call, each one standing in front of his company, with the officers on one side, and a soldier with a lantern on the other to light up the record book. Meanwhile Carluccio, led back to me by the commissary, had run to hide himself between two tents, and stood there frightened and astonished, contemplating the beautiful spectacle of the camp lighted up by the moon. That multitude of tents gleaming in long rows until they were lost to sight among the trees; those five hundred stacks of glistening bayonets; all those people; and the intense quiet, the monotonous voices of the orderly-sergeants growing gradually fainter, from the company near by to the one farthest away, where the lantern hardly appeared as large as a fire-fly; and then the gradual cessation of those voices, and the mysterious silence; and, at a stroke of the drum, the sudden breaking up of the lines and the noisy scattering; and under the tents, in the darkness, that confused shouting and hurried preparation of the beds with cloaks, covers, and knapsacks, until little by little, throughout that immense camp quiet is re-established, and an unseen bugle imposes silence with its lamenting blasts . . . it is a spectacle that moves one. And it would have been much more impressive if any one could have seen inside those tents. How many tapers were secretly lighted between two knapsacks, beside a piece of crushed letter-paper, before a face in which appear from time to time the fatigue of the long march and the fear of the officer of the guard—

God forbid that he should notice the light—and the painful struggle between the affection which breaks out impatiently and the word that one cannot express! That is the place and the hour for melancholy recollections. There, under those tents, when silence reigns all around, there the images of distant relations and friends from home crowd in, images so life-like and speaking; and dear, above all others, are those of the mothers who come to arrange the knapsack under their sons' heads praying down in their hearts: "God grant that this be not his last sleep!" Who has not shed tears at night under the tent in that hour?

When all the regiment had gone to sleep, I called Carluccio, and took him under the officers' tent of my company, where the other two subaltern officers had preceded me (the captain was ill),—two of those young fellows, full of heart, who under the appearance of an ordinary and gentle character hide a soul capable of great things; two of those brave soldiers who, unknown or undistinguished among the many in the ordinary course of life, suddenly spring up giant-like on the field of battle, show themselves heroes, and make people say: "Who would ever have thought it!"; young men who love a soldier's life for this reason, that when occasion demands it they can sacrifice it to a good end.

The tent was lighted by a candle stuck in the ground, and my two friends were seated one here and one there, with their legs crossed over a stratum of straw that our orderlies had hurriedly gathered, during a scamper, from the field. Hardly had we entered when we too sat down and began to chat.

Carluccio kept his eyes down, and scarcely dared raise them

to our faces for a moment when he was questioned. His eyes were still swollen and red from his severe fit of weeping; his voice trembled; and he did not know how to move or where to hold his hands, so embarrassed and confused was he. By dint of questioning him and urging him to talk, we succeeded in loosening his tongue and drawing from him some more particulars about his family. Then little by little he took courage and warmed in his narration, comforted by the signs of assent and compassion that we constantly gave to his words.

"She is not my true mother," he said; "that is why she does not love me. The other was my true mother, and is dead, but she loved me very much; the one I have now . . . is the same as if I were not in the house; she gives me food to eat and a place to sleep, but never looks at me—as if I had done something wrong; and I don't do any one any harm; every one can say that. . . . The neighbors in the house all like me better than she. . . . The other two boys are smaller than I, and there is no danger of her making them cry! Then she never took me to walk with the other two. They are always well dressed, while I seem like a beggar. . . . Sometimes she left me shut up in the house, all alone, those Sunday evenings when you see so many people pass in the street, and I stayed at the window waiting for them to return, but they never came back, and I used to go to sleep with my head on the window. Then when they did return she scolded me; I had been shut up alone in the house, and they had gone to the theatre or café, and the other two boys came and whispered in my ear: 'We went, and you did not'; then they made gestures to provoke me, and if I cried, they laughed at me, and mother never said any thing. These things made me unhappy, because I had never done any thing to them, and every time either of them teased me, and I wanted to do something, I always controlled myself and had patience. There were times when they had finished eating, that mother made me carry away the dishes, and while I carried them the boys said: 'Scullion!' Oh, heavens! if they had given me a blow on the head I should not have felt it as much as I did those words. . . . Once, the evening of a fête day, she returned home late, and her face was all red, her eyes shining; she talked and laughed loudly with the other two, and they all began supper, and mother drank an entire bottle of wine. After they had finished she called me, put all the dishes in my hands, and said: 'Here, carry these away; that's your duty'; she gave me a kick, and all three began to laugh. I said nothing; but when I was in the kitchen I put down the dishes, threw myself on a chair, and began weeping bitterly in the dark until they went to bed. If it had not been for Giovannina, a young dressmaker who lived near us and was kind to me, I should have always been entirely in rags. . . . "

I then asked how he came to think of running away.

"At the beginning," he replied, "I wanted to go off with a company of jugglers, those who play tricks, and when they find boys whom no one wants, they take them with them; but then I was told that there were tricks for which, if they wished to become jugglers, they must have their bones dislocated at the shoulders, and this must be done when they are small, so as I was big, I did not run away. Mother continued to ill-treat me, and gave me little to eat. But one fine day the Italian soldiers began to pass, and all the people welcomed them warmly, and the boys accompanied them outside the city, and there were some who went many miles with them. In fact, I heard that two or three had run away from home, and then came back saying they had eaten the soldiers' bread and slept under their tents. I instantly thought I would run away. I tried two or three times; but when it began to grow dark, I got frightened and went home. But yesterday morning my mother beat me with a stick and hurt me very much; here are the marks on my hands, and then she struck me in the face, and all because I had said: 'May you burst!' to one of the boys who was making fun of my boots, saying they looked like boats. They did not even give me a piece of bread, and then in the evening they left me alone in the house. I stood at the window with tears in my eyes, and was really desperate, when suddenly I heard the band play; I instantly left the house, and as soon as I saw that they were the soldiers of the king who has come to liberate us, I threw myself into their midst, and I have not left them. . . . Then you spoke to me (and he looked at me). Then they told me not to be afraid; they gave me something to eat—I was so hungry!—and told me they would keep me with them. . . . But I don't wish to stay here and eat my bread like a beggar. I want to work. . . . I will brush your clothes (and he touched my jacket). I will bring water to drink and get straw for the officers to sleep on. . . ."

At this point one of my friends cut him short by taking his head between his two hands, and pressing it to his breast with all the pity and love of a father.

## V.

Toward daybreak, before the bugle sounded the reveille, we were waked by the sound of a heavy rain and a violent clap of thunder. I was the first to put my head out of the tent. Not a soul was to be seen in the camp, except the sentinels ; but almost all the soldiers were awake. In fact, at every flash there came from all sides of the encampment a sharp b-r-r-r, such as the puppet-man makes to announce the appearance or disappearance of the devil ; and at every clap of thunder there was a noisy and prolonged shout in imitation of the burst. A short time thereafter the reveille was sounded, and the captain of the guard called the officer of the week to announce that we were to continue our march in three hours. The announcement set me instantly thinking of Carluccio. I had not yet asked myself what was to become of the boy in the end. The son of the regiment ! Beautiful words, quickly said ; but had we the right to keep him from home ? Who would shoulder this responsibility ? I spoke of this to my friends, and they all agreed that it was necessary to provide for the return of Carluccio, by writing to the Syndic of Padua and having recourse to the authorities of the neighboring village. It was a most displeasing decision, but there was nothing else to be done. The duty of writing to Padua I assumed myself, and I did so ; but the other duty of taking Carluccio to the village and giving him into the care of the authorities I would not undertake. " Let the others think of that," I said to myself. " I have done my part," and I begged one of my friends to assume the rest of the responsibility "What have I to do with it ?" one after the other replied. "And I ?" I asked in my turn.

"Well, neither of us have any thing to do with it," and the dialogue ended thus. I returned to the tent quite annoyed, called Carluccio, and said to him:

"You must come as far as the village with me, it is only a few steps away."

A suspicion crossed his mind; he became serious and looked fixedly at me. I had not known how to dissimulate my design by voice or face; I turned the other way, and pretended to look for something in my travelling-case.

"You want to send me home!" he cried suddenly; then broke out into a violent fit of weeping, threw himself on his knees at my feet, and now clasping his hands, now seizing my jacket, began to say, with all his strength: "Oh, no—no, Mr. Officer, don't send me home, for pity sake, for pity sake. I cannot go home, I would rather die first; keep me here, to do any thing you wish. I'll do every thing, and look after my own food. . . . For mercy sake, Mr. Officer, don't make me go home!"

I felt my heart breaking. I controlled myself for a moment, and then said: "No, don't worry, Carluccio; don't cry or be afraid. We won't send you home; you shall always stay with us. We will always love you. . . . I promise you that, rest assured of it; dry your eyes and we won't say any thing more about it."

Then Carluccio grew quiet.

"I was not born for great undertakings," I said to myself as I left the tent; "there is nothing else to do but wait for the reply from Padua—and then . . . then we will see what is to be done."

## VI.

Two days later we encamped in the neighborhood of Mestre, where we remained for nearly a month, until the termination of the last armistice, that is to say, until we returned back toward Ferrara.

No reply came at any time from Padua, and Carluccio remained on with the regiment.

From the very first day we thought of renewing his wardrobe, because his clothes, already worn out, had been so spoiled during the first march that they were literally falling in pieces. We gave him a straw hat, a jacket, a pair of linen trousers, a beautiful red cravat, and two little shoes that fitted his small feet. Oh, how contented the poor boy was! When we presented him with all these things, he did not seem able to believe his eyes; he turned red, twisted his head the other way, almost fancied they were playing a joke on him, tried to push back the unhoped-for gift with his elbows several times, and kept his chin down on his breast. But when he saw that we began to grow angry at his obstinate incredulity, and pretended to move off, saying: "We 'll dress another boy," he took a step toward us, made a motion with his hand for us to stop, and exclaimed in a tear-choked voice: "No! no!" but he was instantly ashamed of that prayer, bowed his head again, and stood motionless with his eyes lowered and full of tears. When he had his clothes on, he was so much embarrassed that he did not know how to walk, act, or speak.

"*Cospetto*, Carluccio!" the soldiers said to him as they made way for him to pass furtively into their midst: "*cospetto*! what luxury!" and he blushed and ran away.

But at the end of little more than a week he became as quick and full of life as a drummer; he was the friend of all the soldiers in our company, of a great portion of the soldiers in the others, and of all the officers in the regiment. Then he began to lead a life both busy and useful to himself and others. He slept in our tent. In the morning at the first roll of the drum he was on his feet and disappeared. We were not well awake when he had returned from the kitchen of our battalion with coffee, rum, or *rosolio*, and "Mr. Officer," he said in a respectful voice, "it is time . . . ." "Time for what?" we muttered in a sharp, rough voice, rubbing our eyes. "Time for you to get up." "Ah! it's you, is it, Carluccio? Give your hand," and we gave him a squeeze of the hand that put him in good-humor for the rest of the day.

He disputed the work with our orderlies; wished to brush our clothes; polish our buttons, swords, and boots; wash shirts and handkerchiefs; he wished to do every thing himself, and he humbly begged first one soldier and then the other to give him something to do, that he would do it so gladly, and try his utmost to do it well, and that it was necessary for him to learn it at any cost. Sometimes we were obliged to take things out of his hands, and say to him with some severity: "Do what I tell you to do, and nothing more." And really we were forced to be very severe, because we could not allow him to play the servant to us. Why, poor boy? Had we brought him with us for this sole purpose? He was afraid that gradually we should grow tired of him, although we did nothing but overwhelm him with caresses, and surround him with care and courtesy. It seemed to him that if he did not work we should think him a useless appendage in the end, and for this reason he tried to show us that he was good for something, or that, if for nothing else, good-will was not lacking on his part. He was even assailed and worried by the fear that he should seem to us importunate. From time to time, while eating with us, seated on the ground around a tablecloth stretched on the grass, becoming suddenly aware that he was being watched, he was ashamed to eat, turned scarlet, dropped his eyes, took small mouthfuls, and if we did not fill his glass he would not dare do it, remaining with his mouth quite dry during the entire meal. Sometimes, in the tent, while we were dropping asleep, he would suddenly be ashamed that he occupied so much space, and would sit up and spread the straw here and there toward our places, reserving only a small portion for himself, then lie down all curled up in a bunch against the linen of the tent, at the risk of catching some severe cold on account of the draught. Not one of his acts escaped me, not one of his thoughts either, and I always tried to dispel his shame, either by addressing him gaily: "Well, Carluccio?" or by pinching his cheeks in a way that signifies: "Have no fear, I am protecting you," and he instantly became reassured. Oh, what a tender pity his delicate sense of shame aroused within me! "Poor Carluccio," I thought, when, the light still burning in the tent, I saw him quietly sleeping, all wrapped up in my cloak, and his face half-hidden under a soldier's cap; "poor Carluccio! why have you no longer a mother? You thought yourself alone on earth, and did not imagine that any one could care for you! No, Carluccio, for boys without father and mother there are the soldiers; they have only a piece of bread in their pockets; but as an offset they have plenty of affection in their hearts, and dispense both freely to any one in need. Sleep quietly, Carluccio, and dream of your mother; be assured that she is looking down upon you, and is content that you are among us, because she knows that under our rough cloaks beat hearts that resemble her own."

He was always busy during the day. He went out of the camp to fetch water for the soldiers when they were prohibited from leaving; and one could see him moving around among the tents laden with flasks and bowls, quite red in the face and dripping with perspiration, accompanied by a crowd of thirsty men who pressed around him, importuning him in this wise: "Carluccio, my canteen"; "my flask, Carluccio!" "I want mine first"; "no, mine"; "I gave you mine before he did," etc., etc. And making signs for them to keep quiet, or pushing them back: "One at a time, like good fellows." "Be kind enough to move off a little, and let me breathe." Then he would wipe his brow and take breath, for he was really so exhausted that he could do nothing more. From time to time some soldier hunted him up to have a letter written home, or to have him read and explain one received. He always did this favor with much gravity. He would be quite pensive for a moment, and then say, gravely: "Let us see." They seated themselves in the tent, and with the forefinger stretched toward the sheet already written, or to be written; finally, Carluccio, turning up his jacket sleeves, knitting his brows, would set to work, pursing up his lips, and uttering an inarticulate sound that signified: "It is a serious affair, but I will do what I can."

He would assist first one and then the other in arranging the tents, and he had such taste in drawing the cords and fastening the poles in the ground that one would have fancied he had done nothing else all his life.

When the men were drilling he would withdraw to a corner of the camp, and from thence would watch in ecstacy all the time the drill lasted. When all the regiment was drawn up and handling their arms, the poor boy was greatly excited. That striking on the ground of one thousand five hundred muskets, in one blow, like a single musket; that long and sharp rattle of the thousand five hundred fixed bayonets, removed, replaced, and sheathed in a moment; that powerful tone of command, and the profound silence of the lines, and all those faces motionless and intent as statues; the sight of those new things fired his enthusiasm, filled him with restlessness, a desire to shout, run, and jump; but he never did this until after the regiment had broken ranks, out of respect for it. At first he contented himself with assuming heroic attitudes, and looking at us with his head raised and a proud glance, without being aware of it; reproducing unconsciously the emotions of his soul, like some one who, in relating us a story, so impresses us that we show by the movements of our intent faces the sense and effect of his words.

When he heard the band he seemed quite crazy. The evenings when some one of us had to go to the outposts he was less gay than usual. "Good-night, Mr. Officer!" he would say, with a long look, when we left, and outside the tent he would watch us until we were lost to sight.

He had this gentle, affectionate way with all, officers and soldiers; and thus all loved him. When he passed among the tents of any company, he was called on all sides; arms were stretched out to detain him; there was a jumping up and running after him by soldiers with letters in their hands: "Carluccio, a moment, a word, only a word." He gave the officers the military salute, and with an expression of more or less respect, according to their grade, which he had learned to distinguish from the very first day. He held the colonel in great fear. When he saw him in the distance he took to his heels or hid behind a tent; and even he himself could give no reason for this. But one day, while he was standing chatting with two or three soldiers near the tent of an adjutant, behold the colonel suddenly appeared. He trembled from head to foot; there was no time to hide himself; he was obliged to look at and salute him; he raised his eyes timidly, and put his hand to his hat. The colonel looked at him, placed his hand under his chin, and said: "Good-by, my good boy." Carluccio went nearly crazy; flew instantly to us, and breathless and stammering related this great adventure.

A strange thing in a boy of his age was that he never took advantage in the slightest degree of the familiarity with which we treated him. He was always docile, humble, and respectful, as on the first day when we picked him up on the road. Of that fortunate day he spoke often, and always with tears in his eyes. He had his melancholy hours, too, especially on rainy days, when all the soldiers were gathered under the tents, and the camp was as silent as a desert. At those times he seated himself under the tent with his face toward the opening, and his eyes fastened motionless on the ground as if he were counting the drops that fell inside. "Carluccio, of what are you thinking?" I asked. "I?—Nothing." "That is not true," I said. "Come here, poor Carluccio, come here beside me; I am only one of the many who are fond of you; but I love you for them all. Come and sit here and we will talk together, and away with all melancholy." He began to cry. Yet they were attacks of melancholy that vanished quickly.

VII.

In a corner of the camp there were two small houses, inhabited by an excellent family of peasants, in which were established the general quarters of the kitchens of all the officers of the four battalions. Fancy the confusion! There were six or eight soldiers, between cooks and scullions, for every kitchen; and consequently a continual squabbling between the former who did not know how to do any thing and wished to teach each other how to do every thing; a continuous conflict between the others who were vying with each other in order to become cooks; an incessant coming and going of orderlies to carry the dinner to the officers on the outposts; and peasants, vendors, and stupefied gamins of the neighborhood.

In one of the empty rooms of one of those houses Carluccio was placed when seized by the fever, which had raged for many days in the regiment to such a degree, that every day from three to five and seven soldiers were taken down in every company. Carluccio had it so badly that it was feared he would die. The surgeon of the regiment took care of him, and all the rest of us lent our assistance.

Between the curtains and door of his room was a constant coming and going of soldiers. They entered on tiptoe; approached his bed quite slowly; looked into his eyes, which he moved slowly around and half closed, or kept motionless for a long time on the face of the persons without giving sign of recognition. They called him by name, placed their hands on his forehead, made signs to one another in order to express their opinion on the subject of the little invalid; then went off in silence, stopped in the door-way to look back again, and went out shaking their heads as if to say: "Poor creature!"

"Carluccio, how are you?" I asked one day when he began to improve.

"I am sorry . . ." he replied, but he left his reply unfinished.

"What are you sorry about?"

"I cannot . . ."

"What can't you do?"

"Do something," and he lowered his eyes and looked at my shoes and trousers, and added: "The others do every thing . . ."

He wished to say that the orderlies cleaned all our clothes alone, without his being able to help them.

"And I am here," he said, in a voice full of tears; "I am here and do nothing—am a burden—I wish . . ." Then he made an effort to sit up, but did not succeed, and his head sank back on his pillow, and he began to cry, murmuring: "If I could only black yours . . . but I cannot. It would really be better if I were dead." And it took all our efforts to comfort him.

### VIII.

Several of us officers used to gather at evening, seating ourselves near Carluccio's bed, and we chatted on sometimes until midnight. There often came to us the communal counsellor of a neighboring village, and the owner of the land which our regiment was occupying. They were two little men of middle age, very jovial, very corpulent, and very passionate, be it understood, about the Italian cause, and quite anxious to make friends with the "*brave*" officers of the Italian army,—excellent sort of people, whose goodness of heart showed in their faces, and who every day, before taking leave, never neglected to repeat most emphatically that with soldiers like ours the fortress of Malghera could be taken with an assault of bayonets. "But believe us," we said, "the thing is not as easy as it seems to you!" "Oh," they replied, smiling with much dignity, "the dash of the Italian soldier . . ." And they finished the phrase with a gesture which signified: they could perform many other miracles.

The conversation ended unfortunately by always falling upon the battle of Custoza, regarding which these two gentlemen had a most pitiless amount of curiosity.

"When you think of it, a retreat must be a very sad sight!" the counsellor was wont to remark, in a melancholy tone.

"Listen," my good friend Albert replied to him one evening (this Albert was one of the most impetuous and dramatic talkers in the regiment); "it is a trial in comparison with which the loss of our fondest hopes and the greatest disappointments of our life are as nothing, and this is the sorrow that filled our souls that evening. . . . In the morning we were happy, wild with joy, filled with an enthusiasm that brought tears to our eyes and made us break out into the maddest shouts, so impatient were we for the battle, so sure of conquering; and a few hours later—behold the army so full of youth, life, and daring, that army idolized by the country, the fruit of so many sacrifices, the object of so much care, the subject of so much trepidation and so many hopes; a few hours later, conquered, disordered, and wandering over the country like a disbanded herd! Ah, it is a spectacle that rends the soul, and which no words can describe! 'Who will give us back the hearts we had in the morning?' one of us asked; 'our pride, faith, strength? Who will call back to our eyes those tears of enthusiasm? Who will raise the edifice on these ruins? And what will the country say?' Heavenly Father, the country! The mere thought fled back astonished; we seemed to hear once more the cries and applause with which the population of the cities had accompanied us to the gates, that applause which went to our hearts and filled them completely. 'Oh, be silent!' we said to ourselves; 'we are soldiers, and our poor hearts are breaking.'"

There followed a moment's silence.

"What a rout there must have been that evening!" said the counsellor.

"And your division?" asked the owner of the house with much sweetness; "about what time did you begin to retreat?"

The tone in which the question was asked expressed the strong desire to know how things really went, and not as they were reported to have done by people and newspapers. The officer understood, and replied:

"As far as I can remember, my division began to retire from the field shortly after sunset. The different corps arrived at quick step from the different parts of the country at the road leading to Villefranche; here the ranks were broken, the regiments mingled, every appearance of order was lost, and a tumultuous crowd rushed into the city, spreading rapidly through the principal streets, squares, alleys, and court-yards of the houses. Burning with thirst, a great portion of the soldiers rushed at the wells with tremendous avidity and a cry of savage joy that was absolutely startling. Ten, twenty, thirty, the first on their faces, the others with their chests on the backs of the first, hung over the mouth of a well, their feet in the air, at the risk of falling headlong into the water, and disputed with trembling hands the rope, the bucket, the pole, pushing each other back with their elbows and by shoves and kicks, threatening to use their bayonets, and shrieking oaths and imprecations into each other's ears; until the bucket, drawn up by ten vigorous arms, came in sight. Then the cries; blows were redoubled, all the arms were bent downward to seize it first; when it appeared, twenty arms caught hold of it, ten burning mouths were nailed to its edges, drawn here and there, the water spilled over their faces, clothes, and the ground. . . . Who has drunk? No one; and so it was everywhere. The majority of the soldiers had scattered over the country; some battalions, but half comprehending the orders received, had not even entered Villefranche, and had taken the road in the direction of Goito by paths through the fields; so that only the nucleus of the different corps remained, one may say—the colonel, flag-bearer, the majority of the officers, and a few soldiers; not one of the band. The crowd which filled the street uttered deafening shouts; there was a calling in a loud voice, a breaking through the crowd by means of pushes, a running hither and thither of officers to seize soldiers by the arm and try and collect them around the flag, a coming and going of aides-de-camp and couriers on horseback; in the middle of the square a hurried grouping of colonels and staff-officers, an anxious questioning, a giving and revoking of orders; all panting, and their faces flaming, wearied, contorted, and full of consternation. Finally, as good fortune willed it, followed by about thirty soldiers, who had to file one by one among a row of carts and the last houses of the place, I got out into the open country, on the road leading to Goito. I found my battalion again, reduced to a little more than two hundred soldiers, and with these I resumed my march. Little by little it grew very dark; we could not see before or around us; half of the road was filled with artillery and provender wagons, which stopped every now and then, so that it was all one could do to avoid breaking his head against points of the bars, and to keep his feet from under the wheels. There were ditches on the right and the left of the road; mile-stones and heaps of stones at every step; from time to time carts overturned in the middle of the road, bags opened, and every kind of provision spread about; within short distances of each other the commissary cart at a standstill, on it a small light, and around it a crowd of soldiers who blocked the way of the persons coming up. From time to time there was some major or staff-officer who came upon us when we least expected it, and ill-luck to him who was not quick in getting out of the way. On all sides there were groups of soldiers who obliged the others to walk zigzag; at every moment gunstocks which came within an ace of putting out our eyes, and great knocks from those who had fallen asleep. There was a dense and continuous cloud of dust, which filled our eyes and mouths; a continuous shouting of artillerymen against the civilian wagoners, who, quite dazed in the midst of that confusion, unluckily filled up the road; an angry screaming of the officers, who were trying in vain to get together the remains of their own squads; soldiers who continually crossed from the fields to the road and from the road to the fields, falling and rolling down the banks of the ditches; in fact, a confusion, a racket, a tumult that is indescribable; it was, in fact, an infernal night. Ah! a retreat is indeed a sad, sad sight!

"The exertions of the day and, more than all, the violent emotions which we had experienced in so short a time, had completely exhausted me. I was dead tired; I caught sight of an artillery wagon where there was an empty place; I took advantage of the moment when it stopped, jumped up on to it; the men made room for me; I seated myself, leaned over, and went to sleep. When I opened my eyes the day was beginning to break. We were within a few steps of the bridge of Goito. It rained; I touched my clothes, and they were wet. I looked up; the sky was covered by a great dark, massive cloud that promised rain for the entire day. I looked around through the fields; there were quantities of soldiers walking slowly along, with their heads lowered and their eyes on the ground. Many of them had taken the linen of the tents and had put it over their shoulders like a shawl, to protect themselves from the water; many others who had lost their knapsacks and linen took refuge under that of a comrade, and so they walked two by two, arm in arm, with their heads completely enveloped; others who had lost their caps had put on their handkerchiefs; others who had thrown away their knapsacks carried their things in a bundle on the end of their bayonets: and all of them dragged themselves along with the greatest difficulty, limping and stumbling at every moment. Some stopped every now and then to lean against a tree or throw themselves on the ground; then rose with difficulty, after a little, to resume their weary way. I passed over the bridge; that bridge upon which, a few hours before, an Austrian and an Italian sentinel stood drawn up, looking doggedly at each other. I entered Goito; turned to the right on the principal street. What a spectacle met my eyes! On the right and left of the street, at the corners, against the walls, under the eaves, in the door-ways of shops and houses,—everywhere, in fact, were soldiers utterly exhausted from their march and fast; some standing with their shoulders leaning against the wall; some sitting all doubled up, with their hands on their knees and their chins in their hands and their eyes wandering here and there with a tired, sleepy look; others were stretched out and fast asleep with their heads on their knapsacks; others who nibbled a piece of bread, holding it tightly in their two hands and glancing around suspiciously, as if some one were threatening to come and drag it away from their very teeth; others re-arranged the things in their knapsacks, or slowly and listlessly dried their arms on the folds of the cloaks. Meanwhile the street swarmed with soldiers who were going toward Cerlungo. Many, glancing here and there with a half-astonished, half-frightened face, passed on; others stopped beside the wall, threw their knapsacks carelessly down, and let themselves down on to them like bundles of rags. From time to time one of those lying down, raising himself on his elbows, rose to his feet with a great effort, and joined and continued his way with the first soldier of his regiment whom he saw pass by. At the doors of the few shops which were open, there was a continual appearance of soldiers by threes, fours, and ten at a time, and a persistent demand for something to eat, for which they would gladly pay, and they stretched out their hands to show the money. 'There is nothing more,' replied a compassionate voice at the end of the shop; 'I am sorry, boys, but there is nothing.' To another shop, then; nothing here either; nothing anywhere, in fact. In passing before certain dens of cafés, they saw the officers sleeping with their arms crossed on the table and their heads resting on their arms; there were three or four heads on every table, and in the centre glasses, bottles, and bits of nibbled bread. Some with their heads on their hands looked out into the street with their eyes fixed and staring: they were all sad, pallid, distorted faces like those of people after an illness; and the waiters, erect at the end of the establishment, their arms crossed over their breasts, stood looking at the scene with an air of sadness. The openings of the side streets were filled with carts and horses, around which people were silently employed, the soldiers of the train and the common wagoners. Meanwhile several batteries of artillery passed through the principal street, and that grave and slow passage, the dull, monotonous noise of the wagons which made the window panes rattle, those robust artillery men so pensive, and serious, enveloped in their great gray cloaks, filled one's heart with a profound sadness. Many carriages containing wounded officers, came slowly behind the artillery, stopping every time the column did. . . . But aside from the noise of the wagons and carriages, over all Goito reigned a mortal silence like that of an uninhabited city.

"The corps of my division had encamped on the left of the road leading from Goito to Cerlungo, and which goes on along the right bank of the Mincio. The camp had a melancholy air. Nothing was to be seen but a few groups of soldiers scattered here and there, who were unfolding their wet tents and cleaning their clothes and arms. All the others were under the tents; at every moment fresh bands of soldiers arrived and wandered uncertainly around the camp in search of their company; and as the majority had lost their knapsacks, sticks, and tent, they stood there near the tents of the companies, their hands folded, mortified and annoyed, looking around with the air of lost travellers. No sound of a drum, trumpet, or voice, was heard, nor any noise; in shutting your eyes you would have fancied the whole army was sleeping.

"Having reached the camp of my regiment, I went into my tent and threw myself down (without saying one word), beside my comrades, who had been there for more than an hour. We did not salute each other, nor speak, nor even look one another in the face; we were as mute and motionless as people who have lost their memory.

"Suddenly, we heard a sharp cry a few steps from the tent; another cry farther away; a third nearer still; ten, one hundred, a thousand voices broke out in concert on all sides of the camp, and we could hear the noise of hurrying steps. What could it be? We dashed out of the tent. Oh, what a magnificent spectacle! The whole regiment was running rapidly toward the road leading to Goito, and not only ours, but those on the right and left of us, and the others farthest away, precipitated themselves toward the road as if for the assault of an entrenchment. I looked in the soldiers' faces; they were changed, trembling, radiant, and they were all uttering loud cries of joy, and prolonged noisy bursts of applause broke out on all sides of the camp. We flew toward the road; two carabineers on horseback with bare swords passed; a carriage appeared; every head was bared, all arms raised, one powerful shout burst from the thousand mouths of the multitude ; the carriage passed, and the soldiers turned back. . . . But the entire aspect of the camp was instantly changed; faith and hope seemed revived ; no one entered the tents ; on all sides there rose and lasted until evening a tumult full of gaiety and life. The bands played marches again ; the dear old friends of our enthusiasms and our hearts experienced for a moment the sublime intoxication of the days before. .'Oh we will fight still ! ' we said ; ' we will fight still ! ' "

" Who was in that carriage ? " asked Carluccio, with intense curiosity.

" The king."

## IX.

Finally Carluccio got up, and the same day the physician held the following conversation with us :

" My dear gentlemen, I feel bound to tell you that this boy ought to return home. He is cured ; but the slightest overexertion may prove fatal. Perhaps if peace is declared within a few days, we shall turn our backs on Venice, go to Ferrara, from Ferrara, heaven only knows where ; we shall be obliged to accept the trifle of a fifteen or twenty days' march, and even more, and it is impossible that this boy should follow us ; he needs quiet and repose, and not to march seven hours a day, and sleep on the ground. This is not the life for a boy who is convalescent ; therefore. . . . You must provide something else."

And he left us. We thought the subject over for some time, but no matter how much we tried to get away from what the physician had said, we could find no good reason for opposing him. There was an indisputable necessity for the boy to return home, but how was it to be managed? But to what home was he to return, poor fellow? In his home he would die of a broken heart. No, that was not to be thought of, but where then could we send him? We thought it over, held a consultation about it, discussed it, and did not succeed in coming to any definite conclusion about the matter, and we were on the point of paying no attention to the advice of the doctor, when an officer from Padua, a young fellow who had enough heart to give a portion to the entire regiment and still retain sufficient for himself, came out with the following:

"I will attend to the matter, but I must know his family name and where he lives. I will put him under the protection of my family; I will write home to-day on the subject. If he were protected by my friends he could return to his stepmother, and if there were any need of it, we would take him into the house and keep him as long as necessary; I give you my word; will that do?"

The proposal was received with a general "Very good, indeed," and a great slapping on the back of the proposer, which took off all the dust that had gathered on his jacket during the manœuvres.

"But now the difficult part comes," he added, disengaging himself from us with a couple of well-bestowed pinches.

"What is it?" we asked.

"To persuade him."

I resolved to assume the responsibility, and we separated.

That evening, before sunset, while ten or twelve of us stood chatting about trifles near the commissary's booth, the Paduan officer raised his voice above the racket of the group, and exclaimed:

"A new armistice has been concluded; we can leave the camp; who is coming to see Venice?"

"I!" we all replied in one voice.

"Shall we go immediately?"

"Yes, immediately."

And all moved.

"Carluccio, come with us; we are going to see Venice."

From our camp, situated in the neighborhood of Mestre, Venice could not be seen; but in much less than an hour we reached a point from which it was clearly visible; that point, at which you turn from the highway leading from Padua to Mestre, toward Venice, into a little road which, on a high embankment, goes as far as Fusina on the banks of the lagoon. At that point there is a group of country houses, and an inn well known and dear for the sake of two of the prettiest little faces that I have ever seen since I possessed this pair of eyes. We took the road to Padua, and started in the direction of those houses. We had scarcely passed the inn, which was the last of the houses, when Venice suddenly presented itself to view. The majority of us had never seen it; and, therefore, when we approached the hamlet, our hearts began to beat furiously. We shall see it at last, we thought,—this blessed city, about which we have so often dreamed, which we have often sighed for and invoked! We counted our steps, and the minutes and seconds, looking at one another and smiling. Finally some one shouted:

"There it is!" All stopped; a shiver ran from head to foot, and my blood was in a tumult. No one opened his mouth.

Before us was stretched an immense tract of barren, uncultivated land, scattered here and there with fords and large swamps, beyond which we could see gleaming in the distance a bit of the lagoon, and beyond the lagoon, Venice. It appeared to us, as if through a thick mist, pale blue in color, which gave it a delicate and mysterious appearance. To the left, that light, enormous bridge; to the right, away in the dim distance, the fort of San Giorgio; and farther still, other forts scattered along the lagoons, which looked like black specks. It was an enchanting spectacle! The place all around was deserted; and a light breeze that was blowing, rustling strongly through the neighboring trees, was the only sound to be heard.

No one spoke; all were absorbed in the contemplation of Venice.

"Come, now!" suddenly shouted one of my companions, a jolly good fellow, rather too much given to the bottle and to sprees, if you will, but as nice as possible. "Come, now, don't let 's stop here and get sentimental. Who will have a drop of wine?"

Some one shouted "I," and the others assented with their heads. Carluccio ran to the inn, and we seated ourselves on the edge of the dyke turned toward Venice.

"Here is the consoler of the afflicted!" exclaimed my friend, pointing to the wine which arrived at that moment. "Take hold of the bottle and up with the glasses!" It is well known that we military men do not mind a drop more or less when we are in company; we tipple with our eyes shut; so it is not to be wondered at if after a few moments some felt in the mood for singing.

"I say, Paduan, teach us a beautiful barcarolle, you who know so many and shriek them into our ears from morning until night, whether we wish to hear them or not."

And all the others joined in : "Yes, teach us a beautiful barcarolle."

"Oh, apply to him," replied the Paduan, pointing to one of his neighbors, who was something of a tenor and a poet. "Make him improvise a romance, that's his profession."

They all approved in chorus : "Courage, Mr. Poet, out with the romance, out with the music, out with the voice, or out with —some banter."

I think my friend, to whom these words were addressed, had a poem all composed in his head, because he accepted the invitation too promptly and with too manifest pleasure, but at all events he did not bring out any thing but very ordinary verses, camp verses, which means rather labored stuff.

"We want a guitar . . ."

"But where can we get a guitar? Do guitars grow here?"

"Wait—wait," shouted a third, starting off on a run for the inn. A short time after, he returned, guitar in hand. "It is all very well to talk about not finding a guitar here within a few miles of the city of gondolas and love."

The poet (pray pardon him) took the guitar, struck an attitude ; all gathered around him, were silent and expectant.

"Listen ; first I will recite the verses and refrain; then I will sing the verse and you others the refrain."

"All right," they all replied ; "start off with the left foot."

And the poet began :

> Pur ti saluto anch' io,
> O Venezia immortale !
> Che infinito desio,
> Cara, ion' avea nel cor !
> Che divino m' assale
> Entusiasmo d' amor !

"What nonsense! what nonsense!" interrupted our jovial friend, who had made the proposal to drink; "what's this stuff? We don't want any melancholy, we want to be gay; give us a barcarolle; go along with your "desire" and your "immortal," that you are improvising, my dear poet! Do you think we look sentimental?"

All those who had taken a little more than was good for them approved his sentiments loudly.

"Fine taste," I observed, "to wish to make clowns of yourselves! There is really a chance of it, with this probability in the air of being obliged to sheathe our swords and take once more the road to Ferrara, and return who knows whither to lead the poppy-like sort of life of a garrison! We ought to turn clowns!"

The sentimental part of the company were of my opinion; the revellers insisted on their rights, the poet held firm, and the party was divided. Half moved off a few steps from us, lighted cigars, and continued to tipple with the best grace in the world; the others took up the interrupted song.

"We will sing you a refrain too, Messrs. Snivelling Poets!" shouted one of the merry-makers, raising his glass: the rest all laughed.

"Sing, do," replied our party.

And the poet (pray pardon him) resumed:

>Che divino m' assale
>Entusiasmo d' amor!

And the chorus:

>Si, Venezia immortale,
>T' abbiam tutti nel cor.

And the revellers:

> Che poeta bestiale!
> Che cane di tenor!

And then a laugh—Carluccio's small voice, tremulous and harmonious, was distinctly heard among all the others.

Then the song began again:

> Ma pur mentr' io ti miro
> E canto e ti sorrido,
> Perchè un lievo sospiro
> Come di mesto amor,
> E non di gioia un grido
> Prorompe dal mio cor?

Then the chorus:

> Ti guardo, ti sorrido,
> Ma non ho lieto il cor.

The tipplers:

> Invece io me la rido,
> E il partito miglior.

At this point there was a great clinking of glasses, and another loud outburst of laughter; the sun had disappeared, and the breeze blew more freshly than ever.

> Ah! da questa contrada
> Che in noi si affida e spera
> Ah! non la nostra spada,
> Non l' italo valor,
> Ma una virtù straniera
> Caccierà l' oppressor!

Then the chorus:

> Quanto è mesta la sera
> Con tal presagio in cor!

And the sponges :

> Che squisito barbèra !
> Che spuma ! Che color !

These two last verses were sung with less vivacity than the others; it seemed as if the solitude of the place, and the dying day, and the sight of Venice, which began to be peopled with lights, filled even the hearts of the most thoughtless ones with a little melancholy.

> O madre, sul tuo seno
> Vorrei chinar la testa
> E sciorre al pianto il freno,
> E infonder nel tuo cor
> Questa dolcezza mesta
> Che mi sembra dolor.

And the chorus :

> Vorrei chinar la testa
> Di mia madre sul cor.

Then two voices of the other group :

> Non mi romper la testa,
> Fammi questo favor.

The others no longer laughed. The last verse was repeated twice. The revellers improvised no more words, and all turned toward Venice. We sang the fourth verse a fourth time; but Carluccio was singing no longer; he understood the meaning of it, poor boy, and it had touched his heart. The hour, the place, and that slow and melancholy music had filled his soul with a sudden sadness.

"What's the matter, Carluccio ? What do you keep your face hidden in your hands for?" I whispered in his ear.

"Nothing!"

"Listen. . . . Suppose we should give you another mamma, who would really love you?"

He looked at me with wide-stretched eyes. I talked to him for a long time in a low voice, and he listened quietly to me. "Well?" I asked when I had finished. He made no reply, but went on plucking at the grass about him. "Well?"

He sprang up, ran to the bank, and hid on the other side of it. A moment later we heard a burst of weeping so violent, so despairing, that it made our hearts tremble.

"What is the matter?" asked the others.

"Just what was to have been expected." They were all silent, and Carluccio's sobs were distinctly heard.

"He must cry himself out," said one; "it's better for him, poor fellow; it will do him good."

They took up the song again:

> O madre, sul tuo seno
> Vorrei chinar la testa
> E sciorre al pianto il freno,
> E infonder nel tuo cor
> Questa dolcezza mesta
> Che mi sembra dolor.

Between every verse we could hear the mournful, tired sobs of the poor child.

The spectacle of Venice at that moment was divine.

"Silence!" said one of our number suddenly. All stopped and strained their ears; the wind brought us now and then the feeble sound of drums.

"It's the fanfara of the Croats of Malghera," exclaimed the Paduan.

We were all motionless for a long time, without exchanging one word, our hearts oppressed at the sound of that sad and inimical music, which seemed to relate to us, derisively, the sorrows of the saddened city, for which we had offered up our lives in vain.

It would be quite useless to try and tell of the weeping fits of despair and prayers of Carluccio; suffice it to say that more than once our pity was so aroused that we were on the point of abandoning our project. But it was a question of his health, and we did not yield. The idea, however, of a good family that would protect him, put him to school, and send him out every day to walk with the small brothers of the officer, and which, if necessary, would take him into the house like a son, and already looked upon him as such, mitigated his grief, especially after we had read to him an affectionate letter from the mother of his host, in which there were a thousand promises and assurances that Carluccio would be the dearest object of her care and affection, and which produced such an effect upon him, that after having tried again and again to turn us from our resolution, he resigned himself to the bitter necessity, sighing: "Well! . . . then, I will return home!"

After a few days we broke up camp and set out *en route* for Padua. We arrived there one beautiful morning at sunrise. We entered by the Portello and passed through nearly the same streets we had traversed the first time. Upon reaching a certain point we saw the Paduan officer leave the ranks and start in the direction of the entrance of a fine house, holding by the hand Carluccio, who was pressing his handkerchief to his eyes. When they were at the door the boy stopped, turned toward us his face streaked with tears, and raising one hand with a convulsive gesture, he shouted between his sobs:

"Good-by, regiment! good-by, Mr. Officers and soldiers! Good-by, all! All so good! I shall always, always remember you! Good-by! good-by!"

"Good-by, Carluccio!" the officers and soldiers replied in passing. "Good-by to the son of the regiment! Good-luck to you, little one. Do not forget us! *Au revoir.* Good-by! good-by!"

The poor boy, not being able to say another word, continued to salute the officers, soldiers, and flag, waving his arm; and then disappeared suddenly, covering his face with his hands.

We never saw him again from that day forth; but the regiment preserved for a long time the recollections of the little adopted son, and every soldier bore in his heart, from garrison to garrison, the memory of that lovely affection, just as he had carried the roses from the gardens of Padua on the point of his bayonet.

# THE CONSCRIPT.

It was a Sunday, toward five o'clock in the evening, and the weather was very beautiful. The barracks were nearly empty. Almost all the soldiers had gone to walk about the city; the few who remained, part in the dormitories dressing themselves, part down in the court-yard waiting, were about to start off too; those down below crying from time to time, "Make haste," and those above replying, "In a moment," while perhaps they were trying to buckle on their belts so tightly as to give them a slender waist. Even the conscripts, who had only joined the regiment two days before, had gone out in part, while the rest were on the point of leaving in sixes, eights, and tens together, pale and serious, their caps on crookedly, their cloaks all bunched up, their hands wide-stretched and stuck into a pair of big white gloves that looked like those the boxers wear; and the soldiers of the guard, seated on a bench at the door of the barracks went on making remarks about them as they passed, although the sergeant grumbled from time to time: "Leave those poor fellows in peace!" The officer of the guard, stretched on the bed in a room on the first floor, was glancing over a newspaper.

In the farthest corner of the court there was a conscript all alone, seated on the steps of a door, with his elbows on his knees and his chin on his hands. He followed his comrades one by one with his eyes as they went out, and when no one was passing he looked steadfastly on the ground. He had the air of one of those good fellows who leave with much pain the family and village where they were born, but come to act as soldiers full of resignation and good-will.—The concise law which enforces this duty, the fact that their names had been placed on the conscript list, the examples of their fathers and their comrades, afford them justification for such a course; and, in fact, as their king calls them, there is nothing to be said, and no one is permitted to make any further investigations on the subject.—But on his face there was something more of that expression, half pensive, half astonished, which is peculiar to conscripts during the first few days; there was melancholy. Perhaps he was repenting not having wished to go out with the others. It is always rather sad to stop at home on Sunday when the weather is fine.

Gradually the quarters were deserted, and an absolute silence reigned.

A corporal in fatigue dress, hastily crossing the court, sees the conscript, stops, and asks him brusquely:

"What are you doing there with your hands folded?"

———"I?" replies the conscript.

"I?" repeats the corporal, drawling, and assuming a stupid expression of face. "This is curious! To whom are you speaking now? the moon? Yes, you. And rise to your feet when you speak to your superiors."

The conscript rose to his feet.

"Who are you? and what company do you belong to?"

———"Company?"

"Company?" asked the corporal in his turn, in a mocking tone. "Do you know that you are a great blockhead, you?"

He approaches, seizes him by the edge of his jacket, and, giving it a great pull which makes him tremble, says: "Look! look how you have spoiled your coat by sitting on the ground like a beggar."

The conscript begins to clean his jacket with his hand.

"Look what a state your shoes are in!" and he gives him a kick on the top of his toes.

The soldier draws out his handkerchief and bends to dust his boots.

"Arrange that cravat, it is going over your ears." And, seizing him by the cravat, he gives him a shake that nearly throws him to the ground.

The conscript raises his hand to his cravat.

"Put that cap on better."

And he carries his hand to his cap.

"And draw up those trowsers if you don't wish to spoil them in a week, straighten the buttons of your coat, take out those earrings which are ridiculous, and don't stand there with your chin on your chest so that you look like a monk, and don't stare at people with that idiotic face. . . ."

The poor young fellow went on touching with trembling hands now his cravat, now his trousers, now the buttons, now his cap; and he did not succeed in doing any thing, for the more he worked the less he accomplished. At that moment the vivandière, who was young and pretty, passed, and she stopped, heartless woman, to look at him. To appear ridiculous in the eyes of a beautiful woman! Ah, it is the most tormenting of all shames! The poor conscript lost his head completely, trifled a little longer with his cravat and buttons, and then felt his arms drop, his chin sink on his breast, and his eyes drop to his feet, and he stood motionless as a statue, utterly annihilated.

The vivandière smiled and went away. The corporal, looking at him and shaking his head with an air of scornful commiseration, went on repeating: "You ape! You ape!"

Then raising his voice: "You must wake up, my dear fellow, and quickly too, or else we shall wake you, I assure you; and how we will do it! Imprisonment and bread and water, bread and water and imprisonment, alternating, just so as not to tire you. Remember that. Now go to your bed and clean your clothes—*march!*"

He reinforced the command by raising his arm with the forefinger pointing toward the window of the dormitory.

"But I . . ."

"Silence!"

"I have not . . ."

"Hold your tongue, I tell you, when you are speaking to your superiors; or the prison is there; do you see it?"

And he moved off mumbling: "Oh, what people! oh, what people! Poor army! Poor Italy!"

"Mr. Corporal!" timidly exclaimed the conscript.

The corporal turned and pointed to the prison again with a pair of terrible eyes.

"I wanted to ask something."

The tone was so quiet and respectful that he could not do less than allow him to speak.

"What do you want?"

"I wished to ask if you knew that there was here in this regiment an officer from my home; there must be, but I do not know if there. . . ."

"From your home? If people from your place are all of your stamp, it is to be hoped that you are the only one in the regiment."

And shrugging his shoulders he moved off.

"What manners!" the conscript murmured sadly, looking at him as he went away. "Yet they certainly told me that he is here," he added, seating himself again. "But why do they treat us so? What are we? Are we dogs? And we have to lead five years of this life! Oh, . . . it is too much! too much!" and he covered his face with his hands and thought of his distant family. "If they could see me in this state!" he said to himself; "poor people!"

He was startled by a burst of laughter at the end of the court; raised his eyes and saw three soldiers of the guard who were looking at him and laughing and talking.

"Oh, what a great blockhead!" the three began saying. "He is in love. He is thinking of his sweetheart. Where have you left her? tell us. Poor thing, she has certainly found some way of consoling herself by this time. Look, look, what eyes you are making!" And then all three exclaimed in one voice, in the tone of a priest who is saying mass: "Oh, what a blockhead!"

The poor young fellow turned pale; they had touched him to the quick; he could not control himself any longer; he rose. . . .

"Who is this man in love?" the officer of the guard said to himself, going to the window with his newspaper in his hand. The soldiers saw him and fled; the conscript raised his anxious face to the window and looked at him. The officer looked at the soldier too, and seeing him give a sign of attention, then one of surprise and contentment without even taking his eyes from him: "Who can this original be?" he thought, as he went down into the court and walked up to him.

"Why are you laughing and twisting your hands about?" he asked in a severe tone.

And the soldier, although a trifle embarrassed, continued to smile.

"But do you know you are an idiot? I ask you what you are laughing at?"

"Well," replied the conscript, dropping his eyes and pulling at his coat with both his hands; "I knew that you were in this regiment, and they have sent me here too. You won't remember me, of course; but I recollect you; it is three years since you went away; I knew you, and your family too; but you did n't know us, though we lived near you, and in the morning I always saw you pass when you went hunting, and . . . we came from the same place, you see."

"Ah! now I understand," replied the officer, looking at him attentively to see who he could be.

"I knew that you had gone to be an officer when you went away, and that you had entered the college, and then you did not come back. . . . Since then they have made over the façade of the dome, and opened a café in the square, almost as large as this court, and it is always full of people."

"Wait, wait; now I remember. Is n't your name Renzo?"

"Yes!"

"You lived in that little house next the church outside the town, I think."

"Exactly! In the little house outside the town, opposite the mill."

And he could hardly contain himself for joy.

"I remember very well. And . . . tell me, how do you like being a soldier?"

The conscript's face changed instantly; he dropped his eyes and was silent.

"Why did n't you go out to walk with the others?"

He made no reply, and looked at his nails as if thinking what he should say; but one could read his thoughts on his face.

The officer understood, and in an affable voice, which went straight to his heart, asked:

"What is the matter?"

This loosened his tongue, and growing more and more animated, he began in a trembling voice: "I . . . ; listen, Mr. Officer; I . . . . I don't know what is the matter, but they treat us in a way that hurts us; that's the trouble. If you ask any thing, they do not reply; and then they say things to us that offend us, and we have to keep quiet or else there is the prison there (and he imitated the voice of the corporal). I understand perfectly that we don't know how to dress, and that we cannot be good soldiers yet; but we have only been here two days, and is it our fault? Can we help it? You know we came on purpose to learn, and they ought to have a little more patience with us, I think. Then they make fun of us before people, put their hands on us, and give us blows, and we have to bear it all, and they laugh. . . I do not see why they ill-treat us so. I came willingly to be a soldier, and said to myself: I will do my duty, and my superiors will like me; but now that I see . . . Perhaps when we get accustomed to it, we shall not notice it, but it hurts us to be so maltreated. We have been accustomed to home, and our family; every one liked us, and here, instead . . . It hurts us; it does hurt us!"

These last words were uttered in a really disconsolate tone; and then he stopped and dropped his eyes, continuing to mutter to himself.

The officer allowed some moments to pass in silence, lighted a cigar, and then, in a careless way, as if he had not understood or did not wish to understand any thing, he said:

"Draw up your cravat a little (and he helped him to do so); so; that's right. Turn around."

The soldier turned; the officer seized and drew down the end of his coat. "Your coat must have no wrinkles; it must be as smooth as a corset. Turn."

He turned; the officer arranged his cap. "This way—a little sideways, for it looks better."

The conscript smiled.

"And stand erect, hold up your head, and when you walk, step off freely and easily, as you did when you played at bowls in our court, do you remember?"

He smiled, and nodded in the affirmative."

"Well, then," continued the officer, leaning against the wall and putting one leg over the other; "look every one in the face, because you need not fear any one, or be ashamed of yourself. Do you understand? Even if the king passed, you are to raise your head and look him full in the eyes, as if to say: 'It is I.' It is self-respect, and we soldiers must always show it in this way, remember."

The soldier nodded in the affirmative and began to grow composed.

"And remember, too, that as soon as you enter the barracks,

you must change your way of speaking; few words, but frank, loud, and sonorous, with any one who addresses you—yes and no, and no and yes—and if you have nothing else to say, so much the better. When you are in the ranks it is exactly as if you were in church, be silent; when the ranks are broken, you are at home, and if the others joke, you must do so too, and not merely stand and look on, because this makes you sad; dash right into whatever is going on. Then you must like your comrades, for you will find warm friends among them, I assure you; you will find young fellows who will love you like a brother. You will see; there may be a great lack of everything, but of heart never. . . . Have you a pipe?"

"No, sir."

"If so, you could smoke. And when a superior scolds—if he is right, listen and take heed; if he is wrong, listen just the same, and don't take it to heart, because in this world we all have our defects, and may all do wrong; we make a mistake in scolding sometimes; but always if we disobey. And you must not think that all the officers who scold have bad hearts, are angry with you, and wish to harm you. There is nothing more untrue. These rough people have better hearts than the others, and like you, and if they were taken away from you, you would all die of melancholy in fifteen days. They shout, scold; it is a habit, an affair of the lungs; nothing more, believe me. You will end by liking them better than the others. You will see, when you go away they will weep. I have seen so many. I saw them at Custoza . . ."

"That battle that went so badly?"

"Yes; I saw a captain who was the terror of his company, and no one could bear him, but they were all wrong; not one man fell that he did not run to help him, look at his wound, and cheer him; he was always in motion though tired to death. 'O captain! captain! don't leave me, captain!' the sufferers shouted, as they seized him by his arm and by the end of his coat. 'No, my boy,' he replied; 'I will stay here with you until you are cured; courage, courage, boy, your captain will not leave you.' Do you understand what a man that was? And there are many like him; you must not judge from appearances; and pity those who seem bad, and be grateful to the good, and above every thing respect all, because they are soldiers, and any day we may see them die under our eyes like valiant men. When we love any one we gladly bear any kind of life, remember that. Ask, look about you, and make your comrades tell you this; you will see that the best soldiers always loved their superiors. Take, for instance, the soldier —what was his name?—the soldier, Perrier, in '48, who threw himself between his officer and the enemy, and fell to the ground with three balls in his breast, shouting: 'Remember me, my good officer; I die happy in having saved your life!' And that other grenadier, I do not recall his name, who, rather than abandon his wounded captain, allowed himself to be beaten to death with bayonets, shouting: 'If you do not kill me, I will not leave him to you.' Then the other eight or ten who, under a shower of bullets, at the battle of Rivoli, went and dragged from the hands of the Germans the body of their officer, as they wished to bury him with their own hands, and give him the last honors in their own camp. Then so many others, whose names and deeds are printed in a hundred books, and remember them all and love them as if they were living. . . . Have you a match?"

The conscript, who up to that point had seemed to be in a state of gaping, wondering ecstacy, hurriedly drew out a match and handed it to him.

"When one thinks of these things and has any heart, certain little troubles, and certain scantiness in the living of the soldiers are quite forgotten; so you must think of these things and they will teach you; and you, who are a good sort of fellow, will keep them in mind, won't you?"

The conscript made a sign in the affirmative, as he could not speak for a moment.

"Certainly," continued the officer, "in order to be a good soldier, one must look above the barracks and the parade ground. Then, there is every thing in habit. The knapsack is so heavy at first, and such a torment; they all say so; but little by little it becomes a trifle. And the food? You certainly don't live like princes, that is well known; but you must have patience, patience, patience, which is the great virtue of a soldier, and not complain and whimper, as some do, with and without reason, of all and every thing; but eat what there is and be content with little. Then the appetite is never lacking when a man works, does his duty, and has a contented spirit; appetite is a great cook. They are only the listless and indolent who find fault with every thing, and are never contented. I see that good fellows always make good soldiers, because their superiors like them, their comrades esteem them, their towns-people respect them, and there are some of them who in five years have never been but one day under arrest, and have left their *numero diciotto* white and clean as a handkerchief; and you will be one of these, won't you?"

The soldier assented quickly.

"Bravo! Now don't think our profession is all thorns; there are flowers for those who know where to look for them, and good soldiers find them. Learn to do your duty well, always be clean, respectful, and willing, and from your captain and officers you will hear certain 'bravos!' that will go to your heart, and increase your appetite and good spirits. The days will pass quickly. Then, in five years, no one knows what may happen; they might make you change garrison ten times, and then time flies, and the months seem days. You will see new places: cities, the country, mountains, seas, a new and varied world, all our beautiful country—Italy—which you now only know by name; statues, churches, palaces, gardens; and in your leisure hours you will go to see every thing, in order to tell every thing to your family and friends when you return home. In the summer we go into camp, eight, ten, twenty regiments, cavalry and artillery, and you will see what a beautiful sight a camp is; what a noise, what gaiety, and how much life there will be every day, and the great manœuvres, and the fêtes they have before breaking camp, with music and dancing, *tombolas*, races; and all the officers and generals join in the fun and amuse themselves with the soldiers, and all the people in the country round about come to see the sight and clap their hands. Then you will know all the soldiers of the corps, you will have a quantity of friends; the regiment will seem like one great family to you. And all the honors bestowed upon the regiment will seem to belong to you, and you will be as proud of your old colonel as you would be of a father. When you see the flag appear in front of the battalion drawn up in line, and the bands begin to play the march of the corps, and all present arms, you will feel your heart beat with joy and pride, and you will tremble with emotion. Little by little you will become fond of every thing: of your arms, your uniform, your trencher, of this court, this staircase, these walls. When you are ready to go away, and have already been to take leave of your captain, officers, sergeants, and all the other soldiers that treat you kindly say to you 'good-by, a fine journey, remember us,' your heart will throb as it did when you left home; then when you are down in the street, you will turn to look for the last time at the windows of the barracks, and you will stop and say once more: 'Farewell! O my second paternal home, where I have loved so many friends, where I have passed so many beautiful days with a clear conscience, where I have thought so much of, and sighed so often for, my dear ones; farewell! my poor little bed; farewell! my good sergeant of the guard; farewell! . . .' What is the matter with you?"

The conscript was motionless, astounded, his face contorted, his breathing labored, and his eyes moist and smiling.

"What is the matter with you?"

He made an effort to control his voice by dropping his head and stretching out his neck, as if to swallow a great mouthful; but he only succeeded in replying hastily in a *mezza voce:* "Nothing."

The officer smiled.

"Do you know how to write?"

"A little," replied the conscript, thickly.

"Well, then, come with me."

He moved off toward his room, and the conscript followed him. When they had entered, the officer made his young townsman sit down at the table, put a pen in his hand, a sheet of paper in front of him, and said: "Write to your father."

The conscript looked at him, open-mouthed.

"Write to your father."

"What shall I say?"

"Tell him what you have seen, what you think, what you feel; in fact, whatever you choose.'

"But . . .

"Keep quiet; until you have finished I shall not permit you to say one word."

And he resumed his newspaper near the window. The conscript continued to look at him with an air of surprise, then bent his head, thought for some moments, and began to write very slowly.

After a quarter of an hour, the officer asked: "Have you nearly finished?"

"It is finished," replied the soldier, quite content.

"Read it, then."

"Read it?"

"Yes."

He was ashamed to do so. '

"Read it, I tell you."

The man prepared to obey.

"But tell me first, have you written the truth? Have you been quite sincere? Have you really said what you think and feel?"

The soldier placed his hand on his breast.

"Read, then."

He began to read with difficulty.

MY DEAR FATHER:

I reached the regiment, and they instantly made me cut off my hair, and then they dressed me. That officer of our town whose name you know, I saw in the court to-day, and we talked together for more than an hour. We don't have the best food, you know; but it is so hard to cook for so many; and then the appetite is never lacking, if a man does his duty. The superiors scold; but they are not so overbearing as many say; for there are soldiers who have died to save them, and would not leave them dead in the hands of the enemy. There are also soldiers who have never been punished, and I hope this will be the case with me. Time passes quickly, because we shall travel, and there are many places to see, and then the manœuvres, then the camp too, and the generals amuse themselves with the soldiers and have *tombola*. Then it is a pleasure to see the flag and hear the music, and to find friends; and the old colonel is like our second father, and we are his sons. Meanwhile I greet you, and I hope you will keep well, etc.

Your most affectionate son.

"Bravo!" said the officer. "And now do me the favor to go and drink a half glass of wine to the health of all conscripts. Take this," handing him a ticket.

"Mr. Officer!" exclaimed the soldier, quite embarrassed, trying to refuse it.

"Eh!" shouted the officer, in a menacing tone.

The conscript took the ticket, and preparing to go out, stammered some words of thanks: "Mr. Officer, . . . I don't know really . . ."

"Silence!"

He left hastily, went down the staircase three steps at a time; gave two or three jumps in the court, rubbing his hands, laughing and muttering to himself as he did so; entered the wine cellar; the vivandière gave him his glass with a lovely smile and manner that made him forget the scene of a short time before; he drank, went out.

Hardly was he outside when he met the corporal, who approached with a more agreeable expression of face and in a more courteous way.

"Tell me, is that officer you were talking to an hour ago your relative?"

"No."

"But you knew him?"

"Very well indeed."

"Is that the officer from your town for whom you were looking?"

"The same."

"I did not understand, you see, when you asked me . . ."

"That makes no difference."

"If I had understood I should have answered."

"Thanks."

The corporal moved off; the conscript, left alone, said to himself: "Well—in the end, he is n't a bad fellow—this corporal!"

Just at that moment the soldiers began to return in groups to the barracks, talking and singing loudly among themselves. Among the others was a band of conscripts, a trifle intoxicated, who were making a tremendous racket.

"When the others make a noise, you dash into their midst, and do the same"; the conscript remembered these words. "I must make a racket too," he thought; "what shall I cry? . . . Ah!" he shouted at the top of his lungs: "Long live the soldier Perrier!"

And the rest, perhaps without understanding what he meant, replied in a loud voice: "Viva!"

Our soldier dashed into their midst, and singing and shouting they went up in confusion to the dormitory.

The officer, who had watched him from the window, said to himself: "That fellow will be a fine soldier."

When it was dark, and the stars were all out, and one could hear in the court-yard that gay noise, and in the street sounded the bugle-call for the retreat, he was filled with an indefinable mixture of generous and noble sentiments, so much so that almost without being aware of it, without knowing the reason, he raised his eyes to heaven and exclaimed affectionately: "Perrier!"

A short time after: "Oh, good Perrier! . . . Where are you? Do you hear your name?"

Because in looking at a beautiful sky at night, the dearest and most revered names spring to our lips.

# A BUNCH OF FLOWERS.

"CURED, yes, entirely cured, and there is not even a scar; look and see if you can find one." Thus said a very young officer (whom I had not seen for fifteen days when we met last year, at the end of February, in the house of a lady friend), as he put out his hand for me to look at. I glanced at it: and there was not a trace of a scar. "And the other man?" I asked. "Oh, he is better," was the reply. "Who? Who is better? Who has been ill?" broke in the lady of the house, coming up to us. My friend and I exchanged smiles. "Shall I tell her?" asked he. "Yes, I would do so, if I were you."

"Well, listen then," began my friend, turning to the lady. "Three days before the end of carnival, one evening about five o'clock, I was standing in front of a café watching the *corso*. I was alone, in no very good humor, squeezed into the crowd, quite white with flour, cursing the moment when I had been seized with the idea of leaving the house and dashing into the midst of all this confusion. From time to time a cavalry soldier passed with unsheathed sword, made a motion to the people to keep back in order not break up the *corso*, and accompanied his gesture with some respectful and courteous words. In front of me were four or five gamins, who, as soon as the soldiers passed, dashed into the middle of the street, between the carriages, and fought with their fists for the comfits and flowers which were scattered over the pavement, at the risk of being crushed by the horses, and to the great annoyance of the coachmen, who, in order to get on, were obliged to shout themselves hoarse in telling them to be careful and get out of the way. One of the soldiers who was on duty, after having warned and scolded them five or six times, seeing that they were behaving worse and worse, lost his patience, put spurs to his horse, and raised his sword, as if to give them a blow on the head, which he certainly never had any real idea of doing. A gentleman who was near me, seeing this, exclaimed : 'Ah !' and when the soldier drew his sabre back to his shoulder, added : ' I should like to have seen him do it !' Then, turning to his neighbor, said : ' This is the result of his education—oppression and brutality.' My blood boiled, I raised one hand, drew it back and thrust it into my pocket, and with all the calmness of which I was capable, and in the most courteous tone, I whispered in that gentleman's ear : ' What education ?' The gentleman turned, gave a start of surprise, paled ; but instantly recovered himself, and answered with insolent nonchalance : ' The military education.' I neither saw him, the crowd, nor the *corso*, and I do not recollect what I said or he replied ; I only remember that the following morning I returned home with a wounded hand, and my friends said that that gentleman had his left cheek laid open. That is all. I was just saying that my hand bore no sign of the scratch, and that the other man is better."

The lady, who up to that time had been listening very gravely, raising her eyes from time to time, and exclaiming : "Heavens ! heavens !" grew more cheerful on learning of the fortunate ending of the duel, and then suddenly broke out with a genuine woman's question : "But why did you provoke him? Would it not have been better to have pretended not to hear?" My friend and I looked at each other, and both burst out laughing.

"Why are you laughing?"

"Listen, my dear lady," my friend replied. "Supposing (which could not be the case) that I ought to have pretended that I did not hear, how could I have done so when my blood was boiling and my head in a ferment? Do you suppose I knew what I was doing at that moment?"

The lady did not appear at all convinced.

"The people all around had heard," continued the officer; "the insult was one that touched the whole army, and those words were a lie; then, just on that occasion the lie was a calumny, the tone of voice in which the calumny had been uttered sounded like a provocation; then that man, as I afterward learned (and it could not have been otherwise, because these are words which reveal a man's soul), was nothing but a . . ."

"Silence! It is not necessary that I should know."

"Then there was another reason still why these words offended me more than they might have another person. And the reason is this. Listen. Fourteen years ago . . ."

"No less than that!"

"Listen; I was at Turin with my family; and only seven years old. The last day but one of the carnival my mother dressed me in a pretty costume of blue and white striped silk, with a red sash, a blonde curly wig, and a green velvet cap, and took me to the *corso* in a carriage. My father and a friend of his, a major in the artillery, were with us. We had a number of bouquets and a large basket of *confetti*. The streets were crowded with people, and there were innumerable carriages, elegant maskers, a great confusion and noise, and a very beautiful *corso*. My mother, according to her custom, took no part in the gaiety of the fête, and rarely spoke. From time to time, when the carriage of some friend passed, she put a bunch of flowers into my hand and had me throw them, holding me by my sash so that I should not fall head first in flinging them. My little friends threw me flowers too, and greeted me with shouts, laughing heartily at my grotesque costume. I laughed at them, and we enjoyed ourselves to our hearts' content. Much more than now,—between ourselves,— for then our glances, thoughts, and desires were not attracted by a beautiful masker stretched comfortably out in a carriage, with a small, shapely foot swinging cunningly out of one door and a *debardeur's* shirt falling on one side."

"That has nothing to do with it."

"We enjoyed ourselves hugely. At a certain point, however, weary with shouting and swinging my arms about, I sat down to take breath. At the entrance of Via Po and Piazza Castello there was a file of cavalry soldiers and carabineers, as grave and motionless as if they were at a funeral. They looked now at the carriages, now at the people, without saying a word, exchanging a smile, or giving the slightest sign of curiosity, pleasure, regret, or ennui; they seemed like automatons. The crowd pressed forward on every side, undulating, mingling, and making a great noise; from the windows of the neighboring house, which were filled with ladies and maskers, fell showers of comfits, from the carriages a shower up at the windows, and from the street another into the carriages. It was a fierce battle, with great clouds of flour which veiled every thing, and a little farther on the band was playing, almost drowned by the racket of the drums and trumpets that fairly deafened one.

"'Poor people!' said my mother to the major, as she pointed to the soldiers. 'They never fail; they are everywhere. It is not enough that they defend us from our enemies, put out fires, quiet riots, and protect our lives and our property; they protect our fêtes too, and secure us our pleasures; they who have neither joys nor fêtes, and suffer so much and make so many sacrifices without ever gaining any thing or obtaining any recompense, not even any consolation, a word of acknowledgment, or a thank you. The people do not as much as look at them; we are every thing for them, they nothing for us—absolutely nothing.'

"The major, solemn as a judge, replied quite gravely, without even looking at the soldiers: 'That is true!'

"'If it is true!' added my mother quickly.—'Look, major; look at the soldier there, the first one on this side, what a melancholy air he has! Can there be something troubling him? Does he feel ill?'

"'Who knows?' replied the major, smiling slightly.

"'Who knows what is the matter with him?' repeated my mother, looking at him pensively. That good woman is so constituted that in the midst of all the racket and gaiety of a fête, a trifle will take her mind from all that surrounds her, and from thought to thought she falls into a state of sadness. The carriage went on and my mother continued talking of that soldier; then she fell to thinking again, and suddenly said: 'If some one at home were ill? That might be the case too.

They do not allow him to go home when one of his family is ill, do they, major?'

"'It is rather rare!' replied the latter.

"'Look!' exclaimed my mother. 'I am willing to wager that that is what makes him sad. And meanwhile he is comdemned to stand there in the midst of all those people who are amusing themselves by singing and shouting . . . I cannot get him out of my mind.'

"The major smiled.

"'How can I help it?' replied my mother; 'I was born so.'

"When the circuit was ended, the carriage was about to pass by the soldier again. My mother, seizing the moment when the major and my father were not looking, handed me a bunch of flowers, pointed quickly to the soldier, and whispered in my ear: 'Throw it to him.' I rose to my feet, and, held as usual by my sash, prepared to fling the flowers. 'You said that one there, did you not?' I asked once more. 'Yes, yes, quick!' We were seven or eight steps away; the carriage stopped, went on, here we are. 'Courage!' said my mother. 'There he is!' I replied proudly. The bouquet had described a beautiful curve in the air, and fallen right on the breast of the soldier, between the buckle of his belt and the hand which held the reins. He started as if in a dream, seized the bouquet almost involuntarily, raised his eyes with surprise, saw me; I made him a sign with both hands; he smiled and looked fixedly at me until the carriage disappeared. My little heart beat furiously; my mother had become calm; the major and my father had not seen any thing. Before making another circuit we left the *corso* and went home.

"I saw the soldier again, ten or twelve days later, in the public gardens. He was with a number of his comrades, and was talking and laughing heartily. 'Look, there is the soldier to whom I threw the bouquet!' I said to my mother, pulling her by the dress. 'Be quiet,' she replied. 'Do not take any notice of him.' I could not understand the reason for this command; I looked at him; he looked fixedly at me, and recognized me, started with surprise, and said, 'Oh!' My mother seized me by the arm and dragged me on. After that day I did not see him for more than a year. The following year, on one of the last nights of carnival, on returning from the theatre with the family, I went to the window a few moments before going to bed, and stood a short time looking out into the street through the glass. The street was dark and it was snowing. From time to time maskers kept coming out of the opposite house, which was a café and hostelry; they scattered, followed each other, disappeared; new ones arrived, and meeting and recognizing each other crowded together, making a terrible racket with their shouts in the falsetto, and confusedly exchanging invitations and salutations. A band of cavalry appeared at that point. The maskers began to dance around them, shouting and clapping their hands as they did so. The soldiers, enveloped in their mantles, passed on without giving any sign of having seen them; but one of them turned toward our house, and seemed to be looking at my window. 'Can it be he?' I thought, as I opened it. At the same moment the soldier put oné hand out from under his mantle, gave a salute, and passed. The following morning I learned from the porteress that some days before a cavalry soldier had entered our portico, glanced at the stairs as if uncertain whether he would go up or not, and had then gone away. A few months later I heard that a regiment of cavalry had left Turin, and I did not see my soldier again, nor did I think of him. Many years passed; '59 arrived. I became infatuated with the army, and manifested to my father my intention of embracing a military career. My father was uncertain. 'Finish your studies,' he said, 'and we will see about it.' In August of '59 I ended them, and from that time forward I had a discussion every day with my father on the subject of my career. As time went on he seemed less disposed to second my desires. But an unforeseen incident settled the question. It was in the beginning of January, '60. One morning I sat writing at a table. There was a rap at the door, and a servant came to say that some one wished to see me. 'Who can it be?' I said to my mother. I rose, she followed me, and we went into the hall-way. There was a man in workman's clothes at the door, wearing a large cloak, a fur cap on his head, and looking pale, thin, with a saddened and weary air. 'He does not even raise his cap,' muttered the servant as we entered. The unknown visitor looked smilingly at me, and said: 'Is it you?' giving my Christian and surname.

"'Yes,' I replied.

"'I am a poor young fellow who is left without work; I have been a soldier, and if you could help me in some way. . . .'

"My mother and I consulted each other with a glance.

"'Give me something,' added the man in a tone of supplication.

"I took and handed him in spite of myself a couple of francs, saying as I did so: 'Take this.'

"'Will you put it into my pocket?'

"'Into your pocket!' I exclaimed, half surprised, half offended. But his glance produced a strange effect upon me; I looked at him for a few moments, and then placed the money in the pocket of his cloak.

"'Thanks,' he replied in a voice full of emotion. 'And now, as I am going home, I beg you to accept a memento of me.'

"My mother and I turned to each other in astonishment.

"'Will you accept it, sir?' he asked timidly, in an affectionate tone.

"'Let us see it,' I replied.

"'Here it is,' he said, and opening his cloak with his elbows, he showed me with his eyes a bunch of flowers that were fastened into a button-hole of his vest.

"'Ah, it is the soldier in the *corso*!' cried my mother.

"'He!' I exclaimed impetuously, and I dashed forward to embrace him; the cloak fell; my mother uttered a cry of terror: 'My God!'

"'What is the matter?' I asked, turning around. At the same time I saw that the poor fellow had no hands.

"He had lost them at San Martino.

"I do not know how it happened; but from that day forward my desire to be a soldier changed into a firm resolution to do so. It seemed almost like an act of homage to that poor young fellow to don the military uniform. And behold me a soldier. This is the reason why every time I see a soldier of the cavalry at the *corso* I feel my heart beat as if for a friend, and I wish to be a child in order to throw him a bunch of flowers."

"And that soldier?" asked the lady quickly.

"He died."

"Where?"

"At our house, in my arms, in the presence of my mother, with a little bunch of flowers at his pillow."

# A NOCTURNAL MARCH.

WHAT a night! No moon, no stars, pitch darkness. There never was such utter gloom seen before. Though it was only the first of October, a fresh autumn breeze was blowing, which whipped sharply across the face, under the clothes, and shrivelled the skin. It was about nine o'clock in the evening; the regiment had folded the tents and was drawn up across the field, their arms at their feet, awaiting the orders for departure. The soldiers, just awakened from a short and uncomfortable sleep, all stood there, doubled up, bent over, shivering, with a bitter, discontented expression of face, their hands in their pockets, the muskets leaning against their arms; and instead of the usual chatting, so lively and gay, nothing was to be heard but an occasional subdued and listless whisper. The darkness was so great that, in looking at the camp from the road, nothing was to be seen but the long line of lanterns hung from the end of the muskets, each one of which lighted up three or four sleepy faces. Over there, in the corner of the field, beyond the extreme flank of the regiment, many little lights were to be seen moving about in a small space, and these served to illumine dimly a confused bustle of people (differently dressed) around certain carts and boxes—the baggage of the sutler. Here and there through the field a few little flames still gleamed; they were the last sparks of the fire which the soldiers had lighted with the straw of the tents, to take off the dampness contracted in sleeping on the ground. Every thing else was in darkness.

Suddenly a loud beating of drums is heard; then silence follows. The companies face about, each in turn; the first lines move, and the regiment starts. After passing a narrow little bridge over the ditch which separates the field from the road, the lines close up, and a mass of lights are seen moving now forward, now backward, according to the motion of the crowd, and start up two by two, extend on the sides of the straight road in a double line, and little by little sink in the distance into two luminous streaks which wind and undulate like two great reins of fire shaken at the end of the column.

On they march, and for a short time is heard a subdued chatting, which gradually dies away into profound silence, broken only by the rough voices of the officers who grumble, "Order!" every time that, casting their sleepy eyes on the soldiers nearest the lanterns, they discover a little falling apart or crowding in the lines. All the others are silent. Nothing is audible but the dragging noise of the foot-falls, and the monotonous clinking of the tin boxes, which keep time to the measured tread.

As the silence increases, sleep (that tormenting and terrible companion of nocturnal marches) begins to take possession of all. Unfortunate he who is seized by it! No former rest, nor chat with friend, nor strong liquor, nor effort of will can conquer it; he must give up to it entirely.

Look at that officer in the middle of the road. He has been struggling with sleep for more than an hour; but now his eyelids, trembling and heavy, are closing irresistibly; his knees are bending under him; his head, raised by force, falls again heavily on his chest, and his arms hang inert and powerless. His mind, little by little, wanders; ideas grow confused, and melt curiously into one another. To his eyes veiled by sleep, the soldiers who are walking before and beside him stagger confusedly along; and the trees and houses on either side of the way, (whose dark outlines are scarcely discernible) present strange, shapeless, wonderful aspects to him. Sometimes he still follows with his eyes the walls of a house when they have already been left behind, or he seems to see a house or clump of trees where there are none. At another moment, there suddenly appears before him, right in the middle of the road, directly in his path, a great obstacle, a large black thing, which he cannot make out, but he sees it; there it is, right there, and he is just about to hit it with his head; he stops, stretches out his arm, shakes it —nothing—there was nothing; so on he goes. Thirty, fifty, a hundred steps, then he begins to dose again. This time he dreams. He seems to be walking alone, in some unknown direction, or to be in another place, far from there, perhaps at home, among other people, in the daytime. . . . Suddenly, the sound of the foot-falls of those around him strikes his ear; he becomes aware of the clinking of the canteens; wakes, glances around, comes to himself, yawns, falls into step, and,—shortly afterward,—the whole thing begins again. With his head on his chest, one hand in his pocket, the other on the handle of his sword, he goes on, leaning on it, in unequal paces and springs, tottering, winding along, three steps here, four there,— five,—six,—a stumble into the knapsack of a soldier. He starts, wakes, looks around with staring eyes, comes to himself again, is ashamed of himself, shakes his head as if out of pity for his sufferings, and then resumes his way with a free and hurried gait. After a hundred more paces, the same thing occurs again. He dashes into a person who is walking in front of him, wakes, looks: "Oh! excuse me, captain."—"Don't mention it, pray! These are things that happen to all."

A companion comes close to you. You walk for a short time, without being conscious of it, side by side. Then: "Are you there?" A grunt is your reply. "Are you sleepy?" "A little. Give me your arm." The arm is given. Shoulder to shoulder, hip to hip, and forward you go as best you can, staggering and stumbling. Eight, ten, twenty paces, sleep seizes you both, and your heavy heads fall on the same side and come into contact with each other. "Ahi!" Then you separate.

All round about is quiet; the pitch darkness continues, the two long lines of light keep waving along the sides of the road, and there is always the same monotonous clinking of the canteens.

Suddenly, an irritable voice bursts out in the middle of the line: "Up with that light there!" and the soldier who is carrying the lantern, and who, overcome by sleep, had slackened his arm and let the musket fall on the head of the man behind him, wakes, draws up his arm, and raises the light.

A few steps more, and a long and sonorous yawn, like the braying of an ass, breaks the silence. Two or three voices try to imitate it; there is a laugh, and all are silent.

A few steps more, and a shrill voice attempts a song. An outburst of protests and disapprobation rises from the lines. "Leave that alone!" At another moment: "Sleep in peace." And the unfortunately inspired singer drives back into his throat the rest of the song, and is silent.

Twenty paces more, and one hears a sharp cry, followed by a raging outburst of oaths. "What's the matter?" "Who is it?" It is a soldier who, overcome by sleep, has dashed violently against a mile-stone with his shin. And on all sides: "Look out where you are going." "I should think so; he is walking with his eyes shut." "You caught it, eh? Keep it!"

A little later, a great laugh breaks out at the end of the column, and an "Uh!" prolonged into a tone of mockery. "What's happened?" "What has happened?" "Who is it?" "It's only a poor devil of a soldier who was walking along the edge of the road, dozing and staggering, and so ended by tumbling into the ditch." "Is it deep?" "Who can see?" "Let's look." "Courage, courage (an officer); what are you doing there? Go on. He'll get up himself. And will *you* hold that light up?"

Then silence, and forward, and increasing darkness, and freezing, biting wind, which scourges one's face and sets one shivering, continue.

"Oh, this drowsiness!" "What time can it be?" "Ten, perhaps, may be later." "What a night!" "One can't see a thing." "Oh! I say, friend, how long have we been marching? . . . Speak. How long?" "He's asleep and does not hear any thing; he'll break his neck in a minute more." . . . "I'm sleepy too. Ah, to be able to sleep." "Well, time is passing with him! What a nuisance not to be able to see any thing! If I could only sleep on foot. . . . I might try, do you say? Phew! how sleepy I am, how sleepy I am, great heavens! . . . the night is dark. . . dark . . . and the wind . . . to sleep . . ."

A moment more and he will fall into the ditch. A blast of the trumpet, "Halt!" He's escaped it. Down they all go like so many dead bodies; they fall where they can, on to stones, among thorns, into the mud, wherever it may happen to be; every thing is comfortable, every thing clean, soft, delicious! There, on a pile of stones, on one side of the road, an entire squad has pitched itself down in a heap, one on top or across the other, just as it happens; the barrel of the guns under the neck, the leather bottle of a comrade under the head, a corporal's foot in the face, the knapsack of another man against the hip; and the hand, sometimes, in the grass, in something damp and soft. . . . But what a heap! The luxury of sleep is so great, so sweet, and powerful, that one cannot pay any attention to any thing, but the utter enjoyment and abandonment of soul and body to it. Oh, the sweetness of the final gratification of a long and harrassing desire! A sense of languid pleasure and gentle exhaustion steals over the frame. . . . "Oh, what bliss! We sleep."

If a ray of moonlight could fall for a moment on to that point of the road, what a strange spectacle would greet our eyes! It looks like a heap of bodies thrown carelessly down: some face upward, others face downward, some stretched out, others doubled up, and here and there arms, legs, feet, and muskets, which protrude between the legs and arms of others still; a muddle, in fact, in which it would be difficult to discover to whom the different members belong. At first, there is a slight movement, a little struggling in that mass of human bodies; each one is seeking, quite gently, the most comfortable position, and this gives rise to a little squabbling: "Get over there! Blood of Bacchus!" "Out of the way with that foot!"

"Draw in that leg; don't you see you are sticking it into my face?" But it is only the affair of a moment, and then all are quiet. A deep, full sleep takes possession of each. At first a quick, heavy breathing is heard; then a feeble, broken sighing; then a dull, rattling moaning; and, finally, a general snoring in every key, bass, baritone, soprano, harmonious and dissonant, shrill and sonorous—an infernal style of music, in fact.

A blast of the trumpet; it is the *Attention!*

In that group no one hears it; no one stirs; all are quiet and motionless as dead bodies. Another blast; which has no effect; all as motionless as before. "I'll make them get up, now!" says a menacing voice above the sleepers. At that voice, behold a leg is straightened there, an arm outstretched here, farther on a head moves more this way, a body writhes, as is the case when a group of snakes turn slowly in the heat of the sun. "Shall we get up or not?" the first voice repeats more angrily than before. One of the sleepers rises to a sitting posture, another rubs his eyes with the back of his hand, another feels around for his cap, a fourth is already on his feet, and a fifth and a sixth . . . all are up: "Oh, at last!" "What misery, what a torment to be waked so roughly, and to be obliged to get up just when one was beginning to enjoy the sleep!" "Where's my cap?" "And my musket?" "Say, give me my cap." "This is mine." "No, it is n't; that other one's yours." "Whose musket is this?" "Mine, give it me." "Go and find the little tassel, now!" and they search, scrape, and poke here and there among the stones on the road, down in the ditch, in the grass and bushes, breathless, puffing, swearing. . . . The trumpet sounds again and the regiment starts.

It is dark still, and the same chilly wind which freezes the face and shrivels the skin keeps on blowing. "Heavens! how cold it is when one stands still! it makes one shiver." The lanterns are all extinguished; an Egyptian darkness reigns. Who knows in what confusion these rascals may be marching! It's lucky for them that they cannot be seen."

After a half hour's silent march, some man begins to distinguish far, far away, a little trembling light, which disappears now and then and reappears like a fire-fly. "What can it be? Let's go on, on, a little farther, another bit." The small light disappears no longer; it seems larger and burns more brightly. "Do you see it?" "It's the lantern at the head of the regiment." "No, no, it's a town." "But what place!" On, on, on, we go. "Ah! . . . You are right, it is a place." The rumor spreads; those dozing rouse themselves; the sleepers wake; a little whisper starts up. "Heaven be praised; here are the houses, the principal street, and we have entered."

The hour is late; the streets are almost deserted, the tread of the regiment resounds distinctly in that solitude, and a whispering is heard on the right and left in those dark and crooked streets. Small ugly houses here and there, all closed and barred, as if it were an abandoned village. But as we proceed, to the left and right, on the ground-floor some little doors half open so that we see the hearths gleaming inside, or the head of some half-dressed woman stuck timidly out; the children run to the threshhold, and in the upper stories now and then a curtain is raised, a light shines through, and behind the window-panes appears a dark figure which looks down to see what this unusual commotion means. . . . Ah! that black figure may have just sprung from the bed, where it was sleeping, and it will soon go back to resume delightfully its quiet, gentle

"That was a large café, lighted and gleaming with mirrors, full of staff-officers, aides-de-camp," etc.

(*Page* 145.)

slumbers. Oh, that bed! We can almost see it; it seems as if the fold of the sheet stretched over the bolster was before our eyes, and that we could pass our hands over it, and perceive the fragrant freshness of the linen just from the wash. Oh, fortunate person who sleeps in there! When shall we too have our beds! Happy and blessed are they who have one!

The street, narrow and tortuous at first, becomes straighter little by little, broadens, widens, and comes out on a square. The beautiful square. Two lines to the right, two to the left: all look around them. Here and there are groups of curious people, some shops open, there a church, here the house of the Syndic, a fountain, an arcade, and over yonder . . oh, . . how tantalizing, a café!

A strange but veritable emotion! Cross a village in the night, after a long and painful march; pass, weary, exhausted, thirsty, covered with dust and dirt, unaccustomed for some time to any pleasant habit or amusement of city life,—pass before a café, and your heart will beat with a certain tenderness, a certain melancholy longing, almost with a sad pity for yourself, and you will cast into that café an eager, envious, bitter look of passionate love, as children do; and you will retain for a long time in your mind the image of the place, objects, and persons seen.

That was a large café, lighted and gleaming with mirrors, full of staff-officers, aides-de-camps, covered with gold and silver medals, plumes, trinkets, and crosses; some inside, some at the door, others out on the square, all gesticulating continuously with arms and legs, and noisily trailing their swords along. A dense cloud of smoke enveloped everything; we could see and hear a great drawing of beer-corks, a running hither and thither of waiters, red in the face, utterly breathless and confused by the unusual splendor and invasion of customers; a wild coming and going from the interior to the outside, from the exterior to the interior, calling to one another, and vieing with each other, until they had completely lost their heads. Before the door was a crowd of people with wide-stretched eyes and mouth, gazing at the broadest galloons and breasts most covered with medals. At the back of the café, quite at the end, in a corner behind a table, surrounded by a younger set of officers, on a raised seat, in a species of niche or temple, was the beautiful little face of a girl, over which modesty and coquetry were amicably disputing the space, amid so many unusual compliments, so many gentlemanly courtesies, passionate protests, audacious petitions, and such a twisting and turning of slender waists and legs incased in buckskin.

All eyes are fastened upon that lovely figure, beautiful face, and there they rest until she disappears from view. They are no sensuous thoughts, images, or desires which she awakens at that moment; oh, no, although she arouses in our hearts (like a weary desire for peace and affection) a vague melancholy, and we suddenly feel ourselves alone, abandoned and discouraged. The woman recalls to our memory the gentle, quiet pleasures of domestic life, which, in comparison with our hard life as soldiers, especially at those hours and moments in which we only experience the discomforts and bitterness, not the consolations nor the proud satisfactions, of such an existence make us seem almost unhappy. That woman's face rouses in our minds the image of our mother, sister, or some one dearer still; and, when it flees from our sight, we bow our heads, think, grow sad; those shadows seem to weigh on our chests, cut off our breath; we look and look again at the sky to see if it is growing light; and in that melancholy wandering of the fancy, it seems as if we would gladly go to sleep for ever, could we only see once more our mother or the sun. . . .

The regiment is outside the village. The same darkness and wind continue. Nothing more is said of the lights, all of which have been extinguished for some time. Well then? Shall we follow the regiment to the station in this cold and gloom, to witness the repetition of the scenes that we have already described? Any one may follow who pleases. I'll let him take his way, hoping that he may find a good camp, and eat a luscious orange, enjoy a long and quiet sleep, because, to tell the truth, these poor soldiers need and deserve it well.

# CARMELA.

### I.

THE affair which I am going to relate occurred in a small island, about seventy miles from Sicily. On the island there is only one town, numbering not more than two thousand inhabitants, in which, however, there were, at the time my story begins, three or four hundred prisoners condemned to hard labor, and on their account, there was stationed there a detachment of about forty soldiers (commanded by a subaltern), who were changed every three months. The soldiers led a very agreeable life, especially for these two reasons: that, aside from the guard at the barracks and prison, some reconnoitring in the interior of the island, and a little drill now and then, they had nothing to do; and the wine, which was delicious, cost only four sous a bottle. I say nothing of the officer, who enjoyed the largest liberty, and had the power of saying: "I am commander-in-chief of all the military forces of the country." He had at his disposal two gendarmes in the quality of employés at the office of the command in the square, a beautiful apartment furnished gratuitously in the centre of the town; passed his mornings hunting in the mountains, the afternoons in a little reading-room with the principal personages of the place, and the evenings in a boat on the sea, smoking excellent cigars at two centimes apiece, dressed just as his fancy dictated, without any annoyances, or superior officers, and as quiet and contented as a man could well be. Only one thing there was to trouble him, and that, the thought that such a delightful life could only last three months.

The town is on the sea-shore, and has a small harbor, near which a postal steamer, plying between Tunis and Trapana, stopped once in fifteen days. It was very rarely that any other boats touched there. So rare indeed was this occurrence, that the appearance of a ship headed in that direction was announced to the town by the ringing of the church bell, and a good portion of the population rushed to the shore, as they would have done to some spectacle.

The appearance of the place is very modest, but gay and smiling; especially in the large square in its centre, which, as in all villages, is to the populace what a court-yard would be to the people living in the same house in a city. This square is joined to the shore by the principal street, which is straight, narrow, and a stone's-throw in length. All the shops and public offices are in the square. There are, or at least, there were, at that time, two cafés: one frequented by the syndic and other authorities and gentlemen; the other by the common people. The house occupied by the commander of the detachment was situated on the side of the square toward the sea, and as the ground rises considerably from the shore to the centre of the town, from the windows of his room (there were two of them) one could see the port, a long stretch of the shore, the sea, and the distant mountains of Sicily.

The island is all volcanic mountains, and great, thick resinous groves.

Three years ago, one beautiful April morning, the postal boat for Tunis stopped at the entrance of the little port.

The bell had been ringing from the moment of its first appearance, and the entire population had gathered, among which was the commander of the detachment, the soldiers, the syndic, the judge, the parish priest, the delegate of public security, the receiver, the commander of the port, the marshal of the carabineers, and a young military physician attached to the detachment for the service of the prisoners. Two large boats approached the ship, and took and brought to shore thirty-two soldiers of the infantry and an officer, a handsome young blonde, of pleasing appearance, who, after having shaken hands with his colleague, and replied courteously to the polite welcome of the authorities, entered the town at the head of his squad, between the two lines formed by the spectators. When he had quartered the men, he instantly returned to the group of personages awaiting him in the middle of the square, and the syndic presented them to him one by one in a serio-comic way, full of cordial familiarity, tempered with a little innocent air of dignity. When this ceremony was over, the group separated, and the officer, left alone with his colleague, was taken to the house destined for him. There, the orderly of the officer who was leaving was engaged in packing the boxes, and that of the new arrival was hastening the moment for the opening of his own by lending a helping hand to his comrade. An hour later every thing was in order.

The detachment that was going away left the same evening about eight o'clock, accompanied to the harbor by the detachment that remained, and our officer, after bidding farewell to his comrade, returned to his home and went to bed, quite worn out with his journey, and, having been busy all day, he felt a great need of sleep. And sleep he did, indeed!

### II.

The following morning, as soon as the sun was up, he left the house. He had not gone ten paces on the square when he felt some one pull lightly at his coat. He stopped, turned, and saw, a couple of steps away, erect and immovable, in the attitude of a soldier giving his salute, a girl with rumpled hair and disordered dress, who was tall, slender, and beautifully formed. She kept two great black eyes fastened on the officer's face, and smiled.

"What do you wish?" the latter asked, looking around with an air of surprise and curiosity.

The girl made no reply, but continued to smile and hold her hand against her forehead in a military salute.

The officer shrugged his shoulders, and went on another ten steps, and another slight tug at the coat. He stopped, and turned again. The girl was still as erect and immovable as a soldier in line. He looked around and saw some one near by, who was watching the scene and laughing.

"What do you wish?" he asked again.

The girl stretched out her hand, with her forefinger pointing to him, and said, smiling:

"I wish you."

"Oh! I understand," he thought; "it's a copper she is after," and taking a few sous from his pocket, he held them out to her, turning to move off. But the girl, folding her arms across her breast, as if to shield herself with her elbow from the hand which was holding the money, exclaimed again:

"I want you."

Then she began stamping, rumpling her hair with her two hands, and uttering a low, monotonous moan, as children do when they are pretending to cry. The persons round about laughed. The officer looked at the people, then at the girl, again at the people, and proceeded on his way. He had nearly crossed the square unmolested, when, on reaching the opening of the street leading to the port, he heard a light, rapid step behind him, as if some one were running on tip-toe, and as he was turning around, a low voice murmured with a strange tone in his ear: "My treasure!"

He felt a shudder run from head to foot; did not turn, but hurried on with quickened pace. Once more that voice murmured: "My treasure!"

"Come now," he cried out angrily, turning entirely around to the girl, who drew back timidly, "leave me in peace. Go about your business. Do you understand?"

The girl looked grieved, then smiled, moved a few steps forward, and, stretching out her arm as if to caress the officer, who quickly drew back, murmured: "Don't be angry, little lieutenant."

"Go away I tell you."

"You are my treasure."

"Go away, or I will call the soldiers, and have you put in prison." And he pointed to some soldiers who were standing at the corner. Then the girl moved off slowly sideways, her eyes always turned toward the officer, putting out her chin from time to time, and repeating, just above her breath: "My treasure!"

"What a pity!" said the lieutenant to himself, taking the street to the port; "she is so lovely."

She was beautiful, indeed; one of the superb models of that proud and bold beauty peculiar to Sicilian women, the love for whom is rather imposed upon you than inspired, generally, by a single long intent glance, that seems to sink to the bottom of your soul, expressing more ardor even than it awakens; the eyes and hair very black, the forehead broad and pensive, and the movements of the brows and lips instantaneous, brusque, full of expression and life. Her voice seemed weary and hoarse, and her laugh convulsive. After she had laughed she kept her mouth open and her eyes wide-stretched for some time.

### III.

'Why don't they keep her shut up?" asked the officer that same evening of the doctor, as he went with him into the gentlemen's café, after having told him what had occurred in the morning.

"And where would you have her shut up, pray? She has been in the hospital for more than a year, and the municipality kept her there at its own expense; but seeing that it was time and money wasted, it had her brought home. There was little or nothing to hope for; the physicians there were the first to say so. Here, at least, she is as free as the air, poor thing; and that can easily be conceded to her, because she gives no trouble to any one but the military."

"And why to the military?"

"Well, it is a rather vague sort of a story, you see. It is told in a variety of ways especially among the common people, to whom the simple truth is not sufficient, and who wish to add something themselves. However, the most probable fact, confirmed too by the few gentlemen of the place, is this: Three years ago, an officer, who was in command of the detachment as you now are, a handsome fellow, who played the guitar like an artist, and sang like an angel, fell in love with the girl, who was then, as she now is, the most beautiful one in the town."

"I should think so," interrupted the officer.

"And the girl naturally fell in love with him, partly on account of his charming voice (they all go mad about music here), partly because of his prestige as commander of all the military forces on the island, but especially as he was a handsome fellow. And how desperately she was in love too! She was one of those fiery characters here, you understand, who was more ardent than the lava of volcanoes, full of jealousy, spasms, furies, and tragedy. Her mother was the only remaining member of the family, a poor woman who only saw through her eyes and was ruled by her entirely. You can imagine what full liberty she enjoyed. . . . The towns-people talked; but facts have proved the falsity of their suspicions (most natural in themselves, and to which the girl's conduct gave rise), so much so, in fact, that all believe and affirm that there was really nothing out of the way in it. . . . It is very strange certainly; indeed, rather incredible, because it is said that the two were together half days at a time. But you know there are such characters, especially in these places; few to be sure, yet they do exist. Bold, independent girls who are under their lovers' feet all day long, and do not seem to have understood any thing about modesty; as austere, however, and tenacious of their good names as the vestal virgins. Though the fact remains that the officer had promised to marry her. She believed him, and had lost her head from pure content. They really say, you know, that there were days when it was thought her brain was affected. I think so too. Who can tell what point the love of women of that temperament may reach? One day, if they had not taken a girl out of her hands, of whom she had become jealous for some unknown reason, she would have killed or injured her severely. Right here, in front of the café, she had seized her, in the presence of every one, and it was a serious affair, I assure you. Nor was it the only one either. No woman, in passing her officer's house, was allowed to glance up at the window, or look at him in meeting him in the street, without her threatening to do her some harm. At last the day for the change of the detachment arrived; the officer promised that he would return in a few months, the girl believed him, and he went away and was seen no more. The poor thing fell ill. Perhaps, in getting well and losing that little ray of hope remaining, she might have forgotten him; but before she had recovered from her illness, she learned, I don't know how, that her lover had married. The blow was unexpected, and was terrible in its effect. She became mad. That is the story."

"What followed?"

"Then, as I told you, she was sent to the hospital in Sicily; then returned, and it is now more than a year since she has been here."

At that moment a soldier came to the door of the café in search of the doctor.

"I'll tell you the rest later; *au revoir*"; saying which he disappeared. The officer, rising to salute him, hit his sword against the table. At that moment a voice was heard crying out in the square: "I heard it, I heard it! He is there!" And at the same time the mad girl appeared on the door-sill.

"Send her away!" cried the officer, bounding quickly to his feet, as if started up by a spring. The girl was sent off.

"I will go and wait for him at home!" they heard her say as she moved away; "I will go and wait for him at home, my dear little officer!"

Among the many persons present was one who, noticing that impetuous movement and his changed face, whispered to his neighbors: "Can the lieutenant have been afraid?"

## IV.

Carmela's mother lived in a wretched house at the end of the town, together with two or three families of peasants, and earned a precarious livelihood by sewing on linen. At first she received assistance, from time to time, from the well-to-do families of the place; but, finally, nothing more. Her benefactors had seen that their contributions were made in vain, for the girl would neither eat nor sleep at home, nor was there any way of making her keep a dress in order for a week. There is no need to tell how much the mother suffered, or how she tried with untiring patience to do something for her daughter each day; but always in vain. Sometimes, after many prayers, she would allow a new dress to be put on, and then suddenly would tear, cut, and reduce it to rags. At others, hardly had she left her mother's hands, nicely dressed and cared for, when she would dash her hands through her hair and in a moment loosen and rumple it like a fury.

She spent a great portion of the day in wandering among the

most rocky and solitary mountains, gesticulating, talking, and laughing loudly to herself. Many times when the carabineers were passing those localities, they saw her from a distance quite intent in building towers with stones, or seated motionless on the summit of a promontory with her face turned toward the sea, or stretched sleeping on the ground. If she espied them, she followed them with her eyes until they disappeared, without replying by voice, smile, or motion to any sign they might have made. At first, sometimes when they were far away, she pretended to fire at them with her two hands; but her face was quite serious all the time. So it was with the soldiers, with whom no one had ever seen her talk or smile. She passed before them or among them without replying to the jokes they flung after her, turning her head, or looking any one in the face. Nor was there any man who would have attempted to touch her finger or pull her dress, because it was said that she gave cuffs that left the imprint of her fingers on their faces.

However it may have been, she made her appearance as soon as she heard the sound of a drum. The soldiers left the town to go and drill on the sea-shore, and she followed them. While the sergeants commanded, and the officer, at a distance, looked on, she would withdraw and mimic with the greatest gravity the attitudes of the soldiers, and imitate with a little stick the movements of the muskets, repeating the command in a low voice. Then, suddenly, she would throw away the stick and go and lounge around the officer, looking and smiling lovingly at him, and calling him by the sweetest and tenderest names, in a low voice, however, covering her mouth with her hand so that the soldiers should not hear her.

When she was in the town she almost always stood on the

square in front of the officer's house, in the midst of a circle of boys whom she amused with every sort of buffoonery. Now she would make a high hat of paper with a large brim, put it sideways on her head, and, leaning on a large stick and grumbling in a nasal voice, imitate the gait of the syndic. Now with some tags of paper in her hair, her eyes lowered, her mouth tightly closed, moving one hand as if using a fan, and swaying her body gently, she caricatured the few ladies in the place when they went to church on fête days. At other times, picking up before the door of the barracks an old cap thrown away by some soldier, she would put it on, draw it down to her ears, hide all her hair under it, and then with folded arms make the circuit of the square two or three times, in slow and measured steps, imitating with her voice the sound of the drum, as serious, stiff, and erect as one of the hardest conscripts. But whatever she did or said, the people paid no more attention to her. The boys, especially the gamins, were her only spectators. However, their mothers tried to keep them away from her, because one day, contrary to her habit, and who knows for what caprice, she had seized one of them, a boy about eight, the prettiest of her spectators, and had given him so many furious kisses on his forehead and neck, that he became frightened and began to cry and shriek for fear she would suffocate him.

Once in a great while she would enter the church, kneel, and join her hands like the others, then mumble some unknown words; but a few moments later she would begin to laugh, assume queer attitudes, and make such strange and irreverent gestures, that the sacristan ended by taking her by the arm and leading her out.

She had a beautiful voice, and when she was herself sang well; but since her brain had been affected she only hummed inarticulately and monotonously, generally when seated on her own door-step, or at the foot of the stairs of the lieutenant's house, nibbling Indian figs, which were, as one might say, her chief nourishment.

She, too, had her melancholy hours, in which she did not talk or laugh with any one, not even with the children, and she generally stayed curled up like a dog at the house-door, with her head enveloped in her apron, or her face covered with a handkerchief, not moving or stirring from her position at any noise around her, or no matter how many times she was called even by her mother. This happened quite rarely, however, for she was almost always gay.

She paid no attention, as I have already said, to the soldiers, nor even looked at them; but reserved all her tenderness for the officers. She did not dispense it, however, in equal measure to all. Since her return from the hospital, the detachment had been changed six or eight times, and officers of every age, aspect, and humor had come. It was noticed that she displayed a much greater sympathy for the younger ones, even when there was only a few years' difference in their ages, and she knew very well how to distinguish between those who were handsome and those less so, although all were equally her "love" and her "treasure." To a certain lieutenant, among the first arrivals, a man in the forties, all nose and stomach, with a stentorian voice, and basilisk eyes, she had never shown any favor. She had addressed a few sweet words to him the first time they met; but he, disgusted, had replied disagreeably, accompanying his words with a threatening movement of the hand, in order to show her, that it was best to desist once for all. And she had desisted, not ceasing, however, to keep behind him every time that she met him in the street, and to pass many hours of the evening seated on the steps of his house. Whether he entered or went out, she never said a word to him, nor moved from the spot. And she conducted herself in the same way with two or three other officers who came after him, and who differed little from him in manners, customs, or appearances. But some young and very handsome ones arrived, and one might say that she went mad about them, if that had not been her state already. Some of them took it into their head that they could cure her by pretending to be charmed and in love with her; but having taken the thing up too lightly, they were wearied after two or three days' trial, and had abandoned their project. Some others, less philanthropic and more material, had asked themselves: "Is it always necessary that a beautiful girl should be perfectly sane?" and having replied in the negative, had tried to persuade Carmela that brains were a superfluity in love-making; but, strange to say, they had met with an unexpected and obstinate resistance. She never said a positive and resolute no, because, perhaps, she did not clearly understand what they wanted of her; but, almost by instinct, at every attitude or act (who can suggest an adjective?) which might seem decisive, she would loosen one hand after the other, draw back her arms, cross them on her breast, and clasp herself tightly, giving a certain strange laugh, like children when they think some one intends to play them a trick, but they do not know what, and, by laughing, wish to show that they have understood it in order to have it explained. At those moments when her face became animated and her eyes sparkled, she no longer seemed mad, and was very beautiful; that self-possession and reserve, giving to her movements and attitudes a certain composure and grace, added an extraordinary brilliancy to the wonderful beauty of her form. In fact, the few who tried to tempt her became convinced that it was a useless undertaking. I was informed that one of these men, in telling the doctor, one day, something of his vain attempts, exclaimed: "Women with virtue in their brains, conscience, hearts, in whatever you like, I have seen many; but women like this one who has it in her blood—in her blood! I confess I have never before encountered." Some said that in every officer whom she liked or fancied, she saw her own, the one who had loved and abandoned her. Perhaps this was not true, because sometimes she would have made some allusion to what had taken place, but, on the contrary, she never said any thing. Frequently she was questioned or spoken to on the subject, but she never gave sign of understanding or remembering any thing about it; she listened attentively and then laughed. When a detachment left she accompanied it to the port, and when the ship was moving off she waved her handkerchief; but did not weep or make any demonstration of grief. She went immediately to offer protestations of her love to the new officer. The last-comer seemed to please her more than all the others.

## V.

The doctor returned a short time thereafter and related to the officer all that we have just finished telling. The latter, on taking leave, exclaimed a second time: "What a pity; she is so lovely!" "Yes, indeed; and what a proud, noble character she must have!" added the physician. The officer went out. It was very late, and not a living soul was to be seen on the square. His house was on the opposite side from the café. Thither he slowly sauntered in an almost melancholy frame of mind. "She will be there," he thought, sighing, and he strained his eyes, turned his head from right to left to see if there was any one before the door; but all in vain, the darkness was inpenetrable. On, on he went, more and more slowly, stopping, meandering, spying about him. . . . "If I knew that a cutthroat, knife in hand, was awaiting me, I could go on more quickly and boldly," he said to himself, then took ten or twelve resolute steps. "Ah! there she is." He had discovered her. She was seated on the steps outside the door; but it was too dark to see her face. "What are you doing here?" he asked, approaching her. She did not reply immediately, arose, came close to him, and, placing her two hands on his shoulders, said, with a sweet voice, in a tone as if talking most sensibly: "I was waiting for you . . . and I went to sleep." "But why did you wait?" asked the officer, removing from his shoulders her hands, which instantly seized his arms. "Because I wish to remain with you," she replied. "What a tone!" he thought; "one would really suppose she was talking like a sane person." Then, taking a match from his pocket, he lighted it, and approached Carmela in order to look into her eyes. The weariness—for she had been wandering around all day—and, more than all, the short sleep from which she had just waked having taken from her face a little of that immoderate and convulsive vivacity which was habitual to it, and in its stead diffused a shade of melancholy and languor over it, so that at that moment her face was enchanting, and she seemed any thing but a mad-woman.

"Oh, darling, darling!" broke out Carmela as soon as she saw the lighted face of the lieutenant, and, stretching out her arm, she tried to take his chin between her thumb and forefinger. He seized her by one arm, she in her turn took hold of the arm which held her, fastened her mouth on his hand, and kissed and bit it. The officer broke away, dashed into the house, and closed the door.

"Treasure!" cried Carmela once again, and then, without saying any thing more, reseated herself on the steps, with her arms crossed over her knees and her head bent to one side. Shortly after she was asleep.

As soon as he had entered the house and lighted the lamp, the officer looked at the back of his right hand and saw there the light imprint of eight little teeth, all around which still gleamed the foam of that convulsive mouth. "What kind of love is this?" he said aloud to himself, and, lighting a cigar, he began pacing the room, thinking over the time-table for his small detachment "I'll think to-morrow," he said suddenly, and he turned his thoughts to something else. He seated himself, opened a book, read several pages; finally decided to go to bed. He had nearly finished undressing when he was seized by an idea; he stood meditating for an instant, ran to the window, stretched out his hand to open it . . . withdrew it, shrugged his shoulders, and went to sleep.

The following morning his orderly, who entered his room betimes on tiptoe, was astonished to find him awake, as it was not his habit to wake himself. And he said, smiling: "That mad girl is down at the door." "What is she doing?" "Nothing; she says she is waiting for you, lieutenant."

The officer tried to laugh, and looking then at the soldier

while he was brushing his clothes, said to himself: "That fellow is working by steam this morning." When he was dressed, he said: "Look and see if she is still there." The soldier opened the window, looked down, and replied in the affirmative. "What is she doing?" "Playing with stones." "Is she looking up?" "No." "Is she directly in front of the door or at one side?" "At one side." "I can escape from her," and down he went. But the sound of his sword betrayed him. "Good-morning, good-morning!" shouted the girl, running up the stairs to meet him, and when she was near him, she kneeled down, drew out a handkerchief, and, seizing him with the other hand, began dusting his boots in the greatest haste, murmuring as she did so: "Wait, wait, one moment more, a little patience, my dear; one moment more, ah! that's it, now you are all right."

"Carmela!" exclaimed the officer severely, as he attempted in vain to free his leg from her little hand; "Carmela!" When he was at liberty he hurried off on a run.

"But is there really no way of restoring her reason?" he asked of the doctor soon afterward. "Ah!" the latter replied, "perhaps so; with time and patience . . ."

## VI.

After a month the doctor and lieutenant were very great friends. The similarity of their characters and ages, and, more than all, their constant intercourse from morning until night in a place where it might be said there were no other young men of their position, resulted in the fact that they grew to know each other intimately and to be as fond of one another as old friends. But during that month one of them, the officer, had changed his habits in a singular manner. During the first few days he had had certain huge books sent him from Naples, and during the evenings of several weeks he had done nothing but read and make notes and indulge in long and abstruse discussions with the doctor, always ending with the remark: "Well, enough of it. I fancy that physicians can do little or nothing in those cases!" "We will see how you succeed," the doctor would reply; and they parted with these words, only to resume the discussion from the beginning the following day.

One day, after having asked certain questions of the syndic, the officer had sent for the only tailor in the town, then had betaken himself to the shop of the sole hatter, and from thence to the only haberdasher's establishment. Four days thereafter he went out to walk on the sea-shore all dressed in Russian linen, with a broad straw hat and a sky-blue cravat. The doctor in meeting him the same evening had asked: "Well?" "Nothing." "Not even a sign?" "Nothing, nothing." "No matter, persevere." "Oh, never fear!"

The receiver of the town had been a singer for many years and knew how to play on several instruments. One day the officer went to him, and without any preamble, said: "Will you do me the favor to teach me to play the guitar?" And the receiver, beginning that very day, gave lessons on the guitar, morning and evening, to the lieutenant, who learned with wonderful quickness, and in a short time was able to accompany himself in singing. "You must have a beautiful voice," the master said to him one day. And in truth his voice was lovely. Then he began to learn to sing, and at the end of a month he sang to the guitar the little Sicilian songs with such taste and feeling that it was a pleasure to hear him. "We had another officer who played very well too!" the receiver once said to him. "There is a little air," he added one day, "which he always sang . . . an air . . . wait; ah, how divinely he sang it! It began . . . he composed it himself, you know; it began:

>  "'Carmela, ai tuoi ginocchi
>  Placidamente assiso,
>  Guardandoti negli occhi
>  Baciandoti nel viso
>  Trascorrerò i miei dì.

>  "'L' ultimo dì, nel seno
>  Il volto scolorito
>  Ti celerò, sereno
>  Come un fanciul sopito,
>  E morirò così.'"

>  Carmela, at thy dainty feet
>    Content I find a resting-place;
>  While gazing in thine eyes so sweet,
>    And kissing oft thy beauteous face,
>  My days will thus glide swiftly by.

>  The last day, upon thy breast
>    My pale brow I 'll lay and keep,
>  Sinking quietly to rest
>    Like a child that 's lulled to sleep;
>  And so I' ll gladly die.

"Say it over again." The receiver repeated it. "Sing it." And he did so.

Another day, after having talked at length with the tobacconist, who had a shop next his house, he went to the marshal of the carabineers, and said to him: "Marshal, they tell me that you are an excellent fencer." "I, oh, heavens! it 's two years since I have had a foil in my hand." "Would you like to exchange a few thrusts with me, from time to time?" "Oh, gladly!" "Then let us appoint the time." And they arranged their meetings. From that day on, every morning all those who crossed the square heard a great clashing of swords, stamping of feet, puffing, and noise in the lieutenant's house. It was the marshal and himself who were fencing. "You may spare yourself this experiment," said the doctor to the officer one day. "Does she give no sign?" "None at all." "But it was worth trying. I was told that he fenced every morning with the marshal, just at that hour, and that she, not liking to stay and look on, went down into the square." "Oh, yes, my dear friend, something else is needed. Something else is needed!"

### VII.

A month and a half had passed since the day of the new detachment's arrival. One night the officer sat at the little table in his own house, opposite the doctor, and with the point of his pen stirring up the flame of the candle burning before him, he said: "How do you think it will end? I shall become mad too; that's how it will end. I am ashamed of myself. Look here; there are moments in which it seems as if every one were laughing at me behind my back."

"Laughing at what?"

"At what?" repeated the other, in order to seize time for a reply. "Laughing at my zeal, my pity for this poor unfortunate creature, my experiments, my useless attempts."

"Zeal! pity! These are not subjects for laughter." And he fixed his eyes on the other's face; then added: "Tell me the truth; you have fallen in love with Carmela?"

"I?" hastily exclaimed the officer, and he stopped in the midst of his question, growing red to the roots of his hair.

"You," replied the doctor. "Tell me the truth; be sincere with me.; am I not your only friend here?"

"Friend, yes; but just because I wish to be sincere I might not like to tell you that which does not exist," answered the other. He was silent for a moment, and then went on talking hastily, now becoming pale, now scarlet, stammering, growing embarrassed and contradicting himself, like a boy caught in mischief and obliged to confess his wrong-doing.

"I, in love? And with Carmela? With an insane person? What are you thinking of, friend? How did you get such a strange idea into your head? The day that that happens, I'll give you the right to say to my colonel that I have lost my reason and ought to be shut up with madmen. In love! You make me laugh. I feel pity for that poor creature; yes, a very strong and lively pity. I don't know what I would not give to see her cured; I would make any sacrifice for her health; I should delight in her recovery as if she were one of my family. . . . That is all very true, but between this and falling in love with her there is a great difference. I like her, this is true too, I like her very much, as I think you do too, because pity always goes with affection. . . . Then I am fond of her because they say she has always been a virtuous, affectionate girl; that her first and only lover she really loved, loved worthily, with the idea of becoming his wife, and without being willing to sacrifice her honor to him before bearing his name. . . . This is virtue, my dear friend, real virtue, and I admire it, you understand; so that poor creature arouses all the more compassion because she deserved a happy fate instead of a misfortune like the one which has fallen to her lot. How could one help having compassion for, and loving her? Is not the character of her madness the expression of a good, loving, lovely soul? From her mouth I have never heard any but sweet and modest words; and that laying of her hands on me, her caresses, her kissing of my hands, are certainly the acts of a mad-woman, but there is nothing in them that passes the limits of decency. Have you ever seen her do any thing out of the way? No, certainly not; and it is for this reason, I repeat to you, that I am attached to her. Poor girl, abandoned by all, . . . forced to lead the life of a dog. . . . Tell me if you are not fond of her too! I tell you frankly that I am sincerely attached to her. Her very beauty (because she is beautiful,—beautiful as an angel; that cannot be denied; look at her eyes, her mouth, her whole figure, her hands; have you ever seen her hands? And her hair? Tumbled as it is she looks like a savage, but it's beautiful. And then dressed in another way. . . . ), well, her very beauty makes my pity all the stronger. Looking at her I cannot help saying to myself: 'What a pity, what a shame that one cannot love those brilliant eyes!' But don't you know that that girl's face, were she sane, would be enough to turn any man's head? Then, too, there are moments in which, if you did not know that she was mad, you would be ready to commit some extravagance; for instance, when she looks you in the eyes, then smiles and says: 'My dear'; and the evening, at dark, when you do not see her face and only hear her speak and say gently that she was waiting for you, that she will stay with you until morning, that you are her angel, and what not besides; at those times she does not seem like a mad-woman. I look at her, I listen to her as if she were herself and really felt what she says to me, and I assure you that, while the illusion lasts, my heart beats, yes, beats as if I were in love with her. I try calling her by name, I don't know why, with the fixed idea that she ought to give me some reply that will show me that she has been suddenly cured. . . . 'Carmela!' I say. And she answers: 'What do you wish?' 'You are not really mad, are you?' I ask. 'I mad?' she replies, looking at me with a certain air of surprise that would make me swear that she was not. 'Carmela!' I cry suddenly, carried away by a sweet hope. 'Tell me once more that you are not mad!' She looks at me astonished for a short time, then breaks out into a loud laugh. Oh, friend, believe me, at that moment I am ready to dash my head against the wall. You know how much I have done to try and restore her reason; but you do not know all. Nearly every evening I have had her brought to my house, I have talked to her by the hour, I have played and sung to her by the hour the songs her lover sang, I have tried to tell her I was in love with her, to calm her by caresses, by pretending to cry and grow desperate, by allowing her to do with me what she chose, to kiss me, embrace me, caress me as mothers do their children. . . . I have tried to do the same to her, and with what a heavy heart I did it, I leave you to imagine, for I could not tell you whether it was a feeling of repugnance, fear, shame, or remorse, or all combined; the fact remains, that, in kissing her, I trembled and grew pale, as if I were kissing a corpse. Sometimes it seemed as if I were making a great sacrifice, and I exulted in it, and, mingling with the kisses, my tears fell on her cheeks. At other times I seemed to be committing a crime, and I felt horrified at myself. I have suffered terribly, dear friend, and all in vain. The more the despair increased, the more this cursed and obstinate fever raged in my heart. . . . I cannot sleep at night, because I know that she is already curled up before my door, and tortured as I am continually by this idea, it seems as if I ought to hear from one moment to the other, another tapping on the glass, and see appear above my window-sill that distorted face, and have those two motionless, staring eyes fastened upon mine! Sometimes I seem to hear her coming up the stairs, and I spring up in my bed, or I fancy I hear down in the square a burst of laughter, and that laugh produces the effect of an icy hand laid on my heart; but I have not the courage to look out of the window. I begin to read, to write, yet my mind, always fixed upon her, is sad, disquieted, almost fearful, I know not why. Then I ask myself when this agonizing life will end, and how; what trace of it will remain in my heart. I do not dare reply, I am afraid of my answer, and I dash my hands into my hair . . . like one desperate. . . . Oh, friend! tell me that I shall not go mad too, because I feel that my heart is breaking and I cannot bear this life . . . I cannot . . . cannot bear it!"

Then he stretched out his hand to seize that of the doctor; the latter drew his chair nearer, and being so moved that he could not utter one word, he placed both hands on his shoulders, looked at him an instant, and then embraced him.

All at once the officer exclaimed with a suddenly quiet face: "If she could become what she once was, if she could regain her reason and the heart she then possessed, and those eyes should lose forever that strange light, that fixed expression which is so frightful; her mouth never give again that horrible laugh, and one day she should say sanely: 'I thank thee, I bless thee, dear; thou hast given me back my life; I am fond of thee, I love thee . . .' and should weep. Oh, to see her weep, to hear her speak, to find her always neat, well dressed, and cared for like other girls; to see her return to church to pray, and blush as she used to do; and to have her experience, one by one, as in a second childhood, all the sweet and pure feelings of affection which have disappeared! Not to find her any more at evening at the foot of the stairs, to be obliged to go to her home in search of her, where, beside her mother, she (quiet and contented) would be occupied with some work. . . . Oh, my friend!" he exclaimed, seizing him by the hands and gazing at him, his eyes filled with tears; "I should feel like a god; it would seem to me that I, too, had created something, possessed two souls, lived two lives, hers and mine; she would seem my own; I should feel that heaven had predestined her for me, and I would lead her into my mother's presence as if she were an angel. . . . Oh, I could not grasp such happiness; I should go mad from joy; oh, if it were true; if it were true!"

Then weeping, he buried his face in his hands.

"Oh, my love!" they heard some one cry in the square. The officer sprang to his feet, and said resolutely to the doctor: "Leave me!"

The latter pressed his hand, said: "Courage!" and went out.

The lieutenant remained motionless for some moments in the middle of the room, then approached the window, opened it, drew back a step, and stood contemplating for an instant the exquisite spectacle stretched out before his eyes. It was a clear, soft, still, enchanting night. Directly under his eyes lay the lower part of the town, the roofs, the deserted streets, the harbor, and the beach, on which the white moon-light fell so brightly that you could have seen a person passing as distinctly as if it were day; then the quiet sea as smooth as glass, and away in the dim distance the mountains of Sicily as clearly defined as if they were near, and over all a profound silence. "If I could but enter this sweet peace," thought the officer, as his eyes swept across the immensity of that sea, and trembling, he approached the window and looked down. Carmela was seated before the door.

"Carmela!"

"Darling."

"What are you doing there?"

"What am I doing? I am waiting; you know it. I am waiting until you let me come up. Don't you want me this evening?"

"I'll come down and open the door."

Carmela began clapping her hands and jumping about with joy.

The door opened, and the officer appeared with the light in his hand. Carmela entered, took the light from him, passed before him and began hastily climbing the stairs, murmuring as she did so: "Come, come, poor fellow," and then turning to stretch out her hand to him, she said: "Give your hand to your little one, you handsome fellow," and so drew him by the hand into the house.

There the officer made her sit down, and with the patience of a saint began to repeat all his former experiments and attempts, invented new ones, tried them several times, always with more active solicitude and ardor, simulating love, hatred, anger, sorrow, despair; but in vain. She looked at and listened to him attentively, then when he had finished she asked him with a loud laugh: "What is the matter with you?" or said: "Poor fellow, you arouse my compassion." Then she took his hands and kissed them with the air of intense pity.

"Carmela!" finally exclaimed the officer in order to try one more experiment.

"What do you wish?"

He made her a sign to come nearer him. She approached slowly, looking lovingly into his eyes, then suddenly threw herself on his breast, clasped her arms around his neck, and, pressing her mouth to it, she cried with a suffocating voice: "My dear! my dear! my dear!" The poor young fellow, who had quite lost his head, passed his arm around her waist, and thus supporting her, bent slowly, she with him, until he laid her down, almost without being aware of it, on the sofa near the little table. . . . Carmela suddenly rose to her feet, looked very serious, seemed to be thinking of something for a moment, and then murmured with a slight expression of disgust:

"What are you doing?"

The officer saw a gleam of hope, and stood watching her silently and anxiously.

Carmela remained pensive, or seemed to be so, an instant longer, then, smiling in a singular way, as she had never done before, said: "Oh, are we already married, we two?"

The officer gave a half cry, and with his eyes toward heaven and the tip of his finger at his lips, pallid, convulsive, he thought for a moment what reply he should make. At that moment Carmela raised her eyes to the wall, caught sight of a high hat hanging from a nail, burst out into a laugh, took it, put it on her head, and screaming and shouting, she began jumping about the room.

"Carmela!" cried the officer, sorrowfully. But she did not heed him.

"Carmela!" he shouted again, dashing toward her. She, frightened, sprang down the staircase, and a moment later was in the middle of the square, still jumping, shouting, and shrieking with laughter.

The officer went to the window.—"Carmela!" he shouted once more in an exhausted voice, then covered his face with his hands and dropped down into a chair.

## VIII.

The following morning, as soon as he was up, he went to the doctor's house. The latter, on catching a glimpse of the red eyes and distorted face, saw that he had come for comfort and counsel, and making him sit down in front of him, began a regular lecture. But the officer did not listen to him, and seemed preoccupied with other thoughts. Suddenly he grew brighter, and clapping his hand to his head, exclaimed: "Ah! I never thought of that before!" "Of what?" asked the doctor. The other made no reply; took a sheet of paper, a pen, and began writing furiously. When he had finished he read the following letter:

LIEUTENANT:

Without any preamble, as is the habit among us military men, I will say that I have been, for a month and a half, in command of the detachment of . . . which you commanded three years ago during the months of July,

August, September. I have learned to know in this town a girl of eighteen or twenty, called Carmela, who has been mad for two years; her insanity having been caused, it is said, by her love for you. What has happened to her since your departure from the island, you must know, and you ought also to be conversant with the especial character of her madness, because I have been told that you have been written to on the subject by some one here. The most unfortunate condition of this girl aroused in me, from the first time I saw her, a profound feeling of pity, and I tried every means to restore her reason. I dressed like you, learned to play and sing like you, informed myself of all your habits familiar to those persons who have known you; I feigned love for her, spoke of you, pretended to be you, but all in vain. You cannot understand how unhappy I have been made by seeing my hopes fall one by one. There is, however, one more thing to try, and this is in your hands; do not refuse me; grant my prayer and you will perform a sacred duty. Listen: It is said that one of the most efficacious means of restoring insane people is to represent before them, with the most minute details and scrupulous exactness, some serious event that preceded their malady, whether it were or were not the direct cause of the same. I have thought that by repeating exactly before Carmela the scene of your departure, I might produce some effect upon her. I have questioned many persons in town and have not succeeded in learning any thing more than the fact that you left at night, and before your departure supped at home in company with the syndic, marshal of the carabineers, and several other people. The particulars of that supper and of your subsequent departure are only remembered indistinctly at best. I beseech you from my heart to do this work of charity, which will cost you little or nothing, and may give life and happiness to the person most interested. Write me all that you remember, tell me of the persons, speeches, occurrences, every thing in fact. And, above all, try to tell me the precise hour or moment in which the most noteworthy incidents occurred; and tell me every thing with clearness and in order. Do me this great service, I pray you, and I shall be grateful to you all through life. I add nothing more. I trust to the generosity of your heart; I press your hand as a good comrade and say adieu.

"What do you think of it?" "Divinely inspired," replied the doctor, who had listened with the greatest attention. "Do you know his name, regiment, and station?" "The syndic knows every thing." "Do you think he will reply to you?" "I am convinced of it."

He did reply; and in a letter of eight pages, in which were written all the details required about the persons, speeches, hours, and all. But there was not a comment, not an allusion to the past, not a single word referring to any thing but the supper and his departure; not a syllable aside from the questions asked, not even an expression of pity for Carmela. But from that bare, crude letter one could see that he must have felt deep pangs of remorse while writing it. If this had not been the case, at least some feigned expression of regret or repentance would have been found therein. In closing he would have said at least: "I hope . . . etc."; but there was nothing of the kind. "At one o'clock at night the steamer left. I salute you." And then the signature.

### IX.

"I understand!" exclaimed the doctor, as soon as his friend had finished reading him the letter; "now I understand why not one of all the persons present were able to relate any of the particulars. I do not doubt it, when they had been drinking like that!"

That same day both began to make preparations for the great experiment. Both of them went to the syndic, judge, receiver, marshal of the carabineers, and the others, all of whom were very intimate; and the one, the doctor, with scientific arguments, and the other with those coming from the heart, by sheer force of talking, explaining, and demonstrating, succeeded in making them understand what it was all about, assuring themselves of their assistance, and teaching each one the part he was to play. "Heaven be praised!" exclaimed the officer on coming out of the receiver's house, which was the last visit;

"the greatest part of the work is accomplished." Then they sent for Carmela's mother, to whom it was far easier to give an explanation of the affair, than to the syndic and other magnates; all of them most excellent people, to be sure, in whom one could confide, but a little dull of comprehension in matters of that description.

Carmela had not been feeling well for some days, and had remained at home almost all the time. The officer and the doctor went to look for her. She was seated on the ground outside the door, with her back leaning against the wall. As soon as she saw them she rose, and moving a trifle more slowly than usual, went toward the lieutenant and tried, as was her habit, to embrace him, murmuring, in a feeble voice, her customary words.

"Carmela!" said the lieutenant, "we have a piece of news for you."

"A piece of news, a piece of news, a piece of news," repeated Carmela, gently passing the palm of her hand three times over the officer's cheek.

"To-morrow I am going away."

"To-morrow I am going away?"

"I, I am going away. I am going away from here. I am going to leave this place. I am going to leave with all my soldiers. I shall go on to the steamer, and the steamer will carry me far, far away."

Saying which he rased his arm as if to indicate a great distance.

"Far, far away," murmured Carmela, looking in the direction the officer had pointed. She seemed to be thinking for an instant, and then said, vaguely, in quite an indifferent tone: "The steamship . . . which smokes."

And she tried to embrace the officer again, while calling him by the usual names.

"It produces no effect," thought the latter, shaking his head.

"You must say it many times," whispered the doctor. "Let us wait until a little later."

And off they went, after speaking severely to Carmela, so that she would not follow them.

The supper was fixed for the following evening. That same evening Carmela went, as was her custom, and seated herself before the officer's door. The latter, on returning home, took her up stairs, where the orderly, according to orders, had turned every thing upside down as if the departure were really to take place. The little table, chairs, and sofa were covered with linen, clothes, books, and papers, flung here and there, and in the centre of the room were two open trunks, in which the soldier had begun to place the clothing.

Carmela made a movement of surprise at the first sight of the disorder, and looked smilingly into the officer's face.

"I am preparing to go away," said the officer.

Carmela looked around the room again, knitting her brows as she did so; a thing she was not in the habit of doing. The officer watched her closely.

"I am going away, far away from here; I am going on the steamship."

"Are you going on the steamship?"

"Yes . . . I am going to-morrow evening."

"To-morrow evening," repeated Carmela mechanically, and seeing the guitar on a chair, she touched a string with one finger and made it sound.

"Are you not sorry that I am going away? Will you not regret never seeing me again?"

Carmela looked at him fixedly, and then dropped her head and eyes as if she were really thinking. The officer said nothing more and began talking *sotto voce* with the soldier, whom he helped to fold the clothes.

The girl stood looking at them without opening her mouth. After a short time, the officer approached her and said:

"Now, go away, Carmela; you have been here long enough. Go home, go."

And taking her by the arm, he pushed her gently toward the door. She stretched out her arms to clasp him around the neck. . . .

"I do not wish you to do so," said the officer.

Carmela stamped her foot two or three times, stretched out her arms again, clasped his neck, passed her mouth over his cheeks without kissing him as if she were thinking of something else, and then went slowly and silently away without laughing or turning back, with a look on her face that expressed nothing, like an abstracted person who is thinking of a thousand things, and of nothing, at once.

"What is this?" thought the officer. "Can this be a good sign? . . . Oh, if God only willed it! Let us hope!"

The following day he did not leave the house, and would not even see Carmela, although he knew that she was seated as usual, at the door. He employed the entire afternoon in preparing for the experiment of the evening. His small apartment was composed of two rooms and a kitchen. Between the bedroom and the entrance, there was a large room, whose windows, like those of the other one, looked out into the square. In this room he had the supper laid. The landlord, his neighbor, lent him an immense dining-table, came himself to cook in the house the few dishes that were needed, and set the table with the greatest possible luxury, as he had done three years before for the other officer. Toward nine o'clock in the evening the doctor arrived, the first comer. "She is down below," he said to his friend on entering; "she was complaining that she had not seen you yet. I asked her if she felt well, and she replied, after looking fixedly at me: 'Steamship,' and she did not laugh. Well! God alone can tell what is passing through her head. Oh, let us see these splendid preparations!"

When both had given a glance at the table, they began to arrange between them the best mode of representing the comedy, or rather the drama, because to them it was a drama and a serious one too. When the matter was settled, the doctor asked: "Have they all learned their parts well?" and the officer replied that he hoped so.

Shortly before ten they heard a shuffling of many feet, and a confused sound of voices. "They are here!" said the doctor, and he looked out of the window. "It is really they."

The soldier went down and opened the door. The doctor lighted the four candelabra at the four corners of the table.

"How my heart beats!" said the officer.

"Courage, courage!"

At that moment they heard Carmela exclaim: "I am going on the steamship too!" and then she began clapping her hands.

"Courage!" repeated the doctor hastily in his friend's ear; "do you hear that? She is beginning to get that idea into her head; it is a good sign; take heart; here are your guests!"

The door opened and the syndic, judge, and all the others who had met at the café, entered smiling and bowing. While the officer was welcoming them, and thanking now one, now the other, the doctor whispered a word in the ear of the orderly, who stood motionless in a corner, and he disappeared. A moment later, without any one's noticing it, he returned with Carmela, and both of them passing close to the wall on tip-toe, entered the other room.

"Let us be seated," said the officer.

All took their places. The noise of the moving chairs and that "Oh!" long and blissful, uttered by the *gourmets* when sitting down at table, did not allow them to hear a slight noise made by the orderly in holding back Carmela, who, exclaiming: "I have not seen him for a whole day!" had opened the door and attempted to dash toward the officer. The orderly held her back, placed a chair near the door, made her sit down; then opened the shutters enough to leave a space as wide as your hand, and she placed her face to the aperture and stood looking on. None of the guests turned in that direction, no one looked then or later, and Carmela made no other movement.

Little by little the confused clatter of forks, knives, glasses, and plates, and laughter and discordant voices that tried to overpower their neighbors', began to increase. All save the doctor and officer were eating with the best appetite in the world, and tippling gayly. They began by giving the loudest praises to the discipline, virtue, valor, and courtesy of the soldiers, corporals, and sergeants of the detachment; then they enlarged upon the choice quality of the wines and viands; then talked of the weather, which was very fine,—an enchanting night,—and of the voyage, which ought to be delightful; then discussed politics, then the soldiers again, once more the voyage, and so, talking more and more loudly, laughing harder, emptying their glasses in greater haste, until all their faces became rubicund, their eyes gleaming, the motion of their lips rather difficult, and their words followed each other without any connection whatsoever. Almost involuntarily each one had taken his part seriously, and represented it marvellously. But the more the others forgot the end for which they had assembled, the more the officer felt his heart-beat increase, and he showed openly on his face the tempest raging in his soul. No one, however, discovered it, save the doctor, who, from time to time begged him in a loud voice not to lose courage, and kept his eye upon Carmela. The latter was always immovable and intent, with her face pressed between the shutters. The orderly, seizing an opportune moment, had taken himself off.

At a certain point three soldiers entered the room, and each took on his shoulders one of the three trunks that were in a corner, and then passed out. Carmela followed all their movements with her eye until they had disappeared, then continued looking at the table.

The doctor murmured a word in the syndic's ear:

"A toast," the latter suddenly exclaimed, rising with difficulty to his feet, his glass in his hand. "A toast to the health of this valorous lieutenant who commands the brave detachment of the town that is going away, and let there remain perpetually and forever in this our town a beautiful, undying, and immortal memory of the brave detachment commanded by this valorous . . ."

He thought a moment, and then went on resolutely:

"Long live the lieutenant who departs!" And they all

rose noisily, clinking their glasses and spilling the wine on the table: "Evviva!"

The syndic fell heavily on to his chair, and there were grounds for suspicion that he was really intoxicated.

Others offered toasts of the same nature, and then they all began talking again, in one voice, of the soldiers, politics, the wine, and the voyage.

"Mr. Receiver, give us a song!" cried the doctor.

All the others echoed this request. The receiver excused himself, allowed them to beg him a little, then smiled, coughed, took the guitar, and sang two or three verses. The guests began to grow noisy again, and interrupted him.

"It's my turn," said the officer, and all were silent. He took the guitar, tuned it, rose to his feet, pretended to stagger, and began. . . . He was pale as death, and his hands trembled as if with fever; notwithstanding which he sang his song with a sweetness and feeling that was really charming.

>    Carmela, ai tuoi ginocchi.
>      Placidamente assiso,
>      Guardandoti negli occhi
>      Baciandoti nel viso
>      Trascorrerò i miei dì.

Carmela listened more and more intently, knitting her brows from time to time, like a person absorbed in deep meditation.

"Bravo! Good! Very well, indeed!" said all the guests in one voice. And the officer continued·

>    L.' ultimo dì, sul seno
>      Il volto scolorito
>      Ti celerò, sereno
>      Come un fanciul sopito,
>      E morirò così.

These were the words and music, and every thing round about was exactly the same as on that night. "Bravo! Good!" repeated all the guests. The officer fell back, as if exhausted, upon his chair; all began to shout; Carmela was as immovable as a statue, and kept her eye steadily fastened on the officer's face. The doctor looked at her out of the corner of his eye.

"Silence!" shouted the lieutenant. All stopped, and, the window being open, they heard the gay music of flutes and violins down in the square together with the noise of a crowd of people. They were the ten or twelve musicians of the place, surrounded by a great portion of the population, who thought the detachment was really going.

Carmela stirred, and turned toward the window. Her face began to grow gently animated, and her great eyes to move restlessly from the window to the lieutenant, from the latter to the guests, and back again to the window, as if she wished to hear the music well and at the same time not to lose the slightest movement made by all those people.

When the music ceased, a great part of the crowd began clapping their hands, as they had done on the same occasion three years before.

At this point the orderly advanced hurriedly:

"Lieutenant, the ship is waiting."

The lieutenant rose to his feet, saying aloud:

"I must go."

Carmela rose softly too, keeping her eyes fastened upon him and slowly moving the chair.

All the guests stood up and pressed around the lieutenant. At that same instant Carmela's mother appeared, entered the other room unseen, put her arms around her daughter, and said: "Be brave; he will return in two months."

Carmela fixed her eyes on her mother's face, slowly removed one arm and then the other, and, without uttering a word, turned her head slowly, and again fastened her eyes on the officer.

All the guests shook hands with the officer, giving rise to a confused murmur of thanks, good wishes, and salutations; he buckled on his sword, put on his cap, slung the travelling-bag over his shoulder . . .

While he was doing this, Carmela had unconsciously opened the door, taken a step forward, and with her wild eyes looked rapidly now at the officer, now at the guests, now at the orderly, finally at her mother who was near her, and with both hands rubbed her forehead, rumpled her hair, sighed wearily, and trembled convulsively all over.

Once more the music in the square began, another burst of applause was heard.

"Let us go!" said the officer resolutely, and he turned to leave.

A shrill, desperate, agonizing shriek broke from Carmela's breast. At the same moment she dashed with one spring upon the lieutenant, seized him with superhuman force about the waist, and began to kiss him furiously on his face, neck, chest, wherever she could, sobbing, shouting, groaning, and feeling his shoulders, arms, and head, as a mother would the son saved from the fury of the waves that had shortly before enveloped him, and from which she had seen him stretch out his arms and beg for assistance. After a few moments the poor girl fell senseless to the floor at the officer's feet.

"At the same moment she dashed with one spring upon the lieutenant, seized him with superhuman force about the waist, and began to kiss him furiously on his face, neck, chest," etc.

(*Page* 186.)

She was saved!

The lieutenant threw himself into the doctor's arms, which were outstretched waiting for him. The mother bent to kiss and bathe her daughter with her tears. All those present raised their faces and arms toward heaven in sign of thanksgiving. The music continued playing.

Four months after, on a beautiful night in September, so clear that it seemed like day, the ship which had left Tunis that evening, and stopped as usual at the harbor of our little town, moved off rapidly toward the Sicilian coast. The water was so calm that the ship hardly seemed to move. The passengers were all on deck, and stood contemplating in silence the clear sky and the sea illuminated by the moon.

Apart from the others and turned in the opposite direction from the ship's course, were a young man and girl leaning on the railing, arm in arm, with their heads so close together that they almost touched. Far away in the distance one could still see confusedly the island they had left, and they were looking at it. They remained a long time without changing their attitudes, until the woman, raising her face, murmured:

"Yet it makes my heart ache to leave my poor little home, where I have suffered so much, where I saw you for the first time, where you restored me to life."

And she laid her head on her companion's shoulder.

"We will return there some day!" the latter said to her, turning her head gently, so that he could look into her eyes.

"And shall we return to your house?" she asked softly.

"Yes."

"And in the evening will we sit and talk by the window from which you once called me?"

"Yes."

"And will you play the guitar again, and sing once more that song?"

"Yes, yes."

"Sing it now!" exclaimed Carmela with joy; "sing it softly."

Then the officer placing his mouth at her ear sang:

>  Carmela, ai tuoi ginocchi
>  Placidamente . . .

Carmela threw her arms around her husband's neck, and burst into tears.

"Poor, dear one," said the latter, pressing her to his breast; "here, here, on my heart, always here!"

The poor thing drew back suddenly, looked around her, at the sea, the island, her husband, and exclaimed:

"Oh, it's a dream!"

And the young man, interrupting her, replied:

"No, darling, it's the waking!"

The ship swept on as if borne by the wind.

---

"Apart from the others, and turned in the opposite direction from the ship's course, were a young man and girl leaning on the railing, arm in arm," etc.

(*Page* 187.)

# THAT DAY.

"It is your turn," a young lady once said to an officer just returned from the war; "tell me what one really feels, what one really experiences in those terrible moments. But be concise, I beg of you. You military men, when you get talking of the war, recount very marvellous tales, and find people who swallow them; but I am not one of the number, I warn you. Tell me the truth and nothing more, without any of the fine rhetoric which I have had too much of already in reading descriptions of battles, for they are all written in the same style."

"Tell, tell, is easily said," replied the officer, "but without any preparation? Give me time at least to collect and put my reminiscences in order, if not I shall give you an account without any head or tail."

"No! my dear sir; no preparations! I do not wish a philosophical dissertation, and, much less, a page of military history. Tell me quickly and as best you can, all that you have seen."

"Do you insist upon it?"

"Yes, absolutely."

"I will begin; but remember, I shall not tell one word more than what I have seen; if the story does not please you, it will not be my fault."

"Be concise, and do not try to be any thing more. Begin!"

"I will begin, and first of all, let me give you an idea of the ground. Give attention. We will suppose that this is a chain of the Alps; that first line up hill . . ."

"Topography? oh, for pity sake!"

"You do not wish it? Well, then, I will explain myself in another way; it will be better so. Let us suppose, then, that we are out in the open country, one beautiful, clear, quiet summer morning. Let us suppose that, beginning here under our feet, the ground rises gradually, until it forms a lovely broad, high hill in regular curves, whose top stands out against the horizon, about half an hour's walk from us. It is a beautiful green hill, sprinkled half way down with hedges, trees, and long rows of grape-vines, ploughed with ditches, and traversed in every direction by paths and low walls of heaped-up stones, such as mark the limits of farms: here, a bit of ground covered with grass and plants; there, broken and reddish, covered with stones; here, an easy bit; there, suddenly steep and barren. Do you see it?"

"Yes."

"Well, suppose one thing more: that a good part of the hill, from the top down, is entirely free from trees and houses, bare and clean, where the sun beats in such a way that every furrow, bush, and person would be visible, if there were any people. You see a person, let us suppose, as tall as this, so that you can tell whether it is a man or woman. Are you laughing? I tell you this to give you an idea of the distance."

"Yes, I understand."

"Well, then, that morning we were at the foot of a hill like the one I have described, and were waiting. Here, there, to the right and left, in the distance, behind the trees and bushes, among the vines, in the ditches, everywhere, in fact, there were soldiers, standing, seated, lying down, some with bare heads, some with coats unbuttoned, some with their muskets on the ground, others with theirs across their knees,—all grave and thoughtful. Although divided and scattered, there was still some appearance of order in the column. The officers were standing in groups, and talked in an undertone among themselves, in few words,—monosyllables and gestures,—raising their eyes, from time to time, to look around and back of them. But the majority looked up, and seemed to be waiting for something from that quarter; every glance was directed toward the summit, as if something would appear from one moment to the other. And, in fact, at a certain point, where there was a thick clump of cypresses, a long black spot appeared, moving slowly, slowly forward, so that it seemed like one of those broad shadows that isolated cloudlets cast in passing before the sun. As it advanced, it broadened out and moved more quickly. It was a column of soldiers, all bristling with bayonets, which sent an undulating flash from one end to the other, like a black torrent covered with silver spangles. We were all silent and motionless, our mouths half open, our eyes fixed on that line, watching its steps, noting all the undulations; not a breath was heard in the whole battalion, not a gesture was seen; the soldiers all seemed statues. Suddenly a voice shouted: 'There, look on the other side!' We all turned the other way. And, in fact, on the right, on the summit, where there was a hovel, another troop, broader, deeper, and gleaming too with bayonets, advanced rapidly, resolutely, and with serrated ranks in an opposite direction from the first. Then an excited murmur rose: 'How many are there?' 'A regiment?' 'No, two battalions.' 'Or one?' 'No, no, two.' 'Three.' 'They look like sharp-shooters.' 'No, infantry.' 'Sharp-shooters.' 'But, no.' 'But yes; see their feathers.' 'They are stopping.' 'Do you think so?' 'Yes, they have stopped, I tell you!' 'No, see how they move!' Meanwhile the ground between the two bodies was diminishing. We measured it from moment to moment. Our eyes ran, without stopping, from one troop to the other, from the latter back with the rapidity of thought, hungrily and expectantly; all our life was in our eyes; all our soul was up there. The ground between the two went on diminishing, and the two bodies were very near, and marched rapidly, a trifle disordered and confused. We, with our eyes dilated, motionless, nailed to the spot, our hearts beating, and our breath bated.

"Suddenly, almost instantaneously, a bright light flashed from those two bodies, fell, and was extinguished; they had lowered their bayonets, and instantly thereafter began running. A shout, that must have been tremendous, came faintly to our ears.

"We replied with a shudder.

"Ah, they are within a few steps of each other; they will clash; have done so; one gives way, spreads, draws back, breaks, and scatters to right and left; it is a rout.

"A fresh shout, a cry of joy reaches us; and this time we respond too. Our shout, ready for so long a time, but suppressed, suffocated, and strangled, came up and burst out from the depths of our souls, and was savagely long and sharp.

"The victorious band stopped an instant, then continued its run, caught up with the fugitives, moved off behind them, became only a black point, and then disappeared.

"At that point a high, vibratory voice resounded in our midst: 'It is your turn now. To your place!'

"It was the voice of our major.

"Try letting drop a flaming piece of paper over one of those large, thick ant hills, which at a few steps' distance seem quite immovable, and look like ugly black spots, which you cannot make out at first. The little troop, quite frightened, turns dizzily in every direction, and rushes toward the subterranean passage. Try the first! The others press forward, dash over one another; that passage is closed? quick, another; this, too? on to a third; this, too? back then to the first. When the greater number have dashed into the hole, many unfortunate ones are wandering around in a desperate manner, quite blindly, more dead than alive, until they, too, find a place of safety, although a trifle late, and, perhaps, at the cost of some burns.

"When the first terror is passed, the same thing occurs among the soldiers at the sound of that voice.

"In a twinkling all were up and in arms; the ranks were quickly formed; there was a great ferment, a whispering, a pushing and squeezing, and then all became quiet. Some ran here and there in search of their places; he who found it pushed into it; he who did not, made one for himself with his elbows: the battalion was in order.

"It was a beautiful spectacle! That multitude a short time before scattered and stretched out with loosened clothes and belts, their arms on the ground, up in an instant in line, motionless and silent, prepared for death. It is sufficient to look them in the eye, to understand that they are men who will see the enemy's backs, or cover the ground with their bodies. The flag is motionless; the arm which holds it does not tremble. In the midst of the soldiers, who form a hedge around it with their bayonets, there are superb faces and flashing eyes.

"'Forward!' sounds the well-known voice.

"An instantaneous movement throughout the column, a shudder, a murmur; then quiet. 'Forward!' the captains repeat.

"Forward, then, up the hill. The company at the head hesitates a moment in front of the first hedge in its way; the companies which are following crowd behind; the heavy column closes up, oscillates and totters from the head to the rear on the uneven ground; then breaks, broadens, draws in, stretches out, forms again, begins crowding again with ceaseless bustle, with sudden starts and stops, unequal steps and bounds. He who is at the rear is thrown back by the knapsack of the man in front of him, which strikes him in the chest; now, a man is suddenly precipitated on to the one in front of him, and staggering, pushes him forward; he who is at the flank, tossed here and there sideways, and by blows from the elbow and knapsacks, goes up zigzag and staggering, his head down, and his legs wide-stretched. Here is a hedge: up with the legs and muskets. There a ditch: quick, it is passed. Here an elevation of ground: courage, up, without any disorder. There an interlacing of branches, which fall across one's face: away with it with the hand, and down with the heads. A vine forms an obstruction: out with the sword, it is on the ground, forward. Grass, vines, hedges, bushes, ditches, paths, all change, every thing falls and disappears under that wave, that weight, that precipitous tread, of that irregular multitude. Here the ground is steep, here stony: the foot slips, many fall; up on the elbows, up, strength, on to the feet, forward. Many help themselves with their hands, the butt-end of the musket, or their knees; the trunks, clods, stones, roots,—every thing, in fact, serves as a support to the trembling hand; the crowd climbs, slips, is piled up, here dense, there thinner, scattered, separated, but tenacious, resolute, and raging. Meanwhile our strength decreases, and the sun drives us mad, and here in our hearts we are burning. . . Not climb any further; courage; give a glance up and see how much remains: a little only. A glance backward: a long line of fallen who stretch out their arms; many try to rise, and fall. We are almost there; they must have seen us. A moment more,—ah! A cry, long, sharp, shrill, and fierce, passes over the heads of the column. A joyful shout, a deep shudder, all on the ground. 'Up with those heads!' shouts the major; 'when you hear the whistle it has passed.' All are on their feet—here we are; they have seen us; let us close up the ranks; down with the bayonets; quicken the pace. Under! Another cry longer, sharper, more penetrating, nearer, and more frightful: all on the ground. 'Up, for heaven's sake, boys!' comes from the same voice; 'look death in the face! Don't be afraid!' Another whistle; another; all unharmed; we are safe; here we are on the crest; let us wait; halt!

"All turn their eyes around in astonishment: What an immense and superb plain! The sky, which was very clear, permitted us to see the most distant horizon. On one side, far away in the distance, mountains behind mountains, high, blue, and clear; on the other side plains. The entire green plain was ploughed here and there by long, slender white lines, which intersected at many points and were lost among the distant trees, raising at certain times great clouds of dust which appeared very pure as they were touched by the sun, and stretched out slowly in the direction of the roads: those white lines were the roads that we had taken that morning; those clouds of dust revealed the advance of the Italian columns. There were a few thatched houses here and there, half hidden among the trees, as if they were afraid and did not wish to see what was taking place up there. Below, quite far down, Villafranca was the nearest and silent spectator. On the other, toward the enemy, there were dark spots among the side green of the fields, and an uncertain gleaming of bayonets, which now advanced, now stopped, now pointing to the left or right, almost as if uncertain toward which point they should move and proceed circumspectly. Nearer us, on the same plain, were four or five Austrian cannon which were roaring slowly and continuously. On the opposite side, directly at the foot of our hill, as many of our cannon were firing like the first but more slowly. Behind us on the slope of the neighboring hill, we could see a dense white smoke, and hear a quick firing of muskets; it was the extreme flank of another division. We saw nothing more, or, at least, I do not remember any thing further. We stood waiting there, contemplating that marvellous spectacle.

"In the time of great excitement, when some strong emotion moves us, the mind often, almost unconscious of what is passing in the soul, becomes abstracted little by little, and wanders and abandons itself to the strangest and most childish thoughts and fancies, as if that passing hour were one of the most idle and quiet of our daily life. Thus, perceiving a distant bell-tower, I thought: 'It is Sunday. The people there this morning, in holiday dress, have gone out joyfully into the street, then to church, then have finished their work, just as on any other day, quietly and contentedly.' Then breaking away from this fancy, I saw all those women on their knees in church, absorbed in their prayers, and I watched their faces and said : 'That one, yes, that one there is the mother of a soldier'; and at every roar of the cannon I saw her grow pale and tremble.

"Suddenly, a sergeant who was seated near me, rose to his feet, took two or three steps with his head raised, a smile on his face, and his eyes fixed on the distance, toward the mountains; then he stretched out his arm, pointed his forefinger in that direction, stopped an instant, looked at his comrades, and shouted in a high, clear voice: 'Boys! come here!' Many rose and gathered around him. 'Look!' he added, keeping his arm stretched out and his finger still pointing in the same direction. 'Do you see that distant tower down there, and that house?' 'Where? where?' many others asked as they hurried toward him. 'There, there, look where I am pointing.' 'I see,' said one. 'I too.' 'I too.' 'We all see.' "'Well?'

"'Well!' he exclaimed in a deep and trembling voice, 'that is Verona!'

"'Verona! Verona!' they all shouted, clapping their hands; the rumor spread; in a moment the entire battalion was there, every face turned in that direction, every arm stretched toward that tower, their mouths open for that shout, looking, as one looks . . . Have you ever been a long time without seeing your mother? If you had been waiting for her arrival, you would have fixed your eyes anxiously along the road by which she was to arrive, and when far away in the distance you discovered a black speck, or a little white cloud of smoke, and the blast of a horn reached your ear, dear reader, what would you have felt in your heart? Just what we felt, fixing our eyes on those most desired towers . . . shouting that dear name. . . .

"All four battalions of the regiment were up there. Suddenly a loud shout is heard, all the soldiers spring to their feet, the officers give the order: 'To your place!' the companies reform, and all are silent. Another shout, and the officers repeat: 'Bayonets fixed!' and all four battalions fix their bayonets, then another period of silence follows. 'What is it? What has happened?' all ask. The colonel's adjutant arrives on horseback, approaches our major, and whispers in his ear. 'Forward!' shouts the major. The battalion moves, passes the summit of the mountain, and descends the slope on the enemy's side. All those behind, and I among the number, stretch out their necks, and put out their heads to the right and left to see where we are going; but we cannot see any thing, as the first company impedes our view. I turn back and see the other battalions following us slowly in the distance. At a certain point, when the last company has reached a slight elevation of ground, I catch a glimpse in the distance, among the trees, a movement, a gleaming . . .

"At the same instant I hear a terrible explosion, and sharp whistles on the right and left, at my feet, above my head, an agonizing cry a few steps from me, and in the distance a great cloud of white smoke, then a powerful shout: 'Charge with the bayonets." The disordered battalion dashes forward on quick step. Another cry: 'Savoy!' The battalion breaks out into a loud shout and starts on a run; nothing but smoke

/

"Oh! here is a door; enter quickly with lowered bayonets; a court-yard, the enemy, a flag; courage, on to them! Around the flag is a bulwark of breasts, bristling with motionless bayonets."

(*Page* 199.)

is to be seen; another explosion; other whistles; forward, forward . . . Halt! The trumpet has sounded the halt. Where are we? Where is the enemy? What are they doing? Oh, what smoke! The battalion is all scattered. Here is a house! It seems as if they were firing from that house. 'Charge with the bayonet!' we hear confusedly in the midst of the musket-firing; the battalion dashes forward; where are we going? how do we get there? There is nothing to be seen. Oh! here is a door; enter quickly with lowered bayonets; a court yard, the enemy, a flag; courage, on to them. Around the flag is a bulwark of breasts, bristling with motionless bayonets. The first, overcome, fall on to the others, firm as a column; the furious assault stops, and then begins a precipitous shower of blows that we hear but cannot see; the bayonets cross and strike, resounding sharply; the broken muskets crack; there are horrible shouts stifled by suffocation, and broken groans that follow the force of the blows; the weapons are straightened, the crowd thickens, the combatants dash at each other, form groups, jammed together, face to face. The soldiers seize the bayonets, take each other by the throat, cross legs and arms, seize and break away from each other, fall, rise pale and breathless, with teeth set, and bare and bleeding heads. One feels the heated breath of the other in his face; at every moment a face becomes pale and a head falls back with distorted eyes; the ground is covered with the fallen; the group around the banner has became thinner; the standard-bearer has been hit in the breast by a bayonet. 'Your turn,' shouts a dying voice; another has seized the flag. Meanwhile they are fighting all over the house. We hear cries of distress from all the rooms. The floors tremble under the weight of hurrying steps, and doors creak and burst open under the blows of the muskets. The besieged wander here and there in despair, hide in the fire-places, behind the furniture and doors; the besiegers rush shouting on to them, scatter them, hunt them, discover them, drive them out, and drag them along, streaking the floor and stairs with blood; the conquered will not surrender; the prisoners revolt, break away, throw themselves from the windows, and dash into the court-yard, or get transfixed with bayonets in their backs, and fall dead in the door-ways; others try to escape by the roofs; others, wounded and dripping with blood, drag themselves out of the fray. The defenders of the flag are at the end of their resources. 'Surrender!' our men shout. 'No! no!' they reply in a stifled voice. 'Death first!' Suddenly a loud shout is heard which resounds through the house, and at the same moment a man dashes out of the crowd with the enemy's flag in his hand, his forehead aloft and shining, but lacerated and bleeding. 'Hurrah!' shout a hundred voices throughout the house. A blast of the trumpet is heard. 'What? What has happened? Retreat? How is that? Why? It is impossible! Silence!' Another blast of the trumpet, and a thundering shout from the major: 'Retreat!' 'Retreat? we? now? why? It is a mistake! It is impossible!' We are out of the house, the major points out the direction of the road, the other battalions are already in motion. Heavenly Father! we retreat! 'Captain, captain, in heaven's name why are we retreating?' The captain, without saying a word, turns toward the enemy and stretches out his arm in the direction of the plain to point out something. 'Look . . .' There was an interminable column of the enemy advancing at our back, and losing itself in the green of the country.

"'But captain! captain! and the other corps and divisions, where are they? what are they doing? why do they not come.?'

"'Humph!' he replied, shrugging his shoulders.

"'Have we lost them?' I shouted in a tone of despair.

'So it seems!'

"I looked around at my soldiers, I looked again at the Austrian column, then at Villafranca, at that superb Lombardian plain, the beautiful sky, and the beautiful mountains. 'Oh, my poor country!' I exclaimed, letting my sword fall to the ground,—and I wept like a child."

The young lady bowed her head on her hand and thought.

---

## THE SENTINEL.

It was one of the last nights of January; it was snowing, and the streets of the city, the squares, the sills and balconies of the houses, and the trees were all white, buried, overloaded with snow; the flakes fell slowly, large, and thick, and on a snowy stratum along the walls a track was hardly made before every trace of it disappeared. The lamps at the corners of the streets gave out a veiled, sad light; at the crossings, no matter in which direction you looked, not a soul was to be seen; on every side there reigned a dead silence, so that you could almost hear the snow fall.

It was one of those nights in which any one who is so unfortunate as to be out hurries home, keeping close to the walls, in rapid, silent steps, like a stealthy phantom, with his eyes on the ground to escape the puddles, the brim of his hat over his ears and nose, his neck down and the coat-collar turned up at the back, one hand stuck into the other sleeve, all huddled up; dashes head down into the door-way, climbs the stairs, stamping his wet feet and shaking the snow-covered garments, pushes the key into the keyhole, enters, off with the coat, down with the hat—what a state to be in! pushes the first chair in front of the fire, drops down on to it, one foot here, the other foot there, drops his head over the fire, and stays there poking and enjoying it, puffing a cigar slowly, making hieroglyphics in the ashes with the tongs, muttering from time to time: "What weather!" One of those nights in which even the bored, disenamored husband draws his chair a little nearer to his wife; the bachelor dreams of the quiet joys of a family, and, renouncing his usual dissipations, dashes under the counterpane betimes, twists about until he has made a warm nest for himself, puts out one hand far enough to hold his novel, and having read two or three pages, falls peacefully to sleep, whetting his own enjoyment of the heat and rest with the picture of the poor benumbed people who have neither home nor bed. One of those nights in which the life of the city is restricted to the domestic hearth, where the usual conversation between the family and most intimate friends extends beyond the customary hour, until the children, overcome with sleep, tug secretly at the mamma's skirt to remind her of the little bed awaiting them, and go to sleep enjoying in anticipation the battle with snow-balls that they shall fight in the morning. One of those nights in which the most ardent desires are three in number, as the *bon vivant* would say: a dear face, a charming book, and a good glass of something.

All, even the poor, seek in such nights the cover of a roof, a little fire, and a little straw; all find a shelter from the snow until the first rays of dawn, at least for those hours in which it comes down so thickly that it seems desirous of burying the houses; all rest, sleep, all but the sentinel—for whom there is neither fire, roof, nor rest; but only a little wooden box, a heavy cloak of coarse cloth, and the corporal's countersign.

Look down there at the end of the square, all white with snow, and lighted all around by four long rows of lamps, near the great door of that black palace, so colossal and old in form, with its huge illuminated windows; look there at that sentinel's box, that muffled man, erect and motionless like a marble statue. He has been there for hours, without moving, without uttering a word, with his right hand quite benumbed on the barrel of his musket, his feet in the snow, his eyes cast down and fixed, so that they seem to be counting the large flakes which fall around him. From time to time his eyes half close, his head drops slowly on his shoulder; but instantly an inner voice warns him, and he raises his head quickly, opens and dilates his eyes, glances around rapidly and vigilantly, as if to compensate his conscience for that moment of languor and inertia. Look at him; even the poorest have a bit of house, fire, and bed; but he has none.

These thoughts passed through my mind one night at the end of January, when I was on guard with about forty soldiers on that square and in front of that palace. And I walked, thinking thus, at a short distance from the door, measuring with slow step a small portion of the square that was free from snow, and turning my eyes now and then up toward the lighted windows, from which there came to my ears a confused harmony of flutes and violins, and a dull, heavy sound of feet, moving in cadence tread over an immense floor. Then I looked into the immense vestibule, at the lamps gleaming with crystal, the carpets and vases of flowers scattered over the marble floor, and the walls covered with tapestries and laurels. Toward the front, between me and the door, was a coming and going of grand carriages, a shouting of coachmen, a continuous mounting and descending of men and women, a hastening to the carriage doors, a reverential opening of these, a respectful presentation of the hand, a long sweeping of dresses, an uncovering of bedecked heads, a curving of spines, and an appearance and disappearance of servants in gleaming gala livery. Here a carriage with a coat of arms approaches, stops; the footman gets hastily down; all gather around; ten hands vie with each other to reach the door-handle; one fortunate hand seizes it; the door opens; the crowd divides into two wings, on the right and left; necks are outstretched, and eyes fixed; a head appears, a foot, then a little hand in a light glove; and another hand stretches out from the midst of the crowd, touches timidly its finger tips, down goes the small foot, slowly, carefully,—a little farther, a trifle farther still, and the small foot is on the ground. Oh, how pretty! How unfortunate it would have been if it had touched a flake of snow! But it kept inside the train of the dress.—What a pity! It must have caught on a nail! Quick—they run in twos, threes, and fours; Where is it caught? Here!—no—there—gently—carefully—delicately—look, look—ah! it is here. The train is free, on the ground, and she is on her feet. What a superb figure! Make way; stand back and look at her. An indiscreet hood only shows the curious eye a wee bit of that charming face; it is the face of an angel! A jealous gown hides from the hungry glances the beautiful hips and white shoulders, but lets one imagine, under its folds, the form which is divine! The beautiful figure advances gracefully, turns, places her foot on the staircase,—one more bit of the dress, and then she has disappeared. What a pity! But follow her with the mind's eye into the midst of the intoxicated throng of those noisy rooms; among all the other beautiful heads bedecked with gems and camelias, distinguish her tresses and flowers, and follow them in the mazes of the dance, amid the conflict of ardent glances which provoke, search, flee away amiably astute, meet amiably audacious, and betwixt the fascination of the soft abandonment and pleasure of the dance, they languish, flush, beseech, refuse, promise, punish, grant, and carry one off to Heaven.

And he is there, I thought, poor soldier! He is there, exposed to the cold, to the snow, alone, silent, sad, without comfort, and without hope. Up there they are playing, dancing, laughing, frolicking, enjoying life's wildest and most charming intoxications; and he, from that darkness and that solitude, is obliged to hear the gaiety going on above his head, and compare it with the sad abandonment, and the weary melancholy of his poor heart. He is obliged to submit to the imageries of those dear faces, beautiful persons, and glances; he, who is alone, far away from his own, who has no woman's face smiling on him, no little hand to press; but who, perchance, to his greater sorrow, will always have fixed in his memory a black braid and two modest eyes that once made his soul tremble with love! Ah! in the midst of those hyacinths and flower-decked heads he dreams of her, and sees those dear tresses, without gems, and without flowers!—"Corporal!"

"Present!"

"Who's the soldier in the sentinel-box?"

"Such and such a one."

"You may go."—My heart told me that it was a conscript. Poor conscript! He has only been in the regiment for a few days, and is still bewildered by this new life; his head and his heart are still at home with his mother, among the quiet habits of his former life; the thought of return does not even pass through his head, or, if it does, it is only a thought of a very distant pleasure! He has no friends in the regiment as yet; he is still suffering from the jokes of the older soldiers, and the first hardships, which are the most painful, of the discipline; not a friendly voice, not an affectionate word, not a smile, nothing but harsh threatening voices and disagreeable faces. After another hour passed there, he will come here, weary and wet, overcome with cold and sleep, and will have a wretched, bare table on which to rest, and will fall into that interrupted, painful slumber, being waked by a jogging of his legs or a handful of snow in his face. He has not even a little fire by which to dry his clothes, not a drop of wine, not even a bit of tobacco,—and probably not even a centime with which to buy some. I could swear that he is suffering at this moment. The music and the gaiety sadden him. I will go and assure myself of the fact. I will go and see him. But no—why not? Yes, indeed, I will go and see him. Why should I not go? Oh, we will see! I will go.

And I started. I passed in front of the box, looked in; it was dark, and I could not see his face. I turned back, hesitated for an instant, and thought: When one is stirred by a very powerful emotion, be it sorrow or joy, the sound of the first word uttered after a long silence must at that moment rouse and reveal that sentiment in question. Let us try. I approached the box, and stopped in front of it. The sentinel noticed me, and came to the opening. I did not see his face, nor he mine. I asked, in an affectedly indifferent tone: "Are you cold?"

He hesitated a moment, and then replied: "No, sir!"

That was enough. There was a slight tremor in the voice; no doubt of it; my supposition had been quite correct, and I had divined the state of his heart.

"Are you really not cold?"

"Oh, no! A little—you know—but not so much so that—rather—"

Poor fellow, he was freezing! He was afraid of appearing lacking in discipline should he tell me he was cold. Just as if he or I had made the snow fall right at his feet, which must have been in a sad state. I was so pleased with his reply, poor fellow! So, do not talk to me of the distance between officers and soldiers at such moments; for the heart is not covered with gilt braid like the cap. Great heavens! how can one be so hard and reserved unless he be made of stone? However, as I did not wish it to seem as if I had gone there to play the pitying consoler, or leave him either before I had cheered him a trifle with a few friendly words, I said, in an indifferent manner:

"How much longer have you to stay here?"

"I really don't know, Mr. Lieutenant. . . . You cannot hear the clock near here . . . on account of the music."

"Yes; well (at this point the ice was broken), certainly to stand still here, at this hour and in such weather, is not a pleasure. But, good heavens! it is our profession. . . . It is all like this, and we must take things as they are. But, my good fellow, this is nothing. If we go to war, then you will see something worse. That is quite another affair, you know, as you will see when you try it. When you are on the outposts, for instance, in a dark wood, under one of those fine drizzling rains that go through every thing and make you thoroughly uncomfortable, quite alone, abandoned, and not seeing a palm before your nose, but there you must stay, firm and erect as a reed, with a vigilant eye and strained ear, because the enemy is in front of you, and from one moment to the other may fall upon you. Then, after a night passed there, you return to the regiment, and there is nothing to satisfy your hunger, no place to sleep, and you are obliged to stretch yourself out in the mud, on stones, or on the damp grass—then you know what a hard life is! This is nothing. Yet brave soldiers lead that life so full of perils and deprivations courageously, and never grumble; when they can sleep, well; when they cannot, patience; when there is bread, hurrah for the bread! when there is none, one can fast, *à la bonheur*, and does not get out of temper for such a trifle. Do you know why? Because they are living among friends and know how to do their duty, to be a soldier who will defend the country where he was born and brought up, where he has his family, home, friends, and . . . sweetheart; all that is dearest and most sacred to us in this world; do you understand? And the consciousness of having done his duty is all that the good soldier needs. See how many poor unfortunates the soldiers have dragged out of the river down there during the summer bathing season! Well, what have those soldiers who have risked their lives to save those of people whom they did not know gained? Nothing; that is, much—the gratitude of the saved, and the consciousness of their courageous deed, and this is enough for a brave man. Then the soldiers who go to fight the brigands? Every day one dies; who knows that he is dead; who will remember his name beyond the members of his family? Yet the soldiers are willing to stop up on the mountains, in the woods and ravines, and to lead that cursed sort of existence, and why? Because they know that they are doing their duty. And the carabineers, poor soldiers too, who wander about the country at night, two by two, among the malefactors hidden in ditches, who treacherously shoot at them from their hiding-places, they too lead a hard life. Yet see how gladly they do their duty! It is the same thing with the sentinel. At night, such nights as these, who sees the sentinels enveloped in their cloaks, curled up at the back of their boxes, motionless and silent; who hears them, knows who they are, or thinks of them? No one. Yet the sentinel must remain at his post, without any melancholy thoughts in his mind, and think: Every one is sleeping; but I watch over the sleep of all; if there were no sentinels, no one would be able to sleep from fear. My little box protects the largest palaces; everywhere people are singing, playing, and enjoying themselves, and they can do so without thought or suspicion, because I am silent, vigilant, and listening for them all; my rough cloak protects the silken and velvet robes of the ladies who go to balls; this shadow protects that light, my silence those sounds. The soldier must draw comfort from the feeling of this truth, of which one is not accustomed to think, or of which many have never thought, but which ought really to be kept alive in his mind and heart, and he ought to comprehend that in this feeling lies the most beautiful reward for his sacrifices and his virtues. Are you convinced of it?"

"Oh, yes, lieutenant."

His voice had trembled, had come from his heart, had found some impediment half way in his throat, I perceived; I went on:

"And after he has sacrificed for five years, five long years, at all hours and moments, his own will, desires, affections, habits, thoughts, every thing in fact; has sacrificed every thing to his duty, his flag—to those three beautiful colors which we ought to hold dearer than ourselves, our life, than every thing in the world ; when after five years passed thus, the country says to him : This is enough, you have done your duty, give me back the musket with which you have defended my honor and my life, and return to your home, for your mother is expecting you, and your sisters wish to see you, and there is another woman, who, standing by the window at evening, looks far away along the road by which you are to return, then, believe me, my good fellow, the being able to return to your old mother's arms, with the consciousness of having been a good soldier,—the being able to return under that poor roof with a high head and your hands hardened from constant handling of the musket is, believe me, a joy that has no equal on the earth—Do you believe it ? "

". . . . Mr. Lieutenant ! . . . ."

" And when you have returned home, at evening, and the beautiful moon is shining, you begin to dance in the meadow, as in old times, and that is the kind of ball which is the most enjoyable, is n't it ? "

He made no reply.

" Am I right or not ? "

" Oh, yes, yes ! " broke out the poor soldier, in a voice whose tone was indescribable, but which still resounds in my ear, as if I had just heard it. " Oh, yes, you are right, Mr. Lieutenant, yes, cer— . . ."

Do you know why he stopped ? Because, affected and agitated as he was, moved solely by affection, by gratitude for my brotherly words, the good fellow forgot for an instant that I was an officer and he a poor conscript, and had stretched out his arm toward me, but recollecting himself, had instantly withdrawn it, not, however, in time to prevent his hand from grazing my cloak slightly.

"Ah! . . ." I exclaimed.

He was ashamed of himself, and quite embarrassed, and, murmuring timidly some words of excuse, dashed back into his box. He seemed to be breathing with great difficulty. Perhaps he was weeping.

I moved off with my heart profoundly touched. I felt so thoroughly contented with myself! I looked up at the lighted windows, went back to listen to the music, to which I had paid no attention for some time, returned in spirit to the ball-room. Pooh, they were all faded imageries.

Poor enjoyment this, I thought, in comparison with mine.

---

# THE CAMP.

THERE is a beautiful, great, level, rectangular meadow, shut in on the four sides by a ditch and a hedge, well covered with grass, and studded with daisies. Beyond the ditch, on one side, a thick clump of mulberries, oaks, thorn trees, and further on, projecting above that mass, a gently sloping hill, green and low, scattered with trees and small white houses. Half way up the slope, a group of higher and more city-like-looking houses, and a high, light bell-tower; round about some bluish and reddish palaces, flowery hillocks, long rows of pines, groups of willows, sandy, winding avenues; and here and there white statuettes and sprays of water, hidden by the trees and bushes. In front of that field, along the side opposite the grove, runs a broad, raised road, which winds around the thickly planted trees, and climbs the hillside to the village. A regiment has pitched its tents in the meadow.

Let us place ourselves on the road and look at the camp. Beginning at twenty paces from the ditch, to the opposite boundary line of the field, there are eight long rows of tents, in parallel lines, divided by a space of about ten paces. In every row there are one hundred tents; three soldiers to each tent; three hundred soldiers in one row; two thousand four hundred, or little less, in all; in fact, an entire regiment. The tents are neat and well stretched; the cords fastened to the ground in straight lines, at equal intervals; every thing in perfect order; it is a camp which looks as if painted. Opposite the openings of the tents, at the back and on the sides, rise the huts and sheds of green boughs (they have despoiled the trees in the poor fields in the neighborhood, so that the colonel got into a perfect rage), and from the branches (like triumphal arches) wave garlands of wild poppies and wheat interlined. Here and there, on the top of a cane stuck into the ground, float several flags, made of a red cravat, a bit of shirt, and a blue handkerchief, which looks like green. In the tents, is a confusion of straw, clothes, knapsacks, rags, cartridge-boxes, gun-stocks, and bayonets. Between the tents are stretched ropes, on which are displayed those half drawers, which are supposed by the government to reach the ankle, but which in reality only come down to the knees on the legs of the soldiers, as nature made them.

To the right of all these tents, in a parallel line with the shortest side of the camp, there is another row of tents, conical in shape and higher, larger, better stretched, and more comfortably arranged than the others; the tents of the officers; from that of the colonel, which is the nearest to the road, down to that of the officers of the last company. Farther to the right, in a parallel line with the tents of the officers, along the dividing ditch, is a long row of wagons overladen with boxes, trunks, bundles, and a hundred various articles. Behind the last wagon, a troop of horses and mules tied to the trunk of the trees. Along the opposite side—the left side—an unending row of black kettles, placed in groups at regular distances, and between each group, ovens made of heaped-up stones and bricks, and piles of ashes and burnt sticks, brushwood, and scattered straw. Beyond the ditch, small trees on the ground split and broken up, thinned out hedges, furrows trampled down and ruined ; all the signs of a great sacking.—Oh, poor colonel, how furious he was !

A little wooden bridge, just made with two trunks of trees and a few boards, unites the camp with the road. Beside the bridge, in the camp, along the edge of the ditch, there are ten or twelve isolated tents in which the prisoners in irons are confined. On the bridge is a sentinel, another in front of those tents, and others around the camp at the different points of exit.

Such is the camp.

The sun was setting; it was a beautiful evening in July. The sky was wonderfully clear, the country still fresh and damp from a recent rain ; and that dark grove, the beautiful green hill, the villas, and the little hamlet still gilded by a ray of the sinking sun, made the scene a fascinating one.

It was an hour of rest and recreation for the regiment. All were in motion. Most of them, in their shirt sleeves and linen trowsers, wandered among the tents, alone, in couples, or in bands ; some were seated or stretched out in groups, or chasing each other, like boys in the court-yard of a school ; others were playing a game with stones; others fenced with sticks in the midst of a circle of spectators ; others, still, having stretched a bit of cord between two tents, jumped on a wager between two rows of admirers ; some, seated on the edge of the ditch, around a rag of table-cloth, devoured a few leaves of lettuce in a friendly way, nibbling at a little white bread (the kind the officers eat) ; some were seated cross-legged over the cart-poles smoking peacefully ; some, dressed in linen waistcoats falling to bits, of which only the white of the past remained, were back among the ovens and kettles, breaking upon their knees the piles of branches, brushwood, etc., for the kitchen; and on every side rose shouts and cries, songs, and continuous and diffused sounds.

How many beautiful pictures for an artist!

There, at the end of the camp, in the middle of the opposite side from the road, the sutler has placed his three wagons in the form of three sides of a trapezium, the opening toward the camp; he has stretched a pieced but torn tent between two side wagons; has set up two or three tables, and three black and rickety benches; has placed a wardrobe door over the two tallest casks and made a counter of it; put the biggest cask behind it and lodged his wife there; has stretched between two wheel-spokes a well-greased cord, and suspended therefrom some long, black, crusty things, which are supposed to be eatable sausages, and which can be enjoyed without danger of death; then, in order to excite the soldiers' appetite, he has exposed to view a couple of baskets of fresh vegetables, a great plate of plucked and rather gamy fowls, a huge piece of raw meat, a row of bottles and badly washed glasses, cigars pregnant with oil, and sheets of letter-paper perfumed by anchovies; then has shouted: "Come on, boys! Here you can eat till you burst!" Which, by the way, is a highly probable statement. The benches are all full; the tables covered with bottles; the men are playing at *mora*, singing, shouting, disputing, and making a racket; the glasses jingle from time to time, and strike each other, and the sutler turns around. What are they doing over there? An officer appears, there is a profound silence; he disappears, and the revelry begins again. Meanwhile, in the open passage between the tables there is a crowd forming, composed of two lines moving in opposite directions, some who are coming to fill their trenchers with wine, and others who, having theirs full, shout: "Make way there," swearing at and cursing the unfortunate man who does not give way and thus makes them spill a few drops. Around the *vivandière* a circle of young corporals has formed; that of the third company, among the others, who is so graceful and so impudent; the husband knows it, and cannot refrain from casting certain sharp glances in that direction which are like so many arrows; and the wife does not neglect to make eyes at her favorites; the husband would like to protest, but the affairs of the shop are flourishing, and much of this is due to the wheedling of madame. "Let us close our eyes," he thinks, "until we have taken in the money." A soldier approaches the counter. "What do you wish?" "A little glass of rum." "Here it is; pay for it." "Take this"; and he presents a bill. "I cannot change it; I have no small money." "Then what shall I do? Ah, that is delightful! try." And the poor soldier stands there, puzzled and confused, fingering the bill and glancing at the little glass with an angry expression of face. Then moves slowly off, murmuring: "They pay us in paper, and to say that there is no specie! But all those who go on horseback put it in their pockets."

Fifty paces nearer there is another picture. It is a captain who has collected about fifty soldiers of his company,—as many as he could pick up round about,—has placed them in a circle, and, after telling them that they will have a great deal of marching to do the following day, and that the first one who gives out will be put immediately in irons, has a small cask of wine brought into their midst, and glancing at one of the quickest soldiers, says: "It's your turn; take out the bung and distribute it." They all gather around, holding out trenchers, canteens, and glasses. "Wait a moment, for heaven's sake! Get out of the way there, or I won't give any one another drop!" They all stand back. And while the soldier endeavors to open the cask with his nails and the point of his bayonet, and the captain stands bending over it, his hand on his knees, directing the operation; all the others, gathered together on one side, smother their laughs of delight, twist their hands around their knees, and, bending their backs, they make mute signs to one another, exchange certain droll gestures, hit each other's elbows, nodding with their head and a half-closed eye at the unusual treat; they pass the back of the hand over the mouth, as if to prepare it for the full enjoyment of the treat, without leaving any other profane taste on the lips; they exchange furtive pinches, and they rub their shoulders against each other. Suddenly, the captain turns. All are erect and motionless, so not to appear quite crazed at the idea of a few drops of wine. The captain makes a sign for them to approach; they crowd forward; the bung is out, a great purple stream comes bubbling forth; ten trenchers are held under it to catch it, after these ten others, another ten, and so on. Down the throat it goes in perfect waves. "Shall we touch glasses?" asks one voice. "Yes," reply twenty others. The trenchers are raised above the heads, they move, turn and return, touch; the wine overflows and spreads over their heads, faces, and hands, staining waistcoats and doublets, and dropping everywhere. But what does it matter? "Hurrah for pleasure! Hurrah for the captain!" exclaims one of the boldest in an undertone. "Hurrah!" reply the others in chorus. "Silence, you dogs!" shouts the captain impetuously, not succeeding, however, in concealing under that show of anger a certain feeling of complacency. "Have you lost your heads? Disperse!" The crowd separate, running in every direction. But the other soldiers, who have sniffed a little festivity in the distance, collect, but too late, however; the cask is empty, and the captain's pocket-book is closed. The new arrivals wander around, glance warily at each other, do, as they say of the Indians, turn their eyes upward to gaze at the clouds, and kick the stones about while yawning indifferently; but all in vain; the captain does not see them, moves off, and every hope is dead. Well, this trifle suffices to make men happy; and they return to the place whence they came, humming in that strained, harsh voice that seems to stick half way in the throat when we are provoked at something and wish, but do not succeed, in dissimulating it.

Now let us look in another direction, down there in the farthest corner. Along that line of wall runs a canal three or four metres in width, and in it are two palms' depth of water between two soft and slippery banks. On one of the sides are standing and sitting the soldiers of the company, whose tents are near by. Suddenly there comes a voice from the group of officers standing on the opposite side: "Who wants to earn a lira? Here it is for the man who can jump this ditch," and a hand with a coin in it is raised in the circle. All turn and run in that direction. "I, I, I, I too." Then an officer exclaims: "Let us see; stand in a row," and he makes a sign with his hand. The crowd of soldiers turn their backs, run twenty paces from the bank, stop, turn around, draw up in a semicircle, the most courageous in the centre, the laziest at the wings; three or four in the middle dispute the best position with their elbows; one finally conquers, puts his left foot well forward, bends backward, measures the ground with his eye, rises on tip-toe to look into the ditch, thinks, hesitates, turns to his neighbor and says: "You jump first." An "oh!" of shame rises on all sides. The neighbor hesitates also; two or three excuse themselves. "Make way, then, I will jump," says a new-comer, opening a path by means of pushes and blows. They make way; he comes forward, prepares, sways backward and forward, glances at the ditch and the ground, and starts. He passes the intervening space, courage, bravo! and he is over, resting on his right foot, with his left one in the air and his arms well extended. The lira is his; away he runs for a drink. The competition is lively; another man has taken the leap, and another lira is won. A third starts. Oh, how short-breathed he is! He reaches the bank, takes the leap, and down he goes flat on to his face, dashing the water over every one. A prolonged shout breaks from every throat, and ends by a general laugh and clapping of hands. The poor fellow has climbed with difficulty on to the bank, all wet and dripping, his hair clinging and matted in bunches over his ears and face, his trowsers clinging to his legs, and his arms hanging. But the officers are moved by pity. "A glass of wine for this poor devil!" exclaims one of them. And the face of the poor devil instantly becomes serene.

Then the circle of singers. One here, one there, around the tents, under the trees, five, ten, and twenty together. One warbles a pathetic ballad with the greatest effrontery; others, half intoxicated, with glistening eyes and inane faces, howl certain bacchanal songs, raising their trenchers in both hands at the end of every verse, burying their noses in them, and taking down the bad wine in long swallows; then a waving of caps in demonstration of their joy, a reciprocal clapping of hands on the back, and a sharp and surly shouting of "Hurrah for the blonde," with certain grins, a monkey-like puckering up of the nose, and the attitudes of satyrs. Around the group of more harmonious voices is a small circle of spectators, and in the midst of the chorus there is a director, who marks the time with his finger, and reproves any one who goes out of tune, performing his part in the most serious way, with a modest face, and glancing around as he does so at the audience, which continues to increase.

Then there are the solitary and melancholy ones who take refuge from all that racket, and to whom the music and shouting, even when heard at a distance, causes sadness and contempt. They wander around the deserted portions of the camp, or seat themselves on the edges of the ditch, with their feet just above the water, poking the sand and stones at the bottom with a willow stick, or else they lie stretched out across the opening of the tent, their faces buried in their hands, the smoked-out pipe in their fingers, and their eyes following in a dazed sort of way the beautiful little flame-colored clouds caused by the setting sun. Their eyes run over the tops of those mountains and they think what may be behind: a plain; then, other mountains; and behind these? another plain; and so on over mountains, valleys, and unknown plains, in imagination, until suddenly they discern the dear and well-known hills of their own home, and they contemplate with a mingling of tenderness and grief that sunset which they have not seen in so long a time. Then, suddenly, they turn their eyes and seem to become aware, at that point, where and among whom they are; they heave a deep sigh, give a toss of the head as if to chase away the feeling of melancholy which begins to creep into their hearts, rise and away they run to join the others, and join in the general racket, since it is no use to grieve over things which cannot be helped.

But not all solitary men change their thoughts so easily. Many of the younger soldiers and some of the older ones remain there the entire evening, thinking and thinking, plucking up the grass about them. Some, seated cross-legged, Turk fashion, polishing their bayonets with a bit of rag, mending their clothes, or attending to some other affair, accompanying their work with a low and monotonous chant, which is sorrowful both in thought and expression. Others seize their knapsacks, spread out on it a sheet of paper, upon which is depicted a soldier starting for the war, or a great heart pierced by a huge arrow; they stretch themselves flat on the ground, draw out the stump of a rusty pen, and squeeze and arrange the stringy sponge of a dried-up inkstand, and, after having looked at the point against the light several times, and pressed it as many times against their nails, they pass and repass the palm of the hand over the sheet, and breathing upon it, drawing in and out their necks as they do so, scratch great crooked words and form wavering pot-hooks, raising their faces heavenward from time to time, as if asking inspiration for a word or phrase which they no longer remember, but which they have certainly read, they could swear to it, in some printed book, the name of which has slipped from their mind. Like the soldiers, the officers, too, have their sad hours, and they sit cross-legged on the boxes, in front of their tents, a book in their hands, or wander around the solitary corners of the camp among the soldiers. "To whom are you writing?" asks an officer, stopping behind a soldier who is writing. "Are you writing home?" "Yes, sir," replies the latter, getting on to his knees in order to rise to his feet. "No, no, stay where you are; and go on." "How long since you have been learning?" "Four months." "Let me see. That's not bad. Bravo!" And on he goes. He stops behind another: "To whom are you writing, your father?" The soldier nods in the negative, smiling as he does so. "To whom then, your mother?" "No." "To whom then?" The soldier continues laughing, twists his head around into his shoulder, and with one hand pretends to play with the sheet in order to hide the first word. "Ah! I understand, you rascal." Both those soldiers are contented; a word sufficed to put them in good-humor; perhaps, later, they will join the others and dance too. A pleasant word costs so little!

Let us look on to the road and see who is coming. Well, will you tell me what it is that the quartermaster-sergeant is carrying? A leather bag swung over his shoulder? Wait until that man has got into the camp, until some one has caught sight of him, until the rumor of his arrival has spread, and then you will see what a tumult, crowd, and confusion there is. Here he comes, and makes with quick, stealthy steps for his tent, looking suspiciously around; he tries to pass unobserved in order to dash into it, and arrange that mass of papers a little, for if he does not do so, it will be almost impossible to distribute them. But it is in vain. A soldier discovers him, turns to his comrades, and gives a shout of joy: "Letters! Letters?" they ask, running around and glancing here and there. "Where is he? where is he?" "He went this way." "No, that." "Ah, here he is!" All dash in that direction. Meanwhile the news has flown to the last boundaries of the camp; two, three, or four soldiers break from every circle, and away they run,—who will arrive first and get hold of the first letter! . . . Ah, the poor carrier is already surrounded, enveloped, squeezed, and suffocated by a restless, impatient crowd, who have their arms in the air, stretch out their hands, and deafen him with a hum of supplicating and persistent voices, and swaying about they bear him here and there just as it happens, until, from all those outstretched arms, two, three, or four hands holding convulsively the wished-for letter, detach themselves, and off go the men, into their tents, to read them in peace and quiet. Little by little the press diminishes, and the crowd is reduced to a group; some disappointed, headstrong creatures still stand there persisting in a lamentable tone of voice: "But really is there nothing for me? It is impossible; look again; do me that favor." "But if I tell you that there is nothing!" "Oh, for heaven's sake give me time to breathe!" The few who remain scatter slowly, their chins on their breasts, their arms hanging; and the poor letter-carrier breathes, draws in a long breath, and wiping his forehead with his hand, exclaims: "Heaven be praised—*that* is over!"

Along the edge of the road, toward the camp, there is a long line of inquisitive people, most of them peasants, men, women, and boys, who have come from the village to contemplate this spectacle, to them so novel and curious. The children sitting on the banks of the ditch, the fathers and mothers standing on the roadside, the grown-up girls a step behind them. All pointing with their fingers to the different details of the great picture, giggling at the shouts of the singers, pitying the prisoners, and breaking out into exclamations of surprise in seeing some jump, and commiserating with a "Poor fellow, he must have hurt himself," those who have fallen. Then they comment upon the structure of the tents and the divisions of the camp, and explain to one another the difference of grade, judging from the bands on the caps, constantly interrupting, and growing quite provoked at each other. At all points of the road where there are two or three, or a group of young and pretty peasant girls, there is correspondingly in the camp, right on the opposite bank of the ditch, an unusual gathering of soldiers, who, like all men when they know women are looking at them, make gestures, assume attitudes, and study their slightest movements, with a careful indifference, an indescribable air of liveliness and effrontery, that is really entertaining; and the peasants laugh and laugh, cover their faces with their hands, hide behind each other, or scatter and group themselves again, still laughing, whispering mysterious words in each other's ears, and sometimes caressing one another, just for the pleasure (the coquettes!) of seeing their admirers envy them those demonstrations of affection, and make them bite their fingers from pure rage.

At one point of the road a band of young ladies, from the neighboring villas, has appeared, in scant, airy, white, rose-colored, blue, and very light dresses, which so fly about at the slightest breath of wind, that they are obliged to place a little hand on them and stand still for a moment to keep them in place. Those young ladies are bare-headed, and that light breeze stirs and disarranges their shining ringlets, and forces à white arm to raise itself from time to time, and a small, patient finger to put the riotous locks in order. Near by, in the camp, there is a group of officers, who glance along the ground. Oh, if there would only come a breath of wind! Ah, it begins to increase, passes, seizes a little white skirt, the same small hand does not arrive in time to prevent it from flying. . . . Oh, what a pretty little foot! Those officers know they are being watched, and how they enjoy it! If this were not the case, that man, to cite one instance, the one nearest the ditch, would not wear his sash with that careless elegance, and would not have run the ring along so that a bow falls over one hip and the other down to the knee; that other one there would not puff clouds of smoke into the air, raising his head so proudly as he does so, and would not stand in a Napoleonic attitude; this third would not feel so frequently at the nape of his neck to see if the small amount of neckband allowed by the colonel were not quite limp and starchless.

Meanwhile a family from the village comes down the road and stops at the entrance of the camp. There is an elderly, lively, strong-limbed, and corpulent papa, with one of those old-fashioned faces, two ships' sails outside the cravat, two locks of gray hair on the temples, a pair of elephant's paws in two gray linen shoes, and a knotted stick under his arm,—the counterpart of a communal secretary, who lives in perfect peace with all, thoroughly satisfied with himself and the remarkable talent for arithmetic developed by his boys at school; the good face of a mamma under à hat in the shape of a Roman helmet; and three boys dressed in their best clothes, well combed, oiled, smoothed, and shining, with their heads still full of a little lesson on the laws of politeness, which was given in haste by mamma just as they were leaving the house. They are old friends of the colonel. What a fortunate chance that he should have camped right there, near their house! The papa, with his round face all wreathed in smiles, and in his loudest voice, begins: "Mr. Soldier," touching the wide brim of his broad hat as he addresses a sentinel, "might one see the Signor Cavalier Colonel, commandant of the regiment?" The sentinel makes him a sign to pass, and points with his hand to the colonel's tent. A gray-bearded sapper runs forward and announces the visit. The family walk slowly on in a most respectful and circumspect manner. The colonel appears, looks about, stops, knits his brow to see better, glances at the sky as if to collect the scattered reminiscences of old times, remembers, and recognizes them, and smoothing his forehead and uttering a prolonged "oh!" of surprise and pleasure, advances to meet his guests with outstretched arms. Then follow the reception and bows, hurried questions and answers, the passing of hands under the chins of the children, who have sprung up in an astonishing way, and have grown pretty. Then: "Oh, madame!" the colonel exclaims, in order to start a conversation, "the effect of the companies is very great, you know. One hundred and fifty men in each; it is quite a delight. What a fine camp, eh? Would you like to see it? Would you like to take a turn?" The family consent with thanks; the colonel, after a little reflection, places himself on the left of the lady, the husband on the right, and the children in front; the troop begins to move. Every one stands aside. The officers salute them. A subdued murmur precedes and follows them. The colonel, a good, rough soldier that he is, forced into the thankless position of *cavaliere servente*, says to the lady: "Look over there! Those are the kettles of the third company, those of the fourth, the others of the fifth. You will probably tell me that they are in a bad condition, which is quite true, but it is because . . ." and then he proceeds to explain the whys and wherefores. And the lady, in the midst of those two rows of soldiers, connot conceal her embarrassment and confusion; but the papa, proud of having a colonel at his side, gives a slow, benignant glance at the soldiers, repeating from time to time in a tone of complacency and admiration: "What a fine thing youth is!" One of the boys approaches mamma, and pointing to the colonel, asks: "But who is that soldier there?" "Be quiet," she replies in an undertone; "he is the one who commands all the soldiers here." "And could he cut off all their heads if he wanted to?" asks the child.

"The music! the music!" they suddenly shout on all sides of the camp. In fact the musicians have come out of the tents one by one, have collected, marched toward the centre of the camp, formed a circle, and stand awaiting the signal of the band-master, holding their instruments in their hands quite ready to place them at their lips. In less time than it takes to tell it, an immense crowd has gathered around them, half the regiment in fact; a deafening noise is raised, loud shouts of joy, and a burst of hand-clapping and whistles; the most furious dancers break through the crowd by means of blows and their elbows, look for and call each other, dash together, and by placing their hands on their chests, pushing into them and treading on their toes, they succeed in opening a circle; the couples prepare, the dancers seize a handful of shirt on their partners' backs (if they were only women), clasp their fingers, put the left foot forward, bend their knees, turn their faces toward the leader: "Well, are you going to play, or not?" The couples grow impatient, tap their feet, shake their fists, twist themselves, puff, shout; the leader makes a sign with his finger, the instruments are placed at the mouths, the tongues protrude and moisten the upper and lower lips; another sign, and they begin to play. The couples are in motion, turn, return, touch each other, meet, dash right and left, forward, backward, back to back, hip to hip, the heels on their neighbors' corns, away they go blindly, just as it happens, fall or not as the case may be; there must be place for every one, if not, they make it by blows and kicks, they push, stagger, shout, and grin. In a moment the grass in the field has disappeared under the heavy feet, the ground is broken up, the couples get mixed, divided, or grouped differently; others fall flat to the ground, and the dancers, pressed over them, stumble and tumble on to them; others were dashed into the midst of the surrounding crowd; but, in the midst of that hurly-burly, the Lombardian continues to dance imperturbably with that swaying of the hips and motion of the head and shoulders, that crossing of legs and sudden bending of the knee as if on the point of falling, that sudden rising as if on springs; the Piedmontese goes on impassible and grave, and takes things seriously, warms up to his work, and is proud too of his robust graces; and the Calabrians, two by two, facing each other, their necks crooked, arms akimbo, their faces in grotesque shapes, upright or doubled, continue to dash rapidly over the ground.

What is the matter?

A sudden deep silence has fallen upon the camp; all faces turn in one direction; he who was on the ground rises; he who was on the edge of the camp comes to the centre; under the sutler's tent the customers have sprung to their feet on to the benches and tables; others have climbed on to the wagons. Every one has come out of the tents. What has happened? What is the matter?

Look up the road. A horseman is advancing on a gallop, enveloped in a cloud of dust; is quite near the entrance, starts toward the colonel's tent, and stops. The colonel comes out; the horseman salutes, hands him a paper, turns, and gallops off.

All eyes are turned in that direction, every one is astonished and silent. One would say that every one was holding his breath; the camp looks like a square filled with people intent on fireworks when the unexpected glare of the Bengal light illumines ten thousand faces with wide-stretched eyes and open mouths.

The colonel opens the paper, turns toward the trumpeter, makes a sign. . . .

Before the first blast has sounded, a universal, prolonged, and very loud shout bursts out like a thunder-clap, rises to heaven from all sides of the camp; the entire scattered multitude starts in every direction with startling rapidity; the benches and tables of the sutler are deserted in an instant; the poor man dashes his hands into his hair; quick! down with the tent, out with the boxes, in with plates, cabbages, sausages, bottles, clothes, chickens, cigars, every thing in confusion; time flies; another blast of the trumpet is imminent; the officers wander hastily about the camp, calling in a loud voice for their orderlies, who arrive breathless and dripping with perspiration. Quick! take hold of the boxes, in with the clothes; boots on top of shirts, combs in the pockets, no matter, only be quick! The boxes will not shut; down with the knees on the cover; more force, more still,—oh! it's closed. Quick! roll up the overcoat; here with the jacket, sword, sack; we are in order at least. And the soldiers around the tents, loosening the knots in the cords with their nails, rolling up covers and linen, filling the knapsacks hastily, buttoning on their gaiters with the confounded cramped fingers which cannot find the button-holes, feeling in the straw for the bowl, tassel, bayonet, with red face, dripping brow, labored breath, and in a perfect fever lest the second blast of the trumpet should sound, with the voice of the sergeant at their backs threatening them with imprisonment if late, with the scarecrow before them of the captain who is stamping his feet, shouting and screaming: "Quick! quick! quick!" Another blast of the trumpet. "Form the ranks!" shout a hundred excited voices. All rush forward just as they are, with their fatigue caps on the back of their heads, their coats unbuttoned, belts in hand, their knapsacks hanging over one shoulder. "To your place, quickly; order—right about." The companies form tumultuously, breaking open at the appearance of every fresh advent of soldiers, then close in, sway backward and forward, undulate from the head to the foot, get out of order, and then form again rapidly. Another blast of the trumpet. The regiment starts. The first company is outside the camp,—the second—the third—the camp is empty.

Such is camp life; sometimes hard and distasteful, but always beautiful and beloved. Who is there who, having tried it, does not love it, and does not recall it with pleasure, and desire it with enthusiasm?

## THE DISABLED SOLDIER.

In the evening, at a certain hour, the aspect of the country produces upon the soul a vague feeling of melancholy, which resembles that oppression of the heart experienced by children who, having escaped from the house to wander about through the fields, from path to path, farm to farm, go on and on until they suddenly discover that they are alone; they look around them, the place is dark and gloomy; they glance back, they have lost their way; they raise their eyes to heaven, the sun has disappeared; the mother, poor woman! is waiting for them. "Oh, dear me, what have I done?" they exclaim, and there they stand quite dazed, with a lump in their throats and their little hearts all in a tumult. This is the nature of the melancholy which gradually takes possession of our souls in the country, when the sun has set, every thing is becoming one hue, and along the mountain tops there is nothing to be seen but a slender streak of sky, pale gold in color, above which the stars are rapidly beginning to appear. It is a sad hour, one which is made sadder still by the monotonous croaking of the frogs and the distant barking of dogs, which break from time to time the deep and solemn silence of the country. Who, walking at that hour through a solitary lane, in the direction of the city, but still far from it, not seeing a living soul about, nor hearing other noise than the sound of his own footsteps, does not find barking of the dogs burdensome? Not that he is exactly afraid, but, well—he could do without it. Passing before the gates of the vegetable- and flower-gardens, he walks on tiptoe in order not to rouse the ugly dog crouched behind them, holds his breath, and listens attentively; he has nearly passed the gate, is almost in safety, when a wretched bark which thoroughly startles him breaks out at his back, and he passes on without even turning, but he seems to see the ravenous beast with his nose at the crack in the gate, and his eyes gleaming with rage. On he goes, but in the middle of the road, as he does not mind the dust, provided he is not obliged to pass too near the hedges; and if he hears the sound of footsteps or the voices of two wayfarers who are talking together, he does not turn back to see who they are, as that would make him appear like a coward, but proceeds with his eyes on the alert, and pretending to glance at the fields, he takes them in with the corner of his eye; then gazing ahead of him he sees appear in the distance two men on horseback, enveloped in huge black cloaks, their heads covered by a two-pointed hat (gens d' armes); he takes courage, quickens his pace, and arriving in front of those two unexpected friends, makes way for them, looking at them with an expression of amiable obsequiousness, and accepting, with a feeling of intense pleasure, the long, searching glance they bestow upon him. When he finally reaches the blessed gates of the city, and perceives the first lamp-post in the nearest street: "Heaven be praised!" he exclaims, as he dusts off his boots with his handkerchief; "here we are at last!" At that hour any one passing the gate of a cemetery does not stop, although the strange fears of the common people and children do not pass through his mind, but goes straight on, turning his face in the opposite direction. In going by the solitary chapels in the country, the children are almost frightened by the sound of their own steps, which, entering by the windows, resounds under the dark vault. At that hour, and until a ray of light is to be seen in the west, the families of the people at the villas live on the terraces, leaning over the railings to contemplate in silence that sad spectacle: nightfall in the country. The boys point out with their little fingers the small lights that appear one by one in the country-houses, or ask papa the names of the stars, and if there are people like us in them. The girls, sitting apart, with one arm on the back of the chair and their heads resting on their arms, fix their eyes dreamily on the distant mountains and are soon lost in thought. But they are not thinking of those mountains. At such times their thoughts withdraw wearily from that silence and solitude; although they are in the midst of their family, they feel quite alone and abandoned. They feel that some great good is lacking, that there is a void in their hearts, that their life is not complete; and their fancy runs irresistibly on to the city, loses itself in the joyous tumult of balls, seeks and finds again the dear faces forgotten for so long a time, enjoys reviving those imageries, in presenting itself upon the spot, and sharing with them that sweet melancholy. They count the time they shall still have to pass at the villa, run over that time in their mind, and enjoy, in anticipation, the pleasures of return and the first sight of those dear faces, waking finally from those sad and lovely fancies as they would from a dream.

Oh! that hour in the country is a sad one. Even if you were beside the woman whom you love, at the height of your bliss, none but sad fancies would pass through your mind, and none but sad words come to your lips.

Just at that hour, one evening, during the early part of May, in 1866, in a deserted lane which ran across the slope of a hill, near one of those country shrines where the picture of the Virgin is painted at the back of a niche, a young girl and a soldier were talking in an undertone: the former seated on a large stone, leaning against a projection of the shrine, her elbows resting on her knees, her chin in her hands; the latter erect beside her, leaning with one shoulder against the wall, and his arms crossed over his breast. He had on his fatigue cap, as soldiers call it, and wore a coat; his knapsack lay at his feet, and in this was a bundle. There was something sad and despairing in the girl's appearance, and she kept her eyes fixed motionless on the ground; a little light, which was burning before the image of the Virgin, cast a veiled gleam over the brow buried in the hands, and showed the imprint of a long fit of weeping around the eyes. The soldier, without his belt or musket, looked like a soldier on leave, and such was the case, for he belonged to one of the classes that had been recalled to arms on the 28th of April, and on the seventh day after the publication of the royal decree they were to present themselves before the military commandants of the district. That soldier must be on the following day in a neighboring city, ten miles, or less, distant from that place.

Judging from the attitudes of the young girl and himself, and from the long silence which followed their few subdued words, it seemed as if they must have been there for some time. Not a living soul was on the road, either near by or in the distance, and a profound silence reigned all around. Only, from time to time, one could hear a confused sound of distant voices, which came from a house situated at the foot of the slope, where lights appeared and disappeared. They were peasants who had returned from the fields and who were replacing their things, putting the oxen to their stalls, and talking loudly to each across the yard. Suddenly the soldier drew away from the wall, took both the hands of the girl, who instantly rose to her feet, and said to her in that faltering tone of pity which is used when giving some one a sad piece of news: "It is late, you know, Gigia. It is time for me to go. I must be in town betimes to-morrow, and the road is long."

Having said which he looked into the girl's face. The latter, without opening her mouth, moved nearer him, placed her two hands on his shoulders, let her head drop on to them, and sobbed. "Courage, Gigia, courage. We'll fire a couple of shots and then return."

"Return!" she said, raising her head slowly, and letting it instantly drop again. "Who knows?" she then added, in a voice full of tears, from behind her hands.

A moment of silence followed, after which the soldier went on: "Well, then, good-by, Gigia." He placed his hands on her temples, raised her head, kissed her on the forehead, stooped, picked up his knapsack, slung it over his back, passing one arm over his head, fastened the straps, bent once more to take up the bundle, and giving his hand to the girl, made ready to start. She, who meanwhile had covered her face with her apron, and stood motionless as if stunned by grief, suddenly started, and seizing the soldier's hand with both of hers, said, in a firm and resolute voice, wishing by this means to delay his departure for a few moments : " You will write—you will write every day ! "

" No, my dear, not really every day," the soldier replied in an affectionate tone.

"And why not ? " she asked hastily, in a reproachful voice.

" But if we are marching every day ? "

" Yes !—" replied the girl in a low tone, dropping her head. " But at least," she went on, suddenly taking courage, " at least every day when there is a battle you will write and tell me you are well ? "

He, who at any other time would have smiled at the charming ingenuousness of that question, felt his heart sink with a compassionate tenderness, which was so strong and sudden, that he was overcome by it, and knew that it was necessary to go off at that moment and without another word. He put his arms around her, kissed her, and away he ran. "Oh ! listen," the poor creature shouted in a supplicating tone, running a few steps after him with her arms outstretched ; "one word more." He did not turn ; she stopped, covered her face with her hands, stood motionless in the middle of the road for a moment, then turned back, and fell on her knees before the shrine, weeping and sobbing bitterly, as children do.

The soldier went hurriedly on his way without turning back. When he reached a certain point where the road divided, he stopped. After a moment's hesitation he turned, looked at the shrine, saw her ; she raised her head at that moment, glanced toward him, seemed to see him, rose to her feet ; he disappeared. He had struck that branch of the road which, descending rapidly, led to the city.

He rejoined his regiment at the beginning of May, and then wrote a letter home almost every day, received one as often from his father, mother, and betrothed; all written, however, by the latter's hand, as no one in his family was able to write; the old father knowing only enough arithmetic for his own special use.

He was at the battle of the twenty-fourth of June. Two weeks elapsed after that day before his family received any news of him. Picture their anxiety, heart-beats, and disquietude. But one fine day, as God willed, a letter came, and how much joy it gave them. They opened it with trembling hands. . . . Ah, but it was not written by him; and they grew pale. After reading it, however, they recovered from their first fright, because he wrote that he had received a wound in his hand on the day of the battle; it was a slight wound, of which every trace would have vanished within a few days, and he should have got out of bed but for a slight fever caused by the loss of a little blood. They were to keep up their courage, because it was nothing to cause any anxiety, and excuse his not having written himself, the right hand being the one wounded, and his fingers still paining him; only a trifle, however, almost none at all. Little by little the family became calm. A week from that day they received the first letter written by him; they knew that he had returned to his regiment, and they said nothing more about that slight misfortune, because something worse might have happened to him, and they ought to thank God that things had gone as they had.

Poor people! if things had gone so, they really might have thanked heaven; but they did not know the truth. The poor soldier had been struck by a rifle ball in the leg, at a hundred paces from the enemy; the bullet had broken two bones, the tibia and the fibula; he had been carried to the hospital, and they had amputated the leg a few inches below the knee.

After forty days, they gave him a wooden leg, a pair of crutches, a passport, and, opening the doors of the hospital, said: "Go home, poor fellow, you have done your part."

Before turning homeward, he wrote to his mother to inform her of his departure, and the day and hour of his arrival; having written which he resolved to tell them of his misfortune, but could not bring himself to do so. Numberless times did he write the first words and instantly scratched them out, almost frightened that they should have fallen from his pen. But the letter had not gone before there came to his mind all the possible consequences, in fact the inevitable and terrible sorrow his pious fraud would cause; he was troubled that he had been silent on the subject of his misfortune, was astonished that he had never thought what sadness might follow his reticence in not telling the truth bravely; and going over in imagination all that would happen at home upon his appearance in this state, picturing the despair of his parents at so unexpected and terrible a sight, and thinking of his betrothed and friends, he dashed his hands into his hair in utter despair, and began wept.

But it was too late.

He arrived in the city near his home the day before that when, according to his letter, he ought to have been with his family. He slept at an inn. The following morning betimes, helped by the landlord, he climbed into the cart of a miller which was to pass the hill, placed his crutches by his side, seated himself on two sacks of flour, the miller gave reins to the horse, and they started.

Passing for several miles along the road down in the valley, the cart did not begin to climb the hill until some hours after their departure. During that time, the poor soldier, who had not been able to close his eyes during the night, oppressed by a rapid and troubled succession of thoughts, imageries, and painful presentiments, had sunk into a species of lethargy, induced by the monotony of the road and the slowness of their pace, and only interrupted now and then by the jolting of the cart over the uneven road. But when, on feeling a stronger light in his eyes and a sharper wind on his face, he became aware that the cart had come out from among the trees and begun to ascend, then he waked quickly, saw that hill, that road, those houses, instantly closed his eyes again, turned away his head as if seized by a sudden fright, and threw himself face downward on the sacks with his face in his hands. His heart beat violently; his blood was in a tumult; his brain became stunned as if he had received a great blow on his head. And he remained a long time in that position.

He changed it little by little, first lifting his head, placing his hands on the sacks to raise himself to a sitting posture, then getting up entirely, but always with his back to the hills, and finally turning his head in that direction, but without glancing upward. Shortly thereafter he began to look at the horse; then a little farther along, on the road, to the right and left and ahead: "Ah! There are those blessed houses!" And his heart gave a bound as if he had got there by accident, and the houses had appeared before him involuntarily. They were still very far away, quite indistinct; they hardly looked as large as white specks half hidden among the trees; yet they seemed quite near to him, and he felt as if he should reach them in a few minutes. Then his parents, relatives, and friends would gather around the cart, and he would have to get down, and how should he do it! And he pictured it to himself, and seemed to see all those dear people, who would certainly be gathered in a group at that hour on the street, at the doors of their houses, or in the yards, waiting for him. He seemed to hear the gay voices come faintly to his ear, and among those voices he distinguished one dearer and sweeter than all. His heart-strings tightened, and he wished those houses farther away, so far that he could not see them yet. On the other hand, they were right there, and seemed to be approaching him more rapidly than he did them, so he closed his eyes and dropped his head in order not to see them. Yet this was a worse torture, for in opening his eyes a moment, and raising them, he seemed to have got over a great deal of the road, a hundred times more than he had done in reality. Then he thought of turning his back to the horse, and, moving the stump slowly, he turned. But he could not remain in this position long, for at every instant he felt an irresistible desire to turn his head back, greatly to the discomfort of his entire body. He then assumed his first position again. And, glancing to the right and left of the road, he discovered, at a short distance, a large oak with its trunk split through the middle, and the thick, leafy branches, under which there was a board, upheld by two stones, which served as a seat. He looked at the seat, touched his forehead with one hand, as if just becoming aware of the sudden outbreak of a recollection; his eyes glistened, his cheeks reddened, he clasped his hands violently, and keeping his eyes fixed motionless on the spot, went on raising and dropping his head, as if to say yes to all the recollections which were waking in him, one recalled by the other. That was exactly the spot where he had come one evening with her, despite the admonition of his mother: "Do not go too far away!" And she had not wished to come, as it was really too far from home, and at that hour, late in the evening, alone with him! But, heavens, how he had begged her! the sky was so clear, the air so mild, and the whole country so fragrant, that she had been obliged to yield and come. They were seated there, on that seat; had exchanged few words, but these were tender, rapid, and faltering; he had sought her hand, and she, frightened by the thought of being alone with him whom she loved, had shut her hand and drawn it from him with gentle force, so that he had been obliged to conquer it finger by finger, for as soon as he succeeded in opening the second the first would close, until at last the little resisting hand opened and was his. Absorbed in the thought of that beautiful evening, the poor disabled soldier (by means of an illusion into which our fancy often drives us at the sight of a place to which we are bound by some tender recollection) forgot the time which had passed since that evening and the present day, forgot all that which had happened meanwhile, —the war, the wound, the amputated leg; the thought that within a short time he would see that girl alone filled his mind, quite separated from the other sad ones which usually followed it; the feeling of a great joy filled his soul, intoxicated and oppressed him; moved by an irresistible impulse of his heart he made an effort to rise to his feet without the aid of his arms, and did so so violently that the nerves of his maimed leg, pressed strongly against the wood, were pained and sent a terrible pain shooting up through his body, which drew a cry from his lips and, casting him cruelly back from the dear illusion to the feeling of sad reality, made him fall face downward on the cart, his hands in his hair, murmuring disconsolately and with a sob: "Oh, she will not wish me in this condition! She will no longer wish me in this condition!"

The miller, who was walking beside the cart, turned and asked: "Are you ill?" The soldier replied in the negative, quite abruptly, and said not another word. The poor fellow remained motionless in that position for a long distance, and it was better for him, because had he glanced about the country, at every step some fresh recollection would have been aroused, and with it new pain.

Meanwhile, at home he was being waited for by his relatives and friends, who, informed the previous day of his expected arrival, had gathered joyfully at the paternal home to receive him with love and honor.

At the first gleam of light, his two old parents had risen and dressed themselves with the joyous haste of children who are preparing for a beautiful walk in the country, and had begun wandering around the house with hurried steps, opening doors and rapping hard on the pillows of the sleepers, shouting: "Wake up; out of bed with you, boys!" The latter, wakened so suddenly, opened their eyes and mouths, glanced sleepily around, and made those wry faces which people do who are disturbed in their slumbers, but on being thoroughly roused, and remembering the reason of that sudden shout, they too became gay, mingled their voices with those of their parents, jumped out of bed, dressed quickly, and away they went through the house, road, gardens, to do their usual work with unusual solicitude, smiling at one another, making signs to each other in the distance, and urging all to make haste. Shortly thereafter came the girl, the betrothed, who lived near by ; she arrived on a run, accompanied by two friends, dressed in gala costume, with a bunch of flowers in her hair, and quite red in the face : met the mother, smiled, blushed, threw herself into her arms, and then breaking suddenly away, and hiding her face two or three times from those who wanted to look into it, she too began wandering about the house as if it were her own. Then all together began dusting and arranging the furniture and the little articles pertaining to the house, sticking the broom into the remotest corners, moving beds from the wall, changing mattresses, folding up clothes-horses, shaking sheets and counterpanes out of the windows, dragging from the wardrobes certain brass candlesticks kept in reserve for grand occasions, and tying boughs and branches of wild flowers on the racks, window-gratings, around pictures, and above the doors, so that at the first appearance of the sun the house was as neat, fresh, and fragrant as a garden, and the house-plot smooth and clean as a marble floor, without one tuft of grass remaining, even if any one had looked for an hour. They could not do less for the reception of a soldier who was coming home wounded from the war! Thus said the good old mother to the other women, when they had finished their work, moving from room to room, and showing them with complacency the beautiful order and neatness of every thing.

Then they went out into the front yard. The mother remained behind, called the girl by name, and as the latter came dancing up, she took her by one hand, led her to her room, and pushing her in front of a small glass, said : " Look, you have spoiled your hair." " Heavens ! " exclaimed the girl, making a woful face, "how could it have happened?" "There are twigs hanging from every side," replied the old woman, "and you are running hither and thither like a mad creature, without looking, or bending your head; sit down." The girl sat down, the mother went behind her, loosened her braids, smoothed her hair, and then taking it all in one hand to keep it tight, in order to part it with the other, made her bend her head backward, dropping her hand little by little, and taking her chin between her forefinger and thumb, or touching the dimple in her throat, so that she twisted about with that convulsive laugh peculiar to girls who are being tickled. She did her braids, put in the hair-pins, passed her open hands two or three times over the hair so that it should be smooth and shining, and then placing her hands on her shoulders, and looking her in the face, she gave her a kiss, and moved off, saying: "Let us go." The young girl rose and followed her, keeping her face turned toward the mirror until she entered the neighboring room. Here, allowing the mother to go out, she raised one foot gently from the ground, and using the other as a pivot, wheeled around twice, and suddenly stopped, threw back her head to look with charming curiosity at the skirts puffed out by the wind, which looked like a dress over hoops. Then, she too ran out into the house-yard.

All the others scattered over the place, some on the road, in front of the house, were in continual motion, as if their feet were scorched when they kept them quiet for a moment. And in that continuous wandering about there never were two who met and looked at each other without exchanging a gay word or a smile, because the glance of the one recalled to the other the happiness of all, and revived in him the same feeling. The brother of the fiancée, in passing, either gave her a pinch in the arm in order to draw forth a scream, or, coming quietly up behind her, seized her by the elbows and pressed them together, and that "Get away with you, you wretch!" which was his punishment, accompanied by a menace of a box on the ear (which was never forthcoming), gave him infinite pleasure. Her friends, drew her aside from time to time to whisper all sorts of things in her ear, which were followed by a burst of laughter, a sudden breaking up of the circle, and a general scattering. From time to time the old father, stopping in front of her, said with a serious face: "He is not coming." "Why not? Who told you so?" she asked excitedly, changing color. "Oh! I fancy so," replied the old man, smiling. "Ah!" exclaimed she, heaving a sigh and becoming reassured instantly, "you were joking. He never has failed to keep his word."

Then turning to the mother, who was outside the gate and kept her eyes fixed on the road: "Mamma," she asked, "don't you see any one?"

"I only see a cart in the distance."

The girl began joking again with the old man, without giving herself any anxiety about the matter.

Meanwhile the cart had come within three hundred steps of the house, and in the heart of the soldier a strange change had taken place. He did not seem to have any true or real appreciation of his condition, nor to know where he was going, and the memory of the places he was passing seemed to be fleeing away, so much so that he kept his eye fixed motionless on his home, the wooden windows and terraces of which began to appear quite distinctly, or he let them wander slowly and listlessly over the fields, houses, and kitchen-gardens near the street. He approached his home as he would have done an unknown place. The sensitiveness of his heart was exhausted. Such is our nature, that we submit with entire impassibility and a species of abandonment to the excess of those sufferings which seemed to us at first quite insupportable. And for this reason that poor unfortunate fellow now gave all his attention, with open mouth and eyes quite fixed, to the noise of the cart, as if the presentiment of the sorrows into which he was about to cast his family had entirely disappeared. Now, giving a blow with his hand to the sack, he looked astonished at the white dust which flew about ; now he buckled and unbuckled listlessly the straps stretched between those two sticks fastened to the wooden opening into which the stump of the leg is put (two sticks that hold the leg quite firmly in its support) ; now, seizing a crutch near the end, he went on beating the handle lightly on the end of his foot. . . . But he had been feeling a slight pain at the end of that poor thigh for some time, although he had wrapped it carefully in some old pieces of linen with which his pockets had been filled when he left the hospital ; and so, almost involuntarily, he unbuckled the straps for the last time, stretched out his arm, took off that wretched apparatus, lifted it, and placed it at his side. When the leg was free, the pain decreased.

On the cart went, and he, without giving himself any other thought, passed and repassed his hand over the leg, as if to soothe the little pain that remained, when, on raising his eyes, he suddenly changed color, clasped his hands, gave a cry, and remained as motionless as a statue. He had seen the shrine where they had parted ; he came to himself ; all the memories which had lain dormant for some time had been roused at that point, and his heart, filled suddenly by a crowd of violent emotions, had given a terrible bound. He gazed for a long time at the shrine with pallid face, dilated eyes, and trembling lips; then stretched out his arms in a supplicating way and cried : " Oh, Gigia ! oh, my Gigia ! " and fell face downward on the cart.

At that point a loud shout reached his ear, and sent the blood rushing from head to foot. He raised his head, looked, seized his wooden leg, put the stump into it, grasped the straps with trembling fingers, and tried, but all in vain, to buckle them. Meanwhile the people were coming nearer, with open arms and lips all set for the shout of joy they could not utter. And all this time the poor fellow could do nothing but pull at his leg like a madman. . . . Ah ! here they are quite near ; the mother first, who, stretching out her arms with a divine smile on her face, dropped her eyes, saw, gave a desperate cry which came from the depths of her soul, seized him groaningly around the neck, and stood still. All the others covered their faces with their hands.

After a moment he was on the ground ; the straps had been fastened without his knowing it. Let him go by himself ! they all thought at once. See him walk like that ? Oh, no ! they must carry him. Carry him ? No ! no ! They carry the dying ; no, they would not carry him ! This thought passed like a flash through their minds. During that instant the poor fellow had placed the crutches under his arms, and to shorten that sad spectacle for his dear ones, he started in long strides toward the house. All looked at him—all except the mother and the fiancée ; they hid their faces in each other's bosom.

He entered the house first; instantly thereafter all gathered around him, took away his crutches, made him sit down near the table; he bent over his crossed arms and let his head rest on them. But instantly a trembling hand was laid on his forehead; he raised his head, saw a breast heaving violently before him, knew who it was without raising his eyes, and hid his face on that bosom. All about there was a great silence, for they could not weep yet.

Suddenly a sob broke out. The wounded man detached himself from his mother's arms, gave one glance around: "Is it you!" he shouted, his eyes glistening with tears, as he opened his arms. The young girl threw herself wildly into them. The mother, struck by a sudden idea, turned to those present, made a sign, and they all disappeared in an instant, she following them.

The girl glanced around the room, and not seeing any one, drew a chair hastily up to that of the soldier, sat down, seized one hand with her left, placed her right one on his shoulder, and with her face covered with tears, and her chest heaving, began to talk quickly, brokenly, breathlessly, in an undertone, giving a glance at the door at every breath, to see if any one was coming.

"Listen, Carlo, and believe me; believe me, for I am speaking right from my heart, I love you better than ever; I will marry you more willingly like this—as you are now, than as if you were as you used to be. I would gladly die at this moment if I am not telling you honestly just what I feel, and if you—listen, Carlo, and don't cry so hard—if you do not care for me any longer I would come and beg you, with clasped hands, to take me, to tell you that I cannot live without you;

so, if you were to say no, I should grow ill from sorrow. But, come now, do not be so despairing. If you had not returned from the war, if I (here she pressed her lips together)—if God had sent me the misfortune of losing you, do you think I would ever have taken any one in your place? No! not even if the king had come. Now, listen; if before I loved you with all my soul, now (saying which she covered her face with her apron and began to weep), now I would fall on my knees before you."

And she slipped down from her chair and fell on her knees before him, who, quite beside himself with joy, in broken groans, inarticulate sounds, and more with the animated expression of face which bore the divine imprint of the thought, and with a convulsive movement of the hands, tried to say one word, only one word; but he had not breath enough to do so, and went on trying, trying, until three times came a sonorous, deep, vehement: "Oh, thanks! thanks! thanks!"

Then he seized her by the arm and tried to raise her.

"No! no!" she replied in a resolute tone, in which one could hear all the force of her girlish love; "let me remain like this, I wish to stay so"; and, drying her eyes, she went on excitedly:

"We will always live together. I will not go to work in the fields any more; I will stay all day near you; I will never leave you alone for a moment; I will work in the house beside you, just as we now are.—But what is the matter, Carlo, that you are crying so hard? Tell me—I love you so well—what is the matter?"

"But," replied the poor fellow, in a timid and trembling voice, "and I . . . ?"

"And you? . . . Well, what do you mean by that? Tell me every thing, Carlo."

But he could not go on.

"And I! I! how shall I work?" and he buried his head in his hands, shaking it in a disconsolate manner.

"But, Carlo, why do you talk to me in that way? Am I not yours? Are we not all here? I am very good at sewing, you know that I don't say it to praise myself. And that lady, you know, who lives in the villa near here, has offered me work several times, and I have always refused it; but now—and all the more when she knows how you have returned—I will bring the work home. Will that do? Then I will work beside you, and you will tell me all you have seen: the towns and places you have passed through, and if you always remembered me, what you did every day, if you had comrades from this neighborhood, and what you all talked about."

On she went in this tone, growing more and more fervent, always on her knees before him, keeping one hand on his shoulder, and twisting the buttons, whose numbers had got upside down, into their places with her forefinger and thumb. Her cheeks were suffused with a brilliant rose-color, her eyes glistening with a soft light, and the words dropped so warmly and spontaneously from her lips, and there was so much ingenuousness and grace in her gestures, looks, and smiles, in her whole person, even in that humble position, that the good soldier looked at and listened to her like one in ecstasy. When she had finished speaking, she fixed her eyes upon him as if to ask for a word of comfort, and he gave her one that was better than any she could have desired: "Oh, Gigia!" he said, "you make me forget all my misfortune!"

"And I never will let you remember it!" the sweet girl cried, with enthusiasm. Then he put his arms around her and they both wept heartily.

The mother's idea had been an excellent one.

At that moment they heard the noise of hastening steps and the confused murmur of many voices coming from the courtyard. The young girl sprang to her feet, and moved off several paces from the soldier. Both turned their eyes in the direction from which the noise proceeded. "Where is he? Where is he? shouted a voice outside. And almost at the same moment a young fellow, pale, breathless, and quite voiceless appeared in sight; and hardly had he seen the soldier when, with one spring, he was in his arms. They had been warm friends for many years. The new-comer was decidedly younger, and belonged to the second division of the class of 1845, called that day to arms. And that very evening the young man, having taken leave, not without tears, of his dear ones, was going toward the city, when, in passing the house of his friend, of whose return he was quite ignorant, he had been called by the family, informed of Carlo's misfortune, and driven fairly into his arms. All the family followed him, and the mother, as soon as she had set foot in the neighboring room, and given a searching glance at the faces of the betrothed couple, still tearful, but lighted up by a deep joy, had understood every thing, been quite comforted, and while her son's head lay in his friend's arms, had communicated this comfort, more by signs than words, to the others.

Finally, the disabled soldier detached himself from that long embrace, made a sign to his friend to sit down beside him, and, having passed the back of his hand over his eyes two or three times, gave him to understand that he had something to say. All gathered about him; the mother and fiancée nearest to him.

"Keep up your courage," he began, turning to his friend, who seemed sad and disheartened; "keep up your courage, comrade. Don't allow yourself to get melancholy. I know that seeing me in this state just as you are starting, after taking leave of your family, now that you are going to be a soldier in time of war, is very painful. Don't you think you understand it, poor fellow? A fine result you will say, from such a profession! But, heavens! what good does it do to get disheartened? You have to serve as soldier whether you are willing or not. Well, then, it is much better to take the matter quietly and leave willingly. You will understand that too. And then, then I will tell you frankly, that if I was destined to have such a misfortune as this, either from falling off a cart, or down the stairs here, or have it happen as it has there, I prefer the latter. It is natural. I do not mean to say that I am content in my present condition; but, in the end, we have not got to stay in this world long, and when there are those who are fond of us, that's all we care for; what does the rest matter? Do you suppose my mother, father, and any one else think the less of me?"

And he raised his eyes to them. The old parents, clasping their hands, exclaimed: "Oh, Carlo!" The girl gave him a long look of inexpressible tenderness.

"More than ever," he went on, his tone and face suddenly becoming quite animated. "And after this misfortune all loved me more than ever. If you had been at the hospital with me, you would have seen things which are hardly to be credited, my dear fellow. After I had been there about twenty days, my regiment passed through the city; all the officers of my company came to see me, and some others too, do you understand? They gathered around my bed, and stayed there for a good half hour; and there was the captain, who looked at me and cried, and another officer, a young fellow without any beard. I saw the tears running down his face. Another officer (I had a little fever) put his hand on my forehead, and his neighbor said to him: 'Take it off; you worry him.' They recommended me to the care of the doctors and nurses, and told me to have some one write to my family, but without telling them what had happened, as it would give them too much pain. And every one of them, from the first to the last, shook hands with me before going away, and the youngest, the one who commanded the second squad in which I was, seized a moment when the others were not looking, and kissed me on my forehead, and when he was at the door he turned and gave me one more salute with his hand. Do you understand? One day came the old general with his breast all covered with medals, and followed by many officers; he approached my bed, cap in hand, and all the others uncovered their heads too. He, the general, asked me how I was, and where I had been wounded, and how; and then when I had told him every thing, —I seem to see him now,—he raised his eyes to heaven, then closed his lips, with a sigh, and said: 'Be brave, my boy.' Then he grasped my hand, he who was a general. His hand was very thin, for he was so old. I would have kissed it, but I was afraid to seem lacking in respect; he seemed to me like another father. Ah! one must have been present on such occasions to know what is felt. One forgets all his misfortunes. Then, even beforehand . . . You will see, comrade; it was one thing to talk of it at a distance, another to be there on the spot, right there in the midst of all those bayonets, the superior officers ahead with their swords in the air, and the flags, music, and all those shouts; your heart fires, your head whirls, and the ball has struck you while you are still shouting: 'Forward!'"

At that moment there came from the street the sound of songs and the music of fifes and shepherd's pipes.

"They are my companions who are starting," shouted the conscript, springing to his feet with a sudden outburst of gaiety.

The disabled soldier's face lighted up; he, too, rose to his feet, supported by his mother and fiancée, and begged them to lead him to the door, saw the conscripts who were leaving: "A pleasant journey, boys; a pleasant journey!" he shouted. They turned toward him, caught a glimpse of his leg, understood, and replied in one voice: "Hurrah for the brave soldiers!"

And he thanked them by waving his hands and shaking his head, for between his emotion and weariness he had no voice left.

"Hurrah for the brave soldiers!" the men shouted as they moved off.

The disabled soldier made one more motion with his hand and head, then, passing one arm around the neck of the young girl who was supporting him on the left, he turned to his mother, standing on the other side, and, in a sweet and affectionate tone, exclaimed:

"Oh, mother, can you believe it? . . . I am content!"
Then he let his head sink on her breast.

The eyes of all present filled with tears, and the music died away, little by little, in the distance down the road.

# A MEDAL.

"I AM always obliged to encounter that cloudy face and sullen look!" Thus said a captain to himself, after having reviewed his company. "But why is it? What have I ever done to him?"

He was thinking of a soldier, an Abruzzese, who had glanced doggedly at him during the review.

There are some proud, savage, and reticent natures in which *amour propre* is so intense and gloomy that they suspect scorn in every smile, a snare in every word, and an enemy in every person. They are good and affectionate characters at the bottom, but appear and are judged as proud and unfortunate ones. They are souls that are retiring sheerly from diffidence; they have no spontaneous affections; never are the first to love; but hardly do they perceive that they have inspired a feeling of affection when they return it with as much greater a strength and effusion as they generally display the contrary qualities with others. When, however, they take an aversion and become envious, they are incredibly obstinate and tenacious in their opinions. Yet they do not hate as they fancy they do. One almost always arrives in time with a hearty hand-shake and a pleasant smile, to dissipate their antipathy (which they believed to be unconquerable) and their rancor (that they swore was eternal).

Such was the Abruzzi soldier who looked so sullenly at his captain.

The first day he joined the regiment with the other conscripts, still wearing their peasant and working dress, the captain had looked at him with an expression of curiosity, had said in the ear of the lieutenant: "Look, what a forbidding countenance!" and then smiled. The soldier had noticed the smile. Upon being taken to the store-house, he had put on the first coat that was given him, and the captain, on seeing him, in passing, so bundled up, with a pair of sleeves which came down below his hands, and with great folds that covered his knee, began to laugh, and said: "You look like a rag-bag!" His face grew clouded, and he gave a sharp glance at the captain. Another time, on the parade ground, when the conscripts were being taught their steps, and were called out from the ranks one by one, and made to walk some distance to the sound of a drum, moving their legs slowly and stiffly like marionnettes, he was so embarrassed when his turn came that he could not take two steps without tottering, stumbling, or making such grotesque and laborious motions that all his comrades were obliged to laugh. His captain arrived at this point and scolded him, so that he became worse than ever. Then the captain, seeing that it was time quite lost, went off, saying: "You are the worst soldier in the company."

Near by were some girls with children, who were looking on, and they began to laugh loudly. He blushed to the roots of his hair, and returned to his place, grinding his teeth like a mad dog.

So he became thoroughly convinced that the captain disliked him, reproved him only from a spirit of malice, and ridiculed him with the hateful intention of enraging and so ruining him. But this was not true. The captain was a fine man; he had nothing more against him than he had against the others; he loved his soldiers, was incapable of a blind or unjust feeling of aversion, and perfectly abhorred intentional persecutions or oppression. Only he had not understood the character of this soldier. Seeing him always so gloomy and sullen, he had fancied him to be of a stubborn, ignorant, and sullen nature, and wished to conquer him; but he was tractable by means of persuasion and kindness, and not with menaces and imprisonment—these made him worse.

One day our soldier stood talking with a girl at a street corner; the captain passed, but the soldier did not see him. The former fancied he had pretended not to see him, in order not to give the salute, so he took him to task in the presence of the girl and many other people who were standing about. The soldier was so ashamed, that as soon as the captain had gone, he too disappeared and was not seen again. But his anger against the captain went on increasing, and became absolute hatred, continually tormented him, left him not a moment's peace, and fairly poisoned his life. Nor could he conceal it, no matter how hard he tried. The captain reproved the soldier, and the latter coughed and kicked his feet; the captain turned angrily around, and he, quite ready, lifted his head and looked at the clouds. During a march, if a soldier was attentive when the captain wished to drink and offered him his leather bottle, he sneered, and, drawing that soldier aside, whispered in his ear: "You imbecile!" When the captain reproved him, he pretended not to understand, rolled his eyes like a madman, shook his head, or smiled maliciously with half-closed eyes, twisting his mouth and sticking out his under-lip. Then there were always that surly glance and gloomy face.

One evening, on the parade ground, while they were drilling, a major reproved the captain in a loud voice; the latter glanced hastily around at his soldiers; the soldier laughed. "Canaille!'" he shouted, blind with rage, and coming up to him planted both fists in his face. The soldier paled, turned toward his neighbor and said: "Some day or other (adding a few words in an undertone) . . . or I am not an Abruzzese." Hardly had he entered the barracks and reached his bed when he threw his bowl and knapsack against the wall. The captain appeared unexpectedly, saw him, and shouted: "Sergeant, put him under arrest," and disappeared. The soldier seized the sheet with his teeth and beat his head with his fists. Three or four comrades dashed upon him, seized and held him, saying: "What is the matter with you? What are you doing? Are you going mad?" Then he came to himself, and said in a low voice, with a gloomy smile: "Yes. . . I am going mad, and you will see one of these days what madmen have the courage to do."

There is a part of the valley of the Tronto, the narrowest portion, in which the ridges rise on both sides to a great height, and forming gulleys, precipices, and dark, deep ravines, stretch out their rocky arms almost to the river banks. The valley at that point presents a sad and gloomy appearance. Between the water and these extreme projections, the ground is all gravel, big stones and enormous rocks precipitated down from the top of the ridges; and from the edge upward, there is a labyrinth of caves, precipices, thick bushes, and mounds, without any pathways. Several narrow paths climb up zig-zag, and are lost in the midst of the great rocks and thickets. A few dwellings appear here and there, half hidden among the projections of the rocks; some bits of level and verdant earth, but on every other side there is only the rough, wild face of nature.

It was a rainy, autumn evening. A patrol of a few soldiers, one behind the other, were passing through that portion of the valley, climbing, descending, and winding according to the elevations of ground and the rocks which filled the small pathway worn by the feet of pedestrians during the long series of years.

A soldier preceded the patrol by about forty paces; another followed it at about the same distance. They were walking slowly and silently with lowered heads, their muskets under their arms.

Suddenly, the soldier who was ahead, heard a sound of hurrying steps, saw three heads appear above a rock, three gun-barrels gleaming, and three flashes, felt his fatigue-cap taken off, and heard two balls whistle to the right and left of his head. In an instant three brigands dashed out upon him. He discharged his musket, and one of them gave a cry and fell to the ground: He rushed upon the other, and with a powerful blow from his musket pushed his carbine aside, and dashed his bayonet into his stomach. But the third, who was behind, attacked him before he could turn against him, seized the musket with one hand, and raised a dagger with the other. The soldier abandoned his weapon, grasped the armed hand of the brigand with his left one, clasped his throat with the right arm, squeezed it like a serpent, and bit and lacerated his ear furiously. A horrible shriek broke from the assassin's breast, and a terrible struggle ensued. They fell and rolled on the ground, a false step and death would be the result; in less than a minute a large portion of the ground was covered with deep tracks; the stones, struck by violent kicks, sprang from the terrible arena; the two enemies clasped, unclasped, and grasped each other again with a marvellous rapidity; they beat each other with their fists, thrusts their elbows and knees into each other's stomach and chests, snorting, gasping, and shouting with suppressed rage; their eyes horribly dilated and gleaming; their foaming and bleeding mouths opening and contracting convulsively, as they gnashed their teeth, so that those two faces no longer retained any semblance to humanity. But the soldier still kept tightly clasped in his iron hand his adversary's fist which held the knife. . . . Suddenly the brigand fell like a corpse, beating the ground about him wildly; the soldier got upon him, seized his throat with both hands, shielded himself on the left with his bended knee, and while the prostrate man wounded him in the left arm, the soldier raised his head from the ground by extreme force, and flung it back against a stone with his entire strength; then taking advantage of the stun caused by the blow, he squeezed the wrist of the armed hand with both of his. The aching hand opened, and in an instant the assassin's knife passed into his possession, and he had driven it into the brigand's throat. The icy blade passed through the uvula and broke the bone of the palate, the blood dashed through the opened throat, mixed with a confused rattle, which was his last utterance.

"Bravo! bravo!" shouted the other soldiers as they came

breathlessly up. They gathered around him and overwhelmed him with questions, while he, motionless, gasping, with pallid face and glaring eyes, was gazing now at the prostrate brigand, now at the bloody knife which he still held tightly clasped.

The patrol had been attacked at the same time by a band of brigands, who fled as soon as they had discharged their guns, and the soldiers followed them for some distance.

The wounded soldier was quite well within a few days. The first time that the captain saw him, in passing in front of him at the review, he looked him firmly in the eye and said: "Bravo!" Instantly thereafter his neighbor whispered in his ear: "You say he has something against you? He said bravo!" "Oh, he felt obliged to do so," he replied, shaking his head, smilingly.

Three months after that day the regiment was transferred to Ascoli. A week had passed since their arrival, when the colonel ordered that on the following day the regiment should be in full uniform to assist at a military ceremony in the principal square of the city. They were to decorate a soldier with the medal for military valor.

"So soon?" thought our captain, when he received the colonel's order. He instantly ran to the quartermaster-sergeant's room, and asked anxiously: "Have you heard the order? Have you done every thing?" "Every thing three days ago," replied the quartermaster-sergeant. "Oh, that's all right; let us see. Give me paper, pen, and inkstand; I want to be quite sure about it."

They seated themselves at the table, and the quartermaster-sergeant began tracing on a scrap of paper some streets and houses, talking all the time in a low voice, and taking up the conversation from time to time as if to explain things more clearly.

After a short time they both rose, and the captain, on going away, added : " Third house to the right, second door ? " " Third house to the right, second door." " Are you quite sure ? " The quartermaster-sergeant made a sign as much as to say: " Go right on, you cannot mistake it."

An hour later the captain was on horseback on the road leading from Ascoli to Acquasanta, a small place on the bank of the Tronto, half way, I believe, between Ascoli and Arquata.

He reached Acquasanta at sunset. Before entering, he unbuttoned his coat to hide the number of buttons, and pushed up the visor of his cap. Then he entered. On hearing the sound of the horse's step, some people came to the doors of the first houses, others approached the windows, and the boys gathered in the street. The captain looked uncertainly to the left and right, then moved toward a door where there was a group of women, who drew up timidly against the wall at his appearance, and looked at him in astonishment.

"Who will give me a glass of water, my good women ? " said the captain, reining in his horse, and affecting a careless air.

" I," replied one of the women quickly. And she disappeared. " It is she," thought the captain ; " it can be no one else."

The woman returned a moment later with a glass of water, and handed it to the captain. The latter looked at her attentively, and began to drink it in slow sips. The woman, meanwhile glanced at him from head to foot, twisted her head from side to side, got on tiptoe in order to discover the number of his regiment, twisted her hands, swayed backward and forward, was not quiet one moment, and by her fixed and excited look, and the rapid movements of her mouth, she showed a timid and anxious content, an irrepressible desire, which she did not know how to gratify. The captain watched her closely.

"Is there no one among you women who has a soldier son?" he asked, with apparent indifference, as he handed back the glass.

"I have," replied the woman who had brought him the water. "I have one!" and she made a sign with her thumb, and stopped to wait for his reply, as immovable as a statue.

"In what regiment?"

The woman told the regiment, and added hastily: "Where is this regiment, Mr. Colonel? Do you chance to know my son? Have you seen him anywhere?"

"I? Oh, no—but how is it that you do not know where he is?"

"Well!" exclaimed the woman, looking very serious, crossing and then letting her hands fall idly, "it is two years since I have seen him. A month ago he was not very far from here; he was fighting the brigands, poor fellow, and he wrote me; but since then I have heard nothing, and he has never sent me another letter. Oh, he may have sent one, but it has not arrived. Those gentlemen who ought to forward the letters, who knows what they have done with them! (And she grew more and more excited, and uttered each word with an increasing expression of sorrow and scorn.) The letters of poor people are known to those gentlemen by the writing, and they throw them into a corner. I know how things go. Those poor fellows write, and their families receive nothing. But the officers who are in command ought to look after these affairs ; you must excuse me, Mr. Colonel, I don't say it of you ; but it does n't seem just to me. We poor women pass entire months without knowing any thing of our sons, and we are always anxious, and my friends here can tell you so, for they see me every day and know what a life I have been leading for some time,—my heart-aches, fears, and the pain I have suffered on account of that poor boy. There are moments in which I really cannot bear it any longer. Oh, no, no, let me finish, Mr. Colonel, it is not just!" Saying which she covered her face with her apron, and began to weep.

All the other women assented by word and gesture ; the captain was silent.

"Look here, my good woman!" he then said suddenly. The woman uncovered her tear-stained face, and glanced at him.

"Look!" repeated the captain, taking off his cap and handing it to her. She took it with a stupid expression of face, looked at it top and bottom, glanced around at her friends as if to question them, then stared fixedly at the captain, as if to show him that she had not understood.

The captain laughed.

"Is there nothing which interests you in this cap?"

The woman began examining it again, and uttered a cry : "Ah! it is the number of the regiment—my son's regiment !" and seizing the cap with both hands she kissed and rekissed it impetuously, and in a moment overwhelmed the captain with so many questions, prayers, demonstrations of gratitude, joy, and affection, that he was overcome, and was obliged to wait, in order to reply one word, until this outburst had quite exhausted her strength and choked her voice.

"To-morrow you will see your son," he then said. "He is at Ascoli, and is expecting you."

The good woman sprang forward to kiss his hand; he drew it back. . . . Half an hour later he started for the city. He had talked for a long time with that poor woman, but had said nothing of the gold medal.

Scarcely had he reached Ascoli and entered his house when he called the orderly, and uttering each syllable distinctly, and accenting each word with his hand, he talked for some time, while the other listened with wide-stretched eyes and mouth. "Have you understood?" he said at last. "Yes, sir." "You will do every thing carefully?" "Rest assured of that." "I depend upon you." And he went out. The orderly followed him with his eyes as far as the door, stood meditating for a moment, then sticking his hand into a boot and seizing the brush with the other he began blacking it with all his might, murmuring as he did so: "You are a good man; you deserve a premium; to-morrow morning your boots shall shine more brightly than any in the regiment."

The following morning, about eight o'clock, the orderly, standing at the corner of a street which opened on the principal square of the city, saw an old peasant woman, in gala dress, with two great hoops in her ears, a beautiful string of coral around her neck, and her skirt speckled with all the colors of the rainbow, coming slowly forward. As she approached she glanced around her with a mingled expression of curiosity, astonishment, and gaiety. He watched her carefully, and then approached her.

"My good woman!"

"Oh, are you the soldier the captain told me about?"

"Yes, exactly."

"Oh, thank you! thank you! And my son? Is n't he here? Where is he? Why did n't he come to meet me? Tell me instantly where he is, my good fellow. Take me right to him."

"Ah! one moment; you must have a little patience; you cannot see him immediately. You must wait about half an hour. You must remain here and see a certain parade that the regiment is going through They are to give a medal for military valor to one of my comrades; it is only an affair of a few moments, and you must be patient."

"A half hour more! Oh, heavens! how can I wait for a half hour?"

"I understand, my good woman; a half hour will seem like half a century to you; but there is nothing else to be done, so you must wait. We will chat a little, and the time will pass quickly."

"Oh, heavens! a half hour! But tell me, tell me, are the soldiers to come into this square?"

"Yes, right into this square from that side—look!"

"But then I shall see him instantly, and I can go and speak to him."

"No, you cannot, my dear woman."

"But it is two years since I have seen him."

"I know; but no one can speak to a soldier when he is in line; you ought to know that too; the regulations are clear enough; the colonel commands here, my good woman; the mothers have nothing to do with the matter; and even if the colonel's mother should come, she, too, would have to be patient and stand on one side and wait. You must understand that women have not made the regulations."

"I do understand; but ·. . ."

At that moment they heard the distant sound of drums, and all the people who were in the square turned in that direction. "Here is the regiment," said the soldier. The old woman felt her heart throbbing wildly, stood quite perplexed for a moment, and then suddenly tried to dash toward the regiment. "Wait!" shouted the soldier, seizing her by the arm, and making a motion with his hand to keep her quiet. "Wait; do me that favor; if he sees you we shall get into trouble. Do you wish to have him put in prison? It does n't take much to do so. If he should turn his head to the left when he ought to turn it to the right."

"That's true!" murmured the woman, and she controlled herself.

"You will only have to wait a quarter of an hour; that's not much, when you have waited two years."

The woman raised her eyes to heaven, sighed, and then fixed them motionless on the opening of the street where the regiment was to appear.

The roll of the drums approaches; the crowd divides into two wings; here are the sappers, the drummers, the band, the colonel on horseback.

"And the soldiers?" asked the old woman anxiously.

"One moment. There are only about ten paces between the colonel and the soldiers. Here they are!"

The woman dashed forward again, and once more the soldier held her back. "Oh, for heaven's sake do be sensible! Do you want him to be thrust into prison at any cost?"

The regiment is drawn up in line.

"I have seen him! I have seen him!" shouted the old woman, clapping her hands, "Look at him!"

"Where?" The woman pointed.

"No; that's not he. You are mistaken, I assure you. You could not recognize him from here; we are too far away."

"Then that other one."

"Which one?" The woman pointed again.

"But no, I tell you, that is n't he; it is impossible for you to see him; he is in the second line."

"In the second line?"

"Yes."

"What do you mean by the second line?"

"Behind the others."

"Oh, holy patience!" exclaimed the woman, as she passed her hand over her brow and sighed, "what are they doing now?"

"Don't you see? The colonel has placed himself in front of the regiment in order to make a speech. Before giving the medal to the soldier they generally make a speech, in which they relate the circumstance, and tell the other soldiers to follow the example of their companion, who is a brave soldier, has done his duty, and has done honor to his regiment, and so forth."

"I don't hear any thing. What is he saying?"

"This is the story: The soldier who is to receive the medal was one day attacked by three brigands, all of whom fired on him at once. He was not hit, and did not get frightened; he discharged his musket at one of the assassins, and killed him; then planted his bayonet in the stomach of the other; and took away the knife from the third and cut his throat."

"Oh, my God!"

"Wasn't that a fine deed?"

"Have they given him the medal?"

"They are doing so now."

"He will be happy, poor young fellow!"

"I should think so; his comrades are so fond of him; his superiors treat him like a son; all respect and esteem him; and he deserves it, he really deserves it; he is one of the best soldiers in the regiment; there are few like him, I can tell you."

"But where is this soldier?"

"In a moment the colonel will call him out of the line."

The colonel ceased speaking.

"Look! look!" the orderly suddenly exclaimed, turning the woman away from the regiment and pointing to the windows in front. "Look how many people are at the windows! In a moment they will all clap their hands."

Meanwhile the soldier had stepped out of the line, come to the colonel's side, facing the regiment, so that the woman in turning toward the soldiers, could not see his face.

"Is that the soldier?"

"Yes."

"What are they doing now?"

"Don't you see? The colonel is putting the medal on his breast."

"Oh, holy Virgin! how my heart beats for him. How happy he must be, poor fellow! Now what are they doing?"

"Now the regiment is going to present arms."

"Really?" asked the woman in astonishment.

"Certainly."

"Oh, what an honor!" exclaimed the good old woman, clasping her hands and remaining motionless in that position, her eyes gleaming with a very beautiful smile, a mixture of content, marvel, and affection.

The colonel turned toward the regiment, and in a loud, senorous, vibratory voice, which echoed through the square, shouted :

"Present arms!"

The woman felt a shiver run from head to foot, drew close to the soldier and seized him as if she were afraid.

At the colonel's shout the four majors of the regiment each turned to his battalion and repeated the command in a powerful voice.

Almost instantaneously, as if moved by a single arm, did the twelve hundred muskets rise, gleaming from the ground, and resound when hit by the twelve hundred hands. All faces were motionless, and all eyes were fixed on the soldier's face. The officers saluted with their swords. The crowd broke out in a burst of applause, and the band began to play.

"But who is this soldier?" asked the poor mother, astonished, moved, and fascinated by that stupendous spectacle.

The orderly turned, looked at her, opened his mouth, uttered some inarticulate sound, glanced at the soldier, and turned again to the woman.

The band continued playing, the regiment was still motionless.

"It is your son!" the orderly shouted.

The old woman uttered a cry, stood immovable for a moment, with wide-stretched eyes and mouth, dashed her hands into her white hair, smiled, groaned, and sobbed; that applause and that music resounded in the depths of her heart like a harmony from paradise; the thousand gleaming muskets all grew confused into a single torrent of light, her mind became suddenly confused, her eyes veiled, she tottered . . . and was upheld.

When she came to herself, the regiment had disappeared; her son was clinging to her neck, and the two hearts were so closely pressed against each other that there was hardly place for the silver medal between them. They remained in this position for some time.

"But how," were the first words of the son, as soon as he was released from that embrace, "how did you know that I was here? Who told you? How did you happen to get here on this day, and just at this hour?"

The woman told him breathlessly, that the previous day an officer on horseback had arrived in her town, stopped at her door, told her where her son was, offered her money so that she could come to the city in a carriage, had given her the money, and she had come, and found the soldier who was waiting, at the officer's orders, for her.

"Where is the soldier?" asked her son. They both looked around; the orderly had disappeared.

"Now I understand, look!" said the woman. "Now I understand why the officer wished me to come this morning; he wanted me to see . . ."

She looked at her son and embraced him.

"He wished me to see every thing, and so told me nothing, in order to give me a surprise; and the soldier was in the plot. What a good man! But how did he learn where I live? And what interest could he have in giving me this pleasure, when he did not even know me! Tell me, my son!"

The son was thinking busily.

"But where is the officer! this man? I want to see him; I want to kiss his clothes. I owe him my life. I want to go to him, my son. Take me to him."

"Immediately!" exclaimed the soldier, coming back from the thoughts in which he had been absorbed.

He took his mother by the hand, and they hastily crossed the square, entered the street where the barracks were, stopped twenty paces from the door, at which almost all the officers were gathered while waiting for the report, and the old woman began to seek eagerly with her eyes, the soldier helping her by motions and words; he, too, searching from instinct, without knowing whom he wished to find.

"Who is he? Have you seen him? Point him out!"

"I have not found him yet."

"Look! Look!"

"That one there; that one leaning against the wall. . . . No, no, I am mistaken; it is n't that one. That other,—the one who is lighting a cigar. Wait till he turns. Wait—no, it is n't he."

"But who is it, then?"

"Ah! there he is! This time I am sure. It is the one who has placed his hand on the shoulder of the man standing near him."

"What!"

"Yes, it is he."

"Mother!"

"I tell you I am sure of it."

"Really? Are you not mistaken? Are you really sure?" shouted the soldier, seizing his mother's hand.

"As sure as I am of the light of day."

The soldier fastened his eyes on the captain, and stood looking at him motionless.

Meanwhile, the mother, whose heart and head were with her son, rather than with the captain, pulled him by his clothes, and taking the medal between her first finger and thumb, drew it closer to her face, looked attentively at it, and said smilingly to the soldier, who still stood motionless looking at the captain:

"I would wager that, after your mother, this is the dearest thing in the world to you." And she raised the medal the entire length of the ribbon.

"No," replied her son, without turning.

"No! Well, what is the dearest thing in this world after your mother?" asked the woman with an affectionate smile.

The soldier raised his arm, and pointing to the captain replied:

"That man there!"

---

# AN ORIGINAL ORDERLY.

OF all the original beings under the vault of heaven—and I can boast I have known many—there certainly is none who can compare with this one.

He was from Sardinia, a peasant of twenty, ignorant of the alphabet, and a soldier in the infantry.

The first time he appeared before me, at Florence, in the office of a military journal, he inspired me with sympathy. His appearance, however, and several of his replies, showed me instantly that he was indeed an original. Seen in front, he was himself; seen in profile, he was quite another. One would have said that his features changed in turning. From the front view there was nothing to say; the face was like many others; but his profile made one laugh. The point of the chin and the end of the nose tried to touch and did not succeed, impeded by two enormous lips that were always open, and which allowed one to see two rows of teeth scattered like a platoon of national guards. The eyes resembled pin-heads, so small were they, and they almost disappeared between the wrinkles when he laughed. The eyebrows formed two circumflex accents, and the forehead was only high enough to separate the hair from the eyes. A friend said to me that he seemed like a man made for a joke. He had, however, a face that expressed intelligence and goodness; but an intelligence, if one may so express himself, which was partial only, and a goodness *sui generis*. He spoke, in a sharp, hoarse voice, an Italian for which he could have demanded with perfect right the patent of invention.

"How does Florence please you?" I asked, because he had only arrived in town the day before.

"It 's not bad," he replied.

For a person who had only seen Cagliari and some small cities in Northern Italy, the reply seemed a trifle severe to me.

"Do you like Florence or Bergamo better?"

"I only arrived yesterday, and cannot judge yet."

When he went away I said: "Adieu"; and he replied: "Adieu."

The following day he entered my service. During the first few days I was several times on the point of losing my patience and sending him back to his regiment. Had he contented himself with understanding nothing, *transeat;* but the trouble was that his difficulty in understanding Italian, and the novelty of every thing, made him half comprehend things and do every thing wrong. If I should say that he took my razors to be ground at Lemonnier's and my manuscripts to be printed at the knife-grinder's; that he carried a French novel to the shoemaker and a pair of boots to a lady's house, no one would believe me; because, in order to credit it, it would be necessary to have seen to what a point (beside undestanding badly) he carried affairs, the mere misunderstanding not sufficing to account for such huge blunders. But I cannot refrain from citing some of the most marvellous of his exploits.

At eleven in the morning I sent him to buy ham for breakfast, and it was the hour at which the *Corriere Italiano* was cried through the streets. One morning, knowing that there was some news I wished to see in the paper, I said to him: "Quick, now—ham and the *Corriere Italiano.*" He never could seize two ideas at a time. He went out and returned a moment later with the ham wrapped up in the *Corriere.*

One morning I was turning over in his presence and that of a friend, a beautiful military map that had been lent me from the library, and I said: "The trouble is, you understand, that I cannot see all these maps at a glance, and am obliged to look at them one by one. To get a clear idea of the battle I should like to see them all nailed on to the wall in a row, so that they would form one picture." That evening when I entered the house—I shudder to think of it—every map in the collection was nailed to the wall, and to make matters worse, the following morning I was obliged to see him appear with the modest, smiling face of a man who is expecting a compliment.

Another morning I sent him to buy two eggs to cook in spirits. While he was out, a friend came to talk about a very important affair with me. That unfortunate wretch returned. I said: "Wait!" He seated himself in a corner, and I continued to talk with my friend. After a moment I saw the soldier turn red, white, and green, and seem to be on thorns about something, so that he hardly knew where to hide his face. I dropped my eyes and saw a leg of the chair slightly streaked with gold color, which I had never seen. I approached; it was the yolk of an egg. The wretch had put the eggs in the back pockets of his jacket, and on entering the house had seated himself without remembering that my breakfast was under him.

These, however, are roses in comparison to what I was obliged to see before having trained him to put my room in order, I do not say, as I wished it, but in a manner that would indistinctly reveal at least the rational being. For him the highest art in putting things in order consisted in arranging them in architectural style one above the other ; and his greatest ambition was to construct the tallest edifice possible. During the first few days my books formed a semicircle of towers which tottered at the slightest breath ; the wash-bowl, turned upside down, upheld a bold pyramid of little dishes and vases, on the top of which my shaving-brush rose proudly ; old and new high hats reared themselves in the form of a triumphal column to a dizzy height. So that often in the dead of night there occurred noisy overturns and tremendous scatterings of my property, which were only restrained by the walls of the room from going on no one knows where. In order to make him comprehend that the tooth-brush did not belong to the family of those intended for the head, that the jar of pomade was quite different from that of the extract of beef, and that the commode was not designed as a receptacle of freshly ironed shirts, required the eloquence of a Cicero and the patience of a Job.

Whether he were grateful for my kindness to him, or felt the slighest affection for me, I have never been able to learn. Once only did he display a certain solicitude about my person, and that in a very strange manner. I was in bed, having been ill for fifteen days, and growing neither better nor worse. One evening he stopped on the stairs my physician, who was a very grave man, and asked him brusquely : " Well, now, are you going to cure him, or are you not ? " The doctor was furious, and gave him a regular wigging. "It is only that the thing has been going on rather long already," he mumbled in reply.

At other times he had tricks at which I laughed instead of reproving him for them, as I ought to have done. One morning he waked me by whispering in my ear in a curious tone of voice: "Lieutenant, he who sleeps catches no fish."

One day he entered the house just as an illustrious person was leaving it, and heard me say to the friend who was with me, that that personage was a "*very conspicuous personality.*" A fortnight later, while I was talking with several friends, he appeared at the door of my room and announced a visitor. "Who is it?" I asked. "It is (he did not remember the name) *that very conspicuous personality,*" he replied. All burst out laughing; the gentleman in question heard; I explained matters, and he joined heartily in our merriment.

It would be difficult to give an idea of the language this curious subject spoke: it was a mixture of Sardinian, Lombardian, and Italian, all chopped phrases and abbreviated words, an infinite number of verbs thrown here and there or left in the air, so that they produced the effect of a speech by a person in delirium. One day a friend came to see me at the dinner-hour, and on entering the house asked: "At what point of his dinner is your master?" "*He is trembling,*" replied the soldier. My friend stood open-mouthed with astonishment. That *trembling* meant *terminating* (finishing).

In five or six months, in attending the regimental schools, he had learned to read and write with difficulty. It was my misfortune. While I was away from home, he practised his penmanship on my table, and used to write one or two hundred times the very same word, generally a word that he had heard me read and which had made an impression upon him. One morning, for instance, he was struck by the name *Vercingetorige*. That evening, on entering the house, I found *Vercingetorige* written on the margins of the newspapers, on the backs of my proofs, on the bindings of the books, on the envelopes of letters, on the paper in the waste-basket,—every where that he found space enough for the fourteen letters so dear to his heart. Another time the word ostrogoth appealed to him, and the day after my house was invaded by ostrogoths. One day the word rhinoceros fascinated him, and the following morning my house was filled with rhinoceroses. I gained, however, on another side, and it was in being able to abandon the use of crosses made with various colored pencils on the letters which he had to carry to certain persons, because it was useless to try and make him remember names, instead of which he would say: "This letter is going to the blue lady (demi-monde), this to the black journalist (who was red), and this to the yellow employés (who was *al verde*, meaning short of funds).

But while speaking of his writing, I discovered something more curious than any thing I have yet cited. He had purchased a copy-book, in which he made extracts from all the books that came into his hand, the dedication of authors to their parents, always taking care to substitute for the latter the name of his father, mother, or brother, to whom he fancied he was thus giving a splendid token of his affection and gratitude. One day I opened this book and read, among others, the following dedications: *Pietro Tranci* (his father, a peasant), *Born in poverty, Was enabled with study and perseverance to*

*Acquire a high position among servantes, and Succor parents and brothers, and Worthily educate his children. To the memory of his excellent father is This book dedicated by The author Antonio Tranci,* instead of Michael Lessona. On another page: *To Pietro Tranci my Father Who in announcing to the Subalpine Parliament The disaster of Novara Fell fainting to the floor, And died within a few days I Consecrate this Poem,* etc. Farther down: *At Cagliari* (instead of Trent) *Not yet represented in the Italian Parliament,* etc., *Antonio Franci,* instead of Giovanni Prati, etc

That which most surprised me in him (for he had seen nothing) was an absolute lack of the sentiment of surprise at any thing, no matter how extraordinary, which he might see. He witnessed, while in Florence, the fêtes attendant upon the marriage of Prince Humbert; saw the opera and ball at the Pergola (he had never seen a theatre); saw the carnival fêtes and the fancy illumination of the Viale dei Colli; saw, in fact, a hundred new things which ought to have astonished, amused, and made him talk, but there was nothing of the kind. His admiration never went beyond his usual formula: "It is not bad." Santa Maria del Fiore. . . . it is not bad; Giotto's Tower. . . . not bad; the Pitti Palace. . . . not bad. I firmly believe that if the good Lord himself should have asked him *in propria persona* what he thought of the Creation, he would have replied that it was n't bad.

From the first to the last day that he remained with me, he was always in the same humor, half serious, half gay; he was always docile, always dazed, always punctual in misunderstanding things, and ever immersed in a beatific apathy, and ever extravagant in a certain way. The day upon which he received his dismissal, he scribbled away, for I know not how many hours, in his copy-book with his customary tranquillity. Before leaving, he came to say good-by to me. The scene of parting was any thing but tender. I asked him if he were sorry to leave Florence, to which he replied: "Why not?" I then asked if he were glad to return home, to which question he responded with a grimace that I did not understand.

"If you ever need any thing," I said at the last moment, "pray write, and I shall be glad to hear from you." "Thank you very much!" he answered. And so he left the house, after having passed two years with me, without giving the slightest sign of regret or joy.

I looked at him as he went down stairs.

Suddenly he turned.

"Now we will see whether his heart has opened," I thought, "and he is coming back to take leave of me in another way."

"Lieutenant," he said, "your shaving-brush I put in the drawer of the big table."

And he disappeared.

## AT TWENTY.

Don't let any one talk to me of the gay life of students and artists; for officers who have just been promoted and are passing through the first few months of regiment life are really the jolly good-fellows after all. A young man of twenty can not be placed in a position more favorable to gaiety and escapades in general. That leap from the college to liberty, from the dagger to the sword, from the refectory to the restaurant; the first delights of command, the new outfit, the ordinance, the new friends, the benign superiors, . . . in way of experiment, and that vague idea of dying some fine day in the midst of a grain field, struck in the forehead by a ball which leaves us not even the time to cry: *Non dolet!* are things which keep us in a state of continuous intoxication, like newly-married people. This kind of officer's honeymoon lasts only a short time, perhaps less than the other one; but it is quite as delightful. How many colonels covered with crosses and laden with money would give their standing in the "Annual" to live over again the twelve months of that enchanting carnival!

Oh, cloudless days and peaceful nights passed in laughing and joking—ah, continue!

As healthful as roaches, strong as oxen, thoughtless as madmen, audacious as adventurers, always in mischief, always hungry, always happy, to see us one would have thought that we were sure of being generals of the army at thirty. That was a gay time! The most cordial laugh of the captains and majors was like the simper of a hypochondriac, a consumptive cough in comparison with our explosions of hilarity, which threw us across the chairs, and made the whole house tremble. We were seven, all belonging to the same brigade, in one of the most beautiful cities of Sicily, and just from the great military manufactory of Modena. Three had come together from Turin on a journey full of incidents. Suffice it to say that we had started from home with a certain sum of money for our current expenses, in the certainty of going direct from Genoa to Sicily, and were obliged to stop at Naples, because the steamer could not leave on account of the cholera, added to which was the disagreeable necessity of being forced to live at our own expense during the quarantine at Palermo, where we passed ten interminable days in the *Bella Partenope*, living on simple macaroni and broth, which we always devoured at an eating-house called the *Villa di Torino* at the end of a little private room, reserved for people in embarrassment, and those under the surveillance of the police. But scarcely had we reached the regiment before our charming existence began. We seven new-comers met on the second day, and one of the number was seized by a brilliant idea. He proposed that we should all live together and have a common mess, and the proposal was accepted. We rented a regular rat's nest, comprising seven rooms and a kitchen. We got an orderly as cook, and each one settled himself in his den, hung up the orders for the day in the dining-room, and off we started with our house-keeping.

It is quite impossible to give any idea of all that was done about the house. It seemed like a hotel, a barracks, and an insane asylum. Fancy seven officers of twenty, seven orderlies of twenty-two,—two Piedmontese, one Lombardian, one Tuscan, and three Neapolitans; fourteen persons in seven rooms as large as the shell of a chestnut, all in motion, from morning until night, like so many lost souls. One went to "mount guard," another returned from picket duty, three came in from the drill, two went out on provision duty, one snored until ten o'clock in the morning, another rose at three in the night, and another returned home at daybreak after the guard. The orderlies arrived to carry dinner to the absent officers, the sappers to bring the orders for the day, the ambulant vegetable-venders to thrust in their wares at the door, the fruit-sellers to toss the oranges in at the windows, the guitarists to sing under the balcony, and so on *ad infinitum*. On one side the windows were scarcely two metres above the street, so that when any one was in haste he simply went out through the window. The house door was always open; the dogs walked in and wandered around at their pleasure. There was not one moment of quiet. The seven soldiers amused themselves by beating their masters' cloaks all at the same time, and made such a noise that people gathered in the street. From the street one could hear all the sounds in the house, even to our conversation carried on in a low voice. One of the seven, to make matters worse, hired a piano, and two more were seized by the mania for fencing with canes. Besides which the house was so wretchedly resonant, that when any one used his handkerchief all the rooms echoed the sound, and from every bed there burst a malediction. Then the rain fell in the dining-room. Yet, despite these discomforts, and the pitiful poverty in the way of furniture and waving curtains and hangings, we all enjoyed it immensely.

The mess, too, went on charmingly, although the cook, as we discovered two months later, was the son of an old apothecary. One of us had assumed the direction of the household and kitchen. Poor caterer! The first day (I shall always remember it) was a sorrowful one for him. His name was Maglietti, and he was a Piedmontese, a capital fellow, sober, orderly, a good house-keeper, economical without being mean. On assuming the direction of affairs he had made his calculations, and had said to us, rubbing his hands as he did so: "Leave matters to me. We will live finely, and spend little or nothing." But he had made his calculations in accordance with his own appetite, not ours. The first time we went to table, after a march, there was such a total destruction of the viands that he was petrified with astonishment. When every thing seemed to have been finished, one of us collected all the leaves of the radishes to be found in the kitchen, made a salad, on which all began to munch, after which we finished a kilo and a half of bread. Poor Maglietti was in despair, almost ready to weep; he rushed into the kitchen, and seizing a handful of uncooked vermicelli, threw it on to the table, saying as he did so: "Take it, and eat till you burst! I refuse to manage affairs any longer. I thought I was dealing with officers, and not with wolves!" Then we burst out into roars of laughter, and it took all our tact to pacify him and make him continue in his office.

However, after this "incident" all went on marvellously. The conversations at table were a joke for the passers-by down in the street. With that delightful freedom and vocal power peculiar to young men of twenty, we discussed every evening a hundred different subjects, from the most difficult ballistic problems to the immortality of the soul; from the regulation of discipline to the music of the future, to bursts of eloquence, to cavils like rascally advocates, to shouts, to cannonades, to explosions of mortars; so that it seemed as if we were in the projectile-car of Jules Verne when Michael Ardan left the oxygen retort open. In this case it was the light wine of Sicily which was working. From time to time two of the party would give each other too hard a blow, and these were ready to fight, to-morrow, this evening, immediately, right there in the room, between one course and another, and would rise to go in search of their swords; but then, after being begged to desist, they would consent to finish their dinner, and by the time the cheese was put on the table they were reconciled. There were some small duels, too, out of the house, just to keep the hand in, and a little crossing of swords now and then; but every difficulty was adjusted at table in the midst of the usual uproar. Little by little, all learned to take jokes manfully without getting enraged; but there was one exception, unfortunately, a man by the name of Cerraghi, a great, big Lombardian, a good sort of devil, but rather fiery. But he was really all the more delightful for this reason. His forte was history, especially modern European history; he read nothing else, and cared to talk on no other subject. He remembered facts, names, and dates in a marvellous manner, and got into a passion when any one said any thing out of the way, although he took a solemn oath every day, with a thump of the fist on the table, that he would allow us to say what we chose without opening his mouth. So of course we amused ourselves by provoking him without letting him see our purpose.

"Have you seen," one man would ask of his opposite neighbor, "at such and such a lithographer's, that magnificent drawing representing Philip II at the battle of Pavia?"

Poor Cerraghi sprang up on his chair, but kept quiet.

"Friends," continued number two, "you really must go to see it. It is a stupendous piece of work. There is really the color of the locality, and the epoch in it. One really breathes the air of the 14th century like . . ."

"Bravo! bravo!" interrupted another, "the battle of Pavia in the 14th century! Well, you have studied history well. You are confounding it with the battle of Legnano."

At this point, poor Cerraghi, the veins of whose throat were almost ready to burst, could no longer contain himself, and he broke out into a shout:

"You asses! you asses! you asses!"

Then, of course, there was a general outburst of laughter which made the window-panes rattle. Another delightful type was Boccetti, a handsome, elegant fellow, a trifle vain, but very good-hearted, who tugged at his coat-sleeves from morning until night in order to display his cuffs, especially when he was at table. So we, for a joke, took to imitating him, vieing with each other as to who could show the most linen, so much so, in fact, that sometimes we stopped eating in order to raise our arms in the air, with our sleeves pushed back to the elbow, like bell-ringers; and, finally, things arrived at such a pitch, that in order to avoid fatigue we calmly took off our cuffs on sitting down at table, and placed them beside our plates, so that every one could admire them at his leisure. Boccetti had a mania for passing as a great *conqueror*, enveloping his *conquests* in a profound mystery; and he had good taste and aimed high—at coats of arms. A month after we were established there were two or three countesses and three or four marchionesses of whom we could not talk at table without a lack of delicacy toward him. And the rascal probably did not know them by sight. Every day a new one was forthcoming.

"Did you see such and such a countess at the theatre last evening?" one of us would ask of his neighbor.

"Yes, indeed! A beautiful little woman, with that charming little rose-colored bodice. I would give the half of my blood to kiss the point . . ."

"I beseech you," interrupted Boccetti, becoming suddenly quite serious, "let us change the topic."

"Come now, is the veto on this one too?"

"I beg you to desist, out of regard for me."

"Well, then, let's change the subject." But there were quiet laughs which were worth a hundred loud ones. That idiot of a Boccetti used to rub his back against the wall at the house-door before coming in, in order to make us believe that he had whitened himself in squeezing some lady of high degree on the staircase of a palace, where she had gone to call upon a friend; and while he was dining, he would jump up from table and rush to the window at the sound of a carriage—only to expectorate, we declared,—and then return to his place with a smile full of condescension, as he stroked his moustache.

His neighbor at table had another passion—that of playing the *Grand Seigneur*. He was born for this rôle, and it fired all his blood. He was empty as air, and not being able to squander in any other way, he did what he could. He lighted his cigar with four matches at a time, the kind which cost four sous a box and are as large as tapers; he would allow his candle to burn all night; gave ten sous as *pour-boire* for a glass of beer; and threw two francs out of the window, with the gesture of an annoyed prince, in order to stop a violin-player who made him nervous. Dear Cavagnetti! He squandered half of his pay in these "expenses for representation." And he said so quite ingenuously: "You understand; one must maintain a certain amount of dignity." And to maintain his own dignity he played like a madman at cards, billiards, chess, dominoes, *mora*, lotta, with any one who came along, at any hour, and upon every occasion, until he had not a copper left; then he would light his cigar with an entire box, and on returning home say quite seriously that he intended to hang himself with his sash, which really meant: "Lend me twenty francs." And he had a curious fancy (developed one hardly knows how) that made us laugh most heartily. He had seized upon a word, which he continually repeated, quite involuntarily, giving a new signification to it each day; the word was cyclop. In speaking of the colonel he would say: "The cyclop was in bad humor this morning." He would call the orderly: "Ho, there, cyclop!". A fourth bottle appeared on the table: "Oh, a fourth cyclop!" and always quite seriously. We asked him the meaning of the word. "How do I know?" he would reply; "it comes quite naturally to me. I like it. Every one has his own particular taste." And he would puff his cigar—*the cyclop*—with intense enjoyment.

After dinner our pianist generally performed, and we had a little ball, each one imitating the mode of dancing of his own—how shall I say it? a Frenchman might say *inclination* (it is strange, but the opposite word would be more gallant). But that pianist was so extraordinary that we stopped as soon as he began. Never in the world had the passion for music been planted in such a disharmonious brain. To hear him play, it seemed as if he were jumping all equipped, and with his baggage to boot, upon the key-board. Yet, despite all this, he was possessed with the idea of composition; he degraded counterpoint, searched for a libretto, and among his other fixed fancies, was the desire to set to music the *Orlando Furioso*, upon which he said he had been working for three years. One day he brought a music-master home in order to ask his opinion about a mazurka, and the latter's sole reply was to ask in a weak voice for a glass of brandy, which of course gave us food for merriment. But our imperturbable friend continued to compose and pound away on the piano in all his spare moments, singing his romances in a voice—strongly resembling a rusty lock—that made one's flesh creep. But he did not attempt this sort of thing at night, however, as, having endeavored to enliven our dreams once with the *Casta Diva*, there was such a shower of slippers and boots in his room, that the following morning there was really a leather carpet over the floor.

But the jolliest, and at the same time the most heedless fellow of the lot, was a man from Romagna, a certain Mazzoni, with a huge frame, who, upon sitting down to table, said: "I am hungry," in such a deep voice, which apparently came from some unknown depth, that the poor caterer fairly paled. And, in fact, it was only the hunger of a trombone-player after a seven hours' concert, of an Esquimaux after a seal-hunt, or a lion who had been fasting for three days, that could be compared to the fury with which he cleared the table. His dinner was not a dinner; it was a regular raid, the "requisition" of a squad of cavalry in time of war, a devastation, a sacking. So much occupied was he in masticating, that he talked little; but amused the company away from the table with every sort of unexpected joke, for which he really had a satanical imagination. Did I say *amuse?* Sometimes he drew forth more curses than there were hairs to his head; but we always ended by laughing. He was quite capable of meditating upon and preparing one of his tricks for seven days running. One night, toward one o'clock, while we were sleeping soundly, we were wakened suddenly by a sense of bitter cold,—all six of us,—and we found ourselves uncovered, with the sheets and counterpanes at the bottom of the bed. We rearranged our beds, and then fell asleep again; an hour later the same thing happened again, and it really seemed as if witches were at work, until one man, having lost his patience, seized a taper, another lighted a candle, and all sprang up, exclaiming: "It's Mazzoni!" Not a bit of it. Mazzoni was snoring, and had not even moved. What is it? What could it be? Finally some one stumbled over a small cord stretched across the room; there was one discovered in every room, and all six were joined in the rascally fist of that imposter who was snoring. Then we went for him. But it was all very fine trying to manage a giant like him, for he drove us all from the room like wasps with just six blows from his pillow, and remained master of the situation. Another time a poor devil who was utterly worn out after a march was waked at midnight by a beautiful Catherine-wheel of various colors, that filled his room with a shower of fire; or we all rose from table with our chairs fastened to the floor; or at the moment we drew out our swords on the review, we would find all the hilts tied to the sheaths by a fine silken cord, with which, at that moment, we would gladly have hanged our dear friend to the nearest lamp-post.

The greatest fun, however, was always at table, where something new was invented each day. For some time we had the habit of unbuttoning our coats, for air, every time an extraordinary statement was made ; and we did little but button and unbutton that garment. For certain canards of Boccetti we all six got into our shirt-sleeves without any ceremony, or we left the table to run and throw open the seven windows of the house ; in fact, one evening he gave vent to such a colossal one, in relating one of his old adventures with a Florentine lady, who, from a marchioness of twenty at the beginning of the tale, changed into a princess of eighteen toward the end, that we all rushed down into the street and obliged him to hold forth from the balcony for some time before returning to the house for dinner. One day we ate in the Oriental fashion, without knives and forks, talking Turkish, that is to say, putting an *a* into every syllable, with a forfeit for every one who made a mistake, which nominally resulted to three hundred lire in one evening. Another day six of us agreed not to allow the seventh to speak, and we silenced him by drowning his voice with a continuous and deafening chorus of disapprobation. Another time no one was allowed to talk except in verses of melodrama, song, or quotations of the master, or title of the opera. Then came the mania for "food-stealing," which was a regular calamity. However, we made a rule by which every one was obliged to abide. Any one who could carry off some tid-bit from a friend's plate had a right to it, and the friend, if he did not wish to fast, was obliged to send the orderly to buy sausage. There was no way of getting out of it. The sufferer might turn red, yellow, green, or black; but he was forced to laugh. The successful onslaughts provoked revenges, so that little by little the game became a rage. We had to defend ourselves like so many dogs. There was no way of dining in peace. The cutlets, side bones of fowls, eggs, and glasses of wine disappeared as if by magic. Some had acquired a fearful dexterity. They even invented instruments for the purpose. That devil of a Mazzoni emptied, with one stroke, a cup of coffee, by thrusting into it with the rapidity of lightning an enormous piece of bread, so shaped that it acted like a pump; and he carried off at one time a half kilo. of maccaroni in broth, by a certain infernal tool, made with a bunch of toothpicks in the shape of a funnel; or with a bed bar, at the top of which he had cautiously tied a fork, he would carry a slice of the fry from one end of the table, which was two metres and a half in length. Then came the thefts by conjury, cords, hooks, wires, and highway robberies. It was something fearful, desperate, and absolutely ruinous. But Mazzoni always said: "You have yet to see the monster theft, the greatest one of all!" And we all trembled. Finally, one evening, while we were disputing with our forks a dish of polenta with small birds, Mazzoni uttered an oath, saying that he had dropped his fork, and stooped to pick it up. . . . Ye heavenly powers! We had not finished our exclamation, when the table was already in the next room, carried off on the back of that gigantic thief, without a single drop of wine having been spilled.

Then came the passion for nocturnal excursions. We went out at night in old citizen's clothes which we had brought from home, dyed, faded, and recolored, which were threadbare, and certain cutthroat-looking hats. We went to sing, under the windows of friends who had fallen asleep, songs for the occasion, for which they generally thanked us with wash-basins or garbage-boxes; or to mysterious dens in the suburbs, to drink punch among English and French sailors, to whom we represented ourselves as journeymen varnishers and cabinet-makers, *en route* to the East. What outbursts of laughter there were with that crazy Boccetti, who, at two in the morning, on returning home through those deserted streets as dark as catacombs, saw behind every blind—he only—a gleam of light, which meant: "Boccetti, my husband has returned; don't come up!" or: "To-morrow at this hour!" And Cavagnetti, who played the grand seigneur even in the dark, by throwing handfuls of coppers to the dogs; and the pianist, who wished to draw rifle-shots upon himself by shouting his superhuman romances under the windows! The nocturnal excursions were generally undertaken after great dinners; because we *did* give dinners despite the "overdrawn accounts" of Maglietti. The guests came half a dozen at a time. We could not write cards of invitation like that in the *Vie de Bohême*: "*Il y aura des assiettes*"; but we managed things equally well. We lighted stumps of candles, and placed on the bureaus and behind vases of flowers heads of lettuce, arranging upon the walls decorations made from cudgels and birch trees. Those who arrived last made themselves comfortable on the beds, in Roman style, drank their wine out of coffee cups without handles, and wiped their mouths on newspapers. Some arranged their little spreads on one side, on a military box set upright; others without any compliments went straight to the kitchen to pilfer from the saucepans. All talked at once; and often a troop of shirtless players in the street enlivened our dinner with music, by singing *Mamma, sto passiarello ;* the soldiers wrangled and disputed in the kitchen as to precedence in the question of rapine, and altogether there was such a racket that the discharge of a gun would not have been heard. That braggart Cavagnetti, however, seized the brief moments of silence, to make the people gathered in the street believe that we were having a supper worthy of Lucullus. "Softly there," he shouted, "with that Johannisberg!" or: "Boccetti! ho, there, Boccetti! have that pheasant with truffles passed!" The conversations changed little by little into choruses from *Ernani;* the brigade scattered to play the devil in the different rooms; then some dressed themselves up, some danced, and others indulged in trials of strength; the neighbors hit each other above and below with sticks; it seemed as if the house were being shaken by an earthquake, for the dust and smoke covered every thing, and in fact one could see nothing, or only indistinctly at best. It even seemed as if we saw, flying around in a giddy waltz, the Rosalies, Concettas, and Neddas, as young as us, but wilder, quite as agile and dark as Bedouins, . . . who melted away in the air.

We had plenty of occupation too, in keeping in order the seven orderlies, who took advantage of our absence for all sorts of wild doings. These malefactors, when we were away (we finally caught them in the act), put on our jackets, lighted our pipes, placed themselves at the windows with our swords in their hands, and played the *Agnus Dei* with those same neighbors to whom we, royal sub-lieutenants, had made eyes. They assumed the attitudes of lovers *à la* Metastasio, the rascals! And we had to keep our eyes open too, on account of the constant coming and going of laundresses, ironers, and pin- and needle-women, because from the very first day we caught, through the cracks of the doors, fragments of Lombardian, Piedmontese, and Neapolitan declarations of love, uttered in tones of voice that demanded the most speedy and vigorous intervention on the part of their superiors. . But this was not the worst. One evening the general caterer goes into the kitchen to change the position of a cask of Marsala wine, which we had purchased three days before for grand occasions, and upon seizing it, he discovers that it is alarmingly light. Our good friends drank, then, and how? While we were swallowing wretched black table-wine, they were indulging like lords in Marsala. Poor Maglietti lost his head; he was ready to stick them all with one blow, like so many spiders. But it was necessary to catch them in the act. The next evening at dinner, taking advantage of a moment of suspicious silence in the kitchen, we all rose softly, approached the door on tiptoe, put our eyes to the crack . . . and what a sight greeted us! There were four of these scapegraces, leaning over the cask, with four long straws stuck into a hole, sucking away blissfully, their eyes half closed like four great cats, with a smile on their lips, so engrossed in their agreeable employment, in such a tranquil state of beatitude, that they were quite unaware of our presence, and continued to enjoy themselves. "Oh, you rascals!" shouted the caterer. The men sprang up like four steel springs, and stood quite breathless. Yet for that piece of impertinence the cook had the face to excuse himself. "Oh, lieutenant!" he murmured, "you are quite right . . . Too good! . . . But . . . well—what can one drink with a straw!" Saying which, however, he dashed behind a wardrobe with one spring, to avoid the cuff that he knew he deserved.

These little domestic calamities, however, gave variety and spice to our beautiful home life. We quarrelled occasionally, but at heart were fond of each other. Whenever it was possible we went out together, so much so that in the brigade we were called the patrol of the seven; our street was called the street of the seven; and it was the custom to say: "I am going to dine with the seven," "I have seen the seven," without any thing more. Just as at Venice they used to say once: "I have seen the ten." We were like brothers. When one was absent at table, the usual good-humor was lacking; the choicest tid-bits from the kitchen were sent to the one on guard; a regular "oration" was made to him who returned from duty; when any man received fifty francs from home he was carried around the house in triumph on a chair; if another was in need of any service he was sure to find the remaining six ready to render it; cigars, watches, candles, sashes, were all common property. Toward the end of the month, when money was scarce, he who had any, gave it freely, and if every one was entirely out of pocket, we all dined together on salad and fresh water, and smoked the stumps which had lain forgotten in the drawers, as gay if not gayer than ever. We were jolly too, because we still possessed that fresh enthusiasm for military life, because the music of the regimental band made our hearts beat, because we wished well to the soldier, but, above all—this is the true reason,—because youth boiled in our veins and beat to our brains, as the venerable Gino wrote, and life . . . but I'll spare my readers a recitation on life.

Every thing has an end; and this was the case with the mess

of the seven too. The first shock came from the illness of the cook, who was replaced by another. We took a Genoese (with a face that would have looked well on the top of a bayonet), who was as bold and secure of himself as an old brave, and who prided himself on having been under-cook in a *great hotel.* When asked what he knew how to do, he modestly replied: "*Every thing.*" "What a marvel!" we said to ourselves. "Now we shall have fine dishes." And we instantly set him to work. . . . He was simply a wretch, a Borgia, a monster without the bowels of compassion. If he had at least been aware of his own ignorance, and had restricted himself to plain cooking! But no, he insisted upon getting up the most aristocratic dishes of his *great hotel*, of which he only retained the most indistinct recollections, and placed upon the table stuff that made him worthy of being shot in the back. For a time we went on with a saintly resignation; but it was useless, we could not stand it. One day he served us an enormous *risotto* flavored with a sauce *of his own invention.* Appearances promised well, we took our places at table, our mouths fairly watering. Ye heavenly powers! The mere odor drove us away from table! And that day matters culminated; we could not procure another cook, because the colonel did not like to dispense with soldiers in service; so we had to make a sacrifice and give up the mess. But it was a genuine sorrow to all. . . . Fortunately a great event came unexpectedly to console us. That same evening, while the excellent Maglietti, surrounded by us all, was closing up his accounts of the mess, and notifying each one of his indebtedness with a melancholy voice, a telegram to the division arrived, ordering the immediate departure of the brigade for Northern Italy. It was the first breath of the messenger of war. All heard and received the announcement with a shout of joy. And we—the seven—after having all run together, like a single sub-lieutenant, to the telegraph office to ask seven money-orders from our respective families, gave, the following evening, in our now famous mouse den, our last Sardanapalus-like feast, at which we drank, in honor of beautiful Sicily, the small quantity of Marsala that had escaped from the rascally straws of our seven revellers.

Two days after, one beautiful April morning, the brigade embarked on a large military transport. The embarkation of a brigade is a spectacle full of poetry. All those boats filled with soldiers, and bristling with gleaming gun-stocks, which crowd around that black, smoking giant, make one think of an ancient fleet, pressing around a solitary fortress, set on fire by its defenders. When we were all aboard we turned toward that beautiful shore, from which thousands of handkerchiefs saluted us. All were gay. The Piedmontese soldier thought: "I shall see my dear Alps again"; the Neapolitan said: "I shall salute, in passing, my Vesuvius"; the Genoese rejoiced in thinking that he would land in his *Superba;* and the Lombardian said in his heart: "We shall pass my country *en route* to the war." Only the Sicilian soldiers, who had never left the island, looked around with a meditative air at their beautiful mountains, which perhaps they might never see again. A certain disquietude took possession of all. We were going to the war, or, in other words, to a mystery. What had the future in store for us? Glory? Humiliation? Promotion? The amputation of an arm? A medal? Or that ball in the forehead, in the midst of a beautiful field of grain? Even at that moment the seven were together, and all looked at Sicily with a slight feeling of sadness. Boccetti touched his eyes with his handkerchief, pretending to weep for his 99th countess ; the *pianista* waved an adieu to that fortunate sky which had heard his divine harmonies for five months ; Maglietti saluted with regret those walls among which he had made so many useless attempts to practise rigid economy ; and even the good Mazzoni contemplated with a certain sweet melancholy the city where he had devoured and imbibed so much, and taken so many turns with his friends. Cavagnetti alone, who had lost seventy-five francs at play two days before, stood on one side, leaning over the parapet, more angry than sad. "What's the matter with you, Cavagnetti?" I asked on approaching him. "Are you thinking with regret of your Sicily?" "Not a bit of it!" he replied, continuing to fix his eyes on the city. "I am thinking with regret of the seventy-five cyclops that I have lost there."

But then he suddenly roused himself, lighted a cigar with eight matches, assumed his usual air of a millionaire, and began promenading with long steps up and down the steamer (which was majestically cutting the waves) laden with so many arms and hopes.

# DEPARTURE AND RETURN.

## REMINISCENCE OF 1866.

My dear friend Alberto, I am going to copy several pages from your reminiscences; do not be annoyed at this, for if these pages do not give you honor as a literary personage, they certainly will not show you to disadvantage as son and soldier. Permit me to take this liberty, and rest assured of my discretion, because if I were really desirous of abusing our intimacy, I could publish many others of your secrets.

### AT HOME.

#### I.

After parting with the joys and illusions of youth, when nought but the comfort of recording them remains to me, I shall think more frequently and with greater emotion of the last days of April and the first ones of May in 1866 than of any others during my entire life.

I had never seen Turin so gay and beautiful. The imminent outbreak of the national war which had been invoked and expected for so many years, had suddenly aroused all the generous and warlike characteristics of that city. It was sufficient to pass an evening in one of the principal streets, to become aware by the bustle, the unusual attitude of persons in general, and the bands of workmen, students, and boys, that there was something stirring the souls of the people, and that some great event had taken place or was about to do so. Every evening seemed like that of a fête.

They were the days when, in meeting a soldier, one looked at and wondered about the horseman who crosses the street with a folded paper buttoned into his coat; and the people stop to see a convoy of the army train pass; and in the boys' schools there is no way of preserving quiet; the old pensioned officers talk in loud voices in groups at the cafés, and bring down their fists on the table; the mothers grow anxious; the young men become quite mad; the women are less looked at than usual, and cease a little to force themselves into all thoughts, desires, and plans, as they always do, with their usual proud tyranny.

Turin felt most profoundly all the poetry of these days. During the morning, on the avenues around the parade ground, were the families, relatives, and friends of the soldiers of the second division, who had been called to arms within a few days and still wore the greater part of their ordinary dress: high hats, red caps, elegant light trousers, and great Alpine-hunters' gaiters, black coats, and ragged jackets,—all equals there. Around the barracks there was a continual wandering of fond mothers with bundles under their arms, a coming and going of officers and messengers of the division and public squares, together with a crowd of curious people before the door; inside, a deafening noise. At evening, behind the bugles and drums, came an immense concourse of people who walked in time, in bands of ten or twelve, arm in arm; and the songs and shouts that echoed through all the neighboring streets. At the point where the music and soldiers re-entered the barracks there were hand-shakings, applause, hurrahs, and the cries: "Till to-morrow! till to-morrow!" They all seemed soldiers. There I felt thee, Piedmont!

## II.

How much better we all were in those days!

The expectation of that solemn war by which liberty was to be vindicated and the country restored to a people so illustrious and beloved, who had suffered so much; the knowledge that even the people of the poorer classes felt that it was a just and holy war; the sight of those poor fellows from the country, rough, ignorant of every thing, who had come to serve as soldiers with so much good-will and heart, and take part so quickly, if not in the enthusiasm, at least in the common gaiety; the report that the same thing was taking place everywhere; that everywhere young men of every condition went by the hundreds to enlist; that the fathers and mothers themselves accompanied them, and the people greeted and blessed them, and in that marvellous unanimity of hopes and good wishes political discords were readjusted, and only one single cry was to be heard;—all this filled people's souls with a calmness and joy so full, so intense, that it seemed a veritable happinesss. Every evil passion fled from the heart; old offenses were pardoned, old rancors stilled; people sought or found in their enemies their mutual friends, and they placed a stone on the past. That ever-present thought, that deep affection which occupied us continually, gave us an energy and a vigorous and unusual vitality which made itself felt by our tone, looks, actions, and steps. What joviality, what affectionate harmony among friends! How pure and elevated were all our thoughts, and how much stronger were all our affections! Spring did not smile in the flowers alone, nor was it felt in the air and blood solely; it laughed in all hearts; it was like a breath of fresh young life that had permeated our entire being. What days! O country! if we could always feel thus!

### III.

From the first day that the possibility of war was mentioned, my head began to grow confused; and the confusion increased little by little, until the probability was changed into a certainty. I say confused, because I can find no other fitting expression. I thought, talked, and worked as if under the influence of some intoxicating liquor. First agitation, then disquietude, then a regular fever; rushes of blood to the head; an itching of the hands to get to work; an intense desire for motion, air, light, music, poetry; and an absolute impossibility of fixing the mind on any one thought. Not even the thought of war, because the representing to myself in imagination events, no matter how marvellous and terrible, was like taking something from that idea of an indefinite and adventurous future which filled me with so much joy and life.

When I entered the house I could not keep quiet. I drew a dozen books down from the shelves, looked over a page in each, panting, working myself around on my chair, and tapping my feet impatiently; then I threw them all into the air. "Books are not enough! they are not enough!" I shouted. "Books do not tell what is boiling within me." I opened a newspaper; in those days the newspapers were on fire; I gave a glance at the customary enthusiastic article and tore the sheet in a hundred pieces. "But this is weak; heavens! this is cold!" And seized by a sudden poetic inspiration, I seated myself at the table and began to write hastily. I will write an article, I said; and instantly thereafter I threw away pen, paper, and ink, exclaiming as I did so: "Every thing is cold! I am growing desperate. Tell me, mother, in heaven's name, are there no verses in Italian literature which will express the fever that is devouring me?" "Berchet," she suggested timidly, "No, not Berchet," I replied in a dramatic tone; "Berchet is irate, Berchet hates, Berchet curses, and I love in this moment, love intensely, love every one; I feel like a brother to all; I could throw my arms around all those whom I meet in the street. I love even the Austrians, dear mother! I would kill many of them; but I love them, because, thanks to them, Italy is thus roused, raises her head, and shows herself to be so powerful, dear, and beautiful, diffusing through all her sons that inexpressible feeling of pride and joy! Death to the Austrians, but hurrah for them too! I never felt so much like a Christian before!"

Then I dashed to the window and grew enraged at the stillness in the street. "Just see what a shameful quiet! How is it possible? Why does not every one go down and make a noise? What sort of people are these? . . . Let me overcome this fever!" Then, shutting myself up in my room and seizing my sword, I pretended that I had facing me an Austrian officer, long and thin, with a pair of bushy moustaches and protruding eyes. I put myself on guard, and down came the blows, the parryings, leaps, and thrusts, until I fell quite exhausted upon the sofa. In other words, I was crazy.

It is quite superfluous to say that the neighborhood were

thoroughly aware of my existence. Besides, my poetic exclamations, which were heard in the street, I used to pass the entire evenings on the terrace in the court; and every one knows what the courts are like in the new houses at Turin. (We lived in one of the three great palaces in Via Nizza, opposite the railway station.) They are great pigeon-houses, where there are more people than stones, and after dinner all rush to the windows, and those above look at those below, those below look at the legs of those above; up in the attics they make love, on the terraces the children play, the employés read the newspapers, and from the roof to the ground-floor, from the ground-floor up to the roof, those on one floor talk illy of those on another, and all bow to and smile at each other like the best friends in the world. We lived on the second floor. We had on one side a charming, cultivated, and clever Neapolitan lady, a great friend of ours; a woman *à la* Cairoli, full of energy and dash, imaginative and prolific, who, one day when her son was to fight a duel, had filled my mother with admiration and surprise in saying to her quietly: "He will do his duty!" On the other side lived an old engineer, a painter and octogenarian, who was blind, and a veteran of Napoleon I, surrounded by a half dozen dear little grandchildren, who were my delight. He was a handsome old man, with a good heart, was fond of me, called me his son, and when I was away and delayed replying to him for a couple of days, would go timidly to ask my mother if I could have taken offence at any thing in his last letter. On the same floor, opposite us, lived a widow, about forty, who was elegant, languid, thin, ugly, a rabid devourer of novels, and had the habit of going to the window every time I was there, casting certain long, languishing glances, drawing up her mouth and drooping her head with its false curls on one side in a melancholy way. In the window next hers usually stood her cook, who was seized with an incipient passion for my orderly (a handsome fellow, in parenthesis); she had a round face, quite purple in color, and so puffed out that it seemed as if she were continually blowing; great lips, large eyes, immense shoulders, with a broad curve here and there, which could be seen even from the most distant quarter of the house. On the third floor above the languid nymph, lived a student of the University, who was very young, a good sort of fellow, crazy about the war, already enrolled in the volunteers, one of the dearest and most curious of jovial people. At any hour of the day, when I clapped my hands, he would spring on to the terrace, with his arms and face in the air like an improvisatore questioning and replying to me in verse, would start discussions on the higher politics, war, philosophy, and literature, declaiming, gesticulating, and humming in a most amusing manner. At the sound of his voice the entire neighborhood would appear at the windows.

. . . . . . . . . .

Then followed a vast amount of hilarity on all the floors. "I like youth like this," murmured the poor old man. And the cook hid behind a blind and burst into a fit of laughter. Her mistress pursed her mouth into a smile which was intended to say: "What dear idiots!" The Neapolitan lady flung a bon-mot at me, my sister ran off, my mother pulled me by the coat, and my brother muttered: "This is too much." Then my cousin, the colonel, when he was there, a stiff, austere soldier, who was really fond of me, but he gave me great wiggings, for which reason I called him *beneficent executioner*, said to me gravely: "*Do be* serious!"

In his presence I cannot deny that I was a trifle embarrassed; but suddenly my friend would break out with another strophe, and then good-by to all gravity, for we grew wilder than ever.

This was the public comedy, which was followed by a private one. The eldest of the old soldier's grandchildren used to come and see me, and I would say to him: "Courage; fall into line!" then taking my mother, sister, and the boy by the arm, I put them in line whether they liked it or not, and made them stay there too. If my mother laughed, I placed my hand on her shoulder and said: "Quiet, my dear lady, erect, and serious, otherwise we shall close the doors and declaim fifty-eight-line stanzas with all the strength of our lungs, and you know we are very robust." "No! no! for pity's sake!" she would reply. "Then silence!" I shouted. "We shall have to stay here," she murmured, laughing afresh, and turning to my sister,—and that laugh of hers was so sweet and gentle. "Attention! march!" My shout was so deafening that my little soldiers would get into disorder, and rush about here and there, holding on to their ears, and I behind them to bring them one by one back to their place; then I set them free, with the understanding that they should all shout together, "Hurrah for the war!". But my mother said to me: "I will not shout." "But you will shout." "Oh, no." "Then take a kiss, you angel!"

But from day to day she became more thoughtful. Several regiments had already started, and from one hour to another we expected the orders for mine to leave. She knew this. Sometimes, when I was making a racket, I caught her looking at me sadly, and I said: "Of what are you thinking?" "My son," she replied sadly, "I am thinking that we have only a few days more together . . . I am glad that you are so gay, and at the same time . . . this gaiety of yours hurts me, because . . . I think that I shall feel all the more painfully the void and silence which will fill this house before long."

"It is true," I thought. Poor women! "Courage! courage!" we say to them,—we who go to the war full of enthusiasm, ambition, with dreams of glory, gay, thoughtless, and surrounded by friends; but they remain here alone without comfort or distraction, always with that thought, that fixed pain.

"I understand, I feel that in these days I am nothing to you. . . ." added my mother. " No, no, let me finish, I do not complain of it, you know ! Poor boy, it is natural . . . but . . ."

"Listen," I said to comfort her; "you have so noble and choice a heart, you can find comfort in yourself much more easily than other women. We are not selfish. Do you think this war ought to take place? that it is just? that it is a solemn duty of the country?"

"Oh, yes, that I admit," she replied, as she wiped her eyes.

"Then if we do not make it, we, the adult generation, our children will be obliged to do so afterward. If there were not now five hundred thousand mothers who are weeping, there would be that number within twenty years. We sacrifice ourselves to our country for the five hundred thousand boys and girls who are still in leading-strings; they have in each other their predestined lovers and wives, shall we not then assure their future, as far as within us lies, from every pain or sorrow, and so act that they may love, marry, and multiply in peace?"

My mother smiled, but instantly became sad again. "All this is true," she said, with a sigh, "but it is not enough to console a mother!"

Then leaning her elbows on a table and burying her face in her hands, she wept silently. I tried to console her. "No, my son; go out, go and hunt up your friends, I do not wish to sadden you; let me weep alone; go."

It was evening; she stayed in the dark in a corner of the room, alone and silent; thinking and thinking.

I have never experienced as I did in those days the marvellous power of imagination over sentiment. I began sometimes, in an idle way, to fancy all possible cases of the war, and then little by little I concentrated my thoughts and buried myself so completely in the imagination of the battles, triumphal entries, and returns, that I really seemed to be present, to feel, and to see; my blood was stirred, I clasped my head in my hands, for it seemed as if it would burst, so great was the tumult of ideas, and my chest was heaving, and I was filled with all sorts of childish impulses.

One night I was on guard at the Madama Palace; alone in my room, seated at a table, with the light in front of me, and giving rein to my fancies, I imagined that I had risen to such a height that I could take in with a single glance the entire country—mountains, valleys, rivers, forests,—and I felt and saw all the streets in the city filled with people, the parade grounds gleaming with bayonets, and from the fortresses, arsenals, and doors came a confused sound of arms and songs, and the dull noise of a hurried, feverish labor. On the railways were interminable, heavy, slow trains, running over the country in all directions, meeting, crossing, following each other, greeted with joy by the people who had gathered. Here and there they stopped to discharge a load of cannon, horses, wagons, and piles of arms. Suddenly a loud sound of drums and trumpets broke out on every side, and from every city there started and spread through the country the columns of the regiments, which converged, united by twos and threes, and advanced slowly to the frontiers, crowning the heights, winding along the rivers, overflowing the valleys, and stretching out in immense battle-lines over the plains. On the mountains of the Tyrol, from Lake Garda, up, up as far as the eye could reach, gleamed in a thousand points the red bands of the volunteers, climbing and descending the slope, disappearing in the chasms, and reappearing on the summits of the rocks. Meanwhile all the vast Lombardian plain was peopled with tents and parks, and the sound of shouts and music was heard. Then came nightfall and all was quiet. Finally, at the break of day, a troop of horsemen started with the rapidity of lightning from the general headquarters, scattered in every direction, and shouts ran on from camp to camp; the whole army began to stir, organize, and advance. . . . Here the imagination not being able to embrace the entire picture of the measureless battle, an immense veil of mist appeared before me, broken here and there in great rents, through which one could see our young regiments dashing to the assault of the hills, receding, and reclimbing again with determination; then squads of horsemen with hanging lances burst *ventre a terre* against the squares; then batteries hastily join other batteries, and from the heights gleam and break the flanks of the retreating columns; then indefatigable troops of sharp-shooters scatter and unite, follow, draw back, hide, and then stretch out again in long chains, and on every side assaults succeed assaults, lines succeed lines, and the very heavens resound with the horrible tumult. When suddenly a deep silence falls over all, the mist disappears, the dust grows thinner, on the tops of all the mountains our battalions are moving, our flags flying, our fanfara echoing, and from one end of Italy to the other bursts out a prolonged shout of joy, which has been suppressed for so long a time. . . . Yes, break out, O shout, and resound through all the vaults of heaven ; but do not drown that undertone which comes from my mother's breast. . . . O God! my head ! my head !

I dashed out of the room, left the palace ; Piazza Castello was as deserted and quiet as the court of an enormous convent ; the hill of Superga was distinctly outlined against a clear and starry sky, and the façade of the Gran Madre di Dio, lighted by the moonbeams, seemed as if only two feet away. "What a beautiful night," I exclaimed. "I am really happy !"

But a picture disturbed my happiness : the picture of a poor woman, seated in the corner of her little room, quite in the dark, with her forehead resting on her hands, thinking and thinking.

---

### THE DEPARTURE.

#### I.

On the 6th of May, toward five o'clock in the evening, a group of ten officers were gathered at the door of the barracks, when we heard a hurried step coming down the stairs, and instantly thereafter the breathless adjutant appeared, shouting : "Gentlemen ! We leave this evening at eight o'clock. Luggage in the barracks at seven. Full marching equipment."

We gave a shout of joy, and without even asking where we

were going, started off on a run. Some to the neighboring café to tell their friends, others to call their orderlies, and the rest home. A moment after in the barracks there was a most awful racket, the drums beat, the news spread through the neighborhood, the people gathered, and in a few moments from house to house, street to street, the rumor flew through half the city, scattering fear in the hearts of all the mothers.

I ran home, climbed the stairs three steps at a time, rapped, and the door was opened by my mother.

"My God! what is the matter with you? what is it?"

I was panting like a horse.

"We must go."

"Oh!"

"Yes; there is no time to lose."

"When?"

"At eight o'clock."

"At eight o'clock," my mother repeated in the same tone, as if in echo, and there she stood without speaking or making any gesture, looking at me with a dazed air.

"Quick, quick, the trunks must be packed; they have to be at the barracks at seven, and the orderly will come for them in a few minutes; meanwhile, we must begin; courage!"

After a moment, on seeing that my mother did not move, I said: "Well?"

"Ah!" she replied, as if coming out of a stupor. "I am ready. Erminia!"

My sister instantly appeared.

"He is going," my mother said hastily; "you must put up all his things; every thing is ready; is it not? Well—now—wait—where is the trunk? But no; it is better first—let me see—or rather . . ."

And she looked here and there, as if she had taken leave of her senses. That good woman is made on purpose to lose her head on similar occasions.

"Well!" she then said (in order to get over her embarrassment) to my sister, who was also standing there as if in a dream.

"Ah!" replied the latter, rousing herself suddenly; "quick; yes, we must hurry."

Then both ran into the other room.

A pull at the bell; I opened the door; it was the orderly. "Here I am!" he exclaimed breathlessly.

"Maria!" shouted my mother, returning in great haste. The servant appeared.

"Go and call my daughter instantly. In passing, tell the porter to come and fetch the trunk. Have Ettore called from the café. Tell them to come quickly."

The orderly carried the trunk on to the terrace; the noise of the trunk brought the languid nymph to the window; the languid nymph called the purple cook; the impetuosity with which the purple cook threw open her window called the other neighbors to the terrace.

Meanwhile my mother was going and coming without doing any thing.

"Friend!" I shouted, clapping my hands.

"Italy!" he replied, appearing at that moment on the terrace in his shirt-sleeves, in an inspired attitude.

"I am going at eight o'clock."

He disappeared, returned dressed, threw up his stick. "I will wait for you at the station!" he exclaimed, and dashed down stairs shouting: "Hurrah for the war!" letting his stick hit every iron in the railing, and creating thus a most dreadful racket.

"Alberto!" exclaimed my mother, stopping in her breathless haste.

"Here I am."

She drew me aside.

"Tell me. . . . Where are you going, do you know?"

"To Piacenza."

"To Piacenza; tell me. Piacenza is a fortified city, is n't it?"

"Yes, it's fortified."

"Shall you remain there?"

"I do not think so."

"But—don't they defend fortified cities?"

"Not that one, because we go further, and it remains behind us."

"Yes, . . ." she said, with the air of one who has lost all hope, and off she went.

Another pull at the bell; I opened the door; it was my elder sister. She pressed my hand and joined the others.

A third ring; it was my brother.

Meanwhile my mother returned, her arms laden with linen. She was so serious and impassible that I was amazed; behind her came the others, all silent, with lowered heads. My mother bent over the trunk; the orderly made a respectful motion to take the things; she waived him aside and replied: "No, let me do it." My sisters stretched out their hands to do the same. "Let me do it," my mother replied again, and stooped to kneel. "Mother!" I said in a tone of affectionate reproof, seizing her by the hand. She looked at me. "I do not wish you to do it,"

I added. Then she said, in a tone even more affectionate than mine: "I ask it as a favor."

She knelt down and packed the things. The orderly looked at me half touched, half surprised, as if to say: "How fortunate you are, lieutenant!" I looked at him as if to reply: "I know it; I am sorry that your mother is not here."

My mother rose and went away. I heard a heavy sigh, turned, and saw my younger sister weeping.

My mother returned with something in her hands, placed it in the trunk, and went away again. I looked: it was her portrait.

She returned with three books, and put them on the portrait.

"What are those, mother?"

"They are *The Promessi Sposi.*"

'Oh, thanks!" and I kissed her hand; she withdrew again hastily—always impassible. We all looked at her in astonishment, and grew uneasy.

"Take off your sash."

"Why?" I asked.

She removed it without saying a word, and put it in the trunk.

"Mother, I must wear it." She made no reply, but went into another room. Another heavy sigh: my elder sister was crying.

My mother returned with a magnificent silk sash, put it around my neck, and said: "I have made it during the hours when you were on the parade ground."

"Mother," I exclaimed, seizing her hand, "this is too much!" She turned her head away.

The orderly looked at her with glistening eyes.

"That is all," she said, turning around; and a moment later: "You can close it."

She lowered the lid, pressed it with her hand, but did not succeed in closing it; she placed her knee upon it, pushing back with her elbows those who tried to help; her foot slipped, she tottered . . .

"Mother! what are you doing?" we all exclaimed, catching hold of her.

A rap at the door; it was the porter who had come to fetch the trunk.

"Here already?" exclaimed my mother, turning around sharply, in a tone of disagreeable surprise. "Take it."

The porter placed the trunk on his shoulders.

"To the barracks of Porta Susa," I said.

"I know where it is," he replied in moving off.

"Stop!" exclaimed my mother suddenly; the latter turned.

"Be careful (she tried to think of something to say)—be careful not to let it fall!"

"Don't be afraid."

Out he went; my mother accompanied him to the door, watched him down the stairs. "He has disappeared"; she pressed her lip together violently, and conquered the rising tears. She returned as impassible as before, and I began to grow alarmed.

Here is the *beneficent executioner*. "Good-evening." No one replied; he understood, looked me in the face, and I raised my head. "That's right; that's not bad," he seemed to say; and we all passed into the neighboring room, where we seat ourselves in a circle. No one spoke. We heard the rustle of a dress, the door opened, and the strong-minded lady appeared. All rose to their feet.

"My good friend," she said, putting out both hands to my mother, with her peculiar grace and her strong and energetic way, "I have only just learned that your son is going away. These are certainly sad moments, but each one of us must suffer for the country. These are great days for Italy! A great war! Believe me, it is impossible that the enemy should be able to withstand for any length of time the wave of fire which will seize it on all sides. The army has a whole people at its back ready to go into the field. These are great days. This is the way nations are made!"

My mother looked at her in astonishment.

"If I could once see a great battle from a distance. To see it at the finest point, when our regiments have driven the enemy from all the hills of the line of battle, and down the slopes; on the other side, horses, soldiers, wagons, cannon,—all flying precipitately! Courage, dear lady; this is a veritable crusade; even the women and children would like to fight too. If the army was broken up, another would form in fifteen days."

"Yes! yes!" broke out my mother with a dash that was meant for enthusiasm, and was in reality nothing but maternal affection veiled in the love of country. "Yes! It is a crusade! Every one ought to go to the war; every one, so that there would be millions and millions, and that the enemy would really be frightened, abandon the idea of resistance, and open the doors of the fortresses."

"Where is my son?" a trembling voice asked in a neighboring room, and at the same moment the door opened, and the old blind man appeared, with his arms outstretched as if calling me to him. I embraced him; he touched my sword, sash, epaulettes, and asked in a trembling voice: "Are you ready?" Then placed his hands upon my shoulders, rested his cheek on my breast, and remained in this position. All were silent. The "*executioner*," erect at the end of the room, contemplated the spectacle with knitted brows and folded arms. My mother looked fixedly at me.

A few moments elapsed, and I, giving a glance at the clock, said with a great effort: "It is time to go!"

All sprang to their feet, and took a step toward me. The "*executioner*" approached me and whispered in my ear: "Be a man!"

"Well!" I murmured, putting on my cap.

"Well!" said the Neapolitan lady resolutely, pressing and shaking my hand at every word. "Courage; do yourself honor; remember us, and write." Saying which, she retired.

"Farewell, Alberto!" exclaimed my brother, throwing his arms around my neck, and kissing me.

My sisters embraced me, sobbing, and then fled.

"Here!" exclaimed the old man, opening his arms. "Here, my son!" And my head on his shoulder, he murmured in a trembling voice: "If this is to be the last time that I embrace you . . . may heaven grant that I be the first one to go!"

The "*executioner*" pressed my hand, looked firmly at me, and withdrew without saying a word.

My mother and I looked at each other for a moment; she threw herself into my arms, put hers around my neck, and covered me with kisses of despair; then seizing my arm with one hand, and pressing the other tightly on my shoulder, close to my side, she allowed herself to be dragged rather than led to the door. There I released myself by force, and dashed down the staircase. At that same moment she uttered a long, heart-breaking cry: "Alberto! Alberto!" as if she had seen me fall over a precipice.

I heard, while going down, the others, who had run forward, —a confused sound of voices; my soldier, among others, who said: "Courage, madame; I will always keep near him; that I promise you!" . . . the despairing sobs of my mother, a last, faint cry of "Alberto!" and then nothing more.

In hurriedly crossing the court, I met the four grandchildren of the old man, who were returning from school; I stopped them, and covered them with kisses: "Oh, you are suffocating me!" shouted the frightened little girl.

"Mr. Lieutenant, if you had seen!" exclaimed my soldier, joining me with his handkerchief at his eyes.

"Be quiet!" I shouted.

And we hurried through the street.

## II.

When I reached the barracks it was almost dark. The companies were already armed and drawn up in line in the court. Outside, there was an indescribable confusion; the street was crowded with people, and illuminated with torches by a large number of the students of the University; the door of the quarters was filled with officers, around whom were a multitude of mothers, sisters, and small brothers, who wished to enter, and who were weeping and begging with clasped hands: "Let us see him once more, one moment only, only for a word!" And the officer of the guard kept pushing them back, shouting and begging too: "Do me the favor to draw back and leave the space open; we cannot allow you to enter; it is forbidden;

we are only doing our duty; you will see them when they go away." Then there was a gathering of the officers' wives with their children, who had come to offer their last words of counsel and their prayers; then a coming and going of other women and girls, who were neither mothers, wives, nor sisters, some of whom were weeping, others pretending to do so in order to arouse a practical sympathy in those who remained, others at one side in melancholy attitudes; troops of workmen who passed singing and waving banners; there were shouts, applause, and a waving and confused murmur like the sea in a storm.

A roll of drums was heard; the officers disappeared, a sudden silence fell upon the crowd. A moment later and out came the sappers of the regiment to clear the street.

I was seized by the thought: "We are going to the station; my God! We shall have to pass under our windows!"

The music began, the regiment is out, flanked by two long rows of torches; the families attacked the lines; the officers and sergeants drove them back; repelled here and there, they returned at another point; the people gathered at the windows waving flags; here and there fall a shower of cigars and oranges; a multitude preceded the regiment singing; another followed it. "Hurrah for the Piedmontese brigade!" "Hurrah for the old regiment 637!" shouted a gentleman from a window, and another cried: "Hurrah for the brave men of Calmasino!"

We reached the Via Santa Therese, the Piazza San Carlo, then the Piazza Carlo Felice; as we advanced my heart grew heavy and my legs trembled: "She will hear the music and these shouts, poor woman!"

I raised my eyes; here is the house and an illuminated window; there is some one there, but it is not she; who can it be? I cannot distinguish the figure; it is waving its hands; looks down, "My God! who can it be?"

Suddenly a light appeared at the window below. "Ah! I see; it is the old blind man. God bless you, papa!"

Here was my friend of the third floor; he embraced me, kissed me, and shouted: "Good luck to you, brother! Hurrah for the war!" and disappeared.

We entered the train; I put out my head; saw the lighted window again, and the old blind man, quite alone, who is waving a salute. "Oh, will the music never cease! Oh, my poor mother!"

We heard the whistle; the train started; my heart gave a tremendous bound. "Who else has come to the window?" I saw two arms stretching out toward me . . . "My God! Did I hear a cry?"

The house disappeared.

"Farewell, my good angel! farewell, my holy and adored mother! May heaven grant that I see you again, or die so nobly that the pride of being my mother will lighten the grief of having lost me!"

"Now it's our turn!" I said, turning quickly and slapping my neighbor on his knee.

My friend, immersed in melancholy at having left his sweetheart, started suddenly and shouted loudly: "Hurrah for the war!"

Then all the others cried: "Let's light our cigars!"

And in a moment the carriage was filled with smoke, noise, and gaiety.

### THE CAMPAIGN.

At this point of the book I find a long series of Alberto's

letters, and beside some of these the answers of his mother fastened to the leaf. From the examination of the mother's writing you could draw out the history of the war; the trembling of her hand is certainly the surest indication of events. Taking them as a whole, her letters always say the same thing,—it is quite natural; but in those of her son there is something to be noted here and there. I will jot down this, which will form an incomplete and disjointed chronicle, but a truthful and lively one, of the different events of the war, or rather of the various impressions which some of them left on my friend's mind:

PIACENZA, 8th May.

Piacenza seems like a barrack. There are more soldiers than citizens, and more medals than soldiers; at every step we meet some one whose breast is covered; at every turn there is a general; and as for colonels, they do not strike us as being any thing at all extraordinary. How I feel my own littleness among all the gilt braid! Great military reunions have this evil, that we poor lieutenants are not looked at even; in fact, we disappear entirely. I am joking, you know; I have you, my soldiers, my friends; my blood is full of fire, my heart full of Italy, my soul full of the future; I am happy, desire nothing, and envy no one. We are quartered in a convent and sleep on straw. It is a desperate sort of business with those conscripts who do not know how to dress themselves, walk, or eat. Things have been done too hastily. If the war were to begin to-morrow, I tell you we should find ourselves in a sorry state; half the regiment does not know how to load; there is a great need of provincial soldiers, who are expected. In the whole barracks they cannot find a room for the officer of the guard. The other night I took refuge in the office of the majority, and I slept on the registers . . .

At the end of the mother's reply I find these words: "Be careful not to injure the registers; they may be important. Did you think to put something under your head? Erminia is ill from the pain of parting with you. The other day, in dusting your things, she began crying. I saw her, and said so. She denied it, but she was really crying. You do not yet know what a good heart she has." The letter ends: "Where are the Austrians?"

In another of her letters she puts this query: "Tell me, Alberto; they say the Austrian battalions are larger than ours. How does it happen? What will you do?"

The son replied: "We will send two of ours against one of theirs."

All these letters and those fastened to them are full of affectionate messages from the old man and the Neapolitan lady, who expects "great descriptions of great things." And now and then there is a postscript from the mother, who asks: "What is the orderly doing?"

I gather from the book that the colonel—the "*executioner*"—was at the headquarters of the army, and from that "superb height" watched lovingly over his obscure cousin by means of letters and indirect information; but the cousin knew nothing of it. The "*executioner*" concealed the protector, so that the colonel should not appear in the matter; and I praise him for it.

Alberto's regiment had been encamped for four days near San Giorgio, within a few miles of Piacenza, and he had only written to his mother on the day of his departure to tell her that he "was to sleep under the tent."

"Four days since he has written! Poor Alberto is sleeping on the ground; he will suffer and be ill. Who knows what may have happened! Oh, my God! I must telegraph to the colonel immediately."

She sent the dispatch: "Give me some news of Alberto, I beg you. I receive no letters, and am trembling for his health."

The colonel instantly replied: "He is very well. But he is so delicate!"

My mother understood the irony; was a trifle angry; seized her pen, and began: "My very dear friend, I do not say that Alberto is delicate, but I think I might . . ." She stops at this point.

The Cugia division has left for Cremona; from Cremona it will go to Goito. A letter from the mother runs thus:

"You will say that I am foolish, that I talk of the things I do not understand; but I certainly see no necessity for passing the Mincio immediately. If I were General La Marmora, I think I should wait a little; one never knows what may happen; at any rate I should have General Cialdini's soldiers go first, because they have the fleet near them, and in any case . . ."

"Could they take refuge there?" asks Alberto in reply. His mother writes back: "This is no time for joking."

The Cugia division is on the Mincio. The mother's letter is hastily written, is all full of exclamation points and words that run into each other, and lines and strokes that are a finger in length.

"For pity's sake, my son, do your duty; I am the first to urge it; but don't do too much. . . . Armies need officers, and if the officers expose themselves more than is necessary, what will be the result? It will end in the soldiers remaining without any guides or discipline, and then . . . what will become of the army? For pity's sake, do think a little of the soldiers! . . . (oh, maternal love, what subtle arguments!) and think of me too; do your duty, yes, but think . . ." Here there are some words which are not comprehensible. Then: "Your life is mine. Oh, my son! what days! what tremendous moments! I will not tell you what is happening at home, in order not to sadden you; I pray for you . . ." The rest is incomprehensible. There is a postscript which begins: "O Alberto!" and then there is nothing more. I see several curves traced by the son, which at first sight might be taken for islands; but I fancy he intended to draw lines around the tears of his mother, and so these figures were the result.

Here I find a page entitled: "That which follows the 28th of June." It says:

"My mother was seated at the dining-table; in front of her was a young fellow, the son of our Neapolitan friend, and by her side my old papa. On the centre of the table was a topographical map.

"'Rest assured, dear madam,' said the young man, 'the Cugia division cannot have taken part in the battle; that is evident.'

"'Oh, yes . . . evident!' exclaimed my mother, shaking her head and passing one hand over her tear-stained eyes.

"'Yes, I believe it; but what is the use of my saying it? The map proves it; look at it. Oh! the Cugia division passed by,' etc. (she pressed and shook each finger of the left hand between the thumb and forefinger of the right), 'and it is impossible that it should have been there at the moment in which . . . Oh, it passed by another road, and in this case it is not admissible that it could have arrived in time. Finally, this is the last, it passed behind the division on its left, and if this is true, it is beyond any doubt, quite clear and indisputable, that it passed beyond the battle-field. Do you not think so, Engineer?'

"The old man, without having understood one word, replied: 'Oh, certainly.'

"My mother continued to look attentively at the topographical map, turning it round on all sides, running over all the roads with her finger, raising her eyes as if to collect her thoughts, and then suddenly broke out weeping : 'Oh, yes, yes, it did not arrive in time ! Who says so ? Who can tell ? The map ? What does the map prove ? The map is not enough. Meanwhile three days have passed, and he has not written me yet ; if something had not happened I should hear, and that means that the division did arrive in time, and that he was there, and that . . . Oh, my boy ! My Alberto ! My poor Alberto !'

"Then clasping her head in her hands she burst into a fit of weeping.

"'Madam ! madam !' the others exclaimed in one voice, 'do calm yourself, for mercy's sake, do control yourself ; nothing has happened, nothing can have happened ! Your maternal love . . .'

"'My God!' cried my mother in a tone of anguish. 'My God, my maternal love ! But if he has n't written ! But if two of my friends, with officer sons, have already had news ! And I nothing ! Oh, Erminia !' My sister ran to her. 'What is it ?'

"'Alberto ! Alberto !'

"'My God ! what has happened ?'

"'Some misfortune ! I feel it ! I shall die ! Quick, a telegram to the colonel; let him ask, search, and be able to tell me something that will relieve my mind . . .'

"Then came a ring at the door. 'Silence !' The servant appears.

"'Here is a letter for you, madam.'

"My mother dashes at the woman, tears the letter from her, looks at it, utters a cry, looks at it again, presses it convulsively to her heart, gasps, smiles, raises her eyes to heaven, and exclaims: 'Thanks! thanks!'—then kisses and kisses again the sheet, presses her daughter's head to her breast, and murmurs in a feeble voice: 'Alberto!' then drops on to a chair. The two friends support her, and try to take the letter from her hands; but it is quite in vain; they are like pincers."

Here are some extracts from the letter:

CERLUNGO, 25*th June.*

I have told you all that I have seen, which is little; I cannot account for certain lapses in my memory, which, if I did not recall many other things, would make me think I had lost all power of retention, so strange and incredible are they. I have quite forgotten where and when my battalion stopped for the first time, and I remember clearly a soldier of another regiment whom I stopped and asked while he was running: "Where do you come from?"—and he pointed to a little house on the slope of the mountain, exclaiming: "*We have made a salad of them,*" which meant that in that house there had been a massacre of the Austrians, and this was quite true. I remember another who had a ball in his finger; while he stooped to touch a dead man, he uttered a cry, looked around astonished, drawing his hand behind his back, and murmuring plaintively: "*It hurts me!*" I remember my major's harangue to the battalion a few moments before we started; it was singularly simple and laconic. "Soldiers!" he said coldly, without even turning his horse toward us, "I am afraid we shall have nothing to do to-day; but in case we should . . . I believe that . . . we are Italians; the devil!" And here he ended with exactly these words. A short time before, in handing his flask full of rum to a small group of officers who did not appear very gay, he had said smilingly: "Take some; it refreshes weak spirits!"

I am thoroughly convinced that true courage comes from the heart and from culture of the mind; and true courage consists less in not being afraid, than in showing one's self and working, while being so, as if this were really not the case; all of which is the effect of reasoning, or rather of an infinite number of reasons, recollections, pictures, and examples, which pass through one's mind at such moments with the rapidity of lightning, and say: "Be firm!" Even entire strophes of patriotic poetry pass through the mind too. Your image passed with outstretched arms, but the forefinger pointing to the enemy, your tearful eyes fastened on mine, and your lips contracted with sobs, but which said in a free and vibratory voice: "Do your duty!" Oh, mother, how near you were to me at those moments!

. . . Do not believe it; the dead do not produce that horrible impression which is supposed to be the case, at least as long as the danger lasts. My battalion was in a column and went forward; the platoons stopped gradually on the edge of a ditch to look at the body of a soldier whose head had been destroyed by grape-shot. I had a tent stretched over it, and no one looked again. It is painful to see those wounded soldiers who, in rolling on the ground and touching it here and there, reduce their linen shirts and trowsers to such a state that not a bit of the white is left, every thing being covered with blood; and generally they are only slightly wounded. At first one is so absorbed in the spectacle of the field that he pays no attention, and does not even think that there will be any wounded. And it is almost always a surprise to see them come down in groups, with their heads bandaged, arms in slings, supported under the shoulders, each carried by two men, as white as death; some pressing one hand on their thighs, some on their chests, and nearly all groaning aloud or uttering feeble moans; the breathless surgeons running here and there, without knowing where to begin or with whom; then the examination, washing, cutting, hasty binding up of one after the other, then all away to the ambulance; then other groups, cries, and laments. Great God! what scenes! I have seen a group of soldiers around a surgeon who was attending to a wounded man, and I have heard the cry: "Oh! oh!" On approaching I found the wounded man already on his feet. "Go to the ambulance—go!" said the doctor. The latter moved off with slow and tottering steps. "Is he already cured?" I asked. "Cured! He may live a few hours," the doctor replied. I was astonished. "They are jokes of the bullets," he added.

I have witnessed beautiful examples of firmness and courage. A sharpshooter came to have a ball removed from his leg, and returned to join his battalion on the battle-field. A soldier in the infantry, who was seriously wounded, was brought in the arms of two of his comrades. He was very pale, his eyes half closed; he still held a cigar stump in his teeth, and put out his under lip in a nonchalant and indifferent way. He passed near my battalion; many ran forward to see him. He turned his eyes slowly around, and seeing that he was watched, made a motion of the mouth as if to take firmer hold of the cigar, which was falling, solely in order to display more *sang-froid.*

. . . One of my best and dearest friends is dead,—one of whom I have often spoken to you; a young sub-lieutenant of the grenadiers, a Lombardian, and very handsome fellow, Edoardo B. He was in my company at college; you have a photograph of us all taken together, hunt it up; he is the first on the right, seated on the ground with a cigar in his mouth—I remember it perfectly. See how he died: his regiment had stopped opposite the enemy's cannon; he was seated on a drum, with lowered head, and poking the clod between his feet with the point of his sword. Suddenly he fell back with a cry; a bit of grape-shot had wounded him in the chest and killed the horse of the adjutant who was behind him. He died after five hours of horrible suffering. Poor friend! Who could have foretold this when we were studying for our last examinations at college, in the wretched little room on the fifth floor, by the light of a taper, with those copy-books and that can of water colored with smoke; when you had so many bright hopes and were so happy! . . .

The answer to this letter is from the brother; the mother had gone into her bed with a fever. "From time to time," the brother writes, "she becomes delirious and calls you."

The army falls back toward the Oglio.

PIADENA, 5*th July.*

. . . It is very sad and painful to be continually crossing villages and cities between two rows of immovable, mute, cold people, who gaze at us with staring eyes, as if we were an unknown army. Who has courage enough to raise his eyes to those people's faces? I seem to read on every countenance: "Good! brave!" Was it worth while to make so much noise to cut such a figure afterward? The regiments file silently by with lowered heads, like a procession of monks. It is a sight that hurts me; my thoughts run back to you, mother; I need you sorely. Pardon me; if I could at least have the consolation of returning home without one arm, I might say: "I have won one arm less at least." But to return home unharmed, healthful, stout, and red enough to cause a pasha's envy, seems really shameful and unbearable. How much bile is stirred up by this little glass which, no matter how hard I work, will persist in showing one chin below the other! I hate this insolent, new-born creature, which seems to laugh at the misfortunes of the country! I am joking, but it is an indigestible joke. We are marching under the mid-day sun; on the right and left of the road are gardens, flowery fields, and villas; through the garden gates we see in the distance, at the end of the avenues, gentlemen in their shirt-sleeves stretched out under the shade of the arbors, young ladies dressed in white wandering about the slopes among pines and myrtles. Oh, happy beings! Not because they are in the shade and rest, but because they do not bear on their souls this terrible weight of discomfort and weariness.

Reply:—" I understand it all; mothers understand every thing. Courage, my son!"

The Cugia division is at Parma; is leaving for Ferrara.

PARMA, 10*th July*.

The blessed soldiers! We seem to love them better after these misfortunes. They are always the same; always resigned and good. On the march, when they begin to bend and limp, I look at and pity them. Sometimes when some one does any thing, I reason for some time with myself that it is really a case for me to get angry, and then I raise my voice: "Come now, it's time to stop that! You can't get on in that way. You try the patience of a saint; now then . . ." "You impostor!" cries a voice within me, "You are not really angry." "That's quite true," I say, smiling, and I stop. Then I propose not to love them any more, or at least not to show it, if not, farewell to all discipline. "We will see," I say; "let us see if they will succeed in melting this stony heart." Then I march quietly on, with an expression of face that ought to arouse any amount of fear, quite sure of my victory. And here is an example: "Lieutenant, shall I carry your cloak for you?" To which I reply brusquely: "No." "You are tired." "No." "Yes!" "How's that? You will see if I am tired because you wish it! Back to your place!" Another comes with a canteen. "Lieutenant, this is fresh." "I don't wish any." "Try it." "I won't try it." "Only a drop, and you will see." "Not a drop!" Then he puts the canteen under my chin. "You will see that it is fresh." "I know how to drink myself." I take the leather bottle, wet my lips, and hand it back to him. "Lieutenant!" "Well, what is it?" "You have not drunk." "Yes I have." "But it is all there!" and he shakes the flask. "Come now, understand that I am tired and cross, and that I can bear nothing more! Go to your place this moment; run, or I'll have you put in the guard-house in the camp for fifteen days. What sort of way is this?" "Impostor!" the same voice repeats. "It is true," I reply again, and I stop. "To-day the lieutenant is in bad humor!" the soldiers say. "No! no!" I hastily say to myself; "no, you set of rascals!"

Reply:—"I often tell your sister Erminia, Alberto has really kept his childish heart. I do not say that it is from any merit of mine; but nevertheless . . ."

The division has left Ferrara in the direction of Padua.

MONSELICE, . . . *July.*

How sad it is to march in the rain! The night had already fallen, and we were still four miles from Rovigo, and it was beginning to rain by the bucketful. In a few moments I found myself reduced to such a state that I seemed to have taken a bath with all my clothes on; the water ran in rivulets down my back and chest; my cloak was so soaked that it was too heavy to carry; there were inches of mud in the road; so you can picture our condition! In passing, we saw through the windows of the peasants' houses "the gleam of the evening lamp," and some shadows which appeared and then vanished. And I thought how you, when I was a child, used to push my small bed near the window, because I liked to hear the rain beat on the panes, and the slow, mournful whistling of the wind, put me to sleep fancying frightful adventures of pilgrims lost in the forests, the mysterious little lights gleaming from afar, and enchanted, hospitable castles. "Oh, poor boy, what a state you are in!" you would exclaim, clasping your hands, if I returned from school a trifle wet. Poor woman; if you could see me now! It was a day of misfortunes. We get near Rovigo, camp in a puddle, and away we start into the town. My friend and I find a wretched little room where we can dry ourselves and rest, in the house of an excellent family; we go to bed and sleep; all dash up at nine o'clock the next morning in order to go to the camp and start . . . Heavenly Powers! I can't get into my boots; I left them near the fire, they have shrunk and hardened so that a child's leg could not get into them. Help me, my friend, for heaven's sake! "That I will!" he exclaims. Up go his sleeves, and we both begin to pull, stop to take breath, and go on again with fresh force, stop again, and try with all the strength of despair. Oh, in vain! The poor tormented legs relax, the exhausted arms hang down, and our heads fall back, with our eyes starting out of their sockets, our foreheads dripping with perspiration. "There is one more thing to try!" shouts my friend; "rip the boots. Let's rip them then!" We seize scissors and penknifes and fall to work. But we cannot see the stitches, and the more we try the less we see. Our fingers are trembling, the boots slip from our hands, my friend has cut himself, so have I too; and time is flying . . . "Ah, there are the drums! We are lost!" The regiment left without us, and we joined it in a carriage an hour after it had camped. "What was the matter?" my friends asked. I reply by showing them my feet, which I had stuck into the first pair of boots that the first shoemaker in Rovigo, whom we had sent for in haste, had put into my hands. They were a spectacle! A moment later, and a warrant for arrest was served upon my friend and self. As soon as I entered the tent, I dashed those boots on to the ground, shouting as I did so: "There, you hangmen!" "But why did n't you, who had no trouble with your boots, come on?" asked the colonel of my friend later. "Colonel," he replied with the utmost gravity, "I have never abandoned my friends in misery."

Reply: "How many times have I preached to you, from your childhood up, against that wretched practice of wearing tight shoes! What will your colonel have said of you! But wasn't there at least a woman with some head in that house at Rovigo who could have helped you out of your difficulty? It seems impossible! Not one with any common-sense!"

IN THE NEIGHBORHOOD OF MESTRE, 20*th July*.

. . . I have seen Venice in the distance. I did not believe it possible that I could so love a city as to experience in seeing it the same sentiment produced upon one by the inamorata. In first seeing it so stupendous, yet so lovely, that it seems floating on the sea, not even a "hurrah!" came to my lips, nor a "beautiful!" as would have seemed most natural; there came a more affectionate and sweeter word, and I exclaimed: "Dear one!" A friend says that Venice, seen from such a distance at evening, produces upon him the effect of a pale, melancholy child leaning on a window-sill, with its head reclining on its hand, and looking fixedly at the horizon of the sea, like one who is thinking and waiting. And hardly had I seen it when I shouted: "I love thee!" Such is the sentiment which Venice inspires at a distance; within it may be grandiose and magnificent and produce an imposing effect; but seen from here it softens and enamours one. Dear mother, you have a formidable rival. . . .

These Venetian peasants are capital people. I was on guard near a hut, was sleepy, and rapped at the door to ask shelter; it was at two o'clock in the morning. A woman opens the door, shows me into the first room, brings me a straw mattress, a coverlid, a pillow, wishes me good-night, and goes away. I lie down and sleep like a prince. In the morning, as soon as I am awake, I go to the other room to thank my hostess, and see her asleep stretched on the ground, on a little straw, with two children, one in her arms, the other at her side, without a sheet, pillow, or even a rag of covering; she had given every thing to me. I was so filled with remorse, anger, and shame, I called myself an unnatural brute, villain, coward, etc. . . . I shall never think of that night without pain."

Reply (oh, you pious but pitiless person!): "You certainly were a trifle wrong but . . . in the end you were tired and were obliged to rise early, while that woman had slept up to that time and could sleep afterward. However, be more careful another time."

IN THE VICINITY OF MESTRE, . . . *August.*

Listen to this which is quite new. Day before yesterday I was on the outposts of the Malghera side. On going off, perhaps a hundred paces from the guard, I saw three ladies coming toward me; one of them elderly, the other two very young (they were her daughters), very beautiful, and vivacious. All three stopped in front of me and made a bow, asked after my health, said they had run off from Venice, were going to Mestre, wished to get to Padua to their relatives, and that meanwhile they were very glad to meet an Italian officer—they had seen no one as yet, I being the first. They gave me a cordial greeting, walk around me, overwhelmed me with courtesy, laughed, clasped their hands in sign of admiration and surprise, and all this with an ingenuity and grace that were really charming. After I had thanked all three with the greatest effusion, the mamma turned to the girls and said: "Show him what you have under your skirts." "Oh, the devil!" I thought. The girls hesitated. "Courage; lift them!" "Lift them!" I thought again. "Courage; what's there to be ashamed of?" I fell from the clouds. The girls hesitated a trifle longer, then, laughing and covering their faces with one hand, they both, while making me a graceful bow, delicately drew up the skirts of their dresses and displayed beautiful petticoats made in three pieces, one green, one white, and one red, with a great white cross in the middle. . .

Reply: "What was that lady doing with her daughters among all you men? Do be judicious. I tell you so because you have so little prudence."

PADUA, 5*th September.*

I was seized by the fever, came to Padua, and am in the hospital of the *Fate-bene-fratelli.* They have taken care of me. I am well, and to-morrow I return to my regiment. That's all. I wished to write you when it was all over, so as to prevent you from coming here, as I knew you would be sure to do. Now you can get angry, cry, write, protest; it's all the same; it is over; and you must be resigned. Do as I wish, dear mother; thank God that it has only been the fever; think of the poor young fellows whom I have around me; some wounded by balls, some by bayonets, condemned to stay in bed who knows how many more months, and fortunate are they who will ever be able to rise again. I have before me a lieutenant in the grenadiers, a Lombardian, who had received a bayonet wound in his chest, at Custoza, from a sergeant of the Croats, yet despite his wound he did not wish to leave the field. He showed me his coat, still stained with blood. He is almost well, gets up, walks, but when he wakes, the motion he makes in sitting up in bed causes him intense pain. He related the affair to me: "I remember very little," he said, "I remember as if in a dream having seen four or five horribly distorted faces running toward us, uttering a prolonged shout, and one of them looked at me. I shall always have before me those two staring eyes and the point of the bayonet; he was a tall, black man, with a huge moustache. I do not recollect how he succeeded in wounding me. I remember that a young, beardless Austrian officer, with an effeminate face, passed before me, waving his sword, and shouting desperately: '*Jesus Maria! Jesus Maria!*' He passed and disappeared. Him I always see and should easily recognize. Several days later, being in the hospital with the fever and delirium, my ears were filled by those shouts and the sound of the clashing muskets, and in the distance I saw a gleaming point come slowly forward in the direction of my heart, as if it were looking at me in order to recognize me. Then I suddenly felt it, cold and hard, entering my flesh, staying there for some time, and then going farther down. It will seem odd to you; but for many days, at every sudden noise I heard, the beating of the blinds or the falling of a chair, I felt a shudder run through my entire frame . . ." This poor fellow, despite his wound, jumped out of his bed in his shirt the other night and came and asked me if I needed any thing, because he fancied that he heard me groan. I *was* mortified. The idea of a simple fever patient being the cause of a wounded man's putting himself out for him!. From that night forward, at every noise he made, if he were only snoring, I jumped up and went to him. The headquarters of the army are at Padua, you know. Yesterday, while I was dosing, I saw a breast covered with medals and crosses gleaming before me; I looked; it was the *executioner*. He remained an hour. I began talking about the war; he let the conversation drop, and never smiled, for he was very sad. He left me with several warm pressures of the hand, saying, as he did so, most gravely: "Be strong!"

The reply is a violent protest, which gradually diminishes in strength from the first to the last word, although it begins : " You are unworthy of the immense love I bear you. Heaven is very cruel to me . . ." and ends : " Heaven be praised, for I see that it protects you ; and receive every blessing, my good Alberto ! "

MARTELLAGO, 25*th* *September*.

. . . Finally ! We are quartered for the first time at Martellago, a short distance from Mestre. I have a room, a bed, a table, and a looking-glass ! Oh, more than human felicity ! You cannot understand, my dear, what it means for us to possess a bit of house after so many months that we have been sleeping on the ground, and washing our faces in the running brooks. " It is mine ! " I exclaim, measuring the length and breadth of my room in slow, grave steps, and turning to look at the walls. " It is mine ; I pay for it, walk in it, enjoy it, and carry the key about in my pocket." The first evening, in getting into bed, I experienced a certain embarrassment and restraint ; I felt like a peasant who has secretly crept into the drawing-room of his master, and that at any moment I might receive a shower of blows. Then when I had placed my knee on the edge and felt it giving way, I thought I was falling, held back, smiled, and climbed up again, with a surprise and pleasure which recalled that which I felt as a boy on opening the box from which jumped the Sabine magician with the long beard. What a delicious sleep ! What a joyful awakening ! . . . A room ! But I am a king ! I wish to amuse myself, to play the *young lord*, and enjoy life. I have begun already. I have had my coffee brought to my bed ; have bathed and dressed slowly, gaping in a luxurious manner, and asking at every moment about the weather and time. I have had the impertinence to send for the barber of the place and receive him stretched out in an arm-chair ; of lighting a cigar, and opening a book . . . It is truly a fine thing to revel in ease and luxury ! My dear, would you believe that I love my little room enough to look out for the symmetrical arrangement of the chairs ? You will laugh, yet. . . . Now I begin to understand why you women so love your houses. I will never laugh again at your care that every thing should be in its place bright and shining. How many things tent life teaches !

Reply : " I should not consider a tent necessary in order to understand some things ! Sleep with your window closed ;

the first days of September are not ones in which to take air; if you have not enough blankets, ask the landlady for more. Apropos: Is your landlady young? Married? Has she children? What kind of a woman is she? These landladies always make me anxious, because they are generally too much inclined to meddle in affairs which do not concern them. You are a blessed boy!"

MARTELLAGO, 16*th September*.

... It is strange, that is to say, it is most natural, but at first it seemed strange to me, that among us, after a campaign, even those who seemed the coldest, most thoughtless, most sceptical, really feel a powerful need of affection, and speak at every moment and with every one of their family (many had even forgotten that they had any), and write here and there, preserve their letters religiously, and beg their distant friends to send them photographs, and hunt up some sort of a love affair on sea or on land. These changes generally follow in the quickest and liveliest manner after an unfortunate war, be it understood. Some have gone to dig up distant cousins, whose name they do not know, and have begun a most desperate correspondence with them. These young lady cousins, surprised and touched by the sudden and passionate expansion of those hearts, reply in a most ardent manner; the irons, as the saying is, become heated, and I foresee marriages. Wars take many sons from the country; but they prepare many. If you could see them as I do, certain Don Juans of eighteen, regular debauchees, who some months since placed the bottle, cigar, and the blonde or brunette above all human affections and happiness; if you could see them at evening, leaning on the window-sill, looking at the moon with melancholy eyes, and complaining to us: "She has not written me for two days." Yes, it is useless to deny it. Woman is always our most revered sovereign and mistress; ambition, glory, any other expected or hoped-for felicity, may sometimes illude us sufficiently to make us believe that we can do without her; hide her, so to speak, from our mind's eye and from the desires of our heart; but then . . . She does not stop us, as Manzoni says, in the superb journey:

> But marks us; watches and waits,
> But catches us . . .

Oh, yes, she always catches us!

Reply: "Whom have you been digging up? For pity sake, do be careful; do be judicious!"

*17th September.*

. . . Another strange phenomenon to be noted after a war, is the passion for reading which awakes again in all, even in the most indifferent, either by nature or from lack of culture, to this kind of occupation and pleasure. All read and hunt up books; the parish priest is obliged to put in circulation all the books in his library. With me, who always go to extremes, as you say, it has become a regular mania; it is no longer a desire for books, but a genuine hunger. Yet I am always faithful to my old friend. During all the leisure hours of the day and evening I read and re-read, thinking over and analyzing that blessed, much-beloved novel "*I Promessi Sposi*." My eternal companion and friend, source of so much sweetness, consolation, and of that even and sweet tranquillity of heart and soul, in which every affection of mine is purified and strengthened, each thought elevated, and things, men, the world, and life are presented to my mind under their best aspect, all surrounded by love and hope. I do not know how it is, but I feel that I love my country, my regiment, you, my friends, better and more nobly, in thinking over that gospel of literature. And there is not one page with which there is not connected some souvenir of our first readings; when you held the book on your knee, I read and you listened, my tears falling on your hands, and at certain points we closed the book and kissed each other. If I read it in my room I left it and came to hunt you up so as to cry in your arms. I have this book before me; I hold it in my hands, pressing it to my heart, and say to it: "By all the tears thou hast caused my mother and me to shed, by all the holy affections that thou hast roused and kept alive in my soul, by all the love that thou hast inspired in men, life and noble and good things, I swear to thee, as thou wert the first book I read, so shalt thou be the last, and as long as my hand can hold thee, my eye see thee, I will always seek thee, thee always, oh, book of paradise!"

After this letter there is the announcement of the departure from Martellago, and then, day by day, a notice of fresh departures and arrivals, from Padua to Rovigo, from Rovigo to Pontelagoscuro, from Pontelagoscuro to Ferrara, from Ferrara to Modena, and from Modena to Parma.

PARMA, 16*th October*.

Just hear what a trick that rascal of an orderly has played me. Two weeks ago, his saint's name-day coming around, I got a bottle of *barbèra* from the sutler, fastened a piece of paper around the neck on which was written: "San Remigio," and seizing a moment when he was absent, put it into his tent. I heard nothing of it; he did not thank me; nor gave any sign, so I fancied some one must have stolen it from him. Last evening, on returning from a walk outside the camp, I enter the tent and see at my place a great pile of fresh straw well gathered and scattered, so that it seemed as if just taken out of a sack. In the place where I put my head, the image of a saint hung from the tent-pole, with leaves and flowers around it, a little wax taper burning before it; by the side, on the cover of the trunk, a wooden box, made with a knife, which might have passed for a cigar-holder; under the case a bundle of cigars tied with a red ribbon. I look at the image; above it is written: "Santa Teresa"; I look at the box—"Santa Teresa"; I look at the ribbon holding the cigars— "Santa Teresa." Imagine how touched I was. I did not think that this poor young fellow, besides being so good, could be so delicate too as to honor, and fête my mother's name instead of mine.

The mother's reply is a regular box on the ear to the regulation of discipline. If Alberto's soldier had suddenly become a general, she could not have written in any other way. And it would seem that Signor Remigio was not illy recompensed for his delicacy, as one day he presented himself before the officer with a letter from home in his hand, his eyes quite moist, and thanked him at length in a trembling voice.

"I understand," said Alberto to himself when he had finished; "the two mothers have become friends."

From Parma to Piacenza, from Piacenza to Pavia, from Pavia to Bergamo; fifteen days' more march, half of which was in the rain. "I am thinking of the state of your poor feet," says a letter from the mother, "and I can do nothing but send you sighs of pain." "Send me some cotton stockings," replies the son.

Bergamo was the last station, from which Alberto's narrative begins again.

### THE RETURN.

It was during the last days of December; I was still at Bergamo with my regiment, amusing myself with books during the garrison duty, which always is (but especially after a war) monotonous and wearying enough to drive one crazy. I did not even think of returning home, because the time for long leaves had not arrived, and I had heard that the colonel did not wish to grant short ones, else all of us would have asked for them. Nevertheless, my mother continued to write me that, absolutely and at any cost, she wished to see me, and could not bear the separation any longer, to which I replied: "Be patient; wait a little longer," and she: "It is impossible"; and I wrote the same again in order to quiet her, and meanwhile days and weeks passed.

One fine morning I hear some one rapping at my door; I open it, and whom do I see, but the colonel!

He salutes me with the utmost gravity, will not sit down, says that he has come direct from Venice, is on his way to Milan, and that he had good news of my family. . . . At this point he looked me firmly in the face, and said with a certain air of pity and reproof: "I understand that you have a perfect mania for returning home."

"Eh! After a campaign!" I replied humbly.

"Campaign! campaign!" he repeated angrily; "don't you call it that; there have been four bad marches and four badly fired shots."

I was silent. He continued in the most serious way: "Get into the habit of considering the regiment your family."

I remained silent, and he went on :

"You really ought to go through a campaign of at least five years in India, in order to harden that small waxen heart of yours, and accustom yourself to the life of a soldier, of which you know nothing yet, allow me to inform you."

I still kept silent, so he continued:

"All this impatience, this great need to attach yourself again to the apron-strings, in fact, to return home, is any thing but soldier-like."

I was still perfectly mute. A brief pause followed, and he added, his voice growing almost imperceptibly sweeter :

"I have spoken to your colonel, and he has given you five days' leave; you can go immediately."

I fell from the clouds; wished to express my gratitude, to tell him that I was indebted to him for a great happiness, which I should always remember; but he stopped me short in telling me to start instantly; took his leave, and turned back at the door once more to say :

"Be a soldier!"

Then he went away. I gave a jump that nearly broke through the floor, and shouted : "Remigio!" Remigio came. "Pack my valise instantly." When he knew where I was going he seemed happier than I. "What a delight for your mother! I can almost see her." "Put in the image of 'Santa Teresa,' the dried flowers, the box, and the cigars." He looked at me in astonishment. "Ah, you don't know where they are! Here they are." And opening a small casket that I always kept closed, I took and handed him every thing. "Did you save them all?" exclaimed that good soldier, clasping his hands in surprise; and he continued, looking for some time, first at me and then at the things, smiling and exclaiming affectionately: "And the dried flowers too!"

Of all that I did before leaving I remember nothing save that, after visiting the colonel, I spun around the city like a top, took all the friends whom I met by the arm, not refraining from magnifying the beauties of Bergamo: "Look, what a sky! Look at the hills! What a superb plain!" And my friends shrugged their shoulders. The orderly accompanied me to the station; I paid for my ticket and forgot to take the change; I sent a dispatch to my mother, saying some ridiculous thing to the operator, who was good enough to laugh; I smoked, or rather bit up, two or three cigars in a few moments, and finally . . . "Mr. Lieutenant," said the orderly, handing me my valise when the bell began ringing, "be kind enough to give my compliments to your mother, and tell her that I have never forgotten her kindness to me and mine, and that I have always—"

"That you have always been fond of her; yes, say it, my good Remigio; I will not forget any thing. *Au revoir.* Good-by."

"A pleasant journey, lieutenant!"

The train was already in motion; I put my head out of the window, and saw my orderly standing behind the station gate; as soon as he perceived me he raised his hand to his cap, and kept it there until I disappeared.

I was due in Turin at ten o'clock in the evening.

When we reached the station at Milan, I saw a battalion of infantry which was just getting into the same train. I recognized an officer, one of my friends, and called him. "We are going to Turin," he said. "We are waiting for them to add other carriages; we have the colonel and staff with us; the headquarters of the regiment will remain at Turin; they write us from there of all sorts of ovations at the station. . . . Only that was lacking! Applause produces a much worse effect upon me than hisses. Oh, hopes! I shall send in my resignation, go and play communal counsellor in my own little town, be captain of the national guard, subscribe to the *Official Gazette*, wear trowsers large at the bottom, take a wife and tobacco, and die a chevalier. That's my destiny. 'Good-by.''

His regiment, whose number I have forgotten, behaved superbly at the battle of Custoza.

That journey from Milan to Turin was unending. "What a torment," I said, "to stay cooped up in this cage of a carriage! There is no air, one cannot breathe; there ought to be some place above. Well, meanwhile let us enjoy our arrival in fancy. Let us suppose that we have already reached the station. No, it is too soon; I wish to enjoy it slowly. Let us suppose that we are outside the circuit of Turin, far outside. The train goes slowly on; here is the enclosure; oh, what a breath! Here are the first walls of the station . . . but no, let us suppose that there is some hindrance; let us stop; this cursed train is going too fast. Forward, we are entering the station, the train stops; no, not yet! What importunate haste! Let me enjoy it at my leisure; so; slowly. My heavens! here I am getting out, there are all the people who are waiting, here . . . How warm I am with this heavy cloak! But how can you others sleep?" I said, looking at the other travellers. "How can you sleep with this fever that I am in?"

Ah, it is no longer fancy! Here are the beautiful hills of Turin, here the boundaries, here the fields, houses, the first walls of the station, and the three palaces of the Via Nizza! Here is that window! Heavens! who is at the window, who is raising and dropping his arms by way of a salute! It is he! it is he! it is papa! What do I hear and see? The music! the torches! Every thing just as on that evening! The train stops, I spring to the ground, run out, here is the crowd, here they all are. They have seen me, and open their arms . . . Ah, my mother! I still feel around my neck the firm pressure of those two trembling arms, I hear that music, and still see that light.

We are at the house door, it opens, I throw myself into the arms of my good papa, who is laughing and crying, without being able to utter one word; here are all his grandchildren, a kiss for each, and such a hearty one that it will leave a mark; here is the Neapolitan lady and her son. "Thanks for the topographical map," I say, and they all laugh. Other neighbors arrive; I am able to hear the impetuous assault of all kinds of greetings, congratulations, pressures of the hand, and questions; my mother catches hold of me, disputes the possession of me with all, looks at me, touches my arms, hands, and shoulders to see if all of me has returned; my sisters take turns in embracing me, and come and kiss me over again; the children jump around me—and it is a regular fête.

Finally, little by little, the neighbors and friends go away; my eldest sister returns to her home, the other goes to bed, with tears in her eyes; my brother leaves the house, and only my mother and I remain.

Hardly are we alone, when we sit down opposite each other, drawing our chairs close together and seizing each other's hands, as if we were lovers when left without any lookers on, and my mother, giving a long sigh, in which one can hear the whole history of the war, begins to say, in a voice full of emotion: "What days I have passed, my son; what anxiety, what terrible heart-beats! I did not write it for fear of saddening you; but this house seemed deserted after your departure. When I could no longer hear your hastening step on the stairs at the usual hour, your gay voice, and that tug at the bell, which made all run to see who would arrive first; the not being obliged to keep near you so that you should not forget the hour for the parade-ground. . . . What fearfully long evenings? And then the days which followed! If the sun shone, 'Poor Alberto,' I thought, 'is marching in the heat!' If it rained, 'Poor Alberto will catch it all!' I was almost ashamed to go to bed at night, when I thought of you as sleeping on the ground, and when it thundered, I waked, lighted the lamp, and said: 'It is impossible for me to sleep in such weather! Who knows where that poor boy is now?' I had almost become superstitious from constantly tormenting myself about you. When I went to look for any thing, I said to myself: 'If I find it no misfortune will happen to him, if I do not find it' . . . like all women. I felt my heart-strings tightening in looking at your clothes, books, and every thing belonging to you. It was a perfect torment to hear and see the gay people in the neighborhood; to see the young fellows of your age walking quietly and contentedly about the city. I went to the windows and looked at the few soldiers who were passing, and watched them until they had disappeared, for it seemed as if there was a little of you about them. I read and re-read all your letters of past years, recalled your and our history to my mind, beginning with the nights when I watched over you as a child, then when you went to school, and I wept if you returned with the 'I think,' and I did it for you, striving to imitate your writing; and I looked (not being able to do any thing else), and bathed with my tears the Latin *Anthology*, when you did not succeed in translating, and grew discouraged over it. Then I remembered the years when you were at college, the time when you were so gay, so happy here, that evening when I heard that music which nearly broke my heart, and I curled myself in a corner of my room, stopping my ears with my hands. The fear of losing you from one moment to the other made my having a son named Alberto almost seem like a dream! It seemed as if only a few months had elapsed since the first day I saw you! At evening, when your sister had gone to sleep, and I remained alone in these rooms, I fell upon my knees, look, beside that bed, and prayed to God as I had never prayed before, and offered Him my life a hundred times over for the preservation of yours, uttering your name a hundred times aloud, as if you were present to hear me, until my strength failed; I felt a weight on my chest, and it seemed as if I should die. . . . But you are here, you are safe, you are mine; I can look at, speak to, embrace you, and press this dear head to my breast. Oh! it seems like a dream! it seems impossible! Tell me that you are really here, Alberto; tell me that you are listening to me, and see me weeping. . . ."

I fell on my knees before her.

"My son, what are you doing? Rise!"

"But, dear mother, what are you saying? Listen to me: if I have suffered, was it not for you, because I love you. Was I tired or thirsty? I thought how that poor woman would suffer did she imagine it. But this intense affection for you gave me strength and courage. 'Am I suffering?' I said. 'Oh, my mother has suffered much more for me; and with what courage she concealed her pain and danger when ill in order not to frighten me.' And thinking of you and your love for me, what esteem you have for my heart and character, the idea, the sole idea of a cowardly feeling on the battle-field filled me with horror because it seemed an outrage to you, and rather than cause you shame I would have died. I too went over your history in my mind during those long evenings passed under the tents; and as children fancy paradise after their fashion, I dreamed of seeing you as a child; and then as a girl when in your garden at Savona you read the books which you first placed in my hands; then as bride and mother; when I was ill, and you made paper hats to amuse me—do you remember? and put them on your head and played the drum with two bits of the chair; brought my coffee to my bed, and I did not wish you to do it, but you said: 'Let me bring it; this is my comfort.' Then all the nursing of my poor infirm father through those long sleepless nights: You dear, holy woman! Then when I returned from college the first time, and you kissed my jacket. 'But who is this woman?' I asked myself. 'What a fool I am! Why does she love and adore me so much that I am her life, her world, and her happiness? Why is it thus? Do I deserve it? Who am I? There are many other mothers who are not and do not do like her; why should God have given me such an angel, or why did he not give her a more worthy son?' No, no, let me finish! how can I be grateful enough to you, how can I reward you? If I should place at your feet the crown of the world, could I give you back the thousandth part of the good that you have done me with your beautiful soul and your holy heart? Listen: I have always said it and I repeat it, and I shall ever say, even at my last moment: 'No one knows you mothers; but if all knew you, if the world were interested in the great mothers as it is in the great citizens, to a mother like you, to an angel like you it would raise a monument.'" . . .

My mother placed her hand on my mouth.

"'A golden monument, and all those who had hearts and souls, and I first of all, would kiss your footprints.'"

"Alberto! Alberto! this is too much! I will not listen!"

Then both of us with tightly clasped hands, and breathing heavily, I on my knees, she leaning over me, looked into each other's eyes, weeping, smiling, and calling each other by name.

. . . "And even now I kiss your jacket!" she exclaimed impulsively as she embraced me and placed her lips on my breast, and I pressed her head to my heart.

A few moments later we both took our lights, she going toward her room, I toward mine.

When we reached the door-way we both turned, laughed, and came back into the middle of the room.

"Alberto! . . . who are you?" she asked lovingly.

"And who are you?"

"You are a *mauvais sujet*?"

"And you are a saint!"

She looked at me, shook her head, and stood motionless in that attitude for a moment, lighted up by the candle, her eyes glistening with tears, with a smile so full of sweet quiet that she really seemed a saint.

How many times, now that I am living far from her, on returning home at night quite alone and *ennuyé*, with the weight of some remorse upon my heart, I seem to see her in the door-way, just in that attitude, as if saying to me : " You are a *mauvais sujet*."

It is a sweet but solemn reproof which resounds in the depths of my soul, and makes me repent, and form the resolution of being from that moment forward better, more honest and more worthy of her.

And on going to sleep, the image of that smiling, luminous face still dances before my eyes.

---

# DEAD ON THE FIELD OF BATTLE.

The artillery, on the battle-field, presents a spectacle that gives rise at the same time to a feeling of surprise and terror. To see that long train of horses and wagons moving, at a sign, from one end to the other, and with a tremendous racket dashing full speed across fields, roads, and vineyards, climbing and descending, and turning with the greatest rapidity, crossing ditches, banks, overthrowing and crushing hedges, plants, and furrows in their impetuous course, and finally disappearing in a whirlwind of dust and stones among the distant trees. Then after a few moments to see it reappear on the top of a hill, break and draw up in line, raise an immense cloud, and fill the valley all about with a loud booming; to see these formidable mouths recede at every discharge as if frightened by their own shouts, and far away in the distance houses destroyed, trees split, and dense crowds of the enemy broken up and scattered over the country, is really a sight that causes surprise and terror.

From the knowledge of the terrible and marvellous strength of weapons, the artillery soldier draws his peculiar character for pride and seriousness, that never leaves his soul or face even after a lost battle, when all the others are prostrate from sadness and despair.

Thus, serious and thoughtful, but not disheartened or dejected, did the cannoniers of a battery of the Piedmontese army enter Chivasso at evening, fifteen days after the battle of Novara. Many wagons, horses, a cannon, two officers, and several soldiers were missing from the battery. The captain and one lieutenant accompanied it. The people witnessed their entrance in silence and sadness, as they would have done the passage of a funeral cortege.

They stopped in the first square. The captain ordered his officer to park the battery, and, dismounting from his horse, he looked about as if in search of some one in the crowd.

A moment later, two young men (one might have been twenty-five, the other eighteen) approached him, took off their hats, and asked timidly : "Are you Captain—— ?"

The captain did not allow them to finish, shook hands with both, calling them kindly by name, and said : "I took the liberty of writing direct to you, without having the honor of knowing you, because I knew of no one else in this city to whom I could turn ; I should have written earlier if I had been able to learn any thing about your family. . . . But not even his friends," he added in a sad tone, "could tell me any thing ; and he had many dear ones, the poor, poor fellow."

Then he put out his hand again to the two young men, who pressed it affectionately.

"Did you say any thing about my letter to your father ?"

They replied that they had said nothing, save that the captain of the battery to which their poor brother had belonged would come within a few days to pay him a visit ; they could not tell him any thing more because he was ill, and they were afraid of exciting him too much ; yet some details of his son's death had reached him two days after the battle, and he had been perfectly inconsolable.

Meanwhile the lieutenant came up to them.

"Here is the officer of whom I spoke in my letter," said the captain in an undertone, as he presented the lieutenant to the two brothers, who pressed his hand, and made many protestations of affection and gratitude, to which he replied with much effusion. After saying a few words more, he returned to the battery. The captain arranged with the brothers that he would go and see their father the next morning at seven o'clock, because at eight he was obliged to leave for Turin, and making them tell him the street and number of the house, he recalled the lieutenant and whispered in his ear: "To-morrow morning, if I am not here at eight o'clock, you can leave with the battery; but do not pass by such and such a street"—naming it. The lieutenant understood the reason, and replied that his orders should be carried out; then the captain moved off with the two brothers.

The following morning at seven, the captain, followed by an orderly with a bundle under his arm, rapped at the door of the two new friends. He was obliged to wait a moment, which seemed like an hour. Was it impatient desire, or timidity which he felt at that instant? Perhaps even he would not have been able to say; but he felt painfully anxious. The door finally opened and the two brothers appeared. They did not give him time to speak; they placed their fingers on their lips, made him a sign to keep his sword from rattling, and greeting him silently they made him enter the house and sit down. The orderly put down the bundle and went away.

"He is sleeping," said the older brother; "but he is much better."

The captain took a chair, and the two brothers sat down

too, drawing their seats near enough to be able to talk in an undertone.

"Do you think I can talk to him without any danger?"

"Oh, yes, indeed," the brothers replied together; "now there is no longer any danger."

"Very well, then. But if you thought to the contrary, I should beg you to tell me quite frankly; I should not wish, in coming here to bring a little comfort, to be the cause of greater evil. Listen: it is only a short distance from here to Turin; I could run off for a few hours within two or three days."

"You are too good!" exclaimed the two young men, pressing his hand. "We thank you from our hearts, but really it is not necessary for you to put yourself out again for us. Our father is really better. If he were any other man, perhaps, even in seeing him better, we should hesitate . . . but believe us, captain, he has a heart so capable of feeling the consolation that you bring him, as not to leave any doubt about the effect which your words will produce upon him. He is a loving father, but a good citizen."

"I believe it," said the captain.

At that moment a door opened and a handsome blonde boy, about ten years old, appeared. On seeing the captain, he started back.

"Come here," said one of the brothers. The boy came forward.

"This is our little brother."

"How much he resembles that poor fellow!" exclaimed the officer.

"Quite true!" said the brothers.

After five minutes more conversation in a low tone, the captain opened the bundle and spoke to the brothers of a surprise for their father, then the second one rose and passed into the other room to wake the sick man.

The oldest brother and the officer pressed each other's hands, and said: "Courage!" to one another.

The young fellow approached his father's bed on tiptoe. The good old man was sleeping lightly with one arm stretched outside the coverlid, and his face turned toward his son. The latter stood for a moment looking at that frank, venerable brow, which even in the quiet of sleep retained the imprint of a deep sorrow, and he thought: "Now I am going to wake you, poor father,—to wake you and call you back to grief; I am taking from you these few moments of peace—but it is necessary. Father!"

The old man opened his eyes slowly and pressed his son's hand with the one he had outside the counterpane. The latter placed his right hand on his forehead, bent and asked him how he felt.

"Much better," was the reply.

"Well then, listen father, there is a person out there who would like to see you."

"Show him in."

The son did not move.

"Who is it?"

"Who is it? . . . It's an officer."

The old man looked at his son without speaking.

"It is a captain."

"A captain?" and he opened wide his eyes. A few moments' silence followed. The son, taking courage, added hastily:

"It is a captain of the artillery."

The father made a sudden effort to sit upright, but the son prevented him.

"No, father," he then said with much sweetness; "do not move; it might make you ill; you know the doctor has forbidden you to get up; lie down, father, and keep quiet."

And he put the arm that was out under the coverlid. The old man's eyes gleamed and he began to breathe heavily. Shortly after, without looking his son in the face, he murmured in a trembling voice:

"And this captain . . . ?"

"He was his captain."

This reply had been expected.

"He has come here on purpose to see you."

The father was silent for a moment, then shook his head, pressed his lips together, and covered his eyes with one hand.

"Father," said the young fellow affectionately, as he kissed him on the forehead, "be brave; the captain has come to bring you some comfort, and he will give it you, I am sure. Don't do so, come" (and he tried to draw his hand from his eyes); "be brave, father!"

"Call him."

"Immediately?"

"Yes, instantly."

"Well, then . . . shall I go?"

"Go!"

"Yes, I'll go; but be brave, father; the captain will bring you comfort; you will see."

So he left the room quickly. The father followed him with his eyes and fixed them on the door. He heard a short whisper, the noise of a sword . . . "Here is the captain." As soon as he appeared, the old man stretched out his arms toward him, and exclaimed sorrowfully: "Oh, captain! captain!" The latter went forward, embraced him, and said affectionately: "Courage, dear sir!"

The oldest son and the little boy placed themselves on one side of the bed, and the second one on the other. The father had laid his head on the captain's arm, and was weeping. For a short time no one spoke.

Suddenly the old man moved, raised his head, and wiping his eyes, said in a resolute tone: "Captain . . . you were there that day; you have seen; . . . tell me . . . relate to me . . . I want to know every thing; I will be strong . . . I am strong . . . I will listen without giving way . . . without interrupting you; but do not conceal any thing . . . I want to know all, I . . . I must know how (and here he broke out weeping afresh) . . . how my poor son died!"

Then he laid his head again on the captain's arm, and shaking it disconsolately, said:

"He was so young!"

"But now he is so great!" replied the captain.

At these words the poor old man started, raised his head, and looked fixedly at the officer; and as he looked, his face, bathed in tears, gradually grew calm and proud, his eyes were animated, and he slowly drew his arm from the captain's shoulder, as if the new thought with which he was occupied were sufficient to sustain him without any other support. This thought, which had lain veiled and dormant in his sorrow, suddenly sprang up in his mind, giving him an unexpected feeling of comfort, and putting into his soul a strength of which he would never have supposed himself capable. "So great!" he repeated to himself, and then in a low, but firm voice he said:

"Speak, captain."

The captain sat down as near the bed as possible, and, playing with the fringe of the counterpane, tried to find some way to begin. He did not succeed immediately, nor would he have found it easy to do so, had not the elder brother come to his assistance.

"Did your battery have much to do, captain?"

"At the battle of Novara? No, not much. That is, as far as firing goes, very little, really; but it had to work as much as if it had done a great deal; for it was running for three or four hours without a moment's rest; backward and forward; almost always on the same road. 'Captain!' they shouted to me, 'go and occupy that height!' And away I went on a gallop. But hardly was I up there, when a counter order arrived, and down we went to our first place. This happened three or four times without stopping. Poor horses, how hard they worked that morning! They really deserved a better fate."

"Were they killed?"

"A great part of them."

"And where did you finally stop?"

"I cannot tell you exactly the point; that is, I could not call it by name; but I remember the aspect of the place perfectly. We were half way down the side of a hill; between that point and the top, the ground caved in so deeply as to hide completely a couple of battalions from the eyes of any coming from the enemy's direction. When I reached it, we could see, off in the distance down on the plain, three long Austrian columns which were slowly advancing, now turning to the right, now to the left, but always keeping in our direction; they were so far away that we could scarcely distinguish their white uniforms and bayonets gleaming in the distance. One of my officers was instantly sent with two cannon to the right side of the hill. I, with my lieutenant and four cannon, remained where we were. At the cannon on the right (here the captain turned to the oldest brother) . . . was your brother."

The old man made no movement; he was intent and impassible. The captain continued:

"He was at the cannon on the right. They instantly began firing. Hardly was the cannon loaded, when your brother, as sergeant, had to 'point it.' 'At the middle column!' I shouted. 'Yes, sir!' he replied, leaning down to carry out the order. 'Let us do ourselves honor!' I added. He smiled, took aim, stepped back, ordered: 'Fire!' and almost at the same moment I saw the trunk of a tree which was in the middle of the centre column dash into the air; the latter began moving confusedly, spreading out and getting into disorder; the wounded officers galloped here and there; then little by little the lines formed again, and continued marching. 'Bravo!' I shouted to him. 'Now, another!' He took aim again, and once more hit the mark."

The old man clapped his hand on the bed.

"He hit the mark perfectly; the column became more disordered than before; the officers galloped around again; the column re-formed, but stopped. At that moment we saw four cannon appear in the distance, reach the line of the columns on a full trot; two of them stop between the centre and left one, the other two between the centre and right, and then begin to fire against us. 'Courage!' I shouted, turning to my soldiers; 'this is an excellent opportunity to let them see who we are.' We began to fire at the enemy's cannon. The columns receded a good deal. The one in the centre approached a little house, and it seemed as if a number of the soldiers entered. 'Sergeant!' I shouted to your son, 'put a ball into that house for me.' 'Yes, sir!' he replied in his usual firm and resolute tone. At that point a colonel of the staff passed behind us on a gallop, heard my words, stopped, and turning toward the cannon on the right, said aloud: 'Let us see!' 'Fire!' shouted the brave young fellow at the same moment. And from the roof of the house we saw rise and fall into the middle of the column, boards, tiles, and beams, and a crowd of soldiers dash out and scatter in every direction."

The father picked nervously at the counterpane with both hands.

"'Well done!' exclaimed the colonel, and off he went on a gallop. But the Austrian cannons were marvellously fired. The balls fell at eight or ten feet around us, buried themselves in the ground, raising clouds of dust and stones which gradually enveloped cannon and cannoniers, hiding them entirely from my eyes. When the cloud disappeared, we could always see your brave son smiling, and taking the dirt out from between his collar and cravat, as quietly and impassibly as if he were in no danger. But we were unfortunate. A ball fell into the middle of the company of infantry which stood as an escort at our backs, and killed three soldiers. After a moment one of our horses was killed, and two badly wounded. This was, however, a lesser evil. Two minutes had not passed when a terrible explosion and loud cry were heard ; a ball had split the wheel of a cannon, and stretched two cannoniers in a shapeless mass on the ground. It was not your son's cannon."

The old man breathed as if some hope remained that his son were still living.

"At that sight, I remember your son struck his head with his hand, and uttered a cry of pain. We were not yet reduced to a desperate condition ; we might have still kept our post for some time ; two new cannon joined the other four of the enemy ; the Austrian columns began to advance again, and we could no longer remain there. Suddenly we heard a confused sound of steps, voices, and arms behind us, and saw two battalions hastily draw up in line on the crest of the hill to repel an assault. Between us and the crest, the ground, as I said, was sunken ; for this reason it would not do for the infantry to advance to our line, and we were obliged to recede. The centre column was coming rapidly forward. I waited for it to arrive within reach, and then ordered : 'Fire with grape-shot !' At the word 'fire' we heard something like a clap of thunder, and a sharp whistle ; a cloud of dust rose and hid the column, and when it thinned, we saw such a confusion and complete rout in the enemy's lines ! But it was late. The enemy, scattered and disordered as it was, continued to climb boldly ; there was no time to be lost, and we must save the cannon. There were not enough horses. 'Back ! with your arms ?' I shouted. Thirty vigorous arms instantly seized the wheels, orillons, mouths, and began to push the cannon back. There was one artillery man lacking at the cannon on the right. Your son took his place, and seized the left wheel. 'Courage !' I shouted; 'strength! strength!' But the ground that he had to get over with his piece was broken up; the wheels sank, and the force they were obliged to use was tremendous; those five brave soldiers made the effort of twenty; one could see the muscles of their hands and necks rise and tremble so that it seemed as if they would burst through the skin; they were flame-colored, dripping with perspiration, and utterly transfigured. 'Courage,' said the soldiers and officers on the crest of the hill. The artillery men, panting and groaning, redoubled their strength. We already felt the heavy step of the Austrian column at our backs, and the voices of the officers; a chain of the pursuers pressed forward by the enemy's left column showered us with balls, we were almost on the crest. . . . At that moment he was wounded!"

"Where? where was he wounded?" asked the poor old man anxiously as if he were hearing the news for the first time.

"In the leg."

"At what point?"

"Here," replied the captain hurriedly, pointing to the calf of the right leg. "Hardly was he wounded, when he turned to look at the leg and shouted: 'It 's nothing! nothing! courage! strength!' and he went on pushing the cannon."

"Bravo!" interrupted the firm and sonorous voice of the sick man.

"Oh, yes, it was brave indeed! and in fact the soldiers who were near by shouted: 'Bravo!' The five courageous men, making a final effort, pushed the cannon on to the crest, and uttering a loud shout: 'It is saved!' they fell exhausted to the ground. They rose immediately, however . . ."

"But they did not all rise!" exclaimed the old man, covering his face with his hands. "Oh, I knew it!"

"He was wounded in the side."

A moment of silence followed.

"Hardly had the cannon passed the crest, when the two battalions of infantry broke out into a heavy fire on the assaulting column. The cannon at the right was dragged thirty paces forward. While they were dragging it (at this point the captain rose to his feet), your brave son, stretched on the ground, pressing one hand against the wound, shouted two or three times: 'Courage! courage!' Then his voice failed him, he made another sign with his hand . . ."

"Oh, that's enough, captain!" cried the old man in a tearful voice.

"Listen. Hardly had our cannon stopped, when the horses from some other pieces that had fallen into the enemy's hands came up; I ordered them to be attached immediately. The lieutenant got out of his saddle, and superintended my orders, standing before the right piece with his back turned toward the enemy; the horses were already attached; he was on the point of turning to say to me: 'We are ready!' when suddenly he felt some one press his knee; he turned and saw. . . ."

The old man sprang up in his bed, seized the captain's right hand, and asked with a shout: "Whom?"

"Your son."

"My son?"

"Your son, who, exhausted and dying, had dragged himself there to take a last farewell of his cannon and comrades. . . . All the cannoniers gathered around him; two seized him under the shoulders and raised him to his knees. He waved both arms and opened and shut his mouth, looking at the lieutenant all the time, as if he wished to say something. 'What do you wish, my brave soldier?' the lieutenant asked, in a tone full of affection and emotion; 'what do you want?' Then he raised his arms and clasped his hands, as if embracing some one. The lieutenant had a capital inspiration, clapped his hand on the mouth of the cannon, and asked: 'Is it this?' 'Yes! yes! yes!' he seemed to try to say, as he shook his head and gave a sign of the greatest joy. The two soldiers lifted him up to the cannon; he encircled it with his arms, pressed it to his breast, uttered a cry, and . . . died."

The father, who had been listening to the captain with ever-increasing emotion, seizing him now convulsively by the hand, now by the sword or the ends of his jacket, feeling of his shoulders and arms, as a blind man would have done to recognize him, broke out at that last word into a violent sob, which was a mixture of laugh and cry; his eyes gleamed, and his whole face was lighted up with an expression of radient joy.

"The sight of that hero's death," continued the captain, "filled us with enthusiasm. The lieutenant seized your son's head with both his hands, and looking into his eyes as if he were still alive, shouted, almost beside himself: 'Dear, brave, sublime soldier!' 'Hurrah!' broke out all the soldiers at once, and I shouted: 'Salute him!' All raised the hand to the cap, and repeated together: 'Hurrah!'"

The old man burst out into a flood of tears.

"Yes, yes," continued the captain, growing more and more excited, "shed those sweet tears; they will do you good; he is the pride of our battery; he will never be forgotten; in twenty years our soldiers, in pronouncing his name, will feel their hearts beat as we do now, a few days after his death; they will say that he was a valiant man, and will love and bless him as they would an absent brother. Yes, yes, weep now; now you can weep; weep here; I wish you to bathe my uniform with your tears!"

Saying which he seized and pressed the white head of the old man to his breast, and held it there for some time. The sons were weeping.

The invalid, exhausted after such long and deep emotion, was hardly released from that embrace when he let his head drop back on the pillow, and said, in a weak and broken voice: "Thanks, captain; thank you from my heart! Your words have done me a great good. It seems as if an immense weight were lifted from my heart. I hardly suffer any more. You have given me great comfort, my good captain, and I thank you for it."

He half-closed his eyes, and remained thus for some time, so that he seemed to be sleeping. Meanwhile all three brothers had gone, one after the other, into the neighboring room, and had returned, each holding one arm behind his back. The captain, too, had assumed that attitude. The sick man noticed nothing.

"Captain!" he finally said, rousing himself.

"Sir?"

"He was your sergeant?"

"Yes."

"Then—perhaps—you have some writing, a letter—or some . . ." and he could go no farther.

"Did you mean some report?"

"Just that, have you any, captain?"

"Yes, I have many of them; and as soon as I reach Turin I will send them to you. Oh, I had thought of this! If you had not spoken of it to me, I should have mentioned it to you."

"Oh, captain!" exclaimed the old man, "how good you are! How much I owe you! I shall always preserve most religiously all that my poor son wrote; I shall read it ten times a day, and always keep it under my eyes. . . . Oh, you will send me a great comfort, captain, in sending me those papers."

"But that will not be the only comfort I can give you."

"What other?" asked the good father quickly, and he sat up again in bed.

"This, for instance," replied the captain, and he handed him the cap of an artillery sergeant, which he had kept hidden behind his back.

The old man uttered a short cry, seized the cap with both hands, and kissed it passionately three or four times.

"Father," then said the oldest son, "I too have some comfort to give you . . . here it is," and he handed him a pair of sergeant's epaulettes.

The father seized and kissed the epaulettes, too.

"I have one also," said the second brother immediately, as he handed his father the yellow full-dress cords.

He took them and kissed them fondly.

"And I," said the boy finally.

"Oh, my child!" exclaimed the father affectionately stretching out his arm to him.

"I too have to give you something in—" he stopped to think

for a moment . . . "in anticipation, as the captain said. Here it is."

And he handed his father a medal for military valor with its ribbon attached.

The father had scarcely caught sight of it, before he had seized and pressed to his breast in one fond embrace the boy's head, the cords, the epaulettes, and the cap, saying as he did so: "Oh, here is my son! my poor son! I feel him!"

Finally he released the boy and fell back exhausted upon his pillow, still holding tightly to his breast, with his clasped arms, those precious objects. From time to time he repeated, with half-closed eyes, just above his breath: "Oh, here is my son! I feel him! I feel him!" And he clasped his arms more tightly still.

All were silent for a short time, until the captain said in an undertone to the brothers that he must leave. It was eight o'clock; and they could not beg him to stay.

"Father!" said one of the young men aloud. The old man opened his eyes.

"The captain must go."

"Go? go already? Oh! why? Can you not remain with us a little longer, captain?"

"I cannot indeed, dear sir, and I regret it much, but I really must leave immediately."

The old man gave vent to an expression of sorrow.

"Dear sir!—press my hand (the old man squeezed it vigorously). I shall return; I shall come sometimes to see you, and I will write you too; do not doubt that. It is impossible that I should ever forget you or this beautiful day. I was fond of you before knowing you, because one cannot help loving the father of a brave soldier, even without having seen him. But now! Now that I have known your generous heart and your noble soul, now I admire and love you a thousand times more than ever. Good-by; be brave, remember me sometimes, and think that I have shared your sorrow, so that I shall always be proud of your pride, and with the same joy with which you say: 'That hero was my son!' I shall always say: 'That hero was my soldier!' Farewell, dear sir!"

"Good-by . . . Oh, I cannot say good-by yet, dear captain! No . . . it is too soon . . . I cannot . . ."

The captain opened his mouth to speak, but the old man made him a sign with his hand as if to impose silence, dropped his head and was motionless, as if straining his ear to catch some distant sound.

"What is it?" asked one of the brothers.

"Silence!" repeated the father. All kept quiet. The captain listened too, made a movement of surprise and regret, and said to himself: "The lieutenant has forgotten or not understood my order." In fact, they heard a distant sound, dull and indistinct, which was gradually increasing.

"Father, what do you hear?" asked the son again.

The father, without moving his head or eyes, stretched out his hand to the captain, seized him by the arm, drew him toward him, and asked in an undertone: "Do you hear, captain?"

"I?—no, nothing!"

At that point they heard a distant sound that seemed like a military command; the noise grew more audible.

"Captain!" shouted the old man impetuously, rising to a sitting posture, "those are cannon!"

The captain trembled.

"It is your battery."

"Nonsense! It cannot be; you are mistaken; that is not my battery, I assure you."

"It is your battery, I tell you! I hear it! I see it! Tell me the truth, captain." His voice and his face had something imperious in them.

"But no!" repeated the captain, raising his voice to drown the noise, and they all did the same. "It is not possible, I tell you; I came here alone; my battery has been two days at Turin; what you hear is a train of military supplies; do believe me; what reason could I have for deceiving you?"

"Do be quiet all of you!" shouted the old man imperiously as he released himself from his sons, who were holding him. "Will you all be quiet!"

It was impossible to disobey; all were silent, and they could distinctly hear the noise of the wagons, the tread of the horses, and the different voices of the commanders.

"Ah! I told you so!" shouted the old man in a tone of triumph, almost beside himself with joy; "I told you so! I felt in my heart that they were cannon! I saw them. . . . Here, quick, give me my clothes, I wish to get up, I wish to go down. . . ."

"But no, father, no! no!" broke out the sons together; "you cannot get up, you are ill, it might do you harm," and they tried to keep him in bed. But he, opening his arms vigorously and pushing them all away from him, shouted: "Leave me, in heaven's name! Do you wish to kill me! Here, give me my clothes immediately, I wish them!" and he started to throw himself from the bed. They prevented him from doing this, but it was not possible to hold him in check; they were obliged to obey; so they handed him his clothes and helped him to dress in haste, not desisting, however, from begging him to stay where he was. "No—no—no!" he kept repeating with a stifled and gasping voice; "I will get up. I wish to see."

Dressed as well as possible under the circumstances, and supported by his sons, he started with unequal steps out of the room. But meanwhile the captain had gone to the window, and calling to the lieutenant, who was passing at that moment, ordered him to put the battery on a trot. The order was instantly executed. The old man reached the street, saw the battery moving rapidly off, uttered a cry of despair, and tried to throw himself at the captain's feet.

The captain could not resist. "Corporal!" he shouted to the first corporal who passed; "tell the lieutenant to stop the column immediately!"

The column stopped. The old man, still supported by his sons, preceded by the captain, moved totteringly toward the battery, which was quite far away.

When the reached the last cannon, the old man turned to the captain, and not being able to articulate one word, made a sign to him.

"No, not this one," the captain replied; "forward."

At that moment the lieutenant came up. They reached the second cannon.

"Nor this one either; go on still."

They reached the third. The captain had no need to speak. The old man dashed forward, with inexpressible affection, on to the cannon, and threw his arms around the middle of it.

The dying son had kissed it on the mouth. "Here! here!" shouted the captain, striking the mouth with his hand. The father stretched his arms toward the mouth, pressed it to his breast, and let his face fall affectionately on it, sobbing as he did so. "Oh, my son! oh, my son!"

Meanwhile, at a sign from the captain, the lieutenant had dismounted, and the two cannoniers who had held the dying sergeant had got down from their seat, and all three placed themselves behind the old man, the officer in the middle and the two soldiers at his side.

"Sir!" exclaimed the lieutenant.

The father, without taking his arms from the cannon, turned, caught a glimpse of the three; the scene which the captain had narrated flashed through his mind; he sprang to his feet, threw his arms around the two cannoniers' necks and laid his head on the lieutenant's breast. The latter, deeply moved, pressed the old man's head between his hands, and gave him on his forehead the kiss which he had given to his son on the battle-field.

"All my sons!" cried the poor father.

The captain made a sign; all the soldiers rose to their feet and gave him a military salute.

The good old man felt his knees giving away under him, and fell into the arms of his sons.

A few moments after, the last cannon of the battery was disappearing at the end of the street, and the father, leaning on his sons' arms and standing at the house door, saluted it with his hand as if his dead son were really leaving with it.

"Oh, father!" said one of the young men, "our brother is not dead!"

And he, raising his head proudly, replied: "And will never die!"

## THE ITALIAN ARMY DURING THE CHOLERA OF 1867.

EVERY time I think how much the army did and suffered for the country during the cholera of 1867, and feel again that lively sense of admiration and gratitude which was aroused in me during those days by the news of every fresh act of charity and courage, I am seized by the doubt that the greater part of those actions has been forgotten by the majority, that many of them have never been known, that all, or nearly all, have been too vaguely mentioned to be as thoroughly appreciated and praised as they deserve. Perhaps the recollection of all those grand actions has been fused by the nation into one single idea—the army did much good; just as after a victorious battle the movements and glory of one hundred thousand soldiers is expressed and exalted in the name of some general. And I am strengthened in this belief when I consider that the country, which is only a spectator, and can, and generally does, notice many things, having been, in the case of the cholera, both actor and victim at the same time in the terrible drama, quite naturally paid little attention to the many passing deeds (although the army was generous), the effects of which were trivial and almost unnoticeable in comparison to the vastness of the evils by which it was so greatly tried. Now there is no one who does not understand how the feeling of admiration and gratitude which arises from the vague mention of the work done by the army for the benefit of the country on that occasion, must be much less deep and lasting, and the example less efficacious, than it would be when knowing the manner in which the work was individually accomplished, the sacrifices which it cost and the perils that accompanied it, the relation of which would produce a deep impression upon the mind, and people thus be able to bestow their admiration upon deeds of daring, and unite their gratitude with names. Some of these facts and these names I mean to revive in the memory of any who have forgotten or never heard them ; and I am induced to this not so much by the thought of the sweet and proud sense of satisfaction that I, as citizen and soldier, shall experience in writing a page so glorious for the Italian army, as by the desire which I have to fulfil a duty of justice by giving light to many virtues, many forgotten or obscure sacrifices, and, besides this, by the firm conviction that it will not be quite a useless task to set forth a splendid example of the way in which the man and citizen should behave in the face of national misfortunes.

Toward the end of 1866, it was hoped in Italy that the cholera, which had invaded many provinces that year, would not return the following season. But on the contrary, as every one knows, it returned with greater force than before, and of all the Italian provinces, that which suffered the most was Sicily, of which I shall write almost exclusively, in order to carry out my design in the clearest and most concise manner.

In the months of January and February of '67 the cholera carried off a few victims in the neighborhood of Girgenti and especially in Porto Empedocle, whence, in the month of March, it spread through the entire province, and from this, in April, into that of Caltanisetta, and increased most terribly in both during the month of May, favored by the summer heat, that made itself felt a month earlier than usual in consequence of the long drought. It did not decrease at all during the month of June, save in the city of Caltanisetta, where it diminished perceptibly. In fact, during the first part of that month, it invaded the provinces of Trapani, Catania, and Syracuse, and at the beginning of July, Palermo, and at the beginning of August, Messina. Meanwhile it had spread through almost all the other provinces of Italy, and particularly in the southern ones; more than all others, in Reggio, where it committed its last and most frightful ravages at the end of the year.

From the first indications that manifested themselves in the provinces of Girgenti and Caltanisetta, General Medici, commanding the division of Palermo, almost foreseeing the terrible course of the epidemic, put in force all the hygienic precautions prescribed by the Minister of War in 1865. He divided the corps into a greater number of detachments, so that no city or village should be without them. He ordered that military hospitals for cholera patients, infirmaries for those suspected of the disease, and houses for the convalescent, should be opened everywhere in the most remote and healthful localities. He instituted a commission for sanitary surveillance in every district, prescribed most thorough and rigorous cleanliness, together with frequent disinfections of the barracks; he suspended every movement of the troops from the infected localities to those that were healthful: obliged every corps and detachment to give its assistance in case of any call from the civil authorities for the service of sanitary cordons, or to re-inforce the national guard in the maintenance of public security ; enjoined upon them to look for and prepare in the neighborhood of the principal cities the best adapted place for the encampment of the troops in case of necessity ; he improved the soldiers' rations by the daily distribution of wine and coffee ; exhorted the officers to prepare the minds of the soldiers for that life of sacrifice, danger, and hardships which every one foresaw in his heart, and expected with his soul resigned and fortified by the experience of the preceding year. An equal number of precautions were taken at the same time by the majority of the divisional commandants in the other provinces of Italy, and everywhere they put up hospitals, disinfected barracks, and there was an unceasing bustle of physicians and officers, a continual giving and receiving of orders, an unusual confusion of people and things, just as at the opening of a war ; in a word, that great agitation of minds which precedes great events, and which is so well expressed by each one in the words : We are ready !

But no matter how well disposed the army and brave, honest citizens were to work for the good of the country, three great inimical forces were bound to render the majority of their labors quite inefficient for a long time : superstition, fear, and poverty, the assiduous companions of contagion in all people and in all ages.

In most of the places, and particularly in the smaller towns, the syndics and many other public officers abandoned their posts at the first appearance of the cholera, and some places were deserted entirely by families with all their worldly possessions. The rich and well-to-do people, and all those, in fact, who might have succored the people most efficaciously, fled from the city and took refuge in their villas. In a few days all the country-houses were crowded with the fugitive citizens, and not only those of the rich, but of any one possessing enough to live several days without work, and hire a dwelling, hut, or any hole, even at a great sacrifice, provided that it was distant from the city, and as far as possible from any other habitation.

Abandoned and frightened by others' fear and the solitude in which they were left, the poor people fled too, and wandered in troops through the country, dragging their lives miserably out amid the sufferings of hunger. The general terror was increased by the recollection of the great sufferings of past years; worse misfortunes were predicted as is always the case; they foresaw such an end from the beginning: in each province they exaggerated most marvellously the ravages of the disease in the others; in the country they narrated horrible things of the mortality in the cities; in the cities just as much again of that in the country-places.

It is quite easy to imagine how the population of the districts became reduced. With the exception of a few cities, the communal administrations having been abandoned, or left in a state of disorder, they neglected the most necessary hygienic precautions. Then the population, declaring firmly that such precautions were unnecessary, refused to render their assistance, without which they were quite useless, no matter how much good-will the authorities, or how much zeal the few citizens who thought and worked with a fixed purpose, displayed. Then let me add that there were many places without any physicians or chemists, and then, even the largest were desolated by the poverty which the famine of the previous year had produced, and increased by the scanty harvest of that season and the enormous mortality in the herds. Most of the merchants had failed ; the construction of railways had been interrupted ; many provincial and communal works had been left half completed ; the men were without work ; the shops for luxuries had been closed first—of late many of those for the necessities of life ; also, the work-shops abandoned ; hundreds of familes reduced to living on herbs and India figs ; on every side famine, discouragement, and squalor.

To culminate the general misfortune there spread and took root in the minds of the people the old superstition that the cholera was the effect of poisons scattered about by the order of the government, which the common people in most of the the southern districts (in consequence of the oppression of a past government) regard as an enemy who is secretly and continually trying to harm them for its own preservation. In Sicily this superstition had been accepted from the conviction that the government wished to inflict punishment for the rebellion of September, and for this reason a great part of the sanitary precautions taken by the government met with a stubborn resistance in the common people ; every action appeared an outrage ; in every order they suspected some rascally design ; from the slightest indication they drew some argument confirmatory of the poisoning, and they saw some attempt in every trifle. The hospitals, disinfections, visits of public officers, were all the objects of diffidence, fear, and abhorrence. The populace could not be induced to allow themselves to be taken to the hospitals, except at the last moment, when every case was useless. The majority of them died ; and just for this reason they believed all the more firmly that the medicines were poisons, and the physicians assassins. They preferred to die quite abandoned, without any assistance or comforts. They did not believe in contagion, and so they lived together in any way, the sick and the well; many families in dark, horrible dwellings, which were the terrible hearthstones of the pestilence. They concealed the bodies to prevent themselves from being isolated, or because they disliked the idea of seeing them buried in cemeteries, instead of in the churches, as is the custom in many places; or, from the obstinate conviction that those attacked by cholera often appear to be dead when they are not, and come back to life after a time. They resorted to every device to elude the researches of the authorities. They often resisted with force the public agents who came to drag the decayed bodies from the houses. They threw these bodies into wells, or buried them secretly inside the houses. In some places, either from carelessness on the part of the authorities, or from neglect on the part of the people who wished to assist at these pious offices, the bodies, although not refused by the relatives, were left several days in the houses, were thrown and left uncovered in the cemeteries, or covered with a few shovelfuls of earth, so that the air all about was poisoned, and no one could be found who was willing to approach the place, thus making it necessary to select other spots for interment. The common superstitions were secretly fermented by the Bourbons and clergy. All the agents of the public force, the carabineers, soldiers, inspectors of the custom-house, and government officials were suspected as poisoners. They scattered, and posted up in the streets seditious proclamations exciting the people to revenge and bloodshed. Little by little the

"Little by little the people, armed with scythes, picks, guns, assembled," etc.
(*Page* 378.)

people, armed with scythes, picks, guns, assembled, ran tumultuously about the country roads trying to put the poisoners to death. They menaced or assaulted the barracks of the carabineers and soldiers; broke into the physicians' houses and sacked them; burst into the pharmacies, and destroyed and displaced every thing; invaded the offices of the Commune, tore the national banner; burned the papers and registers; forced the national guards to hunt the country with them in search of poisoners; looked for them in the houses; thought they had found them; obliged them with daggers at their throats to imagine and confess their accomplices; murdered them, lacerated their bodies, and burned them in the streets and squares. Entire families, accused of poisoning, were suddenly beseiged at night by a crowd of common people; and old men, women, and children fell with their throats cut at each other's feet, without having time to exculpate themselves or plead for mercy. They burned houses and scattered the ruins. At Via Grande, Belpasso, Gangi, Menfi, Monreale, Rossano, Morano, Frassineto, Porcile, in the Potentino, and Avellinese, in a hundred other places there were continuous gatherings, and rebellions, and horrible deeds of bloodshed.

Every day the populace found a stone, a rag, or some object which they fancied was saturated with poison. They gathered in crowds at the syndics, carrying the poisoned object with them; they had physicians and chemists come to experiment with it, and desired that the results of the experiment should be as they declared that they ought to be, or else they threatened them with violence. In some places the madness of the people reached such a point, that the majority of the citizens were obliged to barricade themselves in their houses with some provisions, living shut up like prisoners, from the continual danger of being accused of being poisoners and killed. This course aroused their suspicions more strongly; they assaulted the houses, and a veritable struggle ensued. In the places and during the days in which, on account of the mildness of the disease the people were less brutal, those accused of poisoning were only vituperated, beaten, and then dragged, covered with blood, before the syndic. Sometimes the municipal functionaries, frightened by the exasperation of the crowd, did not dare try to dissuade them from their bloody designs, and exhort them to spare their poor unfortunate victims, so replied, as they did in the village of San Nicola that, "they had better do what they thought best." And the reply had not been made before the wretched creatures lay on the ground immersed in blood and no longer retaining any semblance to human beings. The municipalities, unless one makes an exception of those in the principal cities, menaced and abused every day as they were, had lost all their authority and become quite powerless to put in force the most necessary provisions for the public health, because in fact they were obliged to forestall and grant every wish or desire of the people in order to avoid more deplorable consequences. At first the people insisted that no living soul should be allowed to enter the place, and the municipality established a rigorous cordon around the district, and so all communication was cut off; but hardly did they begin to feel the bad effects of this cessation of intercourse, when they wished to have the cordon removed; they thus increased the epidemic, and once more were obliged to replace the cordon. And the same thing happened with all the other precautions, now desired, now not wished for, according as the malady increased or decreased, according to the distorted fancy of the populace, or by the different manifestations of some supposed symptoms which they thought healthful or otherwise.

In fact every thing was in a state of confusion; in every place was the saddening sight of poverty and fright; the country was overrun by a troop of beggars, and scattered with sick people and bodies that had been abandoned. The villages were half depopulated, all intercourse among people in the cities had ceased, every public place was deserted, every particle of gaiety subdued in the life of the working people, the streets almost deserted, the doors and windows barred for long distances, the air impregnated with the nauseating odor of the disinfectants with which the streets were sprinkled,—on every side a dead silence which was either interrupted by the complaints of the poor and suffering, the laments of the dying, or the shouts of the seditious populace. Such was the condition to which the people of many provinces of Sicily and the lower portion of the Napoletano were reduced, and perhaps the picture which I have drawn only depicts in pallid colors the terrible truth.

But the painful feeling which is aroused in our hearts by the memory of those dark days, comes more from the thought that most of the evils arose from the almost savage ignorance of the common people, and in general from the lack of courage in the citizens of all classes there, than from the knowledge of the terrible ravages which the cholera in itself produced. The most disheartening effect (although perhaps not the most useless one) of the misfortune of the cholera, was perhaps that of showing us that we are more backward in the road of civilization than we are in the habit of supposing, that the way lying before is much longer than it seemed at first, and that we must strike out more seriously and boldly. It would be difficult indeed to prove that on similar occasions in times less civilized than ours, the folly of the common people was carried further, or produced more terrible effects, and that, in the generality of people, to-day more than then, in the presence of misfortunes and common peril reason has conquered instinct, charity selfishness, and duty fear.

But what did the army do?

The disorder of the administrations, the confusion, and general fear had inspired audacity in the highwaymen and bandits, and given them an opportunity to spring up again; so that both scoured the country and cities, committing every kind of depredations and violence. The troops, who could not give up their chase of them, no matter how indispensable their assistance might be elsewhere, found themselves surrounded by a thousand different duties, some more dangerous and fatiguing than others. The numerical force of the corps, which was small in comparison with the needs of ordinary times, proved quite insufficient for the service of the hospitals, sanitary cordons, and public security, at the same time. All these services were performed, however, by dividing the forces as much as possible; so that it happened almost everywhere that the soldiers never slept two successive nights in the same barracks, and no longer ate at prescribed hours, but just as it happened, when, where, and as they could. There was continual motion, continual fatigue. Just during those days when repose, quiet, and every kind of precaution was really most necessary, it is impossible to tell how much the health of the soldiers suffered, and how that kind of life rendered almost useless the great care which was imposed upon all in the cleanliness of the barracks, choice of food, and many other precautions imposed upon them by their superiors, and diligently carried out under their surveillance.

But these services were certainly the least burdensome, because, if not always, at least ordinarily, they were performed by each soldier at certain brief, but regularly established intervals, so that they went forward to meet all fatigues and perils with their minds fully prepared for them. The harder services were those imposed upon them from time to time by the unexpected outbreaks of the people, in the dead of the night, sometimes simultaneously at different points in the same place. A handful of soldiers were obliged to sally forth against an armed multitude a hundred times greater than they, who beat furiously on the barrack-doors, flung stones at the windows, and threatened to set fire to the house, while shouting; "Death to the poisoners! death to the assassins of the people!" together with every other kind of vituperation. These furious cries resounded suddenly through the silent dormitories; the soldiers sprang startled from their beds, dressed in haste; the officers gathered, seized their weapons, and dashed furiously down the stairs to charge the crowd. The crowd opened, scattered, turned, and formed again, shouting, whistling, throwing stones, and the soldiers charged them again; once more they dispersed; and this went on for hours, all through the night, sometimes throughout the following morning. When the mobs consisted of a few people, the soldiers came out unarmed, tried to pacify them by kind words, and all their powers of persuasion; sometimes they succeeded, at others they were attacked, beaten, and then they returned on a run to the barracks, armed themselves, came out again; the rioters shut themselves up in their houses, and fired from their windows, so that they were obliged to break down the doors, penetrate into the houses, and attack them regularly. During the daytime there were continual fatigue; at night short and interrupted slumbers; and danger and anxiety always.

Besides this, in most of the districts the soldiers were obliged to go and take the bodies from the houses, carry them to the cemeteries on the regiment wagons, and dig ditches in which to bury them. At such times the populace offered every possible resistance; they were obliged to penetrate into their lurid dwellings, bayonet in hand, and take possession of the bodies by main force These bodies they sometimes had to go and hunt for in the country, and when the arms of the soldiers did not suffice for the work, they had to force the peasants to render their assistance by threatening and dragging them to the spot. They were obliged to prevent the people from flying from the districts, by following and leading them back by force to their houses, taking by the arm entire families, beggars, and troops of women and children who burst out into tears and cries of despair.

Throughout all the corps and detachments collections were taken up for the poorest families; in some places a certain quantity of bread was distributed every day; in others meat and soup; when nothing else was to be had, they gave the remains of the rations, straw,—old clothes, and something at least. In many corps they formed committees for permanent succor; the officers went every day in turn through the houses of the poor to carry them aid, give advice, and watch over them ; the soldiers gave up their straw mattresses to the hospitals ; offered spontaneously to go and nurse the sick in the lazzarettos and private houses, and went there and performed their duties courageously and cheerfully to the end. In the places where there were no druggists, they went and distributed the medicines in the shops, superintended by military doctors, and they even carried them to the houses when it was necessary, In other places where even the shops for the necessaries of life were closed, they had them opened by force, and they themselves provided for and superintended the sales. Often they were obliged to keep the market open ; a part of them watching over the sale of the articles, and the others maintaining the order and peace which were continually threatened. Very frequently, either in the villages or cities, they had to make and bake bread, a labor which no one wished to perform from fear lest in perspiring they should contract the cholera ; and not infrequently they were reduced to helping the carabineers and policemen sweep the streets and houses of the poor, because there was no one else who would make that dangerous exertion. There were the less humble but not less unusual and difficult duties which often fell to the officers, who were obliged to act as syndics in the villages deserted by the authorities, sometimes as physicians and always as almoners and missionaries of civilization in the midst of a people stupefied and exasperated by fear and sufferings, and fits of fearful passion. This was the case, too, with the military doctors, upon whom was imposed, in addition to the care of the soldiers, that of the people, whose prejudices they were first obliged to destroy, and then overcome their repugnance and hatred by reasoning and arguing with them. This was the case with the commandants of the corps also, who were overwhelmed by a thousand needs, encompassed with as many difficulties and cares, always in apprehension for their troops divided and scattered here and there, and continually in motion and in danger. A terrible sorrow for all was that of having to say farewell every day to so many brave soldiers, good comrades, and dear old friends.

But all these services, sacrifices, and works of charity, which, though barely mentioned, are sufficient to arouse in every good citizen an outburst of grateful recognition, cannot however, as I have already said, be thoroughly appreciated and praised unless one knew intimately with how much zeal and in what way they were performed. This is what I intend to do, and what matters it if it be not particularly understood by those who, in the generous actions of the soldiers, are only accustomed to see and appreciate the immediate and natural effects of the discipline which commands and castigates, but never the natural and spontaneous effects of the heart, which that same discipline educates and softens. It is true, in fact, that in ordinary times, when the soldier does not comprehend or see, or sees too far away in the distance the fruit of the mite which was asked of him in aid of some public misfortune, or when he does not understand the absolute necessity of some other sacrifice, and fancies there is some one else who can or ought to make it in his stead, the desires or suggestions of the superiors generally assume, first, the form, the intention, and therefore the effect of direct and absolute commands, so that the merit of spontaneity cannot be attributed to the acts which follow; but this, for different reasons, could not have happened on the occasion of the cholera, because at that time, in the majority of the cases, the soldiers understood and saw clearly that the health of the districts in which they were, was intrusted to their care; that in certain moments of extremity there was no one but them who could prevent great misfortunes; their every act and sacrifice produced its immediate and visible effect, there was the fleshless hand of some starving person outstretched to grasp every bit of money or piece of bread that they offered. Pity was kept alive by the continual spectacle of misfortune, and there was no room for any doubt or diffidence by which the sentiment of that pity could grow lukewarm or make them hesitate. Neither can one reasonably suppose that the influence of their superiors had any part in the charitable works, that were not performed by the obligation of duty or from any other absolute necessity, for these needs and obligations were so frequent and so grave in themselves that no superior could have made any such pretence without a sting of conscience. Besides which, as the corps were for the greater part divided into very small detachments, and these same detachments performed their labors after another subdivision, the influence which the superior officers could exercise over their subordinates, in order to obtain any thing beyond their duty, was very trifling; it would have been insufficient also in making them do their duty, if there had been in reality any need of such influence. On the other hand, the orders of the superiors never reached the point which the soldier's work did, because certain sacrifices are of such a nature, that they cannot be imposed in any way or for any end; and my readers will see what these were, and how the officers and soldiers of every corps performed them. But if all these reasons should not be sufficient to convince the incredulous, or should the colors of the picture which I place before my readers' eyes appear too vivid or too fanciful, there would always be in confirmation of what I have asserted, the unanimous testimony of the populations, or that, not valid for all, but quite certain and sacred for me, of my many companions in arms and the friends who saw and narrated what the soldiers did or how they did it, with their hearts filled with gratitude and pride. From the light of their eyes and the sound of their voices I attained the deep conviction which moves my heart and pen.

Generally the companies were only united at evening, in the dormitory, at the hour of retreat. While waiting the signal of the drum for the roll-call, the soldiers related to one another what they had seen and done during the day; some of them seated on their beds, others leaning against the windows, the remainder in groups in the middle of the dormitories. There were none of those movements, songs, laughs, or deafening shouts of joy, which in ordinary times are so pleasant in the barracks at evening. Most of the soldiers were motionless, and nothing was to be heard but a subdued whispering, interrupted here and there by some exclamation of surprise, anger, or pity, and long intervals of silence, in which you would have said that all were sleeping. The soldiers who gradually arrived went quietly to their beds, and laying down their fatigue caps and belts, joined the different groups, each one quoting the last rumor in the district, which was always one of misfortune. Any one not knowing it otherwise, would have been able to understand what was being thought and said in those groups, by simply looking in every room at the few faces lighted up by the small lantern placed over the door.

"Do you know," one said, "that they have killed a carabineer at Grammichele? The soldiers found him dead in a ditch; they say that his face was all beaten out of shape, so that it was irrecognizable, and the arms and legs half gnawed by the dogs?" Some one asked why he had been killed. "Because he poisoned people," replied the first, and a bitter smile passed over the lips of the listeners. "Have you heard the news?" said others, "At Belpasso they have killed the delegate of public safety; at Monreale they have fired upon the sharp-shooters; in Ardore they have killed and beaten to pieces the captain of the national guard, and Second Lieutenant Gazzone In some other place they have fastened to the walls a proclamation, which says that they must burn and cut the throats of the soldiers and destroy all the barracks. . . . All this because we poison the people."

A sound of the drum was heard, the companies drew up in line, answered the roll-call; half the soldiers were absent. The quartermaster-sergeant read their names, and when any one was lacking, the corporal of the week, erect beside him, notebook in hand, said in a low voice: "He is ill at the lazzaretto; he is on the patrol in the country; he is on the round in the district; he is on duty at the cemetery; he is dead," and these last words were followed by a movement of surprise and a murmur of compassion. "Silence!" shouted the quartermaster-sergeant; "attention to the duties for to-morrow." And he read the names of those who were detailed for various services on the following day, and generally all present were appointed for the same duty. No one breathed. Some on hearing their names among those detailed for the service of nurse at the hospital, could not restrain a feeling of repugnance and displeasure; so raised their eyes and shook their heads. "What is the matter?" suddenly asked the sergeant, who had noticed the movement. "Nothing." "Then keep quiet." And the poor fellows did not move again, this being the gravest protest made by the boldest and least docile.

On the evenings of the days in which the cholera had committed the greatest ravages throughout the country and among the troops, one could see all the soldiers quite intent at rollcall, motionless as statues, and their faces wearing an expression rather of astonishment than sorrow, their souls being more stunned than saddened by such great misfortunes. "Such and such a one?" asked the quartermaster-sergeant. "He was seized by the cholera a moment ago, and they have carried him to the lazzaretto," replied the corporal. "Such and such another one?" The man called replied from the lines: "Present," but in a forced and weak voice, in which one could hear the effect of the sad news. Then a deeper silence than usual followed.

On such evenings the officer usually gave them some words of encouragement and comfort. He placed himself in front of the company, glanced at the faces in the first line, and then said what he had to say, always ending with a: "Keep up your courage," which was followed by a slight movement along the line, which meant "Thanks." A sign to the quartermaster-sergeant, a word to the sergeant of the week, and then, "Goodnight," he would add, almost involuntarily, as if responding to an imperious movement of his heart, and then go away. And the soldiers followed him with their eyes, which was worth more than a mere good-by. How many times, on going out of that dormitory, the officer said sadly to himself: "Perhaps to-morrow all my good soldiers will not be there!" And how many times the soldiers, in seeing the officer go out, pale and worn, and behind him the orderly with an expression of sad suspicion on his face, have said among themselves: "Perhaps we shall never see our officer again!"

When the officer had gone, the quartermaster-sergeant distributed the letters. Oh, a letter from home in those days and those places! The fortunate ones who heard their names called could hardly restrain an expression of joy; the others impatiently tapped their feet and stretched out their hands. "Mine." "Give me mine." "You have not given me mine yet." "Are you not going to give me one?" "Silence, and back to your place!" shouted the quartermaster-sergeant. Instantly all were silent and motionless as marble, and fancy what self-control they had to exercise in order to conquer that fever! The quartermaster-sergeant stood looking at them for a moment with a frown, then distributed the letters; the company separated in silence, and every one went to bed.

Late at night those who could not sleep heard a sound of slow steps and subdued voices through the dormitories, and raising their heads saw the officer of the guard and the sergeant of the week passing along the rows of beds, stopping before those that were empty, the one questioning, the other replying, then both pausing for a moment in going out, quite motionless in the door-way, as if absorbed in a common thought, which it was easy to divine. "If any thing happens," the officer would say in an undertone, "come and tell me instantly." "Let us hope there will be nothing." "Let us hope so indeed."

And these words were always accompanied by a sigh, which revealed a sentiment quite different, and one, unfortunately, which was generally much better founded. An hour after the expression of that hope the soldiers were suddenly aroused by an outburst of sharp cries, languid moans, and saw their companions spring to their feet, crowd around a bed, heard the officer of the guard come hurriedly in with the doctor and soldiers of the guard, and then in a few moments all make way, and four of the soldiers moving off, carrying a straw ticking with a dying man stretched on it, then a little whispering, and finally to bed once more, and a return of the former silence. In the morning, as soon as they are awake, "Corporal of the week," the soldiers ask anxiously, " . . . well?" "He is dead," the latter replies. "Dead!" and they look one another in the face.

In many corps, and in some more than once, did it happen that an officer and his orderly were seized with the cholera at one time. And in all these corps I have heard it said the same scene was repeated. In the evening, after the roll-call, the quartermaster-sergeant announced the misfortune to the company. "Who will take care of the officer?"

"I." "I." "I too." "But I said so first, and it is useless for you to speak." "Oh! come now! I am at liberty to speak too." "But I was the first." "But I tell you. . . ."

"Will you stop or not?" shouted the quartermaster-sergeant. All were silent. "You shall take care of him," he said, pointing to the soldier who offered first. The latter gave a smile of triumph, and the others were obliged to be resigned. The following morning, before dawn, the generous nurse was beside the sick officer's bed, and there he passed long days, alone, silent, and watchful, watching every night by the light of a lantern, while seated on a chair in one corner of the room. If any one could have been present when the invalid, coming to himself and looking around, and not recognizing him, asked: "Who are you?" and then, hearing the name, asked: "Who sent you?" To which the good soldier replied: "I came because I wanted to do so." "And why?" It cannot be expressed in words what the soldier's eyes replied, and what passed in his heart as he pressed the thin hand that was put out in search of his. At other times, instead, the soldier returned to the barracks after a few days, and as soon as he entered went and seated himself on his bed and began poking the ramrod of his musket into the barrel, this being an occupation in which a man is obliged to keep his head down and can thus hide his eyes.

The officers visited assiduously the sick in the hospitals, and generally went in numbers to visit all, so that no one would have a chance of growing sad or dispirited in seeing his comrades and not himself comforted. Those visits had become an absolute necessity for the poor sick men. At the usual hour they heard the clanking of the swords on the stairs, the sound of the voices, glanced at the door in expectation, and when they appeared and scattered through the wards of the hospital, every face became quieter, and even in the motionless eyes of those most dangerously ill, there lay a slight ray of hope and comfort. Poor young fellows! There were days when the sound of the swords was heard an hour later than usual, and during that time they were all ears and eyes waiting for the slightest noise or movement. They fancied they heard those steps and voices at every moment, and they went on imagining what could have prevented them from coming, what misfortune could have happened, and in that state of anxiety the sense of their sufferings became more intense. "They don't come, and they won't come now, and I am so ill, I shall not last until to-morrow, and I shall die all alone . . Ah ! here they are !" This moment was too sweet for words.

The nurses in the military hospitals were all soldiers, o course ; but in many places they were nurses in the other hospitals too, and for the entire time during which no one was to be found among the populace who would render this service, not even with the promise of large payments, because the fear of death outweighed any cupidity for money, as well as any feeling of pity. The soldiers offered their services spontaneously. The officer of the week asked : "Who will go ?" And half companies took a step forward or raised their hands. When the question was put to an entire battalion, on the parade ground, in the presence of many people, the reply was a solemn and touching sight. One day, on the slopes of Mount Pellegrino, near Palermo, six or seven companies of the 53d infantry were standing drawn up in line of battle, after the drill was over, when the colonel and major, both on horseback, stopped in front of the middle company, and the former made a sign that he wished to speak. The officers ordered silence. The colonel told them in a loud voice of the sad state of the city—the cholera had been raging there for days,—of the hospitals in which nurses were lacking ; of the duty involving upon every good citizen to lend his assistance in the time of public misfortune, and ended by saying, louder still : "I impose no duty upon you ; I exhort you to a sacrifice ; all are at liberty to reply yes or no, according as their hearts dictate. But before consenting each man must measure the strength of his soul, and reflect that the office of nurse is a very noble but a grave one, and one not without danger—and that he must lend his assistance with great courage and great affection—or refuse it. Those who are ready to offer their services, kneel!"

Almost in one instant the whole battalion knelt, as if at a shout of command, and above all those heads appeared, straight and distinct, their four hundred muskets.

But the place where the soldiers exercised their charity most admirably was in the help of the poor.

"When I went in to the barracks," said an officer of the 54th, who had been commanding for some time a detachment at St. Cataldo, "I was accompanied every day by a troop of poor people: the women behind with children hanging to their necks; before and at my side boys with outstretched hands, complaining and crying. Another body of beggars was waiting for me at the door, and all surrounded, pressed about, and seized me by my jacket, and deafened me with groans and supplicating cries. I had all I could do to free myself, and generally, I should not have succeeded if the soldiers of the guard had not come to my assistance, by breaking through the crowd by blows and threats. Many times the mere empty threats did not suffice, they had to seize their bayonets and pretend to charge, and then only did the crowd begin to move away from me, but only for a little while, for if I had not been quick in getting through the door, they would have returned again. Many of those unfortunates were seated on the doorstep all day long; some slept there at night; no one was lacking at the hour of the rations, when the soldiers carried out the kettles with the remains of the soup. Then there was a bustle, and such a shouting that it could not be quieted even by force. They were so hungry that they could not stand, and each one wished to be first to put his spoon into the broth; they all sprang together at the kettles, dashed their soup plates in by tens, pushing and repelling each other, shrieking like madmen,—women, old men, children, altogether; all with thin faces, wearing expressions that were half bitter, half insensate, which aroused at that moment both fear and pity; they were dirty, ragged, half nude, and in a state which excited the greatest repugnance. At such moments the soldiers allowed them to do as they chose, nor could I pretend to hold them to their duty, save in cases where they were inclined to hurt some one; but hardly had the confusion ceased, when we called the women and children (who generally got nothing) apart, one by one, and gave them something to eat, keeping back the others who crowded around and began to beg again. This was an every-day occurrence. I say nothing of the soldiers who were stopped at every moment in the streets by entire families of beggars, surrounded and persecuted, so that they were obliged to remain in the barracks, and content themselves by walking in the court-yard. Yet they preferred remaining in that place where the poor left them no peace, rather than in the others where they fled from them for fear of being poisoned; in fact, they took a sort of satisfaction in being implored and persecuted, in seeing themselves made, in a measure, the slaves of those poor people—a satisfaction which arises from pity when one is able to express and exercise it with benefit. And those good soldiers did feel pity, and they exercised their benevolence with the best heart in the world. Not only did they bestow charity on their own account, when they could do so, and the occasion offered; but every time that I, being obliged by some overwhelming need of the country, had recourse to their pocket-books after having exhausted my own, I found them all, without one exception, generously disposed to give every thing, even to the little wine which they drank on Sundays bought with the few sous saved during the week. I shall never forget how the last collection was taken up for a poor family of the place, whose father and mother had died of the cholera, an entire family of girls, the oldest of whom was only twelve. 'See if we can get any thing,' I said to the sergeant. 'I will,' he replied, 'but you must expect little or nothing, for they are almost more needy than the people here.' 'I understand that,' I added, 'but try in every way; no matter how little you get, that little will be better than nothing.' He went up to the dormitory, the soldiers were seated on the floor in a circle, as if around a great table, eating and chatting, with the little gaiety that was possible in those days and in those localities. The sergeant approached them. 'Give me your attention for a moment!' They were all silent. 'Yesterday morning, here in this place, six children were left without mother or father. Who will give something so that they will not be left to die of starvation?'

"The soldiers looked at each other as much as to say: 'What can we give now? the cover of the account-book to have it boiled?'

"'Courage,' went on the sergeant; 'give me some sort of an answer.'

"One soldier rose, and showing a sou in the palm of his hand, asked: 'Do you want that?'

"'Even that is something,' replied the sergeant, taking the sou. 'Are there any more?'

"'If it is only the question of a sou, I have one too,' replied another, throwing him the sou.

"'Is a sou enough?' asked a third. 'Yes, quite enough.' 'I have one too.' 'I too.' And so all the soldiers handed him their sou one after another, and the sergeant, as he took them, said to each: 'Bravo! Well done! Capital! Ah, what good fellows!' he exclaimed when he had all the sous in his hand, but one thing more.'

"'What?' asked all the soldiers.

"'Bread.'

"'Bread? If that is all,' several replied, 'there is more than enough." And first one and then another cut a slice from his loaf of black bread.

"'Where shall we put it?' asked one.

"A corporal took a ramrod and stuck on to it all the slices as fast as they were handed him. The soldiers laughed.

"'Now who will carry the money and bread to the children?' asked the sergeant.

"'The handsomest man,' replied some voice. All laughed, and approved the proposition.

"'Oh, yes, the handsomest man; let's search for him! Who can this beauty be?'

"'I,' exclaimed a Neapolitan soldier, who had the reputation of being the ugliest in the regiment, and among the laughs of his comrades, he stepped forward, put the money in his pocket, took the ramrod with the bread, and prepared to go out with the sergeant. All the others clapped their hands. 'Oh, come now,' shouted the Neapolitan, turning and facing his comrades. 'Will you stop? What a shame to laugh behind the back of a man who is going to perform a work of charity.' And then he departed while a prolonged laugh broke out in the room. The sergeant met me on the stairs, and fancying that I was going up, said in a voice full of emotion: 'Oh, Mr. Lieutenant! what a good set of fellows we have in our company!'"

This narrative, I heard from an officer of the 54th. And what the soldiers did in that district, the others belonging to the 54th did in the city of Caltanisetta, so that this regiment was a real providence. This was done by the 18th infantry at Terrasini, for the two families who took care of the poor sub-lieutenant, Viale, and the sergeant, Imberti; the 6th battalion of sharp-shooters and the 10th regiment of infantry worked in the same way at Messina; as did also the 58th at Petralia Sottana; the 38th battalion of sharp-shooters at Monreale; the 67th infantry and the 15th battalion of sharp-shooters at Longobucco; the 68th infantry at Reggio di Calabria; the lancers of Foggia at Misilmeri; the 25th battalion of sharp-shooters at Rocca d' Anfo; the 7th infantry at Mantua, together with those at the fort in Bard, and the free lancers of Aosta; and who knows how many other corps did as much, without any notice being taken of it, simply because none of the benefactors wished to speak or write of it. Yet just at that time there were some people who asked severely of the government for what reason it maintained such a "colossal" army, if it expected to "civilize the country with bayonets," if it would not be better to turn so many "lazy" barracks into as many hospitals, and if the money spent in such high pay would not be better employed in alleviating so much misery, etc. These things were being said while the soldier was dividing his bread with the poor, and fighting, suffering, and dying for the health of the country.

Sometimes the municipalities to whom the soldiers rendered great service, offered them in compensation the little money which they had at their disposal; and these municipalities were not a few in numbers. But the money was always refused, and facts and names can be cited to prove it. The municipality of Licata, toward the end of August, offered one hundred lire to the 9th company of the 57th regiment. The evening of the 14th, Captain Pompeo Praga returned to the barracks at the retreat to announce to his soldiers the municipality's offer. They were all drawn up in the dormitory, and the quartermaster-sergeant was calling the roll. The captain interrupted him and gave his news, adding:

"Quartermaster, let this sum be divided among all to-morrow morning before rations."

"Yes, sir."

A moment of silence followed.

"Mr. Captain," murmured an uncertain voice in the lines.

"Who spoke?" asked the captain. No one replied. "Who spoke?" he repeated.

"I," replied a soldier.

"What did you wish to say?"

"I wished to say that, as far as I am concerned (and he glanced bashfully around as if to seek an expression of assent in his comrades' faces), it seems to me that a sou more or less, is the same thing for us, and it would be better, it seems to me . . ."

"Go on," said the captain.

"There are so many poor in this place."

His comrades understood his thought, and whispered: "Certainly, a capital idea! It would be better to do so. It is better to give the money to the poor."

The captain allowed the murmur to subside, and then said: "Listen. I want you all to tell me frankly what you think; I do not wish that any of you should refuse the municipality's offer to please me, for that would cause me great displeasure. Nor do I wish the majority to impose their wish upon the few. You deserve this money; you have worked, suffered, done good, and it is no more than just that you should have this compensation. To advise you to deprive yourselves of it would be unjust, and I refrain from doing so. In fact, I tell you that you would do well to accept it. Courage, be quite frank; if any among you have need of his portion of the money, tell me without fear or shame, as you would a friend; I should not admire a man who accepted it less than one who refused it; I simply wish that any one who needs the money should say so. Courage! Is there no one?"

"No one!"

"Not even one?" and he watched every face.

"No one," they all repeated, and the tone of voice and expression of their eyes attested to the spontaneity of the act.

"Bravo!" exclaimed the captain quickly. "To-morrow I shall go to the municipality, and I shall say to those gentlemen that the 9th company of the 57th regiment offers 100 lire in charity to the poor of Licata."

What they did in Licata they did in Aosta, Scansano, Genoa, and many other places, whose names would fill these pages. But I cannot be silent about you, brave Zamela—a sapper in the engineers, who, having heard of the misfortunes with which your poor Messina was afflicted, sent thirty lire to the syndic, writing him: "They gave me this money because I nursed the cholera patients in my regiment; and I have nothing more; but this little I give with all my heart to the poor of my native place."

Works of charity are always praiseworthy and very estimable, even if the impulse which prompts us to perform them is nothing but the desire for the gratitude and affection of those benefited. But when not even gratitude accrues from the work, and those who ought to love and bless us, return our charity with hatred, and suspect snare in the offer and crime in the benefit; and yet, despite this we persist in doing good, loving and pardoning with no other motive power than pity, without any other comfort than our conscience, then we have a greater right to esteem and praise than is usually bestowed upon the common virtues. I refer to the generous work of the soldiers in those places where it was supposed they were scattering poison by order of the government, and the people hated and cursed them. Unfortunately, these places were not a few in number.

At last, when they saw that the soldiers died also, that all those whom they carried to the hospitals were not poisoned, that in fact the survivors never ceased praising the care and affection with which they had been nursed and watched over, the senseless superstition disappeared. But that the soldiers poisoned the people was at first a universal belief, a profound conviction, a fact which it would not have been proper to doubt. There was no one who would not have sworn to it in perfect faith if the occasion had offered. Every one held, though they had seen nothing, that there were a thousand undeniable indications and proofs of that horrible conspiracy. And one of these proofs, one of the most telling, the common people saw in that very solicitude of the soldiers, in their wishing to go everywhere, meddle in every thing uncalled for and unforced, under the pretence of exercising a charity which they could not believe was really felt by persons like them, who were paid by the government, upholders of the government, and therefore, necessarily, enemies of the people. That charity could only be a mask; those works of beneficence nothing but a pretext, a means to a hidden aim; they could not explain why the soldier, the instrument of an inimical government, should extend one pitying hand to the poor and sick, if it were not to prepare them for death by the other. In consequence of this conviction and fear it is easy to imagine how the common people treated the soldiers.

One of the cities in which there was the strongest belief in the poisoning was Catania, where the 9th regiment of infantry was in garrison.

The soldiers, in their hours of liberty, never went alone into the city; but always in threes, fours, or a larger number, in order to be quite secure from violence, or hold in check any who wished to insult or harm them in an underhand way. They almost always went through the principal streets and not very far from the barracks; sometimes, and only in case of necessity, in the quieter streets; never outside the city, where they certainly would have been provoked and assaulted. But wherever they went, whether in small or greater numbers, they were always regarded with suspicion. If there was a group in the street, those whose backs were toward them turned quickly around, all took a step backward and whispered something in each other's ears. "Here they are," some one would say aloud. And another: "Take care!" The soldiers passed, and the group formed again. Many, on seeing them coming in the distance toward them, would turn a street corner. Others, in meeting them, stood aside, and then stopped to look at them when they had passed with a curiosity mixed with horror and fear. In the quarters of the poor people, many closed their doors at their appearance, and went to the windows; others half-opened the blinds and peeped through the cracks; the women called in a loud voice to the children who were playing in the middle of the street, or caught them by the arms and carried them hastily into the house; the children rushed here and there, turning back to make faces; and as the soldiers went on, the doors and windows were reopened, and the people appeared, once more looking suspicious, interrogating and reassuring each other in turns by signs. Not infrequently the soldiers heard shouts and words from within which they could not understand, but which, judging by angry and mocking tones, seemed undoubtedly intended for them; and raising their eyes to the windows they saw a face slowly appear, which, however, was withdrawn as soon as perceived, or perhaps only a hand put outside the sill and shaken in a menacing way. At other times, in passing, they heard an open insult or a curse muttered at their backs, or some incomprehensible word; they turned and saw a face raised, looking at the clouds in an abstracted manner. To call them to account for any insult would be to gather the people and provoke a perfect tumult, so they kept silence and went on. Sometimes instead of a word, they whirled a stone at their ears; if they turned back to see who it was, questioning those present about it, no one had heard or seen any thing.

In going for provisions, the regiment's carts were only allowed to pass through certain streets, as it was said that they contained poisonous materials which infected the air. In order to carry rations to those on guard, the soldiers were obliged to make a detour around certain quarters; evil to them if they dared pass through them; the mere sight of the kettles aroused the people's suspicions; in less than an instant a crowd gathered, they stopped the soldiers, they wanted to see what they were carrying, forced the carriers to taste the broth in their presence, and then leave a portion for them to try and analyze afterward. Any indication, no matter how slight; any assertion, no matter how absurd; a word, a gesture from one of the crowd, was sufficient to change the doubt into a certainty, and this into madness. There was no time nor way of committing a crime, because the fury of the common people, always foreseen, was frustrated by a quick and ready aid; but they were not always in time to prevent violence, nor could the soldiers be cautious enough to succeed in avoiding, or help provoking, it every time. One day, in a by-street, some common women saw a soldier with a bundle under his arm hurry into a house where a short time before a girl had been seized by the cholera. They began to wonder among themselves why that soldier had entered the door. "Did you see what he had under his arm? Did you observe what a surly face he had, and that he looked around suspiciously?" Every one had noticed something strange and ill-omened. They went toward the house and stopped in front of the door. It was closed; their suspicions increased.

They knocked; no one came to open. They called aloud to those inside; no one replied. There was no longer any doubt that some crime was being committed in that house. They raised a loud cry, beat furiously at the door, flung stones at the windows; in less than a moment the street was full of people armed with sticks, and hatchets, and knives; the door was broken in and the crowd rushed into the house. Suddenly a window is opened, a man in shirt-sleeves springs on to the the sill, gives a shout, jumps down into the street, falls, rises—"It is the soldier who has been poisoning!"—shout the startled crowd who throng around him; he breaks away from them, dashes through the street, and disappears. It was the soldier who had entered the house a short time before to give a bundle of linen from his sergeant to the laundress.

A few days after, something similar happened to an orderly, while he was carrying the dinner to his officer, who was ill at home. In one hand he held a bottle from the pharmacy, in the other the four corners of a napkin with the dishes. He was crossing an alley inhabited by the poor. Every one watched him attentively; some one followed him at a certain distance; four or five women stopped and asked him boldly what was in those dishes. He was unfortunate enough to give them an impertinent reply. In less time than it takes to tell it the dishes, bottle, and napkin were under the feet of a crowd of people who had appeared as if by magic from all the holes in the houses round about. The poor soldier hardly had time to open a path for himself with his bayonet, and was thankful to escape with only a scratch on his face and a stone on his back.

Another time, three soldiers were passing before a group of

houses outside the city ; one of them stopped to look at a child who was digging a ditch with its hands ; he said : "What a beautiful child!" stooped and gave it a caress. A woman near by saw the action, dashed to the door of one of the houses, and shouted in the loudest possible voice : "Quick! quick! the soldiers are killing the child." A sharp cry was heard from within at the same moment, and a woman appeared at the door, saw the soldiers, rushed forward, and caught the child, with a fearful shriek, in her arms, returned like a flash to the house, closed the door, dashed to the window breathless, trembling, her eyes starting out of their sockets, and her face pale and distorted ; she stared at the soldiers, and then, accompanying her words with a vigorous gesture, as if she were throwing a stone, shouted in a stifled voice : "Curse you!" and withdrew. The soldiers stood still, open-mouthed with astonishment. But the woman who had given the first cry had run to call some other people, so that the three poor fellows soon had to think of saving themselves, as there was no time to be lost. They had not gone fifty paces when the armed forerunners of the mob appeared in front of the mother's house.

One evening, at some distance from any habitation, a band of peasants who were on the look-out for poisoners, came across a soldier. Hardly had they seen him, when they ran toward him. The soldier, stupidly, turned to flee. He was caught up with, seized by ten hands, dragged behind a lonely house, placed with his back against the wall, and threatened with death. "Where do you keep the poison?" ten voices asked in one breath. "I have no poison," stammered the soldier, white as a ghost. "Where do you keep the poison?" insisted the others threateningly. One of them took off his fatigue cap, examined it and threw it on the ground; another pulled off his cravat. "Out with the poison!" and the one who had seized him by the collar knocked his head against the wall. "I have nothing," replied the weak and supplicating voice of the soldier. "Oh, you have n't any thing, eh? Now, we will see for ourselves!" snarled the ferocious creatures, and opening his coat and shirt they searched everywhere. "Take off his belt," said one. They instantly seized his belt, pulled him here and there to get it off, but they did not succeed, and they shouted and cursed. "Oh let me alone," implored the poor soldier; "let my belt alone." They loosened it, and threw it away, and forced him to take off his coat, tormenting and beating him, almost sticking the points of their knives into him, shouting in his ears every kind of vituperation and curse. The unfortunate man, who had barely enough strength left to stand, let them do whatsoever they chose without making further resistance, almost out of his senses, with his head and arms hanging like those of a dead person; he murmured from time to time in a weak voice: "My bayonet; I am not poisoning any one . . . let me alone . . . give me my things, my bayonet!" They certainly would have killed him, but as good fortune willed it, a patrol passed, and dashing precipitately forward they dispersed the mob just as it was on the point of shedding the unlucky fellow's blood.

This was one of the least painful affairs which took place, for in Catania at least the soldiers' blood was not spilled, which is more than can be said of other places. What must the soldiers have felt in those days! What must have been their thoughts and conversations, in seeing themselves so brutally execrated by the very people to whom they were sacrificing their rest, health, and life!

But for them, the continual risk of their lives, and the being obliged to defend them so frequently from the violence of an insensate mob, was perhaps a less painful thought and a less grave care than the duty of protecting the lives of other citizens from the same violence, and threatened for the same cause. Every day they were obliged to disarm and quell a mob blinded with fury and thirsting for blood, and to drag from its hands the victims, who were almost always beaten, covered with blood, often half dead, and sometimes already killed. Sometimes when they could not do any thing else, they were forced to fight for the posssession of the bodies, so that they should not be mutilated and dragged through the streets, or given a prey to the beasts or flames. They were obliged to dash one by one into a crowd of armed people, who, pressing and undulating here and there, separated and squeezed them so that they could not have used their weapons had it been necessary to do so, and any one of them could have been stabbed without the others knowing any thing about it. Yet they were obliged to trust themselves to that maddened crowd, and coax and beseech them to be quiet, as every threat would have been in vain, as in rousing their anger, they would have been likely to provoke a tumult, and cause fresh bloodshed, which, unfortunately, not unfrequently occurred. Yet, despite this, many lives were spared, much bloodshed saved and many acts of brutality prevented, especially in those places where the soldiers were not suspected of poisoning, or in those days when this suspicion no longer existed.

One example will suffice for all.

At Bocca di Falco, a small village near Palermo, there was the cholera. The names of those upon whom the terrible suspicion fell ran from mouth to mouth, and the people waited for the opportunity of destroying them. Among these was a poor peddler, who passed through the place every two or three days, on his way to Palermo. He had long hair, a curious way of dressing, a proud face, brusque manners, and was a man of few words ; in fact, there was quite enough about him to make people believe him a poisoner. One day when the cholera had been raging more fiercely than usual in the place, troops of beggars, armed with picks and sticks, went round about the district, indulging in threatening shouts, and firmly resolved to put an end to all the poisoners. One of these troops met the peddler, surrounded him before he was aware of it, and crowding close about him, asked: "Well, how many have you disposed of to-day?" The unfortunate man understood their meaning, but thinking to save himself by a joke, answered: "Ten!" without smiling. That was sufficient. One of the crowd gave a great kick to the box of pins and cravats which he carried suspended from his neck, and sent every thing into the air, saying as he did so: "This will do for the present. Now show us what you poison people with." "I?" replied the former, to his misfortune, not being able to restrain a gesture of indignation. "You are the ones who are killing me!" "Ah! we are the ones!" broke from the furious crowd. And at the same moment a vigorous blow filled his mouth with blood, one hand seized him by the throat, another took him by the hair, a shower of blows and kicks fell upon his unfortunate person, and he was dashed so violently against the wall that the nape of his neck left a bloody imprint.

"Confess your accomplices, assassin!" shouted the foremost, digging their nails into his cheeks and throat, and pressing their knees and sticks against his stomach. "Confess!" And those behind stretched out their hands to seize him, threw themselves here and there, in order to make an opening in the crowd, reach him, and give him a wound also. The luckless man was dripping with blood from his mouth and ears, his eyes seemed starting out of his head, a rattling sound was heard in his chest, and he was a horrible sight. "Confess! confess!" Suddenly a loud shout came from the other side of the street; it was another poisoner whom another band of these madmen had assaulted and beaten; all turned in that direction; the peddler, being free for a moment, threw back with one vigorous push the two who stood at his side, dashed into an open door, and closed it behind him. The crowd, perceiving this, sprang toward the door, and began beating it furiously with stones and picks. The peddler had taken refuge in a small room on the ground-floor, where there was a woman who had witnessed the whole scene from a window. At the appearance of the poisoner she thought she was doomed; courage and the frenzy of despair took possession of her, she dashed at him like a fury; seized him by the neck, and began a terrible battle with teeth and nails. Both falling, they rolled like wild beasts on the floor, holding tightly to each other, one on top of the other as the case might be, their breath and blood mingling; the crowd stretched out their arms through the window gratings, extended their trembling hands to seize their victim, shouting horrid words as they did so. The door began to creak and give way, when, just at that point, a number of voices shouted: "The soldiers! the soldiers!" A moment later the poor peddler heard the approach of hastening steps, saw the gleam of bayonets outside the windows, caught the sound of a powerful voice above the tumult which said: "Bread for all!" and instantly thereafter the blows on the door ceased, the arms of his assaulters retired from the grating, and the raging shouts of the crowd were followed by a low murmur. The woman lay exhausted on the ground, and he was saved. The commander of the detachment had been informed in time of what was taking place, had gathered his soldiers in an instant, made each one take his portion of bread, and had thus come to quell the riot with the double weapons of menace and charity. Not one of the soldiers was suspected in the place, in fact they were always looked upon kindly, and perhaps even loved for their almsgiving and help, which they bestowed so generously in every way, so that at their appearance the mob desisted from violence, and, little by little, became perfectly quiet. Part of the soldiers entered the house and stood guard there; the others remained to watch those poor famished creatures who devoured their bread in silence. How many of these occurrences took place, and how often they were repeated in the same places!

Yet the hardest labor and the most repulsive duty which fell to the lot of the soldiers was that of burying the dead, for which they were obliged to arm themselves with all the strength and courage possible. Sometimes in the middle of the night a messenger from the municipality would arrive at the barracks to say that some bodies had just been discovered in such and such a house, that no one would bury them, and that some steps must be taken in the matter instantly, before putrefaction rendered burial out of the question. A loud beating of the drum waked the whole corps in a moment, and a band of soldiers was gathered. They lighted their lanterns, drew out their carts, took picks and spades, the officer of the guard placed himself at the head of the escort, and they started. They arrived in silence at the place indicated, the streets empty and the houses closed and abandoned. After much difficulty they broke down the doors and an unendurable odor of decay repelled the soldiers. "Courage!" One goes forward with a lantern; the others follow slowly with their hands over their mouths, casting their eyes timidly around the sepulchral chamber. Stretched out on the ground on sacks of straw or rags, nude or illy wrapped, in horrible filth, lay the bodies, side by side, or one on top of the other, carelessly thrown together : the faces swollen, specked with black; the mouth discolored by bloodstained saliva; the bodies swollen, covered with large venous spots and a net-work of green stripes from the intestines and veins; all the members resting on the ground, quite crushed; every semblance of humanity distorted or lost ; and here and there, in those portions which were most decayed, the first manifestations of animal life. Yet they were obliged to approach those horrible couches, and seize and separate the different members, raise those bodies one by one, and carry them to the carts; seeing them change and decompose more horribly at every step, and drop here and there a fetid rag, or some other more filthy trace of itself. Oh, it was quite another thing from seeing the dead on the battle-field stretched out in a pool of blood, torn by shot, or lacerated and mutilated by the cannon-balls! Then, the shouts of a thousand comrades resound about us, we see battalions, gleaming with bayonets, moving here and there through the fields and on the hillside; the flag of the regiment waving near by; hear the distant noise of the batteries which are hastening forward; our blood boils, our souls are exalted, and the bodies we meet on the road do not count, indeed are not seen or looked at, we do not even think that there must be some, or if the eye falls upon them, our hearts exclaim: "Farewell, brother!" and nothing else, as on we go and forget them. But there, in those dwellings, at night, in the midst of that silence, in that quiet, by the light of those lanterns, how horrible the image of death must be! How many of those soldiers, even the strongest of them, must have had the image of these misshapen bodies before him for some time, have felt the contact of those icy and flaccid members, and the noise of those heads as they fell heavily on to the cart! Often some one started back horrified at the sight of the dead, or his arms trembled and his eyes became veiled in the act of touching them. "Oh, friend," he may have said to his neighbor, "I cannot do it!" But the voice of the ever-ready officer would be heard: "Courage, boys! every thing depends upon taking hold of the first. We must become accustomed to it." Then the soldier put his hand timidly on the body, turning away his head and holding his breath as he did so. The band moved toward the cemetery. On reaching it the soldiers placed their lanterns on the ground and part of them dug the graves, while the others stood beside the carts, waiting for a sign to bury the dead. The officer stood motionless at the edge of a grave, superintending the soldiers' work. All were silent. Nothing was to be heard but the stroke of the picks as they were struck into the ground, and the falling of the earth thrown into the air by the shovels. From time to time came a voice: "Courage, boys!" Then they dragged the bodies down from the carts, a soldier held the light so that the others could see where to put their hands, another stood up in the cart to help those who were lifting the bodies one by one from the heap, and said: "Take this one. That one. Be careful of this one, because it is decayed . . ." Ten steps further away nought but the slightest whisper was to be heard, and now and then a louder voice: "Courage!" or: "Look out for your hands!" All about was darkness and silence.

"But why do we have to bury the dead?" asked a soldier once in reentering the barrack. "Oh! that's a fine question," replied a corporal in a tone of profound conviction; "because others will not do it." There was no objection to be made to such a reason, and so all were silent.

What has been told up to the present time is but little in comparison to that which remains to be said. How many sadder and more terrible cases followed, and how far I should still be from the end of my narrative were I to attempt to tell the half I know, and yet I know only so small a portion of them!

At Sutèra, a small place in the province of Caltanisetta, there was a squad of the 54th regiment of infantry commanded by Sub-lieutenant Edoardo Cangiano. On the morning of the 22d of June a peasant arrives at the barrack in a breathless condition, and presents himself before the officer. "Oh, Mr. Officer!" he exclaims in a supplicating voice, "come, for pity's sake, and help us. . . . The cholera has broken out near here, at Campofranco; half the people have fled; the streets are filled with the dead: there are no physicians, nor undertakers; there is not even any thing to eat. . . . it's a perfect desolation; those who do not die of cholera will die of hunger. . . . Oh, come—come immediately!" The squad was instantly armed, a message sent to the syndic, a despatch to the military command at Caltanisetta, a notice to the sergeant to stop there with a few soldiers, and away the rest go toward Campofranco. They had to walk a mile or more through a winding path across the fields. The sun was shining brightly. The soldiers, dripping with perspiration, before leaving the town, proceeded one behind the other in a long file, half walking, half running, listening attentively to the peasant, who, in broken words, described to Cangiano the sad state of the place. "Courage! courage!" the latter replied from time to time; "nothing is done by complaining; this is a time for deeds." He kept quickening his pace, and the soldiers with him, until they ended by actually running. At a certain point they began to see in the distance men, women, and children wandering uncertainly through the fields, pointing the soldiers out to each other, stopping, fleeing, running backward and forward, calling loudly to each other, gathering and dispersing, like people who were being pursued and quite out of their senses from fear. As the soldiers approached the village the fugitives became more numerous, the agitation and shouting increased; entire families roamed about the country carrying or dragging behind them all their worldly possessions; some had put their things on the ground in order to rest; at the sight of the soldiers they took them hastily up and moved off, turning timidly back as they did so. Others fell down, quite worn out; others rose; many farther away, turning toward the soldiers, shouted and waved their arms cursing. "Ah! Mr. Officer!" exclaimed the peasant, "this is nothing!" "No matter," replied Cangiano; "we are prepared for every thing," The first house and the beginning of the first street appeared in sight. The people, who were fleeing in the direction of the soldiers, turned in part at the sight of them and ran back to the town, shouting as if they were announcing an assault of the enemy; the rest dashed right and left into the fields. On first entering the street they saw two bodies stretched on the ground before the door of an uninhabited house. Hardly had they entered, when there was a speedy disappearance of the people in the houses, a hasty closing of doors and windows, the sharp cries of women, the weeping of children, and at the end of the street a rapid gathering and noisy mingling of people, then a general flight. "Quick!" shouted Cangiano; "ten soldiers go around the place and stop these people." Ten soldiers detached themselves from the squad and ran through a side street. The others went on. The frightened people continued to shut themselves up in their houses.

"We do not wish to harm any one!" shouted Cangiano, in a loud voice. "We have come to help you; we are your friends; come out, good people; come out of your houses!"

A few doors and windows began to open; a few people behind the soldiers began to appear; in the houses they heard the weak voices of complaint; in the street, in front of the doors, lay many unfortunate creatures weak and exhausted from hunger, or seized by the epidemic, motionless and torpid as if dead. Here and there were household goods abandoned in the door-ways, or in the middle of the road, and at every step, scattered straw and heaps of rags. In every side alley which lead to the fields were one or more bodies, some covered with straw, some with earth, some with a few rags, among which appeared the blackened and swollen members; others thrown across the door-sills, half in and half out of the houses.

"Look, Mr. Officer!" exclaimed the peasant, sadly.

"We will provide for all," replied Cangiano; "keep up your courage!"

At that point, the crowd of fugitives, who had been driven back by those ten soldiers, came tumultuously toward the officer. "Draw up in line!" he shouted, turning to the soldiers; and they stopped and drew up across the street. Cangiano waited quietly and firmly for the crowd. The latter stopped within ten paces, ceased shouting, and stood looking angrily at the soldiers. They were all poor, ragged people, with pale and thin faces, staring eyes, physiognomies to which their long sufferings had given an expression of deadly weariness and savage pride. "We wish to go away!" shouted a voice from the crowd. All repeated the cry, and the crowd swayed backward and forward. "Why do you wish to go?" asked Cangiano in a resolute voice which was tempered with sweetness. "You must remain where you are and help each other. All must help in a general misfortune. It is a bad thing for each to think of himself and not for all . . . We have come to help you." "We wish to go away!" shouted the crowd, threateningly; and those at the back pressing hard, the foremost were thrown two or three steps forward. "Stand back!" said Cangiano calmly, then added in a loud voice: "Listen to my advice: the women and children shall go into the houses; the men remain to help the soldiers bury the dead." "We do not wish to die!" replied the multitude imperiously, and shouting louder still, they moved and swayed again as if to make a dash at the soldiers. "You wish it? well then," shouted the officer; and turning back he shouted: "Ready!" The squad raised and aimed their muskets, and the crowd, uttering a cry of fright, disappeared in an instant by the side streets. The other ten soldiers joined the first.

"Here, firmness and courage are needed!" exclaimed Cangiano; "the dead must be buried immediately; half of you go into the country and bring back, by force, as many men as you can. You others come with me." Half of the squad started on a quick step out of the town. The others began to run here and there, to enter the houses, and hunt all around for picks, shovels, carts, boards, and benches on which to carry the dead out of the place. In a few moments they found every thing they needed, and part of them began to gather the bodies; when they reached the neighboring cemetery they dug the graves as hastily as possible; others went to work to clear the streets of the worst obstructions and disgusting filth.

Meanwhile Cangiano, followed by a soldier, went in search of a house adapted for the use of a hospital, stopping all the people whom he met on the way, advising, exhorting, and beseeching them to do as he wished; and in passing he hurried the soldiers, gave orders and suggestions, and comforted them with kind words. He found a house, had it cleared, had beds from the deserted houses carried there, went himself with four soldiers to knock at the doors of all the other dwellings, and asked to be allowed to carry away the sick, whom he would nurse and take care of, saying that their families should be assisted. They replied in the negative; he offered them money, begged, threatened; all was in vain. Then the soldiers entered the houses by force; two of them seized the invalid, and two others kept back with their arms the relatives and neighbors. Very often they were obliged to lift away the women from the doorways where they blocked up the entrance with their own bodies ; had to struggle with, repulse them forcibly, and finally drag them off.

After much labor, a large number of the sick were already lodged in the new hospital, and two or three of the soldiers had provided for their needs while waiting the arrival of assistance from Caltanisetta, when the other half of the squad returned to the town dragging by force a band of peasants whom they had arrested in the country. Cangiano ran to meet them, divided them into various groups, and had them led to their different works. The newly arrived soldiers began to work too ; in a short time the bodies which were in the streets had been buried, the streets cleared and cleaned ; they began to go in turn to fetch the sick, and little by little, now by persuasion, now by force, they succeeded in getting the greater part into the hospital. On every side there was a continual coming and going, a calling to one another, and a continuous hurry of soldiers. The people, who began to gather, stood looking at them from a distance, half suspiciously, half amazed ; those scattered throughout the country came gradually nearer the town to see what was going on. The first arrivals, no longer seeing the bodies before the houses, took courage and entered ; many began spontaneously to clear the streets of the remaining filth ; others entered the houses ; some crowded around Cangiano, watching him with astonishment, not uttering a word, still a trifle diffident, but quite prepared to tender thanks for what had been done and to pray also. Cangiano, though never ceasing to run here and there in order to encourage the soldiers, turned from time to time to the people who were following them, and said: "Come now, go and help those poor fellows who have been working so long for you; go and call those who have fled into the country; we can all do something; let us get the town in order; the syndic will return; the gentlemen will come back and help you; so will the bakers and physicians; help will soon arrive from Caltanisetta. Courage! come now, let us all work; there is a remedy for every trouble, and we will remedy even this. We came here for your good, rest assured of that, my good people; what have you to fear from the soldiers? Don't we all belong to the same country; are we not all your brothers and defenders?" These words were followed by a murmur of approbation in the crowd; some instantly detached themselves therefrom and ran to the assistance of the soldiers; others went toward the country; many scattered through the streets; the remainder gathered around the officer with laments and supplications: "We are without bread. We are hungry." "I know it, my good people; have a little patience and the bread will come; I will do all that I can for you; I will send my soldiers to get something to eat at Sutèra; we will give you all that we have. But meanwhile you must work, carry away the dead, nurse the sick, and help each other." Then the people thanked him, began to beg again, complain, and ask for bread.

Suddenly a soldier ran up and whispered in Cangiano's ear. A difficult test of their charity and strength was now to be given! Cangiano saw, very wisely, that every thing must be done secretly, so ordered those present to go and wait for the expected succor on the road leading to Caltanisetta, called fifteen soldiers with their muskets, made twenty peasants with pistols step forward, and went off with them to one end of the village, where there was a little church which had been abandoned. They stopped at the door, tried it, and found it closed. They pulled it down, and all started back together with a cry of horror. In the middle of the church, which was only a trifle larger than an ordinary room, was a heap of twenty decayed bodies. "Forward!" shouted the officer. The soldiers dashed into the church, but the peasants started back. "Forward!" shouted Cangiano again. No one moved. He stepped forward, they took to flight, the soldiers sprang after them, and in a moment had reached and seized them. "Drag those cowards here!" shouted Cangiano from the church door. The soldiers dragged them by the arms with the utmost difficulty, pushing them by blows, and threatening them with their muskets. But as they were about to enter they began a more obstinate resistance, planting their feet firmly on the ground just as restive horses do, struggling and shouting desperately, almost as if they were being dragged to torture. "Out with your bayonets!" shouted the officer, scornfully, as he seized one by the waist and flung him into the church; the soldiers set their bayonets and raised them as if to charge. "Forward, you cowards, or we will stick them into you!" "You want to kill us!" the peasants cried. "We will all die!" replied the soldiers proudly, "but you must enter!" With a final effort, they pushed them all in. Here a terrible piece of work began. The bodies were in a complete state of decomposition and were a shapeless mass, so that they could not even be lifted from the ground. The men were obliged to break up the benches of the church, place two boards under each body, and seizing them by the ends, raise the putrid weight with their arms outstretched, and their faces turned away, as the appearance of those bodies was something too terrible. At every jar they received, a green matter ran from the mouth and ears and spread over the faces, and the black skin of the dangling arms and legs seemed ready to detach itself from the bones and dissolve entirely. Cangiano sent four soldiers to gather wood from the few deserted houses near by. The latter, not finding any thing else, took tables, chairs, blinds, any thing that would burn, and piled every thing up in the middle of a field, a short distance from the church. The bodies were carried out one by one, and thrown on to the heap; fire was set to it, and all were burned. There was not one body left in all Campofranco. Between those buried and burned they had disposed of more than sixty.

When Cangiano saw the first flames starting, he returned to the town, where he continued, in an indefatigable manner, the good work he had begun, until a captain arrived from Caltanisetta, with a good supply of food, medicine, and money, and with these he went from house to house, through all Campofranco, helping the poor and sick, reassuring those who were frightened, and filling all hearts with hope and peace. In a short time all the fugitives returned, the municipality was reorganized, every one resumed his former occupation, the town changed its aspect, and Cangiano and his soldiers returned to Sutèra, accompanied by the benedictions of all. In Sutèra, too, the epidemic was raging, and there also Cangiano performed miracles in the way of charity and courage. On the eleventh of August, the municipal body of the city unanimously acclaimed him the benefactor of the place, and expressed the gratitude of the citizens in a letter full of enthusiasm and affection. May these poor pages have the power of making his name beloved and revered in the hearts of many, as it is in mine!

Let us recall some other facts and names. The sub-lieutenant, Livio Vivaldi, commanded a detachment of the 54th regiment at Palazzo Adriano. The cholera spread there. The syndic, physicians, chemists, and priests all fled; no one but the poor remained. Vivaldi kept every thing in order, and provided for all. During the day, he visited the sick, hastened the burials, had the place cleaned and disinfected, and at night gave chase to the highwaymen who were scourging the country. Once, on the evening of the tenth of July, while he was distributing bread in the houses of the poor, he was informed that a band of malefactors had gathered at a short distance from the place. He ran to the barracks, took ten soldiers with him, went out into the country, surprised the band, attacked it, was wounded, continued to fight, put it to flight, killed the head of it, arrested the others, returned to the town, and the following morning took up again his office of physician and almoner. And this was one instance among many.

At Gangi, in the province of Termini, the cholera broke out toward the middle of June. Half the population fled. Those who remained hid the dead, and shut themselves up in their houses for fear of being poisoned. During the night of the 26th the boldest armed themselves and began rushing about the country, firing blindly into the windows and doors, and against any whom they happened to meet. The sharp-shooters from Petralia Sottana gathered, and gave chase throughout the night to the rioters, dispersed them with great difficulty, and when the riot was quelled, entered the houses by force, found thirteen unburied bodies, interred them with their own hands, though their lives were threatened by the infuriated multitude.

The cholera had broken out at Menfi. The people were without physicians, medicine, money, or 'bread. Twenty-four bodies lay unburied for forty-eight hours. A rebellion was imminent. General Medici was informed of the state of affairs by telegraph. The detachment of Sciacca received instant orders to proceed to Menfi. Twenty-four hours afterward, the general received the following despatch: "The detachment arrived. Buried the dead. Order restored. Medicines and provisions distributed. The communal administration provided for."

At Grammichele, two deaths having taken place from cholera, the populace, suspecting poison, armed themselves, attacked the carabineers, killed one of them, wounded another mortally, so that the rest were forced to shut themselves up in the barracks, where they were besieged all night, an attempt being made at every moment to break down the doors and rush in and kill them. Forty soldiers of the 9th regiment of infantry, commanded by Sub-lieutenant Goi, came from Caltagirone. At their appearance the armed bands dispersed; but, becoming aware of the small number of soldiers, they gathered again, moved against them, insulted and threatened them, shouting that they wished to search their knapsacks, and take possession of the poison therein. The number of rioters was ten times greater than that of the soldiers; a massacre was imminent; reinforcements were demanded from Caltagirone; fresh soldiers arrived in great haste; and all together, after a long struggle, succeeded in getting together fifteen of the national guards, with whom they scoured the country and town all night long, though threatened and assaulted at every moment. Finally, they succeed in establishing quiet. The rioters had attached to one house in the place a proclamation which ran thus: "Courage! Up; courage, companions! Do not desist from what you propose doing; do not be cowards, but vindicators of the country's honor. Are you afraid of a handful of soldiers? Get rid of them and put them to flight. Down with the vile and opprobrious bands of the government; break the murderous pots of poison which your superiors, infamous executors of the royal decrees, kindly place at your lips!" This is an exact quotation.

At Longobucco, a province of Rossano, a certain Guiseppe Citini died of cholera toward the end of July. The common people believed that he had died of poison; they broke, armed, into the syndic's house; invaded Citini's house and sacked it; robbed the house of the chemist, Felicetti, and destroyed the pharmacy; rang the bells violently, ran furiously through the streets during the whole night, shouting that they wished to put to death all property-owners and public officers. The following morning they tried to break into the sharp-shooters' barracks, and hunted again for the syndic in order to kill him. And this they would have done, if the marshal of the carabineers, the quartermaster-sergeant, Allisio, and the sergeant, Cenderini, of the sharp-shooters, had not courageously dashed into the middle of the crowd and succeeded in dissuading them from their iniquitous design; and prevented the burning of various houses and the murder of many citizens. They maintained a little quiet in the place until the following morning, when a company of the 45th battalion of sharp-shooters, commanded by Captain Ippolito Viola, arrived, and dispersed the crowd, which had begun to grow riotous. But the most furious instantly shut themselves up in the houses, and fired upon the sharp-shooters, two of whom fell wounded, and the marshal was nearly killed. Then the sharp-shooters, enraged at this obstinate resistance, broke in the doors of the houses, rushed in, surprised the rebels with their weapons in their hands . . . . and spared their lives. Thus ended the sedition of Longobucco, in which, be it noted, the most wicked deeds were committed by the women.

In Ardore, a commune of Geraci, there were six carabineers and twenty-four soldiers of the 68th regiment of infantry, commanded by Sub-lieutenant Gazzone. On the morning of the 4th of September the people armed themselves and gathered outside the town to the shout of "Death to the poisoners!" When they were sufficient in number, they broke into the place. Gazzone, trusting to the sympathy which the people had shown for him on more than one occasion, moved quietly against the multitude, and tried to quiet it with a few kind words; he was answered by two balls in his chest, which killed him instantly. I will refrain from telling you what was done to his body, in order not to add horror to horror. The soldiers, attacked so hastily, powerless to resist, had barely time to take refuge in the carabineers' barracks, into which three families by the name of Lo Schiavo, whom the populace thought guilty of poisoning, and whose house had been burned, had fled in the morning. An immense crowd gathered in front of the barracks, and demanded that the poisoners should be given into their hands. The head of the families, the elder Lo Schiavo, was courageous enough to go to the window, and from there, with clasped hands, weeping and sobbing in a heart-breaking way, beg the crowd to spare at least the women and children. He was answered that they would all be torn to bits. The poor father, in a fit of desperation, fired into the street. This was the signal for assault. The multitude, uttering a loud cry of fury, dashed with axes against the doors and began to launch a shower of balls and stones against the windows. The soldiers defended themselves from within by shots. The struggle lasted more than an hour. Finally, seeing that all their efforts were in vain, the people set fire to the barracks. A horrible scene followed. The flames, which were already enveloping the entire building, and the walls beginning to crack, played through the rooms; the air was burning, and the beams of the roof bursting; from outside came hisses and shouts of joy, inside were heard the despairing cries of women and children; seven soldiers and Lo Schiavo lay stretched in their blood. Reduced to this extremity, the corporal, Albani, decided to attempt the only means of escape that remained; he gathered the three families into one group; ordered his few soldiers to take the wounded on their shoulders; then he, and the others after him, hastily opened a door, and, with lowered bayonets, dashed head downward into the crowd. The latter, astonished at such incredible audacity, gave way; but hardly had they passed, when the mob fired and killed several members of the unfortunate family; the others saved themselves, partly in the houses, partly in the country; the soldiers were not overtaken. Two days after this three companies of infantry from Gerace, Monteleone, and Reggio arrived in Ardore and restored quiet. Captain Onesti, of the staff, who took upon himself the management of the commune for some time; Major Gastaldini, who was commanding the military forces of Ardore and the neighborhood; and Broglia, doctor of the battalion, behaved in such a way that I cannot find words with which to praise them sufficiently. I say nothing of the soldiers, who there, as elsewhere, worked for the town with indefatigable zeal and earnest pity.

It is not necessary to say how the commanders of the corps and divisions behaved during the time the cholera lasted, because the population, municipalities, and the press awarded them the highest praise and gave full testimony of their deeds. But among the many names dear to the army and country, there is one I cannot withhold, no matter how easily every reader may guess it, and have already divined, perhaps with a spontaneous heart-throb, all that I wish to say of him: it is General Medici.

What he did from the beginning to prevent the spreading of the cholera and to preserve the troops from it, has been already told. It is easy to imagine what he did afterward. At work night and day with mind and body, each moment brought the announcement of some fresh disaster, or of new tumults, which there seemed to be no end to the consultations, orders, and precautions that were necessary. He betook himself now to one place, now to another, in order to assure himself that the military authorities were fulfilling their duties; he visited barracks, prisons, hospitals, and the homes for the convalescent. Noteworthy, among others, was the visit to Messina, where he lost a very distinguished officer of his staff, the good and brave Captain Tito Tabacchi; and that other, in the days when the cholera was raging most fiercely at Terrasini, where he entered the houses of the poor to offer them assistance and comfort, and improvised hospitals, gathered nurses together, and inspired so much confidence by word, deed, and his perfect serenity, that he left the place entirely changed. He was always diligent, provident, and charitable, but at the pillow of the sick, full of divine compassion! He went every week to the two military hospitals of Palermo, Sesta Casa, and Sant 'Agata, visited them thoroughly, asking about and examining every thing, advising and encouraging the physicians, nurses, and sick, with the solicitude of a father. The visit of the fifteenth of August, at the height of the epidemic, is a memorable one. He went to the hospital with several officers of his staff. He was waited for at the door of the first ward by the physicians. At his appearance, the nurses formed two lines along the beds. Some of the sick, the majority dangerously ill, turned their face toward the door. The general approached the first bed; all the others formed a semicircle around him; at his side was the medical director. The patient was very ill, his face was cadaverous, his eyes sunken and bloodshot, his lips black, and his breathing labored and interrupted by heavy sobs. He was quite out of his head. At the approach of all these people, he raised his eyes to the general's face, and kept them there fixed and motionless without any expression. The doctor went up to him and asked, as he pointed out Medici:

"Do you know this gentleman?"

The soldier looked at the doctor without making any sign.

"Do you know him?" the latter repeated.

Then he seemed to understand the question. The physician said in loud tones:

"It is General Medici."

"Medici . . . Medici . . ." murmured the sick man, confusedly; he looked at him, moved his lips as if to smile or say a word, bent his head as a sign of assent, then came a violent sob, his eyes become motionless and senseless, and he gave no other sign of understanding. The general looked anxiously at the doctor. "Not yet," the latter replied, and on they moved.

In one of the neighboring beds was a corporal who died the following day.

He was conscious, but much depressed. The skin of his face was shrivelled, covered with livid spots and glistening with a cold perspiration. When the general approached his bed, he looked at him, now half closing, now dilating his eyes, and uttering an exhausted groan.

"How do you feel?" said the general.

The man shook his head slightly and turned his eyes upward in sign of utter discouragement.

"Courage! my son; you must keep up your spirits; you must think of getting well."

The sick man, making an effort, murmured: "I should not be sorry to—die."

"Die! what are you talking about! You must not despair, my good fellow; you will get well; the physician says that you will recover; is n't it so, doctor, he is going to get well?"

The soldier gave a quick glance at the doctor, made a motion with his head as if to say no, then looked fixedly at Medici, and said in a weak voice: "Thank you, general."

The latter bowed his head, stood thinking for a moment, and then passed to another bed. Here lay a soldier on the road to recovery, who would not take a certain medicine.

"Why won't you take it?" asked the general.

"It hurts me," the former replied timidly.

"No, it does not hurt you, my dear fellow. Will you believe me if I taste it?" and taking a cup which the doctor handed him, he swallowed some it and gave it to the soldier who was looking at him in surprise. "Courage, drink it!" The soldier drank, made a wry face, and then laughed.

The general asked another who was to be removed to the home for the convalescents: "How do you feel now?"

"How do I feel?" replied the soldier. "Ah, Mr. General, very hungry."

So he moved gradually on through the wards; the sick, who were able to do so, rose to a sitting position, or raised themselves slightly on their elbows, listening attentively and stretching out their necks to hear what he was saying, and to look him in the face.

The last one visited was a dying man. His face was distorted beyond recognition, with that imprint of old age, that expression of great fear, which is peculiar to cholera patients, and which, once seen, is never forgotten. He was raving, murmuring indistinct words, moving his arms incessantly, and picking at his counterpane as if looking for something, or raising his hands as if to seize something that was floating before his eyes. He was a young sergeant who, in those sad days of the cholera, had given every possible proof of courage, constancy, and charity. "He has only a few more hours to live," said the doctor in an undertone. The general looked a long time at him with a sad and thoughtful face. He was certainly thinking that that brave young fellow was dying far from his own, without any comfort or any tears; he thought of his family, of so many others dying like him, so many other families like his own, who would be deprived of their dearest members. . . . Suddenly he started, gave a sigh, and moved off, saying: "He has spent his life nobly." And the others all followed him silently.

The last province in which the cholera raged at the end of '67 was that of Reggio di Calabria. It had already ceased in Sicily. During the first days of September, the long and frequent rains having produced a marked depression in the atmosphere, the cholera had begun to decrease slowly in the provinces of Palermo and Messina, and rapidly in those of Trapani, Girgenti, Syracuse, Catania, and Caltanisetta. It broke out again in these two cities toward the middle of September; but only for a few days. After which the general health improved in all parts of the island, so that in the month of October the army only lost twenty men, and November seven, in December none, or one or two at most. From the beginning of the decrease of the epidemic, the cities, villages, and country changed their entire aspect. The first terror, which had crushed every feeling of love of country or charity in the hearts of the majority of the citizens, having subsided, the fugitives, the greater number of whom were rich or well-to-do people, began to return to their homes, and to scatter among the indigent population that assistance, in the way of money, work, and advice, which they had denied at first. And the people took courage instantly, and, as if waking from a profound and painful lethargy, returned little by little to the ordinary duties of life, which had been laid aside or performed at intervals, with an inertia and a species of timid bewilderment under that continuous danger and before that continual spectacle of death. The streets, squares, shops, were filled, the workshops opened once more, commerce began to revive, and the joyful sound of labor sprang up where solitude and silence had reigned before, or only the lament of the dying or beggars had been heard. The public administrations, deserted by dead, fugitive, or expelled officials, were put in working order again; were reorganized, and upheld by those citizens who had abandoned them at first; they began to dedicate themselves to the needs of the country in an active, intelligent, and quiet way. The highwaymen, rendered audacious by the general confusion and fright, and scarcity of the troops, who were interested for the most part in graver duties, had committed every kind of depredation in city and country. On perceiving now, that, with the cessation of the cholera, the military forces would all turn against them with renewed vigor, they began to restrain themselves, and the condition of the public security suddenly improved. The soldiers had a little rest at last, could indulge in unbroken and quiet slumber at night, and during the day they could eat, in peace, their black bread, which had been earned by such long and wearisome labors.

Like the convalescent, who, when returning to the usages of every-day life, is amused by every thing, glad to see every person, and attends with the greatest solicitude and joy to all those duties which he formerly neglected or disliked, so the soldiers, on abandoning that life so full of labor and sadness, took up their ordinary occupations, even those that had seemed most irksome at first, as a sort of amusement; almost all of them felt a freshness of affection and hope, a great joyfulness, a powerful desire to open their hearts to one another, to become expansive, and to fraternize. Throughout the barracks resounded once more the songs, shouts, and that noisy bustle of life which had entirely ceased for so long a time; every thing was changed and revivified.

But in order to form a just idea of the feelings of the soldiers in those days, it was necessary to enter the hospitals of the convalescents, where the rest and silence left their thoughts and minds at perfect liberty.

Let us enter a moment to give a last greeting to our good and brave soldiers.

Toward the end of September, that same year, a soldier of the 9th regiment of infantry wrote me a letter from Catania, begging me to tell in some military journal what had been done for his comrades and himself by the officers of his regiment. He had been ill with the cholera, and was almost well, so wrote me from a convent where his colonel had established a hospital for convalescents, and where he had been for more than a month. "Here we are," says the letter, "after so many perils and misfortunes, still alive, for a wonder." Then follows a long description of the convent, situated on a little hill and entirely surrounded by beautiful gardens, where the convalescents could go for recreation; with a spacious court-yard, filled with large trees, under the shade of which they used to walk a great part of the day, chatting, reading, or playing at draughts with stones! He told me then that each one of them had a cell to himself with a window on the garden; that in his, the ivy had grown about the grating, and that the branches of trees came in through the bars. "We have a good bed, two chairs, and have become as fond of the little rooms as if they were our homes. I keep every thing clean and in order in mine, just like a woman who thinks of nothing but her family and her house." Then he told me of the food, which was excellent, and indulged in encomiums upon and thanks to the directors of the hospital. "It must be confessed that we live very well. Just fancy: meat morning and night, and good wine and soup. We are more than content. In case you desire to publish what I have written, pray be kind enough to give the names of those to whom we are indebted for all this kind care. They are Lieutenant-Colonel Croce and Captain Mirto, the two directors of the hospital; and Dr. Longhi, who has done all that he could for the soldiers, and to whom we are deeply attached." Then he described the groups of convalescents, seated under the shade of the trees in the court, pale, exhausted, with sunken eyes; who talked of past events, dangers which they had encountered, and the sufferings endured, and comforted themselves with the thought of their distant families, to whom sooner or later they should return. "Oh, how gladly," he added, "as you can imagine, after so long a time, so many experiences, and an illness of this kind!" From that letter, written so simply and with so much ingenuousness, I felt in a measure imbued with the calm, weary quiet that must have reigned in that silent enclosure; the first time that I read it I seemed to see those poor, thin, worn faces, and to hear the weak, slow voices. At a certain hour the officers came to visit the soldiers of their companies. It was a delightful sight! One could see those good fellows rise with difficulty to their feet, carry their thin hands to their caps, and in replying to the anxious questions of their officers, show their gratitude by a smile in which affection and respect mingled in the loveliest and gentlest way.

The letter of my soldier ends at this point, and I stop with him,—stop with the picture before my eyes of that smile of gratitude which moves and affects me deeply.

The cholera of 1867 was a great misfortune for the army not less than for the country, but one not without its good results.

The army gained advantage in discipline, and it is easy to understand in what way. Even for those soldiers to whom the discipline seemed hardest, on account of their obstinacy, lack of docility, or because they were quite wanting in any idea of country or nationality and unable to comprehend either it, or the necessity for military rigor,—even for these soldiers, in the midst of the misfortunes caused by the cholera, the discipline lost all that had at first seemed odious and insupportable, and assumed quite a different aspect. Naturally, even the roughest minds, understanding how much there was that was noble and generous in doing and suffering for the public health, saw, too, that if instead of being soldiers, united and subject to discipline, they had been peasants or operatives, who were free and independent, they would probably all have fled from every duty or peril, and each provided for his own individual safety. They felt, therefore, that a part of the merit of their noble work did not belong to them, and they ascribed it tacitly to that discipline, the sad consequences of the lack of which, they saw and experienced every day in the other classes of the population. The more they admitted the good intention of all those laws and of all those measures which they had at first considered as unreasonable and useless aggravations, the more they saw the effects which issued from their own hands, and which they could not help admiring and being proud of, they gradually formed a just idea of discipline, and resigned themselves to it as a salutary necessity. Besides this, that domesticity, that fraternizing which springs up and increases so rapidly between the officers and soldiers in the occasion of great perils or common misfortunes, had made the most obtuse and malevolent understand that if, in the connections of ordinary life, there is a rigorous and unalterable division, that does not arise from a spontaneous desire on the part of the officer, but from custom, from a general rule dictated by the need of discipline and recognized by all as necessary, either from intuition or experience. This being fully understood, there naturally disappeared all those grudges and rancors generally felt by quarrelsome soldiers against the austere and inexorable officers,—an ill feeling which, for the most part, is produced by a false *amour propre*, and which diffidence and timidity only increase; and they did disappear in fact. In the face of that continual spectacle of misfortune, in the midst of that solemn unanimity of affection and good-will, every one understood quite clearly how petty and selfish his personal hates and resentments were, and felt them disappear from his heart of their own accord without his being obliged to fight them. Besides this, the operations of the officers and soldiers had been for a long time of such a nature, that the orders of the superiors mingled, not only in substance, but also in form, with the most simple precepts of religion, taught by mothers to their young children. Certain talks which the officers had with the soldiers might be repeated word for word by a sacred orator on parchment, and certain orders for the day by the colonels were taken purely from the Gospel. Therefore, it was not possible that even the most ignorant and stupid soldiers could rebel at the órders of their superiors, or could doubt the rectitude, discuss the fitness, or deny the duty of obedience. Thus, little by little, the sentiment of religion took the place of that of discipline, and that which would have been done unwillingly from force, was done most gladly from an impulse of charity. On the other hand, that affectionate solicitude which the officers had displayed for the soldiers on every occasion, in visiting them in the hospitals, assisting them with their own money, comforting, counselling, and protecting them, had produced such an effect, that in the hearts of the latter the sentiments of gratitude and duty intermingled in such a way as to take away even the idea that they could be separated or opposed. Understanding discipline as it is and ought to be, understanding the principles upon which it is based and moves, the aims to which it tends, and the effects it obtains, even the intellect of the humblest soldier takes in this great edifice, the army; comprehends the praiseworthy combination and harmony of the forces by which it is ruled; feels that they are foundations for the warmest affections of the family, and the most sacred laws of religion; and as he goes on contemplating the whole, he sees it rise and become illumined on a height which neither the declamations of philosophers nor the complaints of the common people can reach. This was the effect produced upon the soldiers; in this way discipline was enforced.

And the country?

The most splendid proof of the effect produced upon the country by the magnificent conduct of the army was given by the Sicilian people at the end of '67, and has been repeated recently,—the dearest proof that could be given to the army and to Italy,—the admirable result of the conscription. Oh ! that people, so full of pride, daring, and fire, cannot help giving us brave soldiers !

And what was the soldier's reward ?

One evening, after the roll-call at retreat, the quartermaster-sergeant read the colonel's order for the day, in which he said : "*You have done your duty!*"

# RECENT VOLUMES OF TRAVEL.

**Spain and the Spaniards.** By EDMONDO DE AMICIS, author of "Studies of Paris," "Holland," etc. Octavo, with full-page illustrations, $2.00.

"Rarely do we meet with a more generous writer. He tells us that the first feeling that inspires him in visiting a foreign country is sympathy,—a desire not to find any thing to censure, but to pardon what seem to be defects. If there were more of this spirit abroad among us the literature of travel would be oftener enriched by such books as this, where the truth is never sacrificed or exaggerated for effect, and where there is such excellent evidence of honest judgment and acute observation set forth amid picturesque effects."—*N. Y. Critic.*

**Unbeaten Tracks in Japan.** By ISABELLA BIRD, author of "A Lady's Life in the Rocky Mountains," etc. 2 vols., octavo, bevelled boards, illustrated, $5.00. Also "The Popular Edition," 2 vols. in 1, illustrated, $3.00.

"Beyond question the most valuable and the most interesting of recent books concerning Japanese travel. * * * One of the most profitable of recent travel records."—*Evening Post.*

**Six Months Among the Palm Groves, Coral Reefs, and Volcanoes of the Sandwich Islands.** By ISABELLA BIRD, author of "Unbeaten Tracks in Japan," etc. A new and cheaper edition. Octavo, cloth, illustrated, $2.50.

**Norsk, Lapp, and Finn.** By FRANK VINCENT, Jr., author of "The Land of the White Elephant," "Through and Through the Tropics," etc. Octavo, cloth, with frontispiece and map, $1.50.

"Under the above title Frank Vincent, Jr., has produced a book which is full of interesting and instructive matter, and which, we have no doubt, will find a large number of appreciative readers."—*N. Y. Herald.*

"A most interesting book of travel."—*Denver Republican.*

**A Scandinavian Summer**—Up to the Midnight Sun. By KATHARINE E. TYLER. Octavo, cloth, $1.75.

A fresh and picturesque narrative of a summer ramble in the far North by a writer who evidently knows what to observe and how to describe.

**Cuban Sketches.** By JAMES W. STEELE. Octavo, cloth extra, $1.50.

CONTENTS.—Going There—First Impressions—In General—The Cuban at Home—The Spaniard in Cuba—La Señorita—Spanish Rule—War Times—Toilers—The Town—Rural Cuba—Tropical Weather—Domestic Institutions—Municipal Conveniences—Passions and Amusements—Mother Church—What We Eat—Island Ideas—The American in Cuba.

Graphic studies of life and character by an old resident, who has a keen sense of humor and an exceptionally picturesque style.

*⁎* For sale by all Booksellers.

**G. P. PUTNAM'S SONS,   27 & 29 West 23d St., New York.**

## BAYARD TAYLOR'S TRAVELS.

**Eldorado;** OR, ADVENTURES IN THE PATH OF EMPIRE (Mexico and California). 12mo. Houshold edition, $1.50

"To those who have more recently pitched their tents in California, the narrative of Taylor will have interest as assisting them to appreciate the wondrous changes that have been affected in this region since the days of turmoil, excitement, and daring speculation of which the tourist speaks."—*Sacramento Union.*

**Central Africa.** LIFE AND LANDSCAPE FROM CAIRO TO THE WHITE NILE. Two plates and cuts. 12mo. Household edition, . . . . . . . $1.50

"We have read many of Bayard Taylor's readable books—and he never wrote one that was not extremely interesting—but we have never been so well pleased with any of his writings as we are with the volume now before us, 'A Journey to Central Africa.'"—*Binghamton Republican.*

**Greece and Russia.** WITH AN EXCURSION TO CRETE. Two plates. 12mo. Household edition, . . $1.50

"In point of flowing narrative and graphic description, this volume is fully equal to the previous works which have given Mr. Bayard Taylor such an eminent place among modern travellers."—*Harper's Monthly.*

**Home and Abroad.** A SKETCH-BOOK OF LIFE, SCENERY, AND MEN. Two plates. 12mo. Household edition, $1.50

——— (Second Series.) With two plates. 12mo. Household edition, . . . . . . . $1.50

"This is one of the most interesting books that Bayard Taylor has ever made. It is in a large measure autobiographical. Whatever has most impressed him in any part of the earth is noted in some one of these letters."—*Taunton Gazette.*

"A volume from Bayard Taytor is always a pleasure. He not only knows how to travel and how to enjoy it, but he excels in giving entertainment by his narration to others."—*Bangor Whig.*

**India, China, and Japan.** Two plates, 12mo. Household edition, . . . . . . $1.50

"Of all travellers, no one pleases us more than Bayard Taylor. He sees what we most desire that he should see, and he tells us that which we most desire to know."—*New Bedford Mercury.*

**Land of the Saracen;** OR, PICTURES OF PALESTINE, ASIA MINOR, SICILY, AND SPAIN. With two plates. 12mo. Household edition . . . . $1.50

## BAYARD TAYLOR'S TRAVELS.
### (CONTINUED.)

**Northern Travel.** SUMMER AND WINTER PICTURES OF SWEDEN, DENMARK, AND LAPLAND. With two plates. 12mo. Household edition, . . . . . $1.50

"There is no romance to us quite equal to one of Bayard Taylor's books of travel."—*Hartford Republican.*

**Views Afoot;** OR, EUROPE SEEN WITH KNAPSACK AND STAFF. 12mo. Household edition, . . . $1 50

"We need say nothing in praise of Bayard Taylor's writings. He travels in every direction, and sees and hears pretty much all that is worth seeing and hearing. His descriptions are accurate, and always reliable and interesting."—*Syracuse Journal.*

**By-Ways of Europe.** 12mo. Household edition, $1 50

CONTENTS

A Familiar Letter to the Reader.—A Cruise on Lake Lagoda.—Between Europe and Asia.—Winter-Life in St. Petersburgh.—The Little Land of Appenzell.—From Perpignan to Montserrat.—Balearic Days.—Catalonian Bridle-Roads.—The Republic of the Pyrenees.—The Grand Chartreuse.—The Kyffhauser and its Legends.—A Week at Capri.—A Trip to Ischia.—The Land of Paoli.—The Island of Maddalena.—In the Teutoberger Forest.—The Suabian Alps.

**Egypt and Iceland in the Year 1874.** 16mo, cloth extra, . . . . . . . . . $1.50
12mo, uniform with Household edition of the Works, $1.50

## Bayard Taylor's Latest Work.

**Studies in German Literature.** Edited by MARIE TAYLOR. With an introduction by Hon. GEO. H. BOKER. 8vo, cloth extra, . . . . . . $2 00

CONTENTS :

Earliest German Literature.—The Minnesingers.—The Mediæval Epics. The Nibelungenlied.—The Literature of the Reformation.—The Literature of the Seventeenth Century.—Lessing.—Klopstock, Wieland and Herder.—Schiller.—Goethe.—Goethe's Faust.—Richter.

# PUBLICATIONS OF G. P. PUTNAM'S SONS.

### A NEW VOLUME BY "JOHN LATOUCHE."

**PORTUGAL, OLD AND NEW.** By OSWALD CRAWFURD, British Consul at Oporto. Octavo, with maps and illustrations, cloth extra, . . . . . . . . . . $3 50

Mr. Crawfurd, who is better known in literature under his *nom de plume* of John Latouche, has resided for many years in Portugal and has had exceptional opportunities for becoming thoroughly acquainted with the country and its people.

"The whole book, indeed, is excellent, giving the reader not information only, but appreciation of Portugal, its climate, its people and its ways. It is not a book of travel, but a book of residences, if we may say so."—*New York Evening Post.*

" Mr. Crawfurd's admirable book is most opportune, and his long residence in the country, his intimate and critical knowledge of the language, history, poetry, and the inner life of the people, render him an authority as safe to follow as he is pleasant. * * * The book is excellent in every way."—*Athenæum.*

" A more agreeable account of Portugal and the Portuguese could scarcely have been written, and it will surprise us if the book does not live as one of the best descriptions we possess of a foreign nation."—*St. James Gazette.*

**A FORBIDDEN LAND; OR, VOYAGES TO THE COREA.** With full description of the manners, customs, history, etc., of a community of some 16,000,000 people hitherto almost entirely unknown. By ERNST OPPERT. Octavo, with maps and illustrations, $3 00

" The author combines a story of his personal adventures, with a most intelligible description of the country, its inhabitants, their customs, and of everything which would help his readers to form a correct idea of what he himself saw and learned."—*The Churchman.*

" Sure to be eagerly and widely read * * * contains almost the only authentic description of Corea and its people with which the public are familiar."—*San Francisco Bulletin.*

" Full of data of the highest value on the geography and history of Corea, its commercial value and products."—*New York Times.*

" Mr. Oppert has made a book of rare interest."—*New York Evening Post.*

" His personal narrative is one of great interest * * * he is rewarded for his enterprise in being able to communicate so much novel and valuable information in regard to a country which has so long remained beyond the scope of geographical research."—*New York Tribune.*

**ROMAN DAYS.** By VIKTOR RYDBERG. Translated by ALFRED CORNING CLARK, with Memoir of the author by H. A. W. LINDEHN. Octavo, cloth. Illustrated . . . . . . . $2 00

The volume embodies the results of careful historical studies, and gives some legendary matters not heretofore brought forward. The art criticisms are the work of a poet and scholar; the brief historical and topographical sketches, those of a clear-headed philosopher and eager traveller, a quick observer, a man of general and thorough culture. The book is a picturesque mosaic of the many brilliant, sober, gay, comic, dramatic, tragic, poetic, vulgar elements that make up the past history of that wonderful city and the physiognomy it bears to-day.

" We welcome this work from the hardy North for its broad scholarship, its freshness and ripeness. The articles betray an artistic discrimination rare in one not a sculptor by profession and experienced and enthusiastic in that art. Rydberg possesses the pure plastic spirit."—*N. Y. Herald.*

www.ingramcontent.com/pod-product-compliance
Lightning Source LLC
Chambersburg PA
CBHW022106300426
44117CB00007B/615